"Offers both a vision and a road map . . . how entrepreneurial government can work . . . a lively, creative, and important book . . . it will intrigue and enlighten anyone interested in government."
—*The New York Times Book Review*

"A BLUEPRINT FOR A BETTER GOVERNMENT."
—*U.S. News and World Report*

"Chock full of sweeping proposals for change and efficiency."
—*The Philadelphia Inquirer*

"David Osborne and Ted Gaebler are truly original thinkers. *Reinventing Government* will be required reading in the Weld administration."
—William Weld,
Republican governor of Massachusetts

DAVID OSBORNE is the author of the acclaimed *Laboratories of Democracy* and is a frequent contributor to *The Washington Post, Governing,* and other publications. A tireless evangelist for efficiency in government, he has been a consultant to prominent government leaders and candidates, both Republican and Democrat.

TED GAEBLER, former city manager of Visalia, California, and Vandalia, Ohio, is president of the Gaebler Group, a division of MRC, a public-sector management consulting firm, in San Rafael, California.

Reinventing Government

How the Entrepreneurial Spirit Is Transforming the Public Sector

David Osborne
and
Ted Gaebler

A PLUME BOOK

PLUME
Published by the Penguin Group
Penguin Books USA Inc , 375 Hudson Street,
New York, New York 10014, U S.A
Penguin Books Ltd, 27 Wrights Lane,
London W8 5TZ, England
Penguin Books Australia Ltd, Ringwood,
Victoria, Australia
Penguin Books Canada Ltd, 10 Alcorn Avenue,
Toronto, Ontario, Canada M4V 3B2
Penguin Books (N Z) Ltd, 182–190 Wairau Road,
Auckland 10, New Zealand

Penguin Books Ltd, Registered Offices:
Harmondsworth, Middlesex, England

Published by Plume, an imprint of Dutton Signet,
a division of Penguin Books USA Inc
This is an authorized reprint of a hardcover edition
published by Addison-Wesley Publishing Company, Inc

First Printing, February, 1993

40 39 38 37 36 35 34 33 32 31

 REGISTERED TRADEMARK—MARCA REGISTRADA

LIBRARY OF CONGRESS CATALOGING-IN-PUBLICATION DATA
Osborne, David (David E.)
    Reinventing government : how the entrepreneurial spirit is
transforming the public sector / David Osborne and Ted Gaebler
        p.   cm
    Originally published: Reading, Mass. : Addison-Wesley. c1992.
    ISBN 0-452-26942-3
    1. Administrative agencies—United States.   2. Bureaucracy—United
States   3. Government productivity—United States.
4. Entrepreneurship—United States.   I Gaebler, Ted   II Title
[JK469   1993]
353 07'8—dc20   92-30557
                                                       CIP

Printed in the United States of America

BOOKS ARE AVAILABLE AT QUANTITY DISCOUNTS WHEN USED TO PROMOTE PRODUCTS OR SERVICES.
FOR INFORMATION PLEASE WRITE TO PREMIUM MARKETING DIVISION, PENGUIN BOOKS USA INC.,
375 HUDSON STREET, NEW YORK, NEW YORK 10014

To my parents,
Chris and Earl Osborne
—D.O.

To my daughter, Robin,
and my son, Christopher
—T.A.G.

Contents

Acknowledgements

This is a book about the pioneers of a new form of governance. It is not so much about our ideas as it is about the ideas of these pioneers. To them, we owe everything.

Perhaps the single most influential thinker, for us, has been Peter Drucker. His 1968 book, *The Age of Discontinuity,* offered a prescient analysis of the bankruptcy of bureaucratic government. Its basic concepts, repeated in other Drucker books and essays over the years, had an enormous impact—not only on us, but on many of the public entrepreneurs about whom we write and from whom we have learned. We also owe significant intellectual debts to Robert Reich, Tom Peters, Robert Waterman, and Alvin Toffler.

Among the thousands of practitioners and activists who shared their thoughts with us, none was more influential than Ted Kolderie, at the Center for Policy Studies in Minneapolis. Ted and his colleagues in the Public Service Redesign Project have written extensively about several of the principles we discuss in this book, and we have learned an enormous amount from them. Others who have contributed significantly to our understanding of entrepreneurial government include Carl Bellone, Harry Boyte, John Cleveland, John Kirlin, John McKnight, Peter Plastrik, Walt Plosila, Phil Power, Doug Ross, James Rouse, E. S. Savas, Roger Vaughan, and Gale Wilson.

We interviewed hundreds of people in the process of researching this book, and we have worked with thousands more in our various management and consulting roles in government. We are grateful to each and every one for sharing their insights with us. We are particularly grateful to those who went beyond the call of duty in their efforts to help us. We would be remiss if we did not specifically thank John K. Anderson, Doug Ayres, Duncan Ballantyne, Frank Benest, Clement Bezold, George Britton, Belden Daniels, Mitch Dasher, Barbara Dyer, John Falco, Bill Frederick, Bob Guskind, Sandy Hale, Phil Hawkey, Peter Hutchinson, Ron Jensen, Curtis Johnson, David Jones, Tom Jones, Norm King, Jim Kunde, Tom Lewcock, Bob Moore, Joe Nathan, Bob O'Neill, Brenda Robinson, Jim Souby, Stan Spanbauer, Bob Stone, Tom Wilson, Jim Williams, and Bob Woodson.

During the four years in which we labored on *Reinventing Government,* a number of colleagues read and commented on outlines, chapter drafts, or the entire book manuscript. In addition to some of those mentioned above, we have benefited from the astute advice of Arne Croce, Randy Hamilton, John Judis, Barry Kaplovitz, Wallace Katz, Bill Nothdurft, Neal Peirce, Jacqueline and Garry Schneider, Phil Singerman, Brian Sobel, Robert Stumberg, and Ralph Whitehead.

Others offered financial support, without which this book would have taken even longer than the four years we spent on it. We are deeply grateful to Craig Kennedy at the Joyce Foundation, Kavita Ramdas at the John T. and Catherine D. MacArthur Foundation, Doug Ross at the Corporation for Enterprise Development, and John Austin and Allen Charkow at Municipal Resource Consultants (MRC).

Other people supported the book by opening their homes or giving their time. We want to thank Sandy Hale, Deborah Johnston and Bob Thompson, Susan Pearson and John Judis, Gwen Pfanku and Bill Nothdruft, and John and Roxanna Anderson for their gracious hospitality. We are deeply grateful to Donna Hall, without whose hard work and warm spirit we could never have completed the book on time.

We also owe a great deal to several people in the publishing industry. Our agent, Kristine Dahl, believed in the book when the notion of "reinventing government" seemed as foreign as that other revolutionary phrase, *perestroika.* George Gibson at Addison-Wesley was alone among editors in understanding the book's value back in 1986, when he acquired it. Bob Thompson, one of America's best magazine editors, not only commissioned the piece that first brought the two of us together, in 1985, but pushed us to publish a 1990 article in the *Washington Post Magazine* that created an instant audience for the book.

Finally, we are deeply grateful to those who guided us at Addison-Wesley. William Patrick was the perfect editor: absolutely firm about major problems, yet absolutely willing to let us handle the sentence-by-sentence job of writing clean prose. Senior Production Coordinator John Fuller, who shepherded the book to publication in record time, had the patience of a saint.

Our most heartfelt thanks must go to our wives, Rose Osborne and Bonne Gaebler, and to our families. Writing a book of this nature takes an enormous amount of time—time stolen from our families. Without the warmth and patience with which our wives have supported this project, we could never have finished the book. We owe them a lifetime of gratitude. Without the joy our children bring to our lives, the years we spent on the book would have seemed like forever.

—*David Osborne and*
Ted Gaebler
October, 1991
Boston, MA
San Rafael, CA

Preface

We have chosen an audacious title for this book. We know that cynicism about government runs deep within the American soul. We all have our favorite epithets: "It's close enough for government work." "Feeding at the public trough." "I'm from the government and I'm here to help." "My friend doesn't work; she has a job with the government."

Our governments are in deep trouble today. This book is for those who are disturbed by that reality. It is for those who care about government—because they work in government, or work with government, or study government, or simply want their governments to be more effective. It is for those who know something is wrong, but are not sure just what it is; for those who have glimpsed a better way, but are not sure just how to bring it to life; for those who have launched successful experiments, but have watched those in power ignore them; for those who have a sense of where government needs to go, but are not quite sure how to get there. It is for the seekers.

If ever there were a time for seekers, this is it. The millennium approaches, and change is all around us. Eastern Europe is free; the Soviet empire is dissolving; the cold war is over. Western Europe is moving toward economic union. Asia is the new center of global economic power. From Poland to South Africa, democracy is on the march.

The idea of reinventing government may seem audacious to those who see government as something fixed, something that does not change. But in fact governments constantly change. At one time, government armories manufactured weapons, and no one would have considered letting private businesses do something so important. Today, no one would think of letting government do it.

At one time, no one expected government to take care of the poor; the welfare state did not exist until Bismarck created the first one in the 1870s. Today, not only do most governments in the developed world take care of the poor, they pay for health care and retirement pensions for every citizen.

At one time, no one expected governments to fight fires. Today, no government would be without a fire department. In fact, huge controversies erupt when a government so much as contracts with a private company to fight fires.

At one time, governments were active investors in the private economy, routinely seeding new businesses with loans and grants and equity investments. The federal government actually gave 9.3 percent of all land in the continental United States to the railroads, as an inducement to build a transcontinental system. Today, no one would dream of such a thing.

We last "reinvented" our governments during the early decades of the twentieth century, roughly from 1900 through 1940. We did so, during the Progressive Era and the New Deal, to cope with the emergence of a new industrial economy, which created vast new problems and vast new opportunities in American life. Today, the world of government is once again in great flux. The emergence of a postindustrial, knowledge-based, global economy has undermined old realities throughout the world, creating wonderful opportunities and frightening problems. Governments large and small, American and foreign, federal, state, and local, have begun to respond.

Our purpose in writing this book is twofold: to take a snapshot of governments that have begun this journey and to provide a map to those who want to come along. When Columbus set off 500 years ago to find a new route to bring spices back from the Orient, he accidentally bumped into a New World. He and the explorers who followed him—Amerigo Vespucci and Sir Francis Drake and Hernando de Soto—all found different pieces of this New World. But it was up to the map makers to gather all these seemingly unrelated bits of information and piece together a coherent map of the newly discovered continents.

In similar fashion, those who are today reinventing government originally set off to solve a problem, plug a deficit, or skirt a bureaucracy. But they too have bumped into a new world. Almost without knowing it, they have begun to invent a radically different way of doing business in the public sector. Just as Columbus never knew he had come upon a new continent, many of today's pioneers—from governors to city managers, teachers to social workers—do not understand the global significance of what they are doing. Each has touched a part of the new world; each has a view of one or two peninsulas or bays. But it will take others to gather all this information and piece together a coherent map of the new model they are creating.

We hope this book will provide something like that map: a simple, clear outline of a new way of conducting the public's business. We will provide snapshots of existing entrepreneurial governments, and we will outline ten simple principles on which they appear to be constructed. We offer these principles—this "map"—not as the final word about reinvented government, but as a rough draft. We are observing a process of enormous flux, and we believe our snapshot is accurate. But we know that the pioneers will continue their explorations, and we expect that as they discover new lands, newer and better maps will be drawn for those who come behind them.

We have not plucked our ten principles out of thin air—out of our imaginations. They are not what we *wish* government would be. We have developed our map by looking around us, at the successful public sector organizations we see emerging, piece by piece, all across this country. Hence this book is, in a very literal sense, the product of many people's thinking. We, as authors, are not inventing new ideas so much as synthesizing the ideas and experience of others. Those about whom we write are reinventing government. They are the heroes of this story.

We are, of course, responsible for the ultimate shape of the map we have drawn. As such, we feel a responsibility to make explicit the underlying beliefs that have driven us to write this book—and that have no doubt animated its conclusions.

First, we believe deeply in government. We do not look at government as a necessary evil. All civilized societies have some form of government. Government is the mechanism we use to make communal decisions: where to build a highway, what to do about homeless people, what kind of education to provide for our children. It is the way we provide services that benefit all our people: national defense, environmental protection, police protection, highways, dams, water systems. It is the way we solve collective problems. Think of the problems facing American society today: drug use; crime; poverty; homelessness; illiteracy; toxic waste; the specter of global warming; the exploding cost of medical care. How will we solve these problems? By acting collectively. How do we act collectively? Through government.

Second, we believe that civilized society cannot function effectively without effective government—something that is all too rare today. We believe that industrial-era governments, with their large, centralized bureaucracies and standardized, "one-size-fits-all" services, are not up to the challenges of a rapidly changing information society and knowledge-based economy.

Third, we believe that the people *who work in government are not the problem; the* systems *in which they work are the problem.* We write not to berate public employees, but to give them hope. At times it may sound as if we are engaged in bureaucrat-bashing, but our intention is to bash *bureaucracies*, not bureaucrats. We have known thousands of civil servants through the years, and most—although certainly not all—have been responsible, talented, dedicated people, trapped in archaic systems that frustrate their creativity and sap their energy. We believe these systems can be changed, to liberate the enormous energies of public servants—and to heighten their ability to serve the public.

Fourth, we believe that neither traditional liberalism nor traditional conservatism has much relevance to the problems our governments face today. We will not solve our problems by spending more or spending less, by creating new public bureaucracies or by "privatizing" existing bureaucracies. At some times and in some places, we do need to spend more or spend less, create new programs or privatize public functions. But to make our governments effective again we must *reinvent* them.

Finally, we believe deeply in equity—in equal opportunity for all Americans. Some of the ideas we express in this book may strike readers as inequitable. When we talk about making public schools compete, for instance, some fear that the result would be an even less equitable education system than we have today. But we believe there are ways to use choice and competition to *increase* the equity in our school system. And we believe passionately that increased equity is not only right and just, but critical to our success as a nation. In today's global marketplace, America cannot compete effectively if it wastes 25 percent of its human resources.

We use the phrase *entrepreneurial government* to describe the new model we see emerging across America. This phrase may surprise many readers, who think of entrepreneurs solely as business men and women. But the true meaning of the word *entrepreneur* is far broader. It was coined by the French economist J. B. Say, around the year 1800. "The entrepreneur," Say wrote, "shifts economic resources out of an area of lower and into an area of higher productivity and greater yield." An entrepreneur, in other words, uses resources in new ways to maximize productivity and effectiveness.

Say's definition applies equally to the private sector, to the public sector, and to the voluntary, or third, sector. Dynamic school superintendents and principals use resources in new ways to maximize productivity and effectiveness. Innovative airport managers do the same. Welfare commissioners, labor secretaries, commerce department staffers—all can shift resources into areas of higher productivity and yield. When we talk about public entrepreneurs, we mean people who do precisely this. When we talk about the entrepreneurial model, we mean public sector institutions that *habitually* act this way—that constantly use their resources in new ways to heighten both their efficiency and their effectiveness.

Many people also assume that entrepreneurs are risk-takers. They shy away from the notion of entrepreneurial government because, after all, who wants bureaucrats taking risks with their hard-earned tax dollars? But, as careful studies demonstrate, entrepreneurs do not seek risks, they seek opportunities. Peter Drucker, the sage of management theory, tells a story about this that is worth quoting at length:

> A year or two ago I attended a university symposium on en-trepreneurship at which a number of psychologists spoke. Although their papers disagreed on everything else, they all talked of an "entrepreneurial personality," which was characterized by a "propensity for risk-taking."
>
> A well-known and successful innovator and entrepreneur who had built a process-based innovation into a substantial worldwide business in the space of twenty-five years was then asked to comment. He said: "I find myself baffled by your papers. I think I know as many successful innovators and entrepreneurs as anyone, beginning with myself. I have never come across an 'entrepreneurial personality.' The successful ones I know all have, however, one thing—and only one thing—in common: they are not 'risk-takers.' They try to define the risks they have to take and to minimize them as much as possible. Otherwise none of us could have succeeded. As for myself, if I had wanted to be a risk-taker, I would have gone into real estate or commodity trading, or I would have become the professional painter my mother wanted me to be."
>
> This jibes with my own experience. . . . The innovators I know are successful to the extent to which they define risks and confine them. They are successful to the extent to which they systematically analyze the sources of innovative opportunity, then pinpoint the opportunity and exploit it.

Drucker assures us that almost anyone can be an entrepreneur, if the organization is structured to encourage entrepreneurship. Conversely, almost any entrepreneur can turn into a bureaucrat, if the organization is structured to encourage bureaucratic behavior. "The most entrepreneurial, innovative people behave like the worst time-serving bureaucrat or power-hungry politician six months after they have taken over the management of a public-service institution," Drucker writes, "particularly if it is a government institution."

America's crisis of confidence in government has turned books about public policy into a growth industry. Most deal with *what* government should do, and most focus exclusively on Washington. This book is different: it focuses on all levels of government—federal, state, and local—and its subject is not what they do, but *how they operate.*

Although the media is obsessed with the federal government, most government in America actually takes place outside Washington. There are 83,000 governmental units in the United States—one federal government, 50 state governments, and thousands of cities, counties, school districts, water districts, and transportation districts. The majority of our public services are delivered by local governments—cities, counties, towns, and districts. More than 12 million of our 15.1 million full-time civilian public employees work for state or local government.

We care deeply about *what* governments do, but this is a book about *how* they work. For the last 50 years, political debate in America has centered on questions of ends: what government should do, and for whom. We believe such debates are secondary today, because we simply do not have the means to achieve the new ends we seek. After 10 years of education reform and $60 billion in new money, test scores are stagnant and dropout rates are higher than they were in 1980. After 20 years of environmental legislation to clean up our air and water, pollution is as bad as ever. After only a few years of the savings-and-loan cleanup, the projected cost has skyrocketed from $50 billion to $500 billion. We have new goals, yes, but our governments cannot seem to achieve them. The central failure of government today is one of *means*, not *ends.*

We hope this book will illuminate the new means people across America have begun to develop—in fits and starts, by trial and error—to do the public's business. As we researched it, we were astounded by the degree of change taking place in our cities, counties, states, and school districts. Some readers may at first find our findings hard to swallow. But we urge you to suspend judgment and continue reading, until you too have had a chance to see the vast sweep of change coursing through American government. We think you will find it astonishing.

Our purpose is not to criticize government, as so many have, but to renew it. We are as bullish on the future of government as we are bearish on the current condition of government. We do not minimize the depth of the problem, nor the difficulty of solving it. But because we have seen so many public institutions transform themselves from staid bureaucracies into innovative, flexible, responsive organizations, we believe there *are* solutions.

Marcel Proust once wrote, "The real voyage of discovery consists not in seeking new lands, but in seeing with new eyes." Our goal, in writing this book, is to help you see with new eyes. It is our fervent hope that when you put this book down, you will never see government in the same way again. It is our prayer that you will then join the thousands of other Americans who are already working to reinvent their governments.

Introduction:
An American Perestroika

Strangely enough, in the midst of change, the present course may often be the most risky one. It may only serve to perpetuate irrelevancy.
—The Florida Speaker's Advisory Committee on the Future

As the 1980s drew to a close, *Time* magazine asked on its cover: "Is Government Dead?"

As the 1990s unfold, the answer—to many Americans—appears to be yes.

Our public schools are the worst in the developed world. Our health care system is out of control. Our courts and prisons are so overcrowded that convicted felons walk free. And many of our proudest cities and states are virtually bankrupt.

Confidence in government has fallen to record lows. By the late 1980s, only 5 percent of Americans surveyed said they would choose government service as their preferred career. Only 13 percent of top federal employees said they would recommend a career in public service. Nearly three out of four Americans said they believed Washington delivered less value for the dollar than it had 10 years earlier.

And then, in 1990, the bottom fell out. It was as if all our governments had hit the wall, at the same time. Our states struggled with multibillion-dollar deficits. Our cities laid off thousands of employees. Our federal deficit ballooned toward $350 billion.

Since the tax revolt first swept the nation in 1978, the American people have demanded, in election after election and on issue after issue, more performance for less money. And yet, during the recession of 1990 and 1991, their leaders debated the same old options: fewer services or higher taxes.

Today, public fury alternates with apathy. We watch breathlessly as Eastern Europe and the Soviet republics overthrow the deadening hand of bureaucracy and oppression. But at home we feel impotent. Our cities succumb to mounting crime and poverty, our states are handcuffed by staggering deficits, and Washington drifts through it all like 30 square miles bounded by reality.

Yet there is hope. Slowly, quietly, far from the public spotlight, new kinds of public institutions are emerging. They are lean, decentralized, and innovative. They are flexible, adaptable, quick to learn new ways when conditions change. They use competition, customer choice, and other nonbureaucratic mechanisms to get things done as creatively and effectively as possible. And they are our future.

Visalia, California, is the prototypical American community. A leafy oasis of 75,000 people in California's hot, dry San Joaquin Valley, it is the county seat of rural, conservative Tulare County. It is an All-American city: the streets are clean, the lawns are mowed, the Rotary Clubs are full.

In 1978, Proposition 13 cut Visalia's tax base by 25 percent. With financing from one final bond issue that slipped through on the same day as Proposition 13, the school district managed to build a new high school. But as the years went by, it could never scrape together the money to put in a swimming pool.

One hot Thursday in August 1984, a parks and recreation employee got a call from a friend in Los Angeles, who told him that the Olympic committee was selling its training pool. The employee immediately called the school district, and two days later he and an assistant superintendent flew down to take a look. They liked what they saw: an all-aluminum, Olympic-size pool that would likely survive an earthquake. To buy one new, they would have spent at least $800,000; they could buy this one slightly used and put it in the ground for half that amount.

Like any other government agency, the school district needed at least two weeks to advertise the question, hold a board meeting, and get approval for a special appropriation. But on Monday, the parks and recreation employee got a second call. Two colleges wanted the pool, and they were racing each other to get the nonrefundable $60,000 deposit together. So he got in his car and took a check down that afternoon.

How could a third-level parks and recreation employee get a check for $60,000, with no action by the city council and no special appropriation? The answer is simple. Visalia had adopted a radically new budget system, which allowed managers to respond quickly as circumstances changed. Called the Expenditure Control Budget, it made two simple changes. First, it eliminated all line items within departmental budgets—freeing managers to move resources around as needs shifted. Second, it allowed departments to keep what they didn't spend from one year to the next, so they could shift unused funds to new priorities.

Normal government budgets encourage managers to waste money. If they don't spend their entire budget by the end of the fiscal year, three things happen: they lose the money they have saved; they get less next year; and the budget director scolds them for requesting too much last year. Hence the time-honored government rush to spend all funds by the end of the fiscal year. By allowing departments to keep their savings, Visalia not only eliminated this rush, but encouraged managers to save money. The idea was to get them thinking like owners: "If this were my money, would I spend it this way?"

Under the new budget system, Visalia's Parks and Recreation Department had managed to save $60,000 toward a new pool. Arne Croce, an assistant city manager who had worked on the problem, knew that both the school district and the city council wanted a pool. Between them, he was sure, they could find $400,000. (They ended up raising nearly half the money with a community fund-raising drive.) Because Visalia regularly engaged in strategic planning, Croce also understood the city's priorities and values—he knew, for instance, that the council and manager valued entrepreneurial behavior. Although the Olympic pool was a totally unexpected opportunity, he had no qualms about seizing it. "It's something you'd find in private enterprise," said the admiring school superintendent. "You don't have the bureaucracy you have to deal with in most governments."

The Expenditure Control Budget was the brainchild of Oscar Reyes, an assistant finance director in Fairfield, California. City Manager Gale Wilson, one of the pioneers of entrepreneurial government, installed it after Proposition 13. Ted Gaebler, then city manager of Visalia, brought it to Visalia six months later. In Fairfield, in Visalia, and in a dozen other cities and counties that have since adopted it, the way managers spend their taxpayers' money has profoundly changed.

In Visalia, even the man in charge of street sweeping changed his thinking. For years, Ernie Vierra had had the streets swept every three weeks. Quietly, under the guise of equipment problems, he tried four weeks, then five. When he hit six the complaints rolled in, so he eventually settled on four. He did the same thing with the grass in the parks.

Visalia's Police Department pioneered a lease-purchase program for squad cars that was quickly copied by two dozen other cities. The shop that repaired Visalia's vehicles cut its energy consumption by 30 percent. By 1985, with other California governments still crying poor in the wake of Proposition 13, Visalia had $20 million in cash squirreled away—almost as much as its entire annual operating budget. (Ironically, by freezing property taxes, Proposition 13 made it impossible for Visalia to lower its rates.)

The philosophy embodied by the new budget—a philosophy city leaders dubbed "public entrepreneurial management"—permeated the organization. Managers talked of "profit centers," "enterprise budgets," "the CEO," and the "board of directors." They gave bonuses of up to $1,000 per person to reward outstanding group effort. And they encouraged employees to help the city save or earn money by allowing them to take home 15 percent of the savings or earnings their innovations generated in their first year—with no ceiling on the amount.

When Visalia's leaders decided the city needed more cultural life, the convention director coventured with private promoters to bring in headliner acts, limiting their risk by putting up half the capital and taking half the profits. When a citizens' task force found a dearth of affordable housing, the city helped create a private, nonprofit organization, loaned it $100,000, and sold it 13 acres of excess city land. Fifteen months later, 89 families—with incomes ranging from $9,000 to $18,000 a year—moved into their own single-family homes. The planning department officials assigned to work on the project gave up their summer vacations to bring it in on time. But they didn't mind. "We've got one of the most exciting jobs in the city," one of them said. "Its like owning your own business—you spend the amount of time necessary to get the job done."

East Harlem is not the prototypical American community. It is one of the poorest communities in America. Single mothers head more than half of its families; 35 percent of its residents are on public assistance; median income is $8,300. Dilapidated public schools—their windows covered by protective grilles—coexist with crack houses. East Harlem is precisely the sort of community in which public schools normally fail. Yet it has some of the most successful public schools in America.

New York City has 32 school districts. Twenty years ago, Community School District 4, in East Harlem, was at the bottom of the barrel: thirty-second out of 32 in test scores. Only 15 percent of its students—*15 of every 100*—read at grade level. Attendance rates were pathetic.

"It was totally out of control," says Michael Friedman, now director of a junior high called the Bridge School:

The year before I started the Bridge School was probably the worst year of my life. The schools were chaotic, they were overcrowded. There was a lot of violence, gangs roaming the streets. It was sink or swim as a classroom teacher. They closed the door: "That's your class, do what you can." And it seemed like nobody could or would try to do anything about it. You had a lot of people who had been there a long time, and they were just punching that clock.

In 1974, out of sheer desperation, then superintendent Anthony Alvarado, an assistant principal named John Falco, and several teachers decided they had to get the "incorrigible, recalcitrant, aggressive kids" out of the schools, so others could learn. They created an alternative junior high for troubled students.

The task was so daunting that Alvarado told Falco and his teachers to do whatever it took to get results. They created a very nontraditional school, which worked. Two other alternative schools opened that year were also successful, so they tried several more. Soon teachers began proposing others: the East Harlem Career Academy, the Academy of Environmental Sciences, the Isaac Newton School of Science and Mathematics, a traditional school in which children wore uniforms. Each provided a basic core of instruction in math, English, and social sciences, but each also had its own special focus.

Before long, parents and students in District 4 found themselves with a variety of choices. But they could choose only within the "zone" where they lived, and there were only so many spots in the alternative schools. "We had created alternative schools to create good learning environments," says Falco, "but we couldn't let everyone into them. So there was a lot of pressure from parents. It just made sense to go further." In 1983, the district converted all its junior high schools to schools of choice, doing away with assignment by zone. By 1990, District 4 boasted 21 junior high schools, plus six alternative grade schools.

Under the new system, schools were no longer synonymous with buildings; many buildings housed three or four schools, one on each floor. (All told, there were 52 schools in 20 buildings.) Schools were small—from 50 to 300 students—and education was personal. "Kids need to be dealt with personally," says Falco, who now administers the choice program. "The downsizing of the schools has been a tremendous plus."

Alvarado also decentralized authority: he let teachers manage their own schools. Principals still administered school buildings, but actual schools were run by "directors"—most of whom also taught—and their teachers. If a teacher wanted to create a new school, or move to an alternative school, Alvarado usually said yes. This simple change released tremendous energy. "There are teachers who were burned out—they were going nowhere," says Falco. "We put them in an alternative setting, and they flowered."

Before long, the junior highs were competing for students. Teachers and directors began paying close attention to how many applicants ranked their schools number one each spring. And district leaders began closing schools that were not attracting enough students, or replacing their directors and staff. "If you're not operating a program that kids want to come to, you're out of business," says Falco. "You just can't rest on your laurels. You have to continually strive for ways to meet the needs of these kids." Successful schools, on the other hand, were allowed to grow until they hit an upper limit of about 300. At that point, district leaders encouraged their directors to clone them, if space was available for another school.

Ed Rodriguez, principal of one of the last junior highs to become a school of choice, was not eager to compete. But he found the competition a powerful motivator:

> Now that we absolutely have to attract youngsters to our building, we have to really take a long, hard look at ourselves and determine—Are we good enough? Are we going to be competitive enough? We replaced the idea that we're going to be here forever with the idea that we are here with a purpose, and that purpose has to be maximized. The mission, the dream of the school, has to be in everyone's mind and everyone's heart. The level of performance has to increase.

Just as important as competition and a sense of mission is the ownership students and teachers feel for their schools. Rather than being assigned to a school and offered a cookie-cutter education, they are allowed to choose the style of education they prefer. They can choose traditional schools or open classrooms; schools with mentor programs or those that use heavy tutoring; reading institutes for those behind grade level or advanced schools for gifted students; photography programs or computer

programs; experiential education or even a school run in cooperation with the Big Apple Circus.

"When a child chooses the school, there's ownership in that
choice," says Robert Nadel, assistant director of a junior high
called the Creative Learning Center. "There's also ownership
on the part of the parent and ownership on the part of the teachers." That ownership translates into student attitudes very different from those created when a child is simply assigned to a
building. "What you own," says Sy Fliegel, the choice system's
first director, "you treat better."

The results of District 4's experiment have been startling.
Reading scores are up sharply: in 1973, 15 percent of junior
high students read at grade level; by 1988, 64 percent did. Writing skills have improved: in 1988, state tests found that 75 percent of the district's eighth-graders were competent writers.
And the percentage of District 4 graduates accepted to New
York's four elite public high schools, such as Bronx Science and
Brooklyn Technical, has shot up. In the mid-1970s, fewer than
10 of District 4's graduates were admitted to these schools each
year. By 1987, 139 were—10 percent of District 4's graduates,
almost double the rate for the rest of New York City. Another
180 attended a second tier of selective public high schools. And
36 went to selective private schools, including Andover and the
Hill School. All told, more than a quarter of District 4's graduates earned places in outstanding high schools—schools that
were virtually off limits 15 years before.

District 4 is smack in the middle of one of America's most
renowned ghettos. Yet it has a waiting list of teachers who want
to work there. Perhaps the most telling statistic is this: out of
14,000 students in District 4, close to 1,000 come in from outside the district. "On any given day, I receive at least four or
five calls from parents requesting admission from outside the
district," says Falco. "I just have to turn them away."

Bob Stone works in America's archetypal bureaucracy, the
Department of Defense. As deputy assistant secretary of defense for installations, he has at least theoretical authority over

600 bases and facilities, which house 4.5 million people and consume $100 billion a year. Soon after he was promoted to the job, in 1981, Stone visited an air base in Sicily. "We have 2,000 airmen there, and they're out in the middle of nowhere," he says:

> *No families, no towns. They are an hour and a half drive over a horrible mountain road from a Sicilian city of 20,000—and when you get there there's not much to do. So most of our bases have bowling alleys, and we built a bowling alley at this base. I visited them two or three weeks after the bowling center opened/They took me in and they started showing me plans—they're going to take out this wall and add six more lanes over there. I thought, "Gee, you've been open for a couple of weeks, and you're going to tear the place apart and expand it? Why is that?"*
>
> *"Well," they told me, "there's this rule that says, if you have 2,000 troops, you're allowed to construct eight lanes."* [*You can get a waiver to build more—but only after you can prove you need them.*] *I got the book and that is what it says: 1,000 troops, four lanes; 2,000 troops, eight lanes. And it's true if you're in the wilds of Sicily, with no families, or in the northern part of Greenland, where you can't even go outdoors for most of the year.*

The rule book Stone refers to covered 400 pages. The rules governing the operation of military housing covered 800 pages. Personnel rules for civilian employees covered another 8,800 pages. "My guess is that *a third* of the defense budget goes into the friction of following bad regulations—doing work that doesn't have to be done," Stone says. Engineers in New Mexico write reports to convince people in Washington that their roofs leak. Soldiers trek halfway across their bases to the base chemist when the shelf life of a can of spray paint expires, to have it certified for another year. The Department of Defense (DOD) pays extra for special paint, but because it takes longer to establish its specifications than it takes companies to improve their paint, DOD employees pay a premium for paint that is inferior to paint available at their local store.

"This kind of rule has two costs," Stone says. "One is, we've got people wasting time. But the biggest cost—and the reason I say it's a third of the defense budget—is it's a message broadcast to everybody that works around this stuff that it's a crazy outfit. 'You're dumb. We don't trust you. Don't try to apply your common sense.' "

Stone cut the rules governing military base construction from 400 pages down to 4, those governing housing from 800 to 40. Then he decided to go farther. In an experiment straight out of *In Search of Excellence,* he decided to turn one base, called a Model Installation, free from these rules and regulations. If the commander would commit to radically improving his installation, Stone would do his best to get any rules that were standing in his way waived. The principle was simple: let the base commander run the base his way, rather than Washington's way. A corollary was also important: if he saved money in the process, he didn't have to give it back. He could keep it to spend on whatever he felt was most important.

Forty commanders volunteered for the experiment. In the first two years, they submitted more than 8,000 requests for waivers or changes in regulations. Stone can tell stories about them for hours. In the air force, for instance, airmen use complex electronic test kits to check Minuteman missiles. When a kit fails, they send it to Hill Air Force Base in Utah for repair. Meanwhile, the missile is put off alert—typically for 10 days. An airman at Whiteman Air Force Base got approval to fix the test kits himself—and suddenly Whiteman didn't have a Minuteman missile off alert for more than three hours.

Throughout Defense, people buy by the book. Stone holds up a simple steam trap, which costs $100. "When it leaks," he says, "it leaks $50 a week worth of steam. The lesson is, when it leaks, replace it quick. But it takes us a year to replace it, because we have a system that wants to make sure we get the very best buy on this $100 item, and maybe by waiting a year we can buy the item for $2 less. In the meantime, we've lost $3,000 worth of steam." Under the Model Installations program, commanders requested authority to buy things on their own. An entire army command requested permission to let craftsmen decide for themselves when spray paint cans should be thrown away, rather than taking them to the base chemist. Five air force bases received permission to manage their own construction, rather than paying the Corps of Engineers to do it. Shaken by the threat of competition, the corps adopted a new goal: to be "leaders in customer care."

The Model Installations experiment was so successful that in March 1986, Deputy Secretary of Defense William Howard Taft IV directed that it be applied to all defense installations. Stone and his staff then developed a budget experiment modeled on Visalia's system. Normal installation budgets, first drawn up *three years in advance*, include hundreds of specific line items. The Unified Budget Test allowed commanders to ignore the line items and shift resources as needs changed.

In its first year, the test revealed that 7 to 10 percent of the funding locked into line items was in the wrong account, and that when commanders could move it around, they could significantly increase the performance of their troops. The army compared the results at its two participating bases with normal bases and concluded that in just one year, the Unified Budget increased performance by 3 percent. The long-term impact would no doubt be greater. According to Stone and his colleagues, "Senior leaders in the Services have estimated that if all the unnecessary constraints on their money were removed, they could accomplish their missions with up to 10 percent less money." But in a $100 billion installations budget, even 3 percent is $3 billion.

Visalia, East Harlem, and the Defense Department are not alone. Look almost anywhere in America, and you will see similar success stories. We believe these organizations represent the future.

Our thesis is simple: The kind of governments that developed during the industrial era, with their sluggish, centralized bureaucracies, their preoccupation with rules and regulations, and their hierarchical chains of command, no longer work very well. They accomplished great things in their time, but somewhere along the line they got away from us. They became bloated, wasteful, ineffective. And when the world began to change, they failed to change with it. Hierarchical, centralized bureaucracies designed in the 1930s or 1940s simply do not function well in the rapidly changing, information-rich, knowledge-intensive society and economy of the 1990s. They are like luxury ocean liners in an age of supersonic jets: big, cumbersome, expensive, and extremely difficult to turn around. Gradually, new kinds of public institutions are taking their place.

Government is hardly leading the parade; similar transformations are taking place throughout American society. American corporations have spent the last decade making revolutionary changes: decentralizing authority, flattening hierarchies, focusing on quality, getting close to their customers—all in an effort to remain competitive in the new global marketplace. Our voluntary, nonprofit organizations are alive with new initiatives. New "partnerships" blossom overnight—between business and education, between for-profits and nonprofits, between public sector and private. It is as if virtually all institutions in American life were struggling at once to adapt to some massive sea change—striving to become more flexible, more innovative, and more entrepreneurial.

THE BANKRUPTCY OF BUREAUCRACY

It is hard to imagine today, but 100 years ago the word *bureaucracy* meant something positive. It connoted a rational, efficient method of organization—something to take the place of the arbitrary exercise of power by authoritarian regimes. Bureaucracies brought the same logic to government work that the assembly line brought to the factory. With their hierarchical authority and functional specialization, they made possible the efficient undertaking of large, complex tasks. Max Weber, the great German sociologist, described them using words no modern American would dream of applying:

*The decisive reason for the advance of bureaucratic organi-
zation has always been its purely technical superiority over
any other form of organization. . . .*

*Precision, speed, unambiguity, . . . reduction of friction
and of material and personal costs—these are raised to
the optimum point in the strictly bureaucratic administration.*

In the United States, the emergence of bureaucratic government was given a particular twist by its turn-of-the-century setting. A century ago, our cities were growing at breakneck speed,
bulging with immigrants come to labor in the factories thrown
up by our industrial revolution. Boss Tweed and his contemporaries ran these cities like personal fiefdoms: In exchange for
immigrant votes, they dispensed jobs, favors, and informal services. With one hand they robbed the public blind; with the
other they made sure those who delivered blocs of loyal votes
were amply rewarded. Meanwhile, they ignored many of the
new problems of industrial America—its slums, its sweatshops,
its desperate need for a new infrastructure of sewers and water
and public transit.

Young Progressives like Theodore Roosevelt, Woodrow Wilson, and Louis Brandeis watched the machines until they could
stomach it no more. In the 1890s, they went to war. Over the
next 30 years, the Progressive movement transformed government in America. To end the use of government jobs as patronage, the Progressives created civil service systems, with written
exams, lockstep pay scales, and protection from arbitrary hiring
or dismissal. To keep major construction projects like bridges
and tunnels out of the reach of politicians, they created independent public authorities. To limit the power of political
bosses, they split up management functions, took appointments
to important offices away from mayors and governors, created
separately elected clerks, judges, even sheriffs. To keep the administration of public services untainted by the influence of
politicians, they created a profession of city managers—professionals, insulated from politics, who would run the bureaucracy
in an efficient, businesslike manner.

Thanks to Boss Tweed and his contemporaries, in other words, American society embarked on a gigantic effort to *control* what went on inside government—to keep the politicians and bureaucrats from doing anything that might endanger the public interest or purse. This cleaned up many of our governments, but in solving one set of problems it created another. In making it difficult to steal the public's money, we made it virtually impossible to *manage* the public's money. In adopting written tests scored to the third decimal point to hire our clerks and police officers and fire fighters, we built mediocrity into our work force. In making it impossible to fire people who did not perform, we turned mediocrity into deadwood. In attempting to control virtually everything, we became so obsessed with dictating *how* things should be done—regulating the process, controlling the inputs—that we ignored the outcomes, the *results*.

The product was government with a distinct ethos: slow, inefficient, impersonal. This is the mental image the word *government* invokes today; it is what most Americans assume to be the very essence of government. Even government buildings constructed during the industrial era reflect this ethos: they are immense structures, with high ceilings, large hallways, and ornate architecture, all designed to impress upon the visitor the impersonal authority and immovable weight of the institution.

For a long time, the bureaucratic model worked—not because it was efficient, but because it solved the basic problems people wanted solved. It provided security—from unemployment, during old age. It provided stability, a particularly important quality after the Depression. It provided a basic sense of fairness and equity. (Bureaucracies, as Weber pointed out, are designed to treat everyone alike.) It provided jobs. And it delivered the basic, no-frills, one-size-fits-all services people needed and expected during the industrial era: roads, highways, sewers, schools.

During times of intense crisis—the Depression and two world wars—the bureaucratic model worked superbly. In crisis, when goals were clear and widely shared, when tasks were relatively straightforward, and when virtually everyone was willing to pitch in for the cause, the top-down, command-and-control mentality got things done. The results spoke for themselves, and most Americans fell in step. By the 1950s, as William H. Whyte wrote, we had become a nation of "organization men."

But the bureaucratic model developed in conditions very different from those we experience today. It developed in a slower-paced society, when change proceeded at a leisurely gait. It developed in an age of hierarchy, when only those at the top of the pyramid had enough information to make informed decisions. It developed in a society of people who worked with their hands, not their minds. It developed in a time of mass markets, when most Americans had similar wants and needs. And it developed when we had strong geographic communities—tightly knit neighborhoods and towns.

Today all that has been swept away. We live in an era of breathtaking change. We live in a global marketplace, which puts enormous competitive pressure on our economic institutions. We live in an information society, in which people get access to information almost as fast as their leaders do. We live in a knowledge-based economy, in which educated workers bridle at commands and demand autonomy. We live in an age of niche markets, in which customers have become accustomed to high quality and extensive choice.

In this environment, bureaucratic institutions developed during the industrial era—public *and* private—increasingly fail us.

Today's environment demands institutions that are extremely flexible and adaptable. It demands institutions that deliver high-quality goods and services, squeezing ever more bang out of every buck. It demands institutions that are responsive to their customers, offering choices of nonstandardized services; that lead by persuasion and incentives rather than commands; that give their employees a sense of meaning and control, even ownership. It demands institutions that *empower* citizens rather than simply *serving* them.

Bureaucratic institutions still work in some circumstances. If the environment is stable, the task is relatively simple, every customer wants the same service, and the quality of performance is not critical, a traditional public bureaucracy can do the job. Social security still works. Local government agencies that provide libraries and parks and recreational facilities still work, to a degree.

But most government institutions perform increasingly complex tasks, in competitive, rapidly changing environments, with customers who want quality and choice. These new realities have made life very difficult for our public institutions—for our public education system, for our public health care programs, for our public housing authorities, for virtually every large, bureaucratic program created by American governments before 1970. It was no accident that during the 1970s we lost a war, lost faith in our national leaders, endured repeated economic problems, and experienced a tax revolt. In the years since, the clash between old and new has only intensified. The result has been a period of enormous stress in American government.

In some ways, this is a symptom of progress—of the disruptive clash that occurs when new realities run headlong into old institutions. Our information technologies and our knowledge economy give us opportunities to do things we never dreamed possible 50 years ago. But to seize these opportunities, we must pick up the wreckage of our industrial-era institutions and rebuild. "It is the first step of wisdom," Alfred North Whitehead once wrote, "to recognize that the major advances in civilization are processes which all but wreck the society in which they occur."

THE EMERGENCE OF
ENTREPRENEURIAL GOVERNMENT

The first governments to respond to these new realities were local governments—in large part because they hit the wall first. On June 6, 1978, the voters of California passed Proposition 13, which cut local property taxes in half. Fed by the dual fires of inflation and dissatisfaction with public services, the tax revolt spread quickly. In 1980, Ronald Reagan took it national— and by 1982, state and local governments had lost nearly one of every four federal dollars they received in 1978. During the

1982 recession, the deepest since the Depression, state governments began to hit the wall.

Under intense fiscal pressure, state and local leaders had no choice but to change the way they did business. Mayors and governors embraced "public-private partnerships" and developed "alternative" ways to deliver services. Cities fostered competition between service providers and invented new budget systems. Public managers began to speak of "enterprise management," "learning organizations," and "self-reliant cities." States began to restructure their most expensive public systems: education, health care, and welfare.

Phoenix, Arizona, put its Public Works Department in head-to-head competition with private companies for contracts to handle garbage collection, street repair, and other services. St. Paul, Minnesota, created half a dozen private, nonprofit corporations to redevelop the city. Orlando, Florida, created so many profit centers that its earnings outstripped its tax revenues. The Housing Authority of Louisville, Kentucky, began surveying its customers—15,000 residents of public housing—and encouraging them to manage their own developments. It even *sold* one development, with 100 units, to tenants.

The Michigan Department of Commerce adopted a new slogan: "Customer Service Is Our Reason for Being." It surveyed its customers, hired a customer service chief, created classes for employees in customer orientation, and set up an ombudsman with a toll-free telephone line for small businesses. Several of the department's 10 Action Teams embraced Total Quality Management, the management philosophy espoused by W. Edwards Deming.

Minnesota let parents and students choose their public schools—as in East Harlem—and six other states quickly followed suit. South Carolina developed performance incentives under which schools and teachers competed for funds to try new ideas, principals and teachers who achieved superior results got incentive pay, and schools whose students made large improvements in basic skills and attendance got extra money. In the program's first three years, statewide attendance increased, teacher morale shot up faster than in any other state, and Scholastic Aptitude Test scores rose 3.6 percent, one of the largest gains in the country.

Indianapolis Mayor William Hudnut described the phenomenon as well as anyone. "In government," he said in a 1986 speech, "the routine tendency is to protect turf, to resist change, to build empires, to enlarge one's sphere of control, to protect projects and programs regardless of whether or not they are any longer needed." In contrast, the "entrepreneurial" government "searches for more efficient and effective ways of managing:

> *It is willing to abandon old programs and methods. It is innovative and imaginative and creative. It takes risks. It turns city functions into money makers rather than budget-busters. It eschews traditional alternatives that offer only life-support systems. It works with the private sector. It employs solid business sense. It privatizes. It creates enterprises and revenue generating operations. It is market oriented. It focuses on performance measurement. It rewards merit. It says "Let's make this work," and it is unafraid to dream the great dream.*

Surveys even began to pick up the trend. In 1987 and 1988, the consulting firm Coopers & Lybrand conducted a Survey on Public Entrepreneurship, which focused on city and county executives in jurisdictions with more than 50,000 people. Virtually all executives surveyed agreed that demand for public services was outstripping revenues—a conflict they expected to "require continued emphasis on 'doing more with less' and exploring more innovative, cost-effective management techniques." Practices on the rise included contracting for services, performance measurement, participatory management, impact fees, and strategic planning.

When recession hit in 1990, the deficits of large cities and states jumped into the billions of dollars. Finally, out of desperation, even mainstream politicians began to search for new approaches. Gubernatorial candidates talked of "restructuring," "rightsizing," and "partnerships." Democrat Lawton Chiles, a three-term veteran of the U.S. Senate, won the governorship of

Florida vowing to "reinvent government." Republican Bill
Weld, the new governor of Massachusetts, promised to deliver
"entrepreneurial government," which would foster "competition" and focus on "results, not rules." Republican George Voinovich of Ohio said in his inaugural address: "Gone are the
days when public officials are measured by how much they
spend on a problem. The new realities dictate that public officials are now judged by whether they can work harder and
smarter, and do more with less."

It is difficult for the average citizen, who must rely on the
mass media to interpret events, to make heads or tails of these
changes. Their substance is all but invisible, in part because
they take place outside the glare of publicity that shines on
Washington. They also stubbornly refuse to fit into the traditional liberal versus conservative categories through which the
media views the world. Because most reporters are asked to
provide instant analysis, they have little choice but to fall back
on the tried and true lenses of past practice. And because their
standard formula relies on conflict to sell a story, they look for
heroes and villains rather than innovation and change. In the
process, they inevitably miss much that is new and significant.
To paraphrase author Neil Postman, American society hurtles
into the future with its eyes fixed firmly on the rearview mirror.

Over the past five years, as we have journeyed through the
landscape of governmental change, we have sought constantly
to understand the underlying trends. We have asked ourselves:
What do these innovative, entrepreneurial organizations have
in common? What incentives have they changed, to create such
different behavior? What have they done which, if other governments did the same, would make entrepreneurship the norm
and bureaucracy the exception?

The common threads were not hard to find. Most entrepreneurial governments promote *competition* between service providers. They *empower* citizens by pushing control out of the
bureaucracy, into the community. They measure the performance of their agencies, focusing not on inputs but on *outcomes*.
They are driven by their goals—their *missions*—not by their
rules and regulations. They redefine their clients as *customers*

and offer them choices—between schools, between training
programs, between housing options. They *prevent* problems before they emerge, rather than simply offering services afterward.
They put their energies into *earning* money, not simply spending it. They *decentralize* authority, embracing participatory
management. They prefer *market* mechanisms to bureaucratic
mechanisms. And they focus not simply on providing public
services, but on *catalyzing* all sectors—public, private, and voluntary—into action to solve their community's problems.

We believe that these ten principles, which we describe at
length in the next ten chapters, are the fundamental principles
behind this new form of government we see emerging: the
spokes that hold together this new wheel. Together they form a
coherent whole, a new model of government. They will not
solve all of our problems. But if the experience of organizations
that have embraced them is any guide, they will solve the major
problems we experience with bureaucratic government.

WHY GOVERNMENT CAN'T BE
"RUN LIKE A BUSINESS"

Many people, who believe government should simply be "run
like a business," may assume this is what we mean. It is not.

Government and business are fundamentally different institutions. Business leaders are driven by the profit motive; government leaders are driven by the desire to get reelected.
Businesses get most of their money from their customers; governments get most of their money from taxpayers. Businesses
are usually driven by competition; governments usually use monopolies.

Differences such as these create fundamentally different incentives in the public sector. For example, in government the
ultimate test for managers is not whether they produce a product or profit—it is whether they please the elected politicians.
Because politicians tend to be driven by interest groups, public
managers—unlike their private counterparts—must factor interest groups into every equation.

Governments also extract their income primarily through taxation, whereas businesses earn their income when customers buy products or services of their own free will. This is one reason why the public focuses so intensely on the cost of government services, exercising a constant impulse to *control*—to dictate how much the bureaucrats spend on every item, so they cannot possibly waste, misuse, or steal the taxpayers' money.

All these factors combine to produce an environment in which public employees view risks and rewards very differently than do private employees. "In government all of the incentive is in the direction of not making mistakes," explains Lou Winnick of the Ford Foundation. "You can have 99 successes and nobody notices, and one mistake and you're dead." Standard business methods to motivate employees don't work very well in this kind of environment.

There are many other differences. Government is democratic and open; hence it moves more slowly than business, whose managers can make quick decisions behind closed doors. Government's fundamental mission is to "do good," not to make money; hence cost-benefit calculations in business turn into moral absolutes in the public sector. Government must often serve everyone equally, regardless of their ability to pay or their demand for a service; hence it cannot achieve the same market efficiencies as business. One could write an entire book about the differences between business and government. Indeed, James Q. Wilson, the eminent political scientist, already has. It is called *Bureaucracy: What Government Agencies Do and Why They Do It*.

These differences add up to one conclusion: government cannot be run like a business. There are certainly many similarities. Indeed, we believe that our ten principles underlie success for *any* institution in today's world—public, private, or nonprofit. And we have learned a great deal from business management theorists such as Peter Drucker, W. Edwards Deming, Tom Peters, and Robert Waterman. But in government, business theory is not enough.

Consider Deming's approach, known as Total Quality Management. Increasingly popular in the public sector, it drives public institutions to focus on five of our principles: results, customers, decentralization, prevention, and a market (or systems) approach. But precisely because Deming developed his ideas for private businesses, his approach ignores the other five. For example most businesses can take competition for granted, so Total Quality Management ignores the problem of monopoly—which is at the heart of government's troubles. Most businesses are already driven by their missions (to make profits), so Deming does not help public leaders create mission-driven organizations. And few businesses have to be told to earn money rather than simply spending it.

The fact that government cannot be run just like a business does not mean it cannot become more *entrepreneurial,* of course. Any institution, public or private, can be entrepreneurial, just as any institution, public or private, can be bureaucratic. Few Americans would really want government to act just like a business—making quick decisions behind closed doors for private profit. If it did, democracy would be the first casualty. But most Americans would like government to be less bureaucratic. There is a vast continuum between bureaucratic behavior and entrepreneurial behavior, and government can surely shift its position on that spectrum.

A THIRD CHOICE

Most of our leaders still tell us that there are only two ways out of our repeated public crises: we can raise taxes, or we can cut spending. For almost two decades, we have asked for a third choice. We do not want less education, fewer roads, less health care. Nor do we want higher taxes. We want better education, better roads, and better health care, for the same tax dollar.

Unfortunately, we do not know how to get what we want. Most of our leaders assume that the only way to cut spending is to eliminate programs, agencies, and employees. Ronald Reagan talked as if we could simply go into the bureaucracy with a scalpel and cut out pockets of waste, fraud, and abuse.

But waste in government does not come tied up in neat packages. It is marbled throughout our bureaucracies. It is embedded in the very way we do business. It is employees on idle, working at half speed—or barely working at all. It is people working hard at tasks that aren't worth doing, following regulations that should never have been written, filling out forms that should never have been printed. It is the *$100 billion* a year that Bob Stone estimates the Department of Defense wastes with its foolish overregulation.

Waste in government is staggering, but we cannot get at it by wading through budgets and cutting line items. As one observer put it, our governments are like fat people who must lose weight. They need to eat less and exercise more; instead, when money is tight they cut off a few fingers and toes.

To melt the fat, we must change the basic incentives that drive our governments. We must turn bureaucratic institutions into entrepreneurial institutions, ready to kill off obsolete initiatives, willing to do more with less, eager to absorb new ideas.

The lessons are there: our more entrepreneurial governments have shown us the way. Yet few of our leaders are listening. Too busy climbing the rungs to their next office, they don't have time to stop and look anew. So they remain trapped in old ways of looking at our problems, blind to solutions that lie right in front of them. This is perhaps our greatest stumbling block: the power of outdated ideas. As the great economist John Maynard Keynes once noted, the difficulty lies not so much in developing new ideas as in escaping from old ones.

The old ideas still embraced by most public leaders and political reporters assume that the important question is *how much* government we have—not *what kind* of government. Most of our leaders take the old model as a given, and either advocate more of it (liberal Democrats), or less of it (Reagan Republicans), or less of one program but more of another (moderates of both parties).

But our fundamental problem today is not too much government or too little government. We have debated that issue endlessly since the tax revolt of 1978, and it has not solved our problems. Our fundamental problem is that we have *the wrong kind of government.* We do not need more government or less government, we need *better* government. To be more precise, we need better *governance*.

Governance is the process by which we collectively solve our problems and meet our society's needs. Government is the instrument we use. The instrument is outdated, and the process of reinvention has begun. We do not need another New Deal, nor another Reagan Revolution. We need an American *perestroika*.

— 1 —

Catalytic Government: Steering Rather Than Rowing

The word government is from a Greek word, which means "to steer." The job of government is to steer, not to row the boat. Delivering services is rowing, and government is not very good at rowing
—E. S. Savas

Fifteen years ago, St. Paul, Minnesota, was a down-at-the-heels, Frost Belt city that appeared to be dying. Its population had fallen below pre-Depression levels. Its central business district had lost 41 percent of its retail volume over the previous 15 years. A citizens' committee had published a study projecting a continued drain of people and investment to the suburbs.

George Latimer, elected mayor in 1975, knew he would never have the tax dollars he needed to solve St. Paul's problems. So he set out to "leverage the resources of the city"—"combining them with the much more prodigious resources of the private sector."

Latimer started with the downtown, the most visible symbol of St. Paul's malaise. A huge, two-square-block hole in the middle of town had stood empty for so long—waiting for a developer—that residents had begun to call it a historic landmark. Latimer quickly found a private partner and nailed down one of the first federal Urban Development Action Grants, and together they built a passive solar hotel, two high-rise office towers, a glass-enclosed city park, and a three-level enclosed shopping mall.

The worst area was Lowertown, a 25-square-block warehouse district that made up the eastern third of the business district. Latimer and his deputy mayor, Dick Broeker, dreamed up the idea of a private development bank, capitalized with foundation money, to catalyze investment in the area. In 1978, they asked the McKnight Foundation for $10 million to back the idea, and they got it.

The Lowertown Development Corporation brought in developers, offered loans or loan guarantees, and put together package deals with banks, insurance companies, and anyone else who would listen. Over the previous decade, investors had put only $22 million into Lowertown. In the Development Corporation's first decade, it triggered $350 million in new investments—leveraging its own money 30 or 40 to 1. Thirty-nine buildings were renovated or constructed. By 1988, Lowertown generated nearly six times the property taxes it had ten years before, and the Development Corporation was turning a profit.

Latimer and Broeker created a second corporation to develop the nation's first downtownwide hot water heating system; a third to develop affordable housing. They used voluntary organizations to operate recycling programs, to perform energy audits, and even to manage a park. They turned garbage collection and the city's Youth Services Bureau over to the private sector. They used millions of dollars' worth of volunteers' time in the city's parks, recreation centers, libraries, and health centers. And they created more partnerships with foundations than any city before or since.

By constantly catalyzing solutions *outside the public sector*, Latimer was able to increase his government's impact while trimming its staff by 12 percent, keeping budget and property tax growth below the rate of inflation, and reducing the city's debt. Without massive layoffs—in fact, while enriching the lives of public employees—he gave voters what they wanted: a government that did more but spent less.

REDEFINING GOVERNANCE

Latimer had no grand strategy. He was simply responding to the twin pressures of dwindling tax revenues and pressing needs. After a decade in office, however, he understood that he was fundamentally redefining the role of government. In his 1986 State of the City address, he summed up his new vision. To be successful in the future, he said,

> *city government will have to make some adjustments and in some ways redefine its traditional role. I believe the city will more often define its role as a catalyst and facilitator. The city will more often find itself in the role of defining problems and then assembling resources for others to use in addressing those problems. . . .*
>
> *City government will have to become even more willing to interweave scarce public and private resources in order to achieve our community's goals.*

This vision is antithetical to the way traditional mayors and governors and city managers view their roles. For the past 50 years, most public leaders have assumed that government's role was one-dimensional: to collect taxes and deliver services. Before 1930, of course, many "public" services had been provided by nongovernment institutions: religious groups, ethnic associations, settlement houses. But the Progressives and New Dealers believed governments should use public employees to produce most of the services they decided to provide. They worried about the tendency of religious and other private organizations to exclude those not of their own faith or ethnicity. They were determined to stop the widespread corruption that had discredited government contracting. And they lacked the information technology we have today to monitor the performance of contractors. So they put virtually everything in public hands.

By the 1970s, few mayors or governors or legislators could even conceive of another way. They were chained to the wagon of taxes and services. This was fine as long as tax revenues were rising 5.3 percent a year, as they did from 1902 through 1970. But when economic growth slowed and fiscal crisis hit, the equation changed. Now when problems appeared and voters demanded solutions, public leaders had only two choices. They could raise taxes, or they could say no. For officials who wanted to be reelected, this was no choice at all.

In Washington, our leaders escaped the dilemma by borrowing money. But in state and local government, where budgets have to balance, they began to look for answers that lay somewhere between the traditional yes and no. They learned how to bring community groups and foundations together to build low-income housing; how to bring business, labor, and academia together to stimulate economic innovation and job creation; how to bring neighborhood groups and police departments together to solve the problems that underlay crime. In other words, they learned how to facilitate problem solving by catalyzing action throughout the community—how to steer rather than row.

In Indianapolis, Indiana, mayors Richard Lugar and Bill Hudnut worked with the Greater Indianapolis Progress Committee, formed by a group of civic and business leaders, to revitalize the city. Working together to develop a strategic vision and plan, they decided to make Indianapolis the amateur sports capital of America. They created partnerships, tapped foundations, and harnessed the energies of thousands of volunteers—stimulating more than $11 billion of new investment and building 11 new sports facilities in a decade.

"We involved ourselves in a lot of creative leveraging," explains Hudnut:

> When we did the Hoosier Dome we raised $30 million from the non-profits before going to the state for the enabling legislation so the city could do its part with a tax. For the tennis stadium, the city issued a $4 million bond, the private sector came up with $3 million. . . .
>
> In running a city you've got to recognize that the dialogue is more important than the agenda item—getting people talking and working and thinking about who we are and where we want to be going, not just about specific agenda items. The mayor is more than a deliverer of services. That's become clear in the '80s. A mayor is a deal maker, who pulls the public and private sectors together.

In Lowell, Massachusetts, another depressed industrial city, then Congressman Paul Tsongas persuaded the city's bankers to set aside one-twentieth of their collective assets to make low-cost loans to businesses wanting to expand or relocate in downtown Lowell. Working with local government leaders, he then developed the Lowell Plan—an agreement that every important business in town would do a major project to improve Lowell. The efforts of a united business and political leadership convinced Wang Laboratories to build three office towers in town, the state government to create its first Urban Heritage Park in Lowell, and the federal government to follow suit with the nation's first urban national park. These efforts helped transform Lowell, in 10 years, from a city of 16 percent unemployment to a city of 3 percent unemployment.

By 1980, the tax revolt had radically changed the fiscal equation for most American cities. Suddenly the strategies used in desperation by Rust Belt cities like St. Paul and Indianapolis and Lowell began to appear throughout the nation:

- Newark, New Jersey, turned to community organizations and private sector initiatives to deal with problems from housing to AIDS to homelessness, as it pared its payroll from 10,000 in 1980 to 4,000 in 1988.

- Massachusetts boosted its funding of nongovernmental organizations to provide social services from $25 million in 1971 to $750 million—spread over 3,500 separate contracts and grants—in 1988.

- San Francisco, Boston, and other cities pioneered "linkage" programs, in which corporations that wanted to construct buildings downtown had to provide quid pro quos, such as child care and low-income housing.

- The California Department of Transportation negotiated franchise agreements with four private consortia to build toll highways.

As we surveyed governments across America, we found no less than 36 separate alternatives to normal public service delivery—36 different arrows in government's quiver. Some, like regulation, tax policy, contracting, and grants, were long established. Others were more startling. We found governments investing venture capital, creating private financial institutions, using volunteers to run parks and libraries, swapping real estate, even structuring the market to encourage energy conservation, recycling, and environmental protection.

Surprisingly, the federal government already relies heavily on many of these alternatives. "This heavy reliance on third parties to carry out public objectives has, in fact, become virtually the standard pattern of federal operation in the domestic sphere," according to Lester Salamon of Johns Hopkins University. This form of "third-party government" uses "government for what it does best—raising resources and setting societal priorities through a democratic political process—while utilizing the private sector for what it does best—organizing the production of goods and services. In the process it reconciles the traditional American hostility to government with recent American fondness for the services that modern society has increasingly required government to provide."

Even the leading symbol of New Deal liberalism, Governor Mario Cuomo of New York, has articulated the new approach. "It is not government's obligation to provide services," he told the *New York Times*, "but to see that they're provided."

SMALLER BUT STRONGER

Today's entrepreneurial leaders know that communities are healthy when their families, neighborhoods, schools, voluntary organizations, and businesses are healthy—and that government's most profound role is to steer these institutions to health. As Governor Lawton Chiles of Florida said during his 1990 campaign: "We believe the central purpose of state government [is] to be the catalyst which assists communities in strengthening their civic infrastructure. In this way we hope to empower communities to solve their own problems."

As they unhook themselves from the tax-and-service wagon, leaders such as Lawton Chiles and George Latimer have learned that they can steer more effectively if they let others do more of the rowing. Steering is very difficult if an organization's best energies and brains are devoted to rowing. As Peter Drucker wrote in his 1968 book, *The Age of Discontinuity*:

MANY ARROWS IN THE QUIVER

The 36 alternatives we have found to standard service delivery by public employees range from the traditional to the avante-garde. We have arbitrarily grouped them in three categories:

Traditional

1. Creating Legal Rules and Sanctions
2. Regulation or Deregulation
3. Monitoring and Investigation
4. Licensing
5. Tax Policy
6. Grants
7. Subsidies
8. Loans
9. Loan Guarantees
10. Contracting

Innovative

11. Franchising
12. Public-Private Partnerships
13. Public-Public Partnerships
14. Quasi-Public Corporations
15. Public Enterprise
16. Procurement
17. Insurance
18. Rewards
19. Changing Public Investment Policy
20. Technical Assistance
21. Information
22. Referral
23. Volunteers
24. Vouchers
25. Impact Fees
26. Catalyzing Nongovernmental Efforts
27. Convening Nongovernmental Leaders
28. Jawboning

Avant-Garde

29. Seed Money
30. Equity Investments
31. Voluntary Associations
32. Coproduction or Self-Help
33. Quid Pro Quos
34. Demand Management
35. Sale, Exchange, or Use of Property
36. Restructuring the Market

Many of these methods can be used in combination. For example, when the city of Visalia helped create its nonprofit housing corporation, Visalians Interested in Affordable Housing (VIAH), it jawboned the private sector, catalyzed a nongovernmental effort, provided seed money, sold property to VIAH, and offered technical assistance.

For definitions and examples of each of the 36 methods, see appendix A. Several methods are also discussed in chapter 10, pp. 290–298.

Any attempt to combine governing with "doing" on a large scale, paralyzes the decision-making capacity. Any attempt to have decision-making organs actually "do," also means very poor "doing." They are not focused on "doing." They are not equipped for it. They are not fundamentally concerned with it.

If a government does less, one might ask, is that not a weaker government? Are we not talking about undermining the power of the public sector? A traditional liberal, who equates dollars and numbers of employees with power, might make that case. Yet the governments we saw that steered more and rowed less—like St. Paul—were clearly stronger governments. After all, those who steer the boat have far more power over its destination than those who row it.

Governments that focus on steering actively shape their communities, states, and nations. They make *more* policy decisions. They put *more* social and economic institutions into motion. Some even do *more* regulating. Rather than hiring more public employees, they make sure *other* institutions are delivering services and meeting the community's needs.

In contrast, governments preoccupied with service delivery often abdicate this steering function. Public leaders who get caught on the tax-and-spend treadmill have to work so hard to keep their service systems together—running faster and faster just to stay in the same place—that they have no time left to think about steering. School boards get so busy negotiating contracts and avoiding layoffs that they forget about the quality of their schools. Transit directors get so wrapped up in keeping the buses running and begging more subsidies that they never question whether the transit model of the pre-automobile age—a centralized system operated by public employees—still makes sense. Federal leaders get so preoccupied with the ever-rising cost of Medicare and Medicaid that they ignore the overall dynamics of our health care system.

The irony is that while our governments pay 40 percent of all health bills, they let private doctors, hospitals, and HMOs shape the marketplace. While Congress finances a $500 billion bailout of failed savings and loans, it lets banks, insurance companies, and investment firms determine the overall shape and health of the financial marketplace. In other words, traditional governments get so preoccupied with rowing that they forget to steer. Are these governments strong or weak?

The ability to steer is particularly important today, with the emergence of a global economy. Most people understand the impact global competition has had on American industry. They know about the collapse of the steel industry, the massive layoffs at auto plants. But they don't understand the impact global competition has had on government. Stop and think about it for a moment, and it becomes obvious.

If corporations are to succeed in today's supercompetitive global market, they need the highest quality "inputs" they can get—the most knowledgeable workers, the most groundbreaking research, the cheapest capital, the best infrastructure. This makes government's various roles as educator, trainer, research funder, regulator, rule setter, and infrastructure operator far more important than they were 30 years ago. In 1960, it hardly mattered that 20 percent of General Motors' workers were functionally illiterate; 20 percent at Ford and Chrysler couldn't read either. But when the Japanese began selling cars made by workers who could *all* read, the Big Three found that they couldn't compete.

In the 1980s, it suddenly dawned on business and government leaders that our economy would suffer unless we improved our schools, upgraded our training systems, and got control of our health care costs. To do such things, however, we not only have to restructure institutions and markets, we have to force change on some of the most powerful interest groups in the country—teachers, principals, unions, doctors, hospitals. We are experiencing exactly the same shock monopolistic industries like autos and airlines experienced when thrust into competitive environments. Suddenly there is enormous pressure for change, and leaders have to enforce the general interest over the special interests who want to preserve the status quo.

When combined with voters' refusal to pay higher taxes—in part because global competition is also driving the average standard of living down—this new pressure demands very different behavior by government. Suddenly there is less money for *government*—for "doing" things, delivering services. But there is more demand for *governance*—for "leading" society, convincing its various interest groups to embrace common goals and strategies. This is yet another reason why our visionary public leaders now concentrate more on catalyzing and facilitating change than on delivering services—why they provide less government, but more governance.

SEPARATING STEERING FROM ROWING

In today's world, public institutions also need the flexibility to respond to complex and rapidly changing conditions. This is difficult if policy makers can use only one method—services produced by their own bureaucracy. It is virtually impossible if their employees cannot be transferred when needs change, moved into the employ of nongovernmental organizations when they can do a better job, or fired for poor performance. Bureaucratic governments can do none of these things easily, thanks to their civil service regulations and tenure systems. In effect, they are captive of sole-source, monopoly suppliers: their own employees. (If you doubt this is really the norm, ask yourself why anything else is called "alternative service delivery.") No business would long tolerate such a situation.

Monopoly suppliers become a problem as soon as policy makers decide to change their strategies. When police departments decide to attack the roots of crime by working with communities to solve their social and economic problems, their officers rarely have community organizing skills—but they're stuck with them. When city councils require that sprinkler systems be installed in all new buildings, they gradually need fewer firemen—but they're stuck with them. When welfare departments go into the business of training and placing their clients in jobs, their eligibility workers rarely have the career counseling skills needed—but they're stuck with them. When managers try to go around their employees, by using private organizations to provide the necessary services, public employee unions often sue, strike, or protest.

As a result, entrepreneurial governments have begun to shift to systems that separate policy decisions (steering) from service delivery (rowing). Drucker long ago noted that successful organizations separate top management from operations, so as to allow "top management to concentrate on decision making and direction." Operations, Drucker said, should be run by separate staffs, "each with its own mission and goals, and with its own sphere of action and autonomy." Otherwise, managers will be distracted by operational tasks and basic steering decisions will not get made.

Steering requires people who see the entire universe of issues and possibilities and can balance competing demands for resources. Rowing requires people who focus intently on one mission and perform it well. Steering organizations need to find the best methods to achieve their goals. Rowing organizations tend to defend "their" method at all costs.

Entrepreneurial governments increasingly divest rowing from steering. This leaves "government operating basically as a skillful buyer, leveraging the various producers in ways that will accomplish its policy objectives," explains Ted Kolderie, whose Citizens League and Public Services Redesign Project have stimulated an enormous amount of new thinking in Minnesota. Government agencies remain as service producers in many cases—although they often have to compete with private producers for that privilege. But these public service producers are separate from the policy management organizations, and "in-house production" is only "one of the available alternatives."

Freeing policy managers to shop around for the most effective and efficient service providers helps them squeeze more bang out of every buck. It allows them to use *competition* between service providers. It preserves maximum *flexibility* to respond to changing circumstances. And it helps them insist on *accountability* for quality performance: contractors know they can be let go if their quality sags; civil servants know they cannot.

Frank Keefe, former secretary of administration and finance in Massachusetts, sums it up this way: Contracting with private

vendors "is cheaper, more efficient, more authentic, more flexible, more adaptive. . . . Contracts are rewritten every year. You
can change. You cannot change with state employees who have
all sorts of vested rights and privileges."

Steering organizations that shop around can also use *specialized* service providers with unique skills to deal with difficult
populations: an organization of recovered alcoholics to work
with alcohol abusers; ex-inmates to work with young convicts.
This was not so essential 40 years ago. But as the *Boston Globe*
points out:

> *Many of the services provided by the government today were
> not even thought of back in the old days when the state ran
> huge institutions and provided direct service itself. Crack ba-
> bies, the AIDS epidemic and the stunning level of child
> abuse did not exist in the 1950s. Because of the implosion of
> so many families, 16,000 children are wards of the state to-
> day. They are housed in small community-based residential
> facilities.*

Steering organizations that shop around can even promote
experimentation and learn from success. Nature experiments
through natural selection: the evolutionary process rewards new
adaptations that work. Competition in the private sector works
the same way: successful new ideas draw customers, and unsuccessful ones die out. Using many different service providers
helps the public sector take advantage of the same phenomenon. "We need multiple providers out there, and we need sens-
ing systems to learn from their experience," says Brian
Bosworth, former president of a steering organization called the
Indiana Economic Development Council. "Then we need ways
to transmit what we've learned to the others."

Finally, steering organizations that shop around can provide
more *comprehensive* solutions, attacking the roots of the problem. They can define the problem—whether it is drug use,
crime, or poor performance in school—in its entirety, then use
many different organizations to attack it. They can bring all the
stakeholders into the policy process, thus ensuring that all

points of view are heard and all significant actors are motivated
to take part in the solution.

In contrast, governments that put steering and rowing within
the same organization limit themselves to relatively narrow
strategies. Their line of attack is defined by programs, not
problems.

In 1986, a White House report documented 59 "major public
assistance programs," 31 "other low income grant programs,"
and 11 "low income loan programs." Another study found that
"a low income family in one county with a population of roughly
half a million' would have to apply to 18 separate organizations to
reach all the different sources of assistance for which its members
were eligible." As the White House report concluded:

> *Each program began with its own rationale, representing the*
> *intent of public officials to address a perceived need. But*
> *when the programs are considered as a system they amount*
> *to a tangle of purposes, rules, agencies and effects.*

Successful antipoverty efforts, on the other hand, are usually
holistic. As Lisbeth Schorr reports in *Within Our Reach: Break-*
ing the Cycle of Disadvantage, they involve service providers
from different professions and agencies who don't ordinarily
work together. The only realistic way to develop such holistic
strategies is to separate steering from rowing, so the policy managers can define a comprehensive strategy and use many different oarsmen (oarspeople?) to implement it.

PUBLIC EMPLOYEES:
VICTIMS OR BENEFICIARIES?

The great fear of using nongovernment institutions to row is, of
course, that it will cost many public employees their jobs. This
fear is legitimate. In fact, the prospect of massive layoffs is one
of the barriers that keeps governments from moving into a
more catalytic mode.

We have found that the transition can be managed without
significant layoffs, however. The typical government loses 10

percent of its employees every year. By taking advantage of this attrition, governments can often avoid layoffs. They can also shift employees to other departments or require contractors to hire them at comparable wages and benefits. Los Angeles County, which has more than 100 separate contracts with private firms, has successfully relocated people within county government. The federal government requires contractors to give workers who are displaced by a contract first crack at job openings. Other governments do both.

Public employees do not have to be the victims of entrepreneurial government. In places like St. Paul and Visalia, they are its primary beneficiaries. The total number of jobs created by such governments does not change very much; some of those jobs simply shift to private firms and community organizations. But the job satisfaction of the workers increases dramatically.

Many employees in bureaucratic governments feel trapped. Tied down by rules and regulations, numbed by monotonous tasks, assigned jobs they know could be accomplished in half the time if they were only allowed to use their minds, they live lives of quiet desperation. When they have the opportunity to work for an organization with a clear mission and minimal red tape—as in Visalia or St. Paul or East Harlem—they are often reborn. When they are moved into the private sector, they often experience the same sense of liberation.

Governments that move from rowing to steering have fewer line workers but more policy managers, catalysts, and brokers. They have fewer paper pushers and more knowledge workers. Consider the Community Redevelopment Agency in Tampa, Florida. In 1985, it (and an agency with which it later merged) had 41 employees. They were traditional bureaucratic organizations, using federal funds to make rehabilitation loans on low-income properties. In 1985, these 41 employees made 37 loans.

When Sandy Freedman campaigned for mayor that year, she promised to do something about housing. Almost a third of the city's housing units needed some degree of rehabilitation. She and Community Redevelopment Director Fernando Noriega decided the city could never get at the problem with its traditional approach. So they decided to use the city as a catalyst and broker, to reshape the marketplace. They convinced several of the city's banks to create a $13 million Challenge Fund. The banks would make loans with low interest rates and 15-year repayment schedules to owners, to renovate their buildings. The city would guarantee each loan for its first five years, to limit the bankers' risk. A nonprofit Methodist agency would process the loans—on the theory that low-income people would be more comfortable dealing with a community organization than with bureaucrats or bankers.

In the process, Noriega merged his two housing organizations and trimmed them down to 22 employees. (He accomplished most of this by attrition, laying off only five people.) He retrained his employees, opted out of the civil service system, and structured his agency like a bank. He increased salary levels by 50 percent and began to treat his employees like professionals. He gave them monthly goals—for loan volume, dollar volume, and related measures—but turned them free to do the job as they saw fit. Today, says Noriega, they are "happier, more productive, better paid employees." They also have far greater impact. With half the people and less federal funding, the agency now facilitates *1,000* loans a year—a productivity increase of 3,000 percent.

"The answer to cuts in federal funds is not to cut services, but to find new ways of doing things," Noriega declares:

For some reason the philosophy in the public sector is, "When funds are cut, there's no other way but to cut services." But in my opinion, sometimes the best opportunities come because you're forced by budget cuts to find new ways to do things. We were forced to use the private sector—where else could we go?

CREATING "STEERING ORGANIZATIONS"

When governments separate policy management from service delivery, they often find that they have no real policy management capacity. Their commerce departments, welfare departments, housing authorities—all are driven by service delivery.

Policy management is done on the fly—or not at all. As governments embrace a more catalytic role, they are often forced to develop new organizations to manage the steering role.

Steering organizations set policy, deliver funds to operational bodies (public and private), and evaluate performance—but they seldom play an operational role themselves. They often cut across traditional bureaucratic boundaries; in fact, their members are sometimes drawn from both the public and private sectors.

- The Private Industry Councils set up under the federal Job Training Partnership Act bring local public and private leaders together to manage job training activities within their region. Primarily, they use performance contracts with other organizations to produce the actual training.

- Ohio uses local boards to manage its outpatient mental health and mental retardation services. Most of the boards play no operational role; they contract with almost 400 nonprofit mental health institutions to operate drug abuse programs, day treatment centers, family programs, and other services.

- In Pittsburgh, the Advisory Committee on Homelessness, made up of government, university, community, and religious leaders, coordinates the city's response to homelessness. It uses federal, state, and corporate funds to fund dozens of food banks, soup kitchens, counseling centers, job training programs, and housing initiatives. "This kind of broad-based response to homelessness has helped this city of 387,000 dodge the bullet that is crippling cities like New York, Chicago and Washington," reports the *Washington Post*.

- Montgomery County, Maryland, has created a Transportation Management District, in Silver Spring, that enlists all employers with more than 25 employees in a concerted effort to reduce commuter traffic. By coupling financial incentives and discounts with a requirement that all such employers develop traffic mitigation plans and participate in an annual commuter survey, it has brought the percentage of commuters who drive alone down from 66 to 55 percent. Although the Transportation Management District is an arm of county government, it has an advisory board made up of citizens and business leaders.

- Oklahoma Futures, which describes itself as the "Central Economic Development Policy Planning Board for the State of Oklahoma," has a five-year strategic plan that spells out the actions it expects from more than 25 separate organizations—from the AFL-CIO to the state Department of Education. Oklahoma Futures oversees the state Department of Commerce and approves the annual business plans of several other state development authorities.

Taking this principle one step further, the Arizona Department of Health Services actually contracts out the steering role. It contracts with nine nonprofit agencies and local governments—which must compete every three years for designation as "administrative entities"—to manage its adult mental health system. This method has reduced the cost of administration within the system to less than 7 percent, while allowing the Department of Health Services to function with only 62 full-time employees (excluding the state-owned hospital and mental health center).

The administrative entity in South Phoenix, one of Arizona's poorest areas, is the Community Organization for Drug Abuse, Mental Health and Alcoholism Services, Inc. CODAMA, as it calls itself, was born 20 years ago as an activist community organization. Today, it is a perfect example of a steering organization. It manages almost $17 million in state contracts with more than 50 drug, alcohol, and mental health treatment programs in South Phoenix. Every year it reviews each contract. Organizations that perform well are kept on; those that don't are cut off; those with high overhead costs are forced to slim down.

In CODAMA's first year as an administrative entity, it cut the administrative overhead among its service providers from 21 to 17 percent. It forced South Phoenix's largest mental health center to cut its overhead by $150,000. The next year the center applied to run a new residential treatment program, and lost.

"They were real mad," remembers CODAMA's executive director, Alan Flory, "so I said, 'Let's talk' ":

> There were three competitors for this new contract. I said, "The reason you didn't get funded was real clear: You were gonna do it for $300,000, they were gonna do it for $200,000, they were gonna hire 15 staff members, and you were gonna hire six!" I said, "I'll be damned, that doesn't make any sense to me!"

Flory is quick to enumerate the advantages of using nongovernment organizations like CODAMA as steering bodies:

> We can respond a lot quicker. We don't have the restraints of state government. It takes the state three to six months to get a contract amendment through the system; I can take care of a contract amendment in a day. The state uses civil servants; they can't switch those people. They went through cutbacks a few years ago, and they ended up with all the people that had been there for years and years. They're burned out. And the state can't fire anybody. My people—I can push 'em, I can make 'em work hard.

Flory has contracted with nonprofit organizations, local governments, and for-profit firms. "The nonprofits are clearly the best," he says. Many social services are simply not well suited to companies whose basic motive is profit. How much profit is there, after all, in helping poor people deal with alcoholism? "The for-profits and the government agencies have both been real problems for us. The for-profits are in business to make money, and the public sector agencies have little interest in saving money."

PUBLIC SECTOR, PRIVATE SECTOR,
OR THIRD SECTOR?

Most people have been taught that the public and private sectors occupy distinct worlds; that government should not interfere with business, and that business should have no truck with government. This was a central tenet of the bureaucratic model. But as we have seen, governments today—under intense pressure to solve problems without spending new money—look for the best method they can find, regardless of which sector it involves. There are very few services traditionally provided by the public sector that are not today provided somewhere by the private sector—and vice versa. Businesses are running public schools and fire departments. Governments are operating professional sports teams and running venture capital funds. Nonprofits are rehabilitating convicts, running banks, and developing real estate. Those who still believe government and business should be separate tend to oppose these innovations, whether or not they work. But the world has changed too much to allow an outdated mind-set to stifle us in this way. "We would do well," Harlan Cleveland writes in *The Knowledge Executive*, "to glory in the blurring of public and private and not keep trying to draw a disappearing line in the water."

When people ask themselves which sector can best handle a particular task, they also tend to think only of two sectors, public or private. But as Alan Flory made clear, "voluntary" or "nonprofit" organizations are often quite different from both public organizations and private, for-profit businesses.

The voluntary sector plays a role in American life that is seldom fully appreciated. By 1982, nonprofit organizations employed 8 percent of all workers and 14 percent of all service workers in the United States. Between 1972 and 1982, they were the fastest growing sector of the economy, in terms of employment. A 1989 Gallup survey on voluntary activities found that roughly half of all Americans 14 years of age or older—93.4 million people—volunteered their time in some way. The Independent Sector, which commissioned the poll, estimated the dollar value of their time $170 billion.

Defining this sector can be tricky. Neither the word *voluntary* nor the word *nonprofit* offers an accurate description. Organizations like the Red Cross, or Blue Cross/Blue Shield, are hardly voluntary: they employ thousands of professionals on salary. Nor does the phrase *not for profit* describe them accurately. In 1985, Blue Cross/Blue Shield of Massachusetts served three million members, earned a "gain" of $43 million, and was indistinguishable in its behavior from a for-profit business.

This sector, it seems to us, is made up of organizations that are privately owned and controlled, but that exist to meet public or social needs, not to accumulate private wealth. By this definition, large, nonprofit firms that exist primarily to accumulate wealth would not qualify. But for-profit institutions that exist to meet social or public needs (development banks, for instance) would qualify. For lack of a better term, we call this group of institutions the "third sector."

When governments shift from producing all services themselves to a more catalytic role, they often rely heavily on the third sector. Most of us assume that government does the important things and voluntary efforts fill in the cracks. But according to Lester Salamon, who lead a multiyear research project on nonprofit organizations at the Urban Institute, the third sector is actually society's *"preferred mechanism* for providing collective goods." It existed long before most government services existed. It coped with social problems long before governments took on that role. Governments stepped in only when the third sector proved incapable of dealing with particular problems. To this day, cities with a high level of third sector activism, such as Pittsburgh and the Twin Cities, are by far the most effective in dealing with social problems. In fighting homelessness in Pittsburgh, says Allegheny County official Robert Nelkin, "individuals and churches are the mainstay. Government is the Johnny-come-lately."

It is startling to see how many "public" services are actually delivered by third sector organizations. Even a decade ago, according to a survey by Salamon's team at the Urban Institute, nonprofit organizations delivered 56 percent of all social services financed by government, 48 percent of employment and training services, and 44 percent of health services. Government was by far their most important source of income. Our old assumptions blind many of us to this fact, but it is obvious to anyone who works in the human services field.

Ronald Reagan often argued that by cutting public sector spending, we could liberate voluntary efforts from the oppressive arm of government. Where we followed his lead—particularly in low-income housing—we often had the opposite effect, crippling community-based organizations. Such are the perils when one acts based on outdated assumptions.

PRIVATIZATION IS *ONE* ANSWER, NOT *THE* ANSWER

Conservatives have long argued that governments should turn over many of their functions to the private sector—by abandoning some, selling others, and contracting with private firms to handle others. Obviously this makes sense, in some instances. Privatization is one arrow in government's quiver. But just as obviously, privatization is not *the* solution. Those who advocate it on ideological grounds—because they believe business is always superior to government—are selling the American people snake oil.

Privatization is simply the wrong starting point for a discussion of the role of government. Services can be contracted out or turned over to the private sector. But *governance* cannot. We can privatize discrete steering functions, but not the overall process of governance. If we did, we would have no mechanism by which to make collective decisions, no way to set the rules of the marketplace, no means to enforce rules of behavior. We would lose all sense of equity and altruism: services that could not generate a profit, whether housing for the homeless or health care for the poor, would barely exist. Third sector organizations could never shoulder the entire load.

Business does some things better than government, but government does some things better than business. The public sector tends to be better, for instance, at policy management, regulation, ensuring equity, preventing discrimination or exploitation, ensuring continuity and stability of services, and ensuring social cohesion (through the mixing of races and classes, for example, in the public schools). Business tends to be better at performing economic tasks, innovating, replicating successful experiments, adapting to rapid change, abandoning unsuccessful or obsolete activities, and performing complex or technical tasks. The third sector tends to be best at performing tasks that generate little or no profit, demand compassion and commitment to individuals, require extensive trust on the part of customers or clients, need hands-on, personal attention (such as day care, counseling, and services to the handicapped or ill), and involve the enforcement of moral codes and individual responsibility for behavior. (For a discussion of the particulars, see appendix A.)

Likewise, private markets handle many tasks better than public administrations—but not all tasks. Our private market for higher education works extremely well, but without public universities, public community colleges, and public financial aid, many Americans would be denied the opportunity to go to college. Our public administration of elementary and secondary schools has many problems, but if we turned all education over to the private marketplace, many Americans could not even afford elementary school. Even if we used public vouchers, we would lose one of the fundamental benefits of public education—the chance for children to rub elbows with others from many different walks of life. (Those who could afford to would add their own funds to the voucher and buy a "better" education for their children, leading to extreme segregation by income group.) This shared experience may not be efficient, in market terms, but it is effective in making democracy work.

Those who support privatization in all cases because they dislike government are as misguided as those who oppose it in all cases because they dislike business. The truth is that the ownership of a good or service—whether public or private—is far less important than the dynamics of the market or institution that produces it. Some private markets function beautifully; others

do not. (Witness the savings-and-loan crisis.) Some public institutions function beautifully; others do not. (Witness public education.)

The determining factors have to do with the incentives that
drive those within the system. Are they motivated to excel? Are
they accountable for their results? Are they free from overly re-
strictive rules and regulations? Is authority decentralized
enough to permit adequate flexibility? Do rewards reflect the
quality of their performance? Questions like these are the important ones—not whether the activity is public or private. Often when governments privatize an activity—contracting with
a private company to pick up the garbage or run a prison, for
example—they wind up turning it over to a private monopoly,
and both the cost and the inefficiency grow worse!

It makes sense to put the delivery of many public services in
private hands (whether for-profit or nonprofit), if by doing so a
government can get more effectiveness, efficiency, equity, or accountability. But we should not mistake this for some grand
ideology of privatizing government. When governments contract with private businesses, both conservatives and liberals
often talk as if they are shifting a fundamental public responsibility to the private sector. This is nonsense: they are shifting
the delivery of services, not the responsibility for services. As
Ted Kolderie once said, "The fact that a road is built by a private contractor does not make that road a private road." When
governments contract activities to the private sector, those governments still make the policy decisions and provide the financing. And to do that well, they must be quality governments.

Even Peter Drucker, the first advocate of privatization (he
coined the term, originally calling it reprivatization), argued
that we needed more governance, not less. Drucker did both in
1968, in *The Age of Discontinuity*:

> *We do not face a "withering away of the state." On the con-*
> *trary, we need a vigorous, a strong, and a very active govern-*
> *ment. But we do face a choice between big but impotent*
> *government and a government that is strong because it con-*

fines itself to decision and direction and leaves the "doing" to others.

[We need] a government that can and does govern. This is not a government that "does"; it is not a government that "administers"; it is a government that governs.

–2–

Community-Owned Government: Empowering Rather Than Serving

The older I get, the more convinced I am that to really work programs have to be owned by the people they're serving That isn't just rhetoric, it's real There's got to be ownership
—George Latimer, Former Mayor of St. Paul

In 1982, Lee Brown became chief of police in Houston, Texas. The Houston police force was beset by charges of racism and brutality. Brown, who is black, set out to transform it. The vehicle he chose was "neighborhood-oriented policing": the notion that the police should not simply respond to incidents of crime, but also help neighborhoods solve the problems that underlie crime.

Brown assigned most of his officers to neighborhood beats. He set up 20 storefront ministations in the neighborhoods. He instructed his officers to build strong relationships with churches, businesses, PTAs, and other community organizations. In one high-crime area, he had officers on the beat visit more than a third of all homes, to introduce themselves and ask about neighborhood problems.

"What we're doing is revolutionary in U.S. policing," Brown told one columnist. "We're redefining the role of the patrol officer—we want him to be a community organizer, community activist, a problem solver. . . . I want people as committed to neighborhoods as young Americans were to the Peace Corps."

Now the police chief in New York City, Brown is a leader in what political scientist James Q. Wilson calls "the most significant redefinition of police work in the past half century." Wilson and others call it community-oriented policing. The basic idea is to make public safety a *community* responsibility, rather than simply the responsibility of the professionals—the police. It transforms the police officer from an investigator and enforcer into a catalyst in a process of community self-help. Sometimes this means police officers help neighborhood members clear out vacant lots and rusting cars. Sometimes it means they help organize marches in front of crack houses. Sometimes it means they work with community leaders to keep neighborhood children in school.

"You can't rush in with the police car, handle the call, and leave," says Tulsa Police Chief Drew Diamond. "Then what you've done is reactive, a momentary solution to the problem, and you're going to be back."

Under Chief Diamond's leadership, the Tulsa police studied arrest trends, school dropout statistics, drug treatment data, and the problems of the city's public housing developments. They concluded that teenagers from one section of town were creating most of the city's drug problems—so they began to work with the community to attack the problem at its roots. They organized the residents of one apartment complex, and with their backing prosecuted and evicted residents who were dealing or helping dealers. They created an antidrug education program in the housing projects. They set up job placement programs and mentoring initiatives for young men and women. They set up a youth camp for teenagers. And they worked with the schools to develop an antitruancy program.

Community-oriented policing is under way in more than 300 American cities, from Newark, New Jersey, to Dallas, Texas; Charleston, South Carolina, to Madison, Wisconsin. In addition some 18,000 "neighborhood watch" groups, with a million members, work with local police forces to help defend their communities against crime, according to the National Association of Town Watch. To make a long-term impact, most experts have concluded, such groups need to focus on their community's underlying problems. Community-oriented policing turns the local police officer into their ally.

The real key, says Hubert Williams, president of a research institute called the Police Foundation, "is the ability of the police to act as a catalyst to draw together community resources, to provide resources, backup and training."

In short, the police can be most effective if they help communities help themselves. This is really just common sense. We all know that people act more responsibly when they control their own environments than when they are under the control of others. We know that owners take better care of homes than renters. We know that workers who own a piece of the company are more committed than those who simply collect a paycheck. It stands to reason that when communities are empowered to solve their own problems, they function better than communities that depend on services provided by outsiders.

Empowerment is an American tradition, as old as the frontier. We are a nation of self-help organizations. We create our own day-care centers, our own babysitting cooperatives, our own Little Leagues, our own Girl Scout and Boy Scout troops, our own recycling programs, our own volunteer organizations of all kinds.

And yet, when we organize our public business, we, forget these lessons. We let bureaucrats control our public services, not those they intend to help. We rely on professionals to solve problems, not families and communities. We let the police, the doctors, the teachers, and the social workers have all the control, while the people they are serving have none. "Too often," says George Latimer, "we create programs designed to collect clients rather than to empower communities of citizens."

When we do this, we undermine the confidence and competence of our citizens and communities. We create *dependency*. It should come as no surprise that welfare dependency, alcohol dependency, and drug dependency are among our most severe problems.

Latimer likes to quote Tom Dewar, of the University of Minnesota's Humphrey Institute, about the dangers of "clienthood":

Clients are people who are dependent upon and controlled by their helpers and leaders. Clients are people who understand themselves in terms of their deficiencies and people who wait for others to act on their behalf.

Citizens, on the other hand, are people who nderstand their own problems in their own terms. Citizens perceive their relationship to one another and they believe in their capacity to act. Good clients make bad citizens. Good citizens make strong communities.

PULLING OWNERSHIP OUT OF THE BUREAUCRACY, INTO THE COMMUNITY

Clienthood is a problem that emerged only as our industrial economy matured. Before 1900, what little control existed over neighborhoods, health, education, and the like lay primarily with local communities, because so many products and services, whether public or private, were produced or sold locally. It was only with the emergence of an industrial economy of mass production that we began to hire professionals and bureaucrats to do what families, neighborhoods, churches, and voluntary associations had done.

We started with the best of intentions, to heal the new wounds of an industrial, urban society. We moved ahead rapidly when the economic collapse of the Depression strained the capacities of families and communities to the breaking point. And we continued on after the Depression, as prosperity and mobility loosened the old bonds of geographic community, leaving the elderly far from their children, the employed uninvolved in their neighborhoods, and the churches increasingly empty. But along the way, we lost something precious. The Progressive confidence in "neutral administrators" and "professionalism" blinded us to the consequences of taking control out of the hands of families and communities.

The reaction was not long in coming. During the 1960s, neighborhoods fought against the urban renewal schemes dreamed up by professional city planners. Minority communities fought for control over Great Society programs like Community Action and Model Cities. By 1970, a welfare rights movement had emerged to demand more control over the welfare system, a tenants' rights movement had emerged to demand more control over public housing, and a neighborhood movement had emerged to demand more control over urban development and public services. Soon middle-class America joined in, with a consumer movement, which sought to give consumers more control over the products made by private corporations; a holistic health movement, which sought to give individuals more control over their own health; a deinstitutionalization movement, which sought to give mental patients more control over their environments; and a general effort to force authorities of all kinds to share their power, through "sunshine" laws, freedom-of-information acts, right-to-know laws, open-meeting laws, and the like. These movements were animated by a common sense that real control over our lives had been lost to the megainstitutions of society: big business, big government, and big labor.

Slowly, government has begun to respond. Community-oriented policing is not an isolated phenomenon. The same themes of community ownership and empowerment appear in virtually every segment of American public life. Our governments are beginning to push ownership and control of public services out of the hands of bureaucrats and professionals, into communities.

During the huge refugee resettlement effort for those fleeing Southeast Asia, the federal government did not pay professionals or bureaucrats to help people find homes and jobs; it used churches.

As recycling became a priority, the city with the best track record, Seattle, credited part of its success to voluntary block captains who helped their neighbors figure out how to make curbside recycling work.

Most housing initiatives now use community development corporations, tenant cooperatives, and the like to develop

low-income housing. Boston even let one community organization take over abandoned buildings and lots through eminent
domain.

In education, parents are beginning to assert control over the
schools. According to John Chubb, coauthor of *Politics, Markets and America's Schools*, "The largest estimated influence on
the effectiveness of school organization is the role of parents in
the school. All other things being equal, schools in which parents are highly involved, cooperative, and well-informed are
more likely to develop effective organizations than are schools
in which parents do not possess these qualities." And yet most
public schools let parents handle little more than bake sales,
fund-raising, and PTA meetings.

In Chicago, every public school is now run by a council of six
parents, elected by parents; two community members, elected
by community residents; two teachers, elected by the school
staff; and the principal. This council acts as the board of directors: it hires the principal (on a four-year performance-based
contract), prepares a school improvement plan, and prepares
the school budget, in accordance with its improvement plan.
Principals are now hired and fired based on merit rather than
seniority. After the first year, 81 percent of parents and 62 percent of teachers said their schools were operating "better" than
before the reform. Seventy-eight percent of parents reported
improvements in safety and discipline, 61 percent saw improvements in the physical plant, and 83 percent reported progress in educational programs.

"Lots of people told us we were making a terrific mistake,
because we were turning power over to illiterate, underclass
people, taking it away from those who had the professional
knowledge," says Don Moore, whose advocacy organization,
Designs for Change, spearheaded the reform effort:

*They said we wouldn't get people to run for the councils.
But 17,000 people ran, and we had a higher turnout than
they get in suburban school board elections. We see the
councils as a new democratic unit in the community. We
expect that the people who serve on councils will probably*

get involved in other issues, like housing, economic devel-
opment, and adult education. These are real seedbeds for
leadership development.

New Haven, Connecticut, tried something similar back in 1968. At two failing, inner-city schools, it set up Governance Management Teams made up of parents, teachers, other staff members, and the principal. By 1978, students at the two experimental schools had caught up to grade level. By 1984, they scored third and fourth highest in the system and had the best attendance records. By 1990, the specific model, called the School Development Program, was used in all 42 New Haven schools—and in more than 60 other schools in eight states. Professor James Comer of Yale, who initiated it, was even planning to introduce it in six Chicago schools.

The same trends are evident in early childhood education. From its inception, Head Start has "made an all-out attempt to use the parent as part of the teaching process," in the words of one expert. Even where parents do not teach, they work as aides, serve on boards, and help with field trips and other activities. "The best Head Start programs in this country learned a long time ago that when the parents really feel like they're in charge, like they've got ownership, you get a different performance out of that kid," says Curtis Johnson, a former college president who, as director of the Citizens League, has been a key force behind education reform in Minnesota. Today, Head Start is considered by many one of our most successful antipoverty programs.

Several states have gone even further, developing programs that encourage parents to teach their own children. Arkansas imported its model—the Home Instruction Program for Preschool Youngsters (HIPPY)—from Israel. Every day, 2,400 welfare mothers spend 20 minutes teaching their children at home, with simple workbooks. A trained HIPPY worker—often a former HIPPY mother—visits once a week to help plan the next week's work. In 1989, the percentage of children testing at or above national averages jumped from 6 percent going into the program to 74 percent at the end of the year. "In one project, 18 of the 39 participating welfare mothers enrolled in education courses for themselves after the first year," says Governor Bill Clinton. "The HIPPY program builds in its own follow-up by changing the parent into the child's first teacher, which is what every parent should be."

Even job training agencies are beginning to empower workers. The Massachusetts Industrial Services Program, which provides training for dislocated workers, uses some of those very workers to help staff its 30-odd centers around the state. When a plant announces a closing or major layoff, the state sets up a temporary center and hires a staff to provide counseling, training, help in finding another job, and related services. It hires several of the dislocated workers, then keeps those who excel to staff other centers. In some centers, every staff member is a former dislocated worker.

These workers know firsthand the problems their colleagues face, and they are determined to do something about them. "I love these people in the plant, and I've worked with them for 25 years," says Richard Wisniewski, a former machinist who became a career counselor at one center. "I wish I could change and take away their hurt, but I can't do that. But maybe I ease the pain just a little bit by giving 110 percent to my job."

The program is one of the most effective in the country. Over its first five years, it served more than 37,000 dislocated workers, placing 80 percent in jobs that paid, on average, 92 percent of their former wages.

In criminal justice, community-oriented policing is just the beginning. San Francisco uses Community Boards, with voluntary mediators, to resolve the kinds of everyday conflicts that often erupt into violence. Pioneered in the late 1970s by neighborhood activists, these boards now handle and settle more cases than the San Francisco Municipal Court. They save a tremendous amount of money, but more important, they build a sense of empowerment, a sense that people working together in neighborhoods can solve their own problems. A third of their volunteers are people who have found themselves in a neighborhood dispute, used a Community Board to resolve it, and liked the process so much they volunteered.

Some community organizations are even taking ownership of the justice process *after* a criminal is arrested. Florida paroles first-time convicted criminals into the care of the Salvation Army—25,000 of them at any one time. Massachusetts closed its traditional, prison-like juvenile corrections institutions and moved its juvenile offenders into small, community-based group homes. A 1989 study by the National Council on Crime and Delinquency found that this system not only led to lower rearrest rates than most states and fewer violent crimes, but cost less than incarceration.

David and Falakah Fattah opened their own home in Philadelphia to 15 teenage gang members in 1969. Since then, they have "adopted" more than 500 former gang members, with such success that the juvenile courts have begun to send many of their worst cases to the Fattahs' House of Umoja. Those who stay abide by strict rules: they must rise by 6 A.M. every morning for a conference to set goals for the day; they must do chores; and they must attend a weekly meeting to review their behavior. In return, they get the support of a strong, dedicated family. In a study of recidivism, the Philadelphia Psychiatric Center found the rearrest rate of ex-offenders sent to the House of Umoja to be just 3 percent. At the city's far more expensive correctional facilities, rearrest rates ranged from 70 to 90 percent.

Health care is a system thoroughly dominated by professionals, but even here a shift toward community is evident. Our health care system was set up to deal with acute care: life-threatening illnesses and injuries. It was so effective that today most people die of chronic, degenerative problems—of "old age." Yet we continue to respond with an acute care system of high-technology hospitals and highly trained doctors. Ironically, it was our very success at acute, professional care that left us with an elderly population desperate for something more.

"Chronic care requires a fundamentally different response, one grounded in the meaning and familiarity of community, family, and friends," explains David Schulman, who runs the Los Angeles City Attorney's AIDS/HIV Discrimination Unit. "That explains the powerful growth of hospice—providing a homelike setting for supportive care of the terminally ill."

Between the late 1970s and the late 1980s, Schulman reports, the number of hospices in the United States swelled from a few dozen to a few thousand. The home health care industry also exploded. State governments developed extensive programs to help the elderly stay in their own homes rather than go into nursing homes. Most health insurance companies began covering home health care. One even began to pay family members, trained by nurses, to provide care at home. By 1989, home health care was a $7 billion industry.

AIDS catalyzed perhaps the most profound shift from the old model to the new. "The San Francisco gay and lesbian community adopted the hospice model," explains Schulman. "They got teams of friends and volunteers together to care for people with AIDS at home—at a fraction of the cost of hospital care. It not only works better, it helped San Francisco soften a blow that may yet bankrupt it."

In a powerful article in the *Washington Monthly*, Katherine Boo described the process. It began when a gay nurse at San Francisco General Hospital, Cliff Morrison, convinced his superiors to let him suspend the normal hierarchical, bureaucratic rules on the AIDS ward. He let patients set visiting rules, recruited hundreds of volunteers to help AIDS patients—often just to sit with them—and set up a special kitchen and other facilities.

But "a comfortable hospital is still a hospital," as Boo put it. So Morrison and his staff "began suturing together a network of local clinics, hospices, welfare offices, and volunteers that would get patients out of the ward and back into the community." For two years, Morrison spent much of his time "battling the higher-ups." But when San Francisco's average cost of AIDS treatment dropped to 40 percent of the national average, they finally understood.

The idea spread quickly to other cities. In some, the new communities of care even began helping AIDS patients do battle with Medicaid and welfare bureaucracies. "For the first time in recent history, AIDS brought members of the organized middle class into the ghetto of the human services bureaucracy," Boo wrote. "They found the system lacking, so they changed it.

Outside the fragmented, assembly-line world of social services, with an army of volunteers, the gay community built a new way of caring for some of society's most vulnerable members."

"This is how effective social service programs work: intimately, aggressively, with feeling."

PUBLIC HOUSING: A CASE STUDY

To understand just how profound a force community ownership can be, let us take a close look at one example: the transformation that occurs when public housing tenants take control of their own environment.

Public housing began as transitional housing for working people who had come upon hard times, during the Depression. It was an inexpensive, safe, stable environment for families while they got back on their feet. Public housing authorities had rigid standards, and residents had clear responsibilities: they had to pay their full rent; they were generally not welcome if they were on welfare; if they had children, they had to be married; and if they found jobs and could afford better housing, they had to move.

Public housing worked well for two decades, even though it was a classic example of the centralized, top-down, bureaucratic model. Then, during the prosperity of the 1950s, a dramatic change took place. Working families moved out of public housing, and poor, illiterate blacks from the rural South poured in. Bureaucratic organizations are slow to respond when conditions change, and housing authorities were no exception. As this radically different population moved in—most of whom had never *seen* a high-rise building, let alone lived in one—few housing authorities changed anything.

Meanwhile, Congress decided to deny welfare to most families if the father was present—thus driving many fathers away. It also gave welfare mothers in public housing subsidized rent, which meant that their rent often tripled or quadrupled if they left welfare to work. These changes created powerful incentives to stay single and unemployed.

Before long, public housing developments were functioning as traps, not safe havens. In many cities, they sank into a vicious cycle of drugs, crime, teenage pregnancy, and welfare dependency. Because all the control lay with a central bureaucracy—the local housing authority—residents were powerless to enforce standards of behavior or evict criminals. If someone dealt drugs out of the apartment next door, residents could complain—but the system rarely responded.

The Kenilworth-Parkside development, in northeast Washington, D.C., was a classic example. By 1980, its main street was an open-air drug market, and violence was so common that the management company put a bulletproof barrier around its office. Residents went without heat or hot water for months at a time. The roofs leaked, the grass died, and the fences were torn down. Rubbish was picked up so infrequently that rats infested the buildings.

Over the next ten years, however, Kenilworth-Parkside's residents transformed their community. By 1990, the drug dealers were gone, crime was negligible, and the buildings were under repair.

The catalyst for this transformation was an extraordinary woman named Kimi Gray.

When she got her first apartment at Kenilworth-Parkside, in 1966, Kimi Gray personified the stereotype many people have of the welfare mother: 21, black, divorced, on welfare, with five children. Today she is an example not of dependency but of the mountains people can move when they decide to take control of their own lives.

In 1974, Gray remembers, "some students came to me and said, 'Miss Kimi, we want to go to college.' What the hell did I know about going to college? [But] I said, 'Let me check it out, let me see what I can do.' " Soon she and several recruits were tutoring students, helping them find summer jobs, enrolling them in Upward Bound, helping them fill out college applications, and drumming up scholarship money. The students called their project College Here We Come. They held bake sales and raffles, got part-time jobs, and opened bank accounts. After Kimi had hustled all the scholarships and loans and work-study jobs she could, and a student still needed $600 or $1,000, College Here We Come kicked in the rest.

Seventeen kids left for college the first August. Word spread quickly: "Man, this stuff is real! People really going to college! These children couldn't believe that," Kimi says. "Poor people, from public housing, their mothers on welfare, absent fathers, going to college?"

In the 15 previous years, two residents of Kenilworth-Parkside had attended college. Over the next 15 years, 700 did—and three-fourths of those graduated, according to Gray. Today even 16-year-old boys on street corners look up to those who attend college.

The second phase of the transformation began in 1982. For several years, Kenilworth-Parkside's residents had been pressuring the mayor to let them manage the property. Finally, grudgingly, he agreed. The tenants wrote their own constitution and bylaws, their own personnel and policy procedures, their own job descriptions.

The bureaucrats "*could not* believe it," Kimi says. "Public housing residents? I said, 'The worst it can do is have wrong grammar in it. But at least we would understand and we would know clearly what was in it, right? So therefore we could enforce what we knew we had written.'" Besides, if the Department of Housing and Urban Development (HUD) wrote it, there would be ten lawyers in the room, writing "rules for things that don't even exist. I mean the crime hasn't been committed and they got a rule for it already."

The Kenilworth-Parkside Resident Management Corporation hired and trained residents to manage the property and do the maintenance. They held monthly meetings of all tenants. In their Bring the Fathers Out of the Closets campaign, they hired absentee fathers. Believing that peer pressure was the key to changing their environment, they set up fines for violating the rules—littering, loitering in hallways, sitting on fences, not cutting your grass. They created a system of elected building captains and court captains to enforce them. They started mandatory Sunday classes to teach housekeeping, budgeting, home repair, and parenting. And they required mothers who enrolled their children in the day-care center to work, attend school, or get job training.

Based on the results of a needs survey, the Resident Management Corporation created an after-school homework and tutorial program for kids whose mothers worked full-time. They set up courses to help adults get their high school degrees; contracted with a doctor and a dentist to set up part-time office hours and make house calls at the development; set up an employment office to help people find training and jobs; and began to create their own businesses, to keep money and jobs within the community.

The first was a shop to replace windows, screens, and doors, owned by a young man who could neither read nor count. In return for a start-up loan from the residents council, he trained ten students, who went on to market their skills elsewhere in Washington. The board fired the garbage collection service and contracted with another young man, on condition that he hire Kenilworth-Parkside residents. Before long they had a cooperative store, a snack bar, two laundromats, a beauty salon, a barber shop, a clothes boutique, a thrift shop, a catering service, a moving company, and a construction company that helped renovate vacant apartments. All the businesses employed residents, and all were required to hire young people to work with the adults. At one point, 120 residents had jobs at Kenilworth.

Gradually maintenance improved as well. The managers and maintenance men lived on the property; if the heat went out over the weekend, they got cold too. "It has to be someone who's there all the time, on the property," says Renee Sims, head teacher at Kenilworth's Learning Center. "Because if you have someone outside managing it, and a pipe bursts over the weekend, you're not going to get it done."

Kimi and her managers estimate that in 1982, when they began, less than half the residents were paying rent. Resident Manager Gladys Roy and her assistants began going door to door, serving 30-day eviction notices. They explained that if people didn't pay the rent, they couldn't afford the repairs people needed. If people did not have the cash, they worked out payment plans or collected what they could. By 1987, rent collections were up to 75 percent.

Perhaps the worst problem at Kenilworth-Parkside was drugs. Every evening hundreds of dealers lined Quarles Street. Many of the worst offenders lived at Kenilworth, but the police were reluctant to enter the neighborhood because residents were hostile. Mothers kept their children barricaded indoors.

Finally, Kimi called a meeting and invited the police. At first most residents stayed home, afraid to be seen as snitches. Kimi and the few who did attend asked for foot patrols at Kenilworth. Then they suggested a temporary station—a trailer— right on the grounds. The police agreed.

"By putting guys over there, on a regular basis, they began slowly to develop a sense of trust in us," says Sergeant Robert L. Prout, Jr. "And they began to give us information. . . . And now, it's got to the point where we have mothers that have sons that if they're wanted for something, they'll pick up the phone and call us."

Kimi remained the role model. She turned in anyone who was selling drugs—even members of her beloved College Here We Come. (Her own son was arrested for dealing in southwest Washington.) She made sure a 30-day eviction notice went to every household in which someone was dealing. If nothing happened, the Resident Management Corporation started litigation.

"We got with the attorney down at the Housing Department and we wore 'em to death, 'til we got them to take our cases to court," Kimi explains. "Now once we got to court, we were alright, because we would take residents with us down to court to say, 'No, your honor, that fella cannot stay in our community any longer.'" Four families were evicted. "That's all it took. People seen, 'Hey, they serious.'"

Evictions did not stop the dealers who lived elsewhere, of course. Finally, in 1984, the residents decided to confront the dealers head on. "We got together and we marched," says Denise Yates, assistant manager of the Resident Management Corporation. "Day after day, and in the evening too. We marched up and down the street with our signs. We had the police back us. Maybe half the community would march. A lot of teenagers and little kids, in addition to mothers."

After several weeks of disrupted business, the dealers began to drift away. Some resisted, and for a time things got nasty. Someone cut the brake lines in Kimi's car, put sugar in her gas tank, slashed her tires. But she refused to bend, and her confidence rubbed off on the others.

"When she didn't show any fear of being seen with the police, or riding through the neighborhood with us, then they more or less followed suit," says Sergeant Prout. By 1989, the crime rate had fallen from between 12 to 15 crimes a month—one of the highest levels in the city—to 2.

The lesson is clear: the police can make raid after raid, but only if a community decides to take responsibility for its own safety can the police be truly effective. "We tell them, 'The police can't be here all the time,'" Prout explains. ' "You live here, you know more about what goes on, you know who does what. It's just a matter of whether you want your community, or whether you want them to have your community.' "

In 1986, the accounting firm Coopers & Lybrand released an audit of Kenilworth-Parkside. During the first four years of tenant management, it reported, rent collections increased 77 percent—seven times the increase at public housing citywide. Vacancy rates fell from 18 percent—then the citywide average—to 5.4 percent. The Resident Management Corporation helped at least 132 residents get off welfare: it hired 10 as staff and 92 to run the businesses it started, while its employment office found training and jobs for 30 more. (Others received part-time jobs.) Overall, Coopers & Lybrand concluded, four years of resident management had saved the city at least $785,000. If trends continued over the next six years, it would save $3.7 million more—and the federal government would reap additional savings.

Since the Coopers & Lybrand audit, a complete renovation of Kenilworth has been done, under HUD's normal renovation program. In 1990, the residents bought the development—for a grand total of $1. A community of 3,000, once characterized largely by single-parent families on welfare, is now a community of homeowners, the majority of whom work.

Expectations are powerful. Before they took control of their own environment, people at Kenilworth-Parkside expected things to happen to them. They *expected* to lose their heat or hot water. They *expected* to be victimized by crime. They *expected* their roofs to leak. They *expected* their sons to get into drugs, their daughters to get pregnant. They expected to have no power to change any of this, because all the power in their environment lay with the housing authority, the police, or the criminals.

As they took control of their environment, their expectations began to change. "There is a conversion experience that people go through," says David Freed, a real estate consultant who specializes in low-income tenant buy-outs in Washington, D.C. "It happens when there is a process that renters go through together and there is a change in people's view of themselves and their neighbors. I see it again and again. It's what's exciting about my work: it's that conversion experience."

Today, more than 15 tenant organizations around the country manage their own public housing projects, and more than 200 groups have received formal training for the management role. Several want to buy their developments, as Kenilworth-Parkside residents have.

"Development begins with a belief system," says Robert Woodson, whose National Center for Neighborhood Enterprise has functioned as an informal staff for the tenant management movement:

> *What Kimi and other tenant leaders have done is just self-confidence, and they've passed that self-confidence on to others. Only when you overcome the crisis of self-confidence can opportunity make a difference in your life. But we act with programs as if opportunity carries with it elements of self-confidence. And it does not.*

PROFESSIONAL SERVICE VERSUS COMMUNITY CARE

The empowerment of communities like Kenilworth-Parkside not only changes expectations and instills confidence—it usually provides far better solutions to their problems than normal public services. John McKnight, director of community studies at Northwestern University's Center for Urban Affairs and Policy Research, spent several decades as a community organizer in Chicago. His experiences convinced him that by pulling ownership of services out of the community and into the hands of professionals and bureaucracies, we have actually weakened our communities and undermined our people. "There is a mistaken notion that our society has a problem in terms of effective human services," he says. "Our essential problem is weak communities."

McKnight provides an illuminating series of contrasts between professional service delivery systems and what he calls "associations of community"—the family, the neighborhood, the church, and the voluntary organization. For example:

Communities have more commitment to their members than service delivery systems have to their clients. Kimi Gray and her staff are more committed to their residents than any housing authority could be. Those who join Mothers Against Drunk Driving are more committed to their mission than any government agency could be. The nonprofit organizations CODAMA contracts with in Arizona are more committed to their patients than any hospitals or psychiatrists could be. "In our organizations, bachelor-level counselors are working for around $15,000," says Alan Flory. "They tend to be very committed people. Some of them are recovered alcoholics, or people who've had alcohol or drug problems in their families."

Communities understand their problems better than service professionals. No bureaucrat could know more about problems in a public housing development than the people who live there. No state employee can understand the problems of unemployed workers better than their coworkers. "I'm from manufacturing, and I speak their language," says Barbara Gillette, a former sugar refinery worker who joined the staff of a Worker Assistance Center in Massachusetts. "The key to what I do is to let people know I've experienced it. I had difficulty and I had losses too, but I came through it."

Professionals and bureaucracies deliver services; communities solve problems. McKnight describes a neighborhood organization in Chicago that tried to forge a partnership with the local hospitals to improve health care. When the effort yielded few results, the organization gradually began to look "not at more professional service, but instead at the question of what brought their people to the hospital in the first place." The answers were predictable: automobile accidents, interpersonal violence, accidents, alcoholism, and dog bites.

When this became clear, the people in the neighborhood immediately saw that what they needed was not really more and better medical/hospital service, but to work down the volume of auto accidents, interpersonal violence, accidents, alcoholism, and dog bites. . . . They began with dog bites. It occurred to them to offer kids in the neighborhood a bounty for bringing in dogs running loose. They had been paying something like $185 for the treatment of a dog bite. They paid a $5 bounty for dogs. And they gradually began to be aware, as this went on, that though there is a market for professional service, there is not really a market for problem solving. Nobody puts up money to reduce dog bites; they put up money to stitch up dog bites. Most of the activity and the money nominally addressed at solving problems is, in fact, simply going to pay for services.

As we write, the city of Boston is forcing its hospitals to expand their services for pregnant women in Boston's black neighborhoods, where infant mortality is on the rise. But anyone who reads the newspaper knows that the problem is not simply a lack of medical services. The problems are poverty, drug addiction, teenage sex, and the dissolution of the black family. More medical services will have very little impact.

Institutions and professionals offer "service"; communities offer "care." Care is different from service. Care is the human warmth of a genuine companion; care is the support of loved ones as a family copes with tragedy; care is the gentle hand of a helper when one is bedridden. Economist Steven E. Rhoads describes one example in his book *The Economist's View of the World:*

Over 6,000 people in our community of 100,000 perform volunteer work. One hundred participate in the "Meals on Wheels" Program, donating a few hours a week and driving expenses to take hot meals to elderly people who cannot cook for themselves.

This program is the perfect example of the kind of in-kind redistribution program economists typically attack. The charge would go something like this. "Why have a separate bureaucracy charged with one small thing—delivering hot meals to the elderly? What is so special about a hot meal anyway? Why not give the poor the money we spend on the program to do with as they wish?"

This analysis misses something. The most important thing that the volunteers bring the elderly is not the hot meal, but the human contact and the sense that someone cares. Volunteers can do this more convincingly than bureaucrats.

Communities are more flexible and creative than large service bureaucracies. Kenilworth-Parkside is a perfect example. An Illinois initiative called One Church, One Child provides another. A decade ago, the Illinois Department of Children and Family Services was having trouble placing black children for adoption; it had a backlog of 1,000. The problem, according to black leaders, was the bureaucracy. Its members brought the same middle-class standards to black adoptions that they used for white adoptions. They turned down black families because they lived in apartments rather than houses, they did not have enough formal education, they lacked middle-class incomes, or they had only one parent.

In 1980, the department turned to the black community for help. Working with black ministers, it asked each black church to find at least one family willing to adopt a child. The first person to volunteer was an unmarried black minister. The churches have since found homes for more than 3,000 black children, and the backlog of black children waiting for adoption has fallen below that for whites.

Communities are cheaper than service professionals. One Church, One Child saved Illinois an estimated $15 million in just three years. Florida saves $180 million a year by financing home care and community care to keep people out of nursing homes. The community mental health organizations with which Arizona contracts save the state millions of dollars every year. (In fact, the state makes them raise 25–50 percent of their budgets on their own; by 1989, this amounted to $12 million a year.)

"The professional servicers take increasing proportions of public money, desperately needed by the poor, and consume it in the name of helping poor families," says McKnight. His center at Northwestern University did a study of government spending on the poor in Cook County, which includes Chicago. They found that in 1984, federal, state, and local governments spent $6,209 per poor person in Cook County—enough to get everyone over the poverty line. Yet only 35 percent of this money reached the poor in the form of cash. Another 13 percent came as food stamps and rent vouchers. The majority, 52.6 percent, went to service providers: hospitals, doctors, nursing homes, social service agencies, job trainers, lawyers. The Community Services Society of New York did a similar study, with similar results. Of the roughly $7,000 in public and private money expended per low-income person in New York City in 1983, only 37 percent reached the poor.

Communities enforce standards of behavior more effectively than bureaucracies or service professionals. Several years ago a Catholic church in Brooklyn closed down a shelter for homeless men, which provided a bed, clothing, and help in finding a job. The church had run it successfully for 10 years, but when the city opened a shelter nearby, most of the men left. Why? Because they preferred the city shelter—where no one forced them to give up alcohol and drugs, to wash up, or to look for a job.

Sister Connie Driscoll runs a nationally recognized shelter for homeless women and children in Chicago. Those who stay have to take classes, do chores, and save 70 percent of their welfare checks. In seven years, 6,000 women have moved through the shelter, and according to Driscoll, only 6.5 percent have returned to the shelter system. Driscoll believes other shelters should start requiring things like education—"if you can get the liberal left to get off the bandwagon about 'You can't force people to do things because you think it's right.' Well, maybe they can't, in publicly operated shelters and publicly funded shelters. But, as a private shelter, we can make it a part of our contract—and we do."

Like public bureaucracies, professionals are also reluctant to impose their values by telling clients how to behave. In fact, by treating problems as "diseases," professionals often avoid the question of values and behavior altogether. Family members, church members, and community members are not so reluctant.

"One of the things that this community has brought back is a kind of old-fashioned shunning," says Dr. Alice Murray, a psychologist who runs Kenilworth-Parkside's Substance Abuse Prevention project. "It's a way of saying, 'This is behavior we will not tolerate. Should it happen, then we put you through all the services, but we don't expect it to happen ever again.' It's done in a very kind and gentle and loving way, but there's shame when it occurs—which is not the case in the outside community."

Communities focus on capacities; service systems focus on deficiencies. Communities like Kenilworth-Parkside depend on the capacities of their members to get things done. Think of your church, your synagogue, your voluntary organization. It wants a contribution from you, in time, talent, or treasure. Hence its entire attention is on your *capacities*—on what you can bring to the task. In contrast, job training programs, social work agencies, police departments, and welfare programs focus on your deficiencies: what you don't know, what you can't do, how you have been victimized. Most professionals "basically see the family as a client in need of treatment and therapy," says McKnight. This has "the increasing effect of convincing families that they are incompetent to know, care, teach, cure, make, or do. Only certified people can do that for you."

MANAGING THE TRANSITION
FROM SERVICE TO EMPOWERMENT

If community ownership is the goal, what role can government play? How can it empower stakeholders? Does it simply abandon services delivered by bureaucrats and professionals?

Of course not. Public housing again provides a useful illustration. In the mid-1980s, Robert Woodson asked Kimi Gray and other tenant management leaders to draw up a list of policy changes that would remove barriers to their success. Based on that list, they developed seven amendments to the federal Housing Act. The resulting bill gave resident councils a clear right to manage their own developments; gave them priority for HUD renovation grants; set up procedures by which resident management corporations could buy their projects after three years of successful management; and appropriated $5 million to train residents in self-management at 50 projects. When Jack Kemp became secretary of housing and urban development, he made tenant management and ownership one of HUD's top priorities. By 1993, he hopes to have moved 250 public housing developments through training for tenant management.

Government cannot force people to take control of their housing or schools or neighborhoods. When HUD and the Ford Foundation tried to stimulate tenant management from the top down, during the 1970s, most of their attempts failed. But governments *can* structure things so that people can take control, if they want it. "I'm not suggesting that we're going to force it down people's throats, and I'm not suggesting that everybody might want to do it, and I'm not suggesting that everybody should be treated in exactly the same manner," says Kemp. "But I at least want the opportunity out there for everybody."

Kemp's strategy includes many of the specific steps government can take: it can remove the barriers to community control; encourage organized communities to take control of services; provide seed money, training, and technical assistance; and move the resources necessary to deal with problems into the control of community organizations.

Public organizations can create a spectrum of opportunities, which different communities can seize as they are ready. Many public housing authorities create resident advisory boards, give tenants seats on the board of directors, or encourage residents to form tenant councils at each development. Some encourage tenant councils to hire and fire private management firms. A few encourage tenants to form their own corporations and manage the property themselves. And a handful, including those in

Washington and Louisville, have allowed tenants to buy developments.

None of this is easy, or automatic. In poor communities, enormous leadership is necessary to make something like tenant management work. "The Kimi Grays are rare," says Andrea Duncan, who runs the Housing Authority of Louisville. "Most public housing residents are women who are very dependent, who don't have a lot of confidence, who have a long way to go just to deal with their own sense of wellness, their own life management." But it takes enormous leadership to create any successful enterprise—whether Kenilworth-Parkside Resident Management Corporation or IBM. So why not create more opportunities in poor communities and see how many leaders emerge?

It would be wrong to force people who have long been dependent to suddenly manage on their own, without some kind of transitional support. "You can't take residents of public housing who spent most of their lives in a colonial state and expect them to turn around and have the attitudes of entrepreneurs and the skills of private sector administrators," says Robert Stumberg, a housing expert with the National Center for Policy Alternatives, in Washington, D.C. One solution, he argues, is some form of "intermediary ownership structure, such as a mutual housing association—a corporation owned by its residents:

People have a vested interest in how it's run, they have a direct democratic vote in management, they are encouraged and involved in policy making about such things as rent structures and resident obligations, and they get a financial cut in terms of personal tax benefits and the rewards of sweat equity in maintaining their own units. But they still have corporate accountability in terms of making the whole thing work. There are professional managers who are hired and fired by the residents.

Even in the best situations, there will be problems. Corruption has plagued some tenant management corporations. The

Housing Authority of Louisville quit contracting with one of its resident management corporations because the corporation began to cheat. But Louisville's experience also demonstrates the answer: it discovered the corruption because it had strict, measurable performance standards in its contract. When performance began to fall off—because the corporation was engaging in nepotism and other self-dealing practices—the performance measures quickly showed it. The success of empowerment is thus directly dependent on the success of other concepts in this book, including accountability for results.

When governments push ownership and control into the community, their responsibilities do not end. They may no longer produce services, but they are still responsible for making sure needs are met. When governments abdicate this steering responsibility, disaster often follows. The massive deinstitutionalization of mental patients in favor of community-based treatment during the 1970s was a perfect example. It worked in a few places, but most governments abdicated their steering responsibilities. They failed to make sure that community treatment centers and homes were in place, with adequate funding, and they failed to monitor what happened to patients who left their hospitals. As a result, many of the mentally ill ended up on the streets, homeless.

EMPOWERING CITIZENS THROUGH PARTICIPATORY DEMOCRACY

The ultimate form of ownership is not ownership simply of problem solving or of services, but of government. In theory, our representative system of democracy gives us that ownership. In reality, few Americans feel that they "own" or "control" their governments. By 1989, three out of four Americans surveyed agreed that "most members of Congress care more about special interests than they care about people like you." By 1990, efforts to take control back—through term limits, campaign finance reform, and a broader use of ballot initiatives—had begun to sweep the country.

Campaign finance reform is obviously a precondition to recapturing our governments. Many people have recommended other forms of democratic participation, from neighborhood assemblies to a national initiative and referendum process. Many cities and states have used "futures projects" to generate widespread discussion of issues. (See chapter 8.)

Most of these ideas make eminent sense. We would no doubt be better off if they were adopted by every government in America. But there is a reason they have not been. Americans are not clamoring for more elections, more opinion polls, and more meetings to attend; most of us are far too busy making ends meet and raising our children. America already holds more elections than virtually any other country on earth—national elections, state elections, city elections, county elections, school board elections, water board elections, transit board elections . . . We already have 504,404 elected officials, one for every 182 voters. We all know the sinking feeling that comes in the voting booth, after we get through the national and state and city council races, when we see pages of names we do not know and contests for offices we know nothing about.

What Americans *do* hunger for is more control over matters that directly affect their lives: public safety, their children's schools, the developers who want to change their neighborhoods. They care so much about these things, in fact, that many of them devote precious hours every week to volunteer work in the schools, on neighborhood watches, or in community organizations. It is precisely here that participatory democracy is becoming real within American governments.

In St. Paul, for example, George Latimer pushed ownership of dozens of services into the community, from home energy audits and weatherization to the replacement of trees killed by Dutch elm disease. He was so intent on getting citizens to feel like they owned the city that he published an *Owner's Manual* listing all city services and departments. His principal instrument was a remarkable system of 17 elected district councils. (Several other cities, including Dayton, Cincinnati, Birmingham, Seattle, and Portland, Oregon, have similar systems.) The city subsidized an office and an organizer for each council, and the councils acted as sounding boards for city government, set priorities for half a billion dollars' worth of public works investments, initiated special projects funded by the city, and delivered services.

Some district councils remained essentially reactive, but others actively attacked problems in their neighborhoods. Many sponsored neighborhood watches. One managed the city park in its neighborhood. Another organized a Chore Service that paid neighborhood kids to do chores for the elderly. Still another organized a Block Nurse Program, through which neighborhood residents and nurses provided nursing care, companionship, and help with household chores to elderly residents, so they could stay out of nursing homes. Church groups trained the volunteers, church youth groups helped out with things like lawn care, Boy Scouts painted houses, and local stores provided goods.

Kathy Tarnowski, the paid organizer for the District 14 Community Council, summed it up well: "The strength of our process is not in reactive governance. The strength is that we're solving our own problems. That's the kind of thing a politician—an alderman—can't do."

—3—

Competitive Government: Injecting Competition into Service Delivery

The issue is not public versus private It is competition versus monopoly.
—John Moffitt, Chief Secretary to Massachusetts
Governor William Weld

In 1978, in the throes of a tax revolt, Phoenix decided to contract garbage collection out to the private sector. Predictably, the union protested. The city council met, discussed the issue, and eventually voted to go ahead. After the vote, the mayor turned to Public Works Director Ron Jensen: "You *are* going to compare the bids with your costs, aren't you?"

"Mayor," Jensen replied, "we'll bid [for the job] too."

"I said it just like that, without any thought," Jensen remembers. "It was a halfway humorous remark. When I got back to the office, my staff said, 'What do you mean we'll bid it too?' I just said, 'Why not?' "

So began one of the nation's most extensive experiments in public-private competition. The Public Works Department divided the city into districts and began bidding them out on five-to seven-year contracts—roughly one a year. The city adopted a no-layoff policy; it required private contractors to hire Public Works employees who were displaced, and it transferred those who wanted to stay with the city to other jobs (sometimes at lower pay). To make sure the bidders included all their costs, the city auditor's office examined each bid, public or private.

Three times Public Works submitted bids, and three times it lost. The fourth time its bid was virtually identical to that of the lowest private bidder, but the council decided to go with the private company.

The losses forced Jensen and his employees to rethink the way they did business. They were already converting from three-person to one-person trucks, with mechanical arms that picked up trash barrels. When given the opportunity to compete, however, the private companies followed suit. So Jensen and his managers had to look elsewhere for an advantage. They asked their drivers to redesign their routes and work schedules, because the drivers knew better than anyone else where efficiencies lay. They created quality circles, called "partnership teams," and a labor-management Productivity Committee, to come up with other improvements. They developed a new cost accounting system, so they would know precisely how much their services cost, per household, per month. They installed a suggestion program that gave employees 10 percent of the savings generated by their suggestions—up to a maximum of $2,000. And they gave monthly and quarterly awards to the best drivers.

Gradually the department's costs came down. In 1984, a seven-year contract came up for the city's largest district. Public Works was determined to win it. All competitors in Phoenix, public and private, were using trucks that held 25 cubic yards of garbage. Jensen and his colleagues heard that Sacramento had picked up on the idea of one-person trucks, but had put the mechanical arm on 32-cubic-yard trucks. "So we had one of our guys go look at them," Jensen says. "He liked them. We had the auditor take a look, so we could include that in our bid. The private contractors were still using 25-cubic-yard trucks, so we beat them by more than $6 million."

Morale soared. Management held a dinner for all employees and handed out new hats with the city logo and "Sanitation #1" printed across the face. "It was amazing, when they finally whipped the private people morale went way up, because now they could prove that they had done it well," said Mayor Terry

Goddard. "They weren't just city bureaucrats, they weren't just people that had a cushy job. They had proof, out of the competitive process, that they were good."

The private companies quickly converted to 32-cubic-yard trucks as well. ("We learn from each other," says Jensen. "That's what competition does.") But Public Works kept finding new ways to drive its costs lower. It won a second district, then a third. By 1988, it had won back all five districts. "Over a 10-year period, you see the costs for all other city programs going up," says Jensen. "Solid waste costs have gone down by 4.5 percent a year, in real, inflation-adjusted dollars."

Charles Fanniel, the union president, would prefer the comfort of guaranteed jobs for his employees. He is critical of a "lowball" contract the city once awarded to a firm that quickly failed to fulfill its obligations; after virtually a complete breakdown, the city had to hand the contract to another firm. But overall, Fanniel agrees that working conditions, pay and morale are better than they were before 1978. Communication between labor and management is good, and formal grievances have virtually disappeared. "We've done well," says Fanniel. "And we've got some good incentives for performance." But, he adds, his people work very hard. "What happens with this bidding system is you cut out all the fat."

Phoenix has used competition not only in garbage collection but in landfill operation, custodial services, parking lot management, golf course management, street sweeping, street repair, food and beverage concessions, printing, and security. Between 1981 and 1984, it moved from 53 major private contracts to 179. Some proved better than their public competitors, some did not. The city eventually decided that ambulance service, street sweeping, and maintenance of median strips were better handled by public employees. But overall, the city auditor estimates savings of $20 million over the first decade, just in the difference between the bids the city accepted and the next lowest bid. Since competition has forced *all* bid levels down, this is but a fraction of the real savings.

City Auditor Jim Flanagan has overseen the process from the beginning. There is no truth to the old saw that business is always more efficient than government, he has learned. The important distinction is not public versus private, it is monopoly versus competition: "Where there's competition, you get better results, more cost-consciousness, and superior service delivery."

In government, of course, monopoly is the American way. When the Progressives embraced service delivery by administrative bureaucracies, they embraced monopoly. To this day, we deride competition within government as "waste and duplication." We assume that each neighborhood should have one school, each city should have one police force, each region should have one organization driving its buses and operating its commuter trains. When costs have to be cut, we eliminate anything that smacks of duplication—assuming that consolidation will save money. Yet we know that monopoly in the private sector protects inefficiency and inhibits change. It is one of the enduring paradoxes of American ideology that we attack private monopolies so fervently but embrace public monopolies so warmly.

"I often ask people how they would like it if there were one airline in this country," says General Bill Creech, who used competition and decentralization to turn the Tactical Air Command around, as we will see in chapter 9. "By the theory of centralization, it would be very efficient. How efficient? Just ask anyone who flies on Aeroflot, the Soviet airline."

Entrepreneurial leaders such as Creech know that competition between *policy agencies*—otherwise known as turf war— only makes it harder for government to play a steering role. In policy management, coordination between different interests is vital. Similarly, they know that competition makes little sense in most regulatory functions. But they have discovered that when *service providers* must compete, they keep their costs down, respond quickly to changing demands, and strive mightily to satisfy their customers. No institution welcomes competition. But while most of us would prefer a comfortable monopoly, competition drives us to embrace innovation and strive for excellence.

Competition will not solve all our problems. But perhaps more than any other concept in this book, it holds the key that will unlock the bureaucratic gridlock that hamstrings so many public agencies. This is not to endorse cutthroat competition, which can bring out the bad as well as the good. If competition saves money only by skimping on wages or benefits, for instance, governments should question its value. Nor are we endorsing competition between *individuals*. Merit pay for individual teachers, to cite one example, just sets teacher against teacher and undermines morale. But merit pay for *schools* is another matter. Competition between teams—between organizations—builds morale and encourages creativity.

THE ADVANTAGES OF COMPETITION

The most obvious advantage of competition is greater efficiency: more bang for the buck. E. S. Savas, chairman of the Department of Management at City University of New York, is one of the nation's leading experts on competition in public service. He came to the issue in an interesting way, when he served under New York City Mayor John Lindsay.

> We had a disastrous snowfall which had serious political overtones. To make a long story short, we discovered that the department responsible for cleaning the snow was really working only about 50 percent of the time during this emergency. The rest of the time was consumed by work breaks, warm-up breaks, coffee breaks, fueling breaks, lunch breaks, and wash-up breaks. Being curious about how this department functioned when there was no emergency but only the normal work of refuse collection, I decided to compare the New York City Department of Sanitation with the private sector in and around the New York City area. We discovered that it cost private contractors about $17 per ton to collect refuse, whereas it cost the city agency $49 a ton, almost three times as much.

When these findings attracted media attention, Mayor Lindsay appointed a commission to look into the option of contracting out garbage collection. But when the unions objected, Lindsay buried its report.

After leaving government, Savas convinced the National Science Foundation to fund a large-scale comparison of public and private garbage collection. "The results were quite striking and irrefutable," he says. "Private firms under contract were equally effective, equally responsive, but vastly more efficient than government agencies."

Since then Savas has studied other services and reviewed countless other studies. They show, he says, that on average public service delivery is 35 to 95 percent more expensive than contracting, even when the cost of administering the contracts is included. "Nevertheless," he adds, "I have seen situations— and have helped bring about situations—where the government matches the performance of the private sector. It does that in a situation like Phoenix, or Minneapolis, or Kansas City, or Newark, when the government competes continually with the private sector."

Other studies confirm Savas's points, although estimates of the savings from contracting vary. James Q. Wilson presents an exhaustive review of the literature in his book *Bureaucracy*. It shows that in most cases, private firms deliver services more economically than public organizations. But where public and private organizations (of similar size) function in the same marketplace—as in health care and electrical utilities—their costs and quality are roughly the same. If anything, publicly owned utilities are cheaper.

Where private service providers do not have to compete, on the other hand, they are just as inefficient as public monopolies. Consider Massachusetts, which like other states relies on private companies to provide automobile insurance, but unlike most states does not let them compete. Their prices are set by a regulatory commission, just as a utility's would be. As a result, insurance companies have no incentive to lower their costs, to find efficiencies, or to control fraud. They show as little interest in their customers as do the worst government bureaucracies. Not surprisingly, Massachusetts has the highest average premium rates in the country, the highest claims frequency, and the highest auto theft rate.

Competition forces public (or private) monopolies to respond to the needs of their customers. Consider the U.S. Postal Service—with 760,000 employees, our largest civilian monopoly. We all know the Postal Service is inefficient: if the ever-rising cost of first-class mail is not evidence enough, consider the fact that the Postal Service spends more than 80 percent of its budget on labor, while United Parcel Service (UPS) spends less than 60 percent. The Postal Service is also *unresponsive.* In 1973 it tried, unsuccessfully, to suppress private courier services—even though it was not willing to offer same-day service itself. In the 1970s, it refused to offer overnight express service—until Congress let its private competitors into the market. In 1988, it met its own third-class delivery standards only 30 percent of the time—and it *lost* 3.5 to 15 percent of all third-class mail. The trade association of bulk mailers, the Third Class Mail Association, became so frustrated that it finally endorsed competition in third-class delivery as well.

Competition has forced drastic improvements in some areas, such as express mail. But with the Postal Service's monopoly on first- and third-class mail intact, old habits die hard. While Federal Express and UPS have produced a constant stream of innovation, earned millions of loyal customers, and kept their prices steady, the Postal Service has struggled. In 1971, it had half the market for package delivery; by the late 1980s it was down to 8 percent. In 1981, it had 26 percent of the overnight market; by 1989, it was down to 12 percent.

In contrast, public monopolies that are thrust fully into competition have little choice but to please their customers. Countries all over the world have discovered this as they have privatized their state-owned enterprises. Consider what happened when New Zealand simply allowed one airline to compete with its state-owned line. Roger Douglas, a former Labor Party finance minister, tells the story:

Air New Zealand, as a state owned business, had always done a first-class job for customers on international routes. They had to—they were competing with Pan Am, Quantas, British Airways and the best in the world. But at home in New Zealand, where they had a domestic monopoly, it was a different story.

Passengers all trudged through the rain from the terminal to their aircraft. They waited up to 20-30 minutes at the other end for their luggage. Nobody realized what we had been missing until the present government decided to break Air New Zealand's monopoly by letting Ansett come in alongside them.

Suddenly, overnight, to the utter amazement of the New Zealand public, we found that we too could have covered access to planes, just like the rest of the world. The capital city had been using a grotty old prefabricated building as a terminal ever since World War II, and nobody had been able to get it upgraded. Suddenly we had two totally modern terminal buildings. We got more flights, cheaper flights, better food, friendlier service and virtually a zero wait for luggage.

People began to see, often for the first time, that the central issue in safeguarding their own interests as consumers was not, in fact, ownership—it was competition.

Competition rewards innovation; monopoly stifles it. Competition in service delivery favors "the survival of the helpful," as two British socialists once put it. It is a form of natural selection. "Nature's incessant experimentation with mutations enables species to evolve, adapt, and survive despite drastic environmental changes," writes Savas; "some of these 'experiments' turn out to be better suited to the new surroundings than the original model and ultimately replace it."

Normal government practice discourages natural selection. Rather than the survival of the helpful, we find the survival of the already entrenched or the politically powerful. Service decisions are made based on what was done last year, which provider organizations have political clout, who gave campaign contributions, and where the unions stand. Successful experiments all too often remain marginal, if they have no political clout. And when budgets are cut, marginal programs are the first to go.

When service organizations are put into genuine competition, everything changes. Those who deliver poor service at high prices are gradually eliminated, while those who deliver quality service at reasonable prices grow larger. Competition on the margin forces organizations to shed their skins, time and again. If accurate measurement of quality is in place, natural selection proceeds almost automatically. Politicians may try to interfere, but when they do, they have to argue against the facts.

Competition boosts the pride and morale of public employees. Most of us assume that public employees suffer when they have to compete. They certainly lose a degree of security, and for that reason their unions often oppose any threat to their monopoly status. We believe that efforts to minimize the pain, such as Phoenix's no-layoff policies, are critical. Governments can easily guarantee their employees a job, without guaranteeing the job they currently hold. But we have also found that once public employees find themselves in competition—if their job security is not at stake—they enjoy it.

"People want to do fine work," says John Cleveland, formerly of the Michigan Commerce Department:

> They find that when they get into a competitive situation, they work a lot harder, but it's far more exciting. They may have to be pushed into it, but they discover that it's much more rewarding. And there's no question about when they're doing a good job. The world knows it, because they're winning in competition with others.

THE VARIETIES OF COMPETITION

Phoenix is hardly alone. Since the tax revolt of 1978, governments all across America have begun to use competition to lower their costs. They have developed almost an infinite variety of methods.

Public versus Private Competition

Some people believe government cannot compete with business. But as we saw in Phoenix, not only can it compete, it can win. Arizona's adult mental health system, described in chapter 1, pits public hospitals and agencies directly against for-profit and nonprofit providers for contracts. In job training, competition between public agencies and private firms has become relatively common. When Tennessee recently decided to build three new prisons, it let a private firm handle one and the state operate the others—to see who could do it more cheaply.

Beginning in 1984, the federal Department of Transportation asked local transit authorities that wanted federal funds to include private firms as potential service providers. By the late 1980s, at least two dozen cities, including Los Angeles, Kansas City, Miami, and Denver, were bidding out some transit routes competitively.

New York City's Sanitation Department, which claims to have the largest nonmilitary vehicle fleet in the free world, used public-private competition as one element of a remarkable turnaround. By comparing the costs of its internal repair shops with those of private shops—and posting charts of each public shop's resulting "profit" or "loss"—Deputy Commissioner Ron Contino and his employees increased productivity enough to save $2.4 million a year. Now that they "could see how their shop compared with other shops," Contino says, his employees "were no longer just city workers." They thought "of themselves now as competitive individuals, working for a competitive shop." Almost inevitably, they began looking for other business—bidding for jobs other departments had contracted out. By 1989, they were pulling in $700,000 a year, in what they dubbed their Contracting-In program.

Even the Postal Service uses some private contractors, although it doesn't expect its employees to compete with them. To handle 4,500 of its rural routes, it contracts with private individuals—at *half the cost* of its 40,000 other routes. To operate some of its small community post offices, it contracts with private merchants—also at half the cost of its own community post offices. Were it willing to build such competition into its core services, it could no doubt save billions of dollars a year.

Private versus Private Competition

This is by far the most common approach: governments ask private firms to compete to produce some public service.

Load shedding is perhaps the simplest method. By simply backing out of public provision, governments turn services over to the private market. George Latimer did this in St. Paul with garbage collection, for example. By setting the rules, governments can structure the marketplace so it meets public needs. But because public agencies give up direct control over service producers, load shedding reduces government's ability to hold firms accountable. If customers do not have the information or leverage necessary to hold them accountable—principally by threatening to switch to a competitor—load shedding can leave them vulnerable. (We will return to this subject in greater depth in chapter 10.)

Procurement is another common avenue governments use to force private companies to compete. Typically, public agencies have to secure competitive bids for any procurement contract over a set amount—say, $5,000. Governments spend hundreds of billions of dollars this way every year—on health care, on highway construction, on building maintenance.

Consider health care. More than half the states have experimented with competition between prepaid medical plans to provide Medicaid and/or coverage for state employees. Medicaid is "the Pac-Man of state budgets," as a National Association of State Budget Officers executive put it—and health insurance for state employees is right behind it. In recent years, Medicaid costs have shot up by almost 20 percent a year. States like Massachusetts, which still rely primarily on traditional third-party payment systems, find their costs doubling every five years. By 1991, Medicaid consumed 20 percent of Massachusetts' entire budget. The state had to eliminate $250 million in other spending every year, just to feed its Medicaid habit.

Prepaid plans such as health maintenance organizations (HMOs) tend to be less expensive, because they compete fiercely on price. In Massachusetts in 1989, for instance, traditional health insurance for public employees cost almost $200 per month per employee, while prepaid plans cost between $104 and $138.

Arizona was the first state to use prepaid plans to provide all Medicaid coverage. An in-depth study by SRI International showed that during the program's first five years—fiscal years 1983 through 1987—its per capita inflation rate was only 23 percent (5.3 percent a year). A traditional Medicaid program in Arizona, SRI estimated, would have experienced a 37 percent inflation rate. Quality of care was also higher in Arizona than in a comparable traditional program.

Studies in Wisconsin estimate that the state is saving roughly 15 percent a year by putting its welfare population in Milwaukee County into HMOs. Many governments, including Milwaukee's, have also bid their public employees out to HMOs on a competitive basis. "We didn't slash any benefits, and we didn't shift costs to employees," Milwaukee's deputy budget director told *Governing* magazine. "We're using the competitive free-market process to force HMOs to compete for the city's business."

Contracting is another common method of injecting competition into public services. By 1987, the federal government contracted out $196.3 billion of work, while state and local governments contracted out $100 billion. (Not all contracting is competitive, of course—witness Defense Department contracting.) The average city contracted out 27 percent of its municipal services.

Contracting is one of the most difficult methods a public organization can choose, because writing and monitoring contracts require so much skill. Many governments act as if their job is done once they have signed a contract. As a result, too many private contractors fail to deliver what they promise—or worse, commit fraud. The AFL-CIO has filled books with the resulting horror stories.

To do it right, cities often spend 20 percent of the cost of the service on contract management. (When they keep services in-house they also have management costs, of course.) Typically, they have to hire new people, with particular expertise. "We found out that a foreman who can supervise a crew does not often have the skills to administer a contract," says Phoenix's Ron Jensen. "So we created a position called contract monitor, and we recruited people who had those skills."

Cities like Phoenix have learned a great deal about how to manage their competitive contracts. Phoenix ties reimbursement closely to performance and puts withholding clauses in its contracts, so contractors who do not perform are not paid. It tracks citizen complaints by area and incidence, so managers can tell a contractor exactly where the problem is and defer payment until it is solved. And it uses inspectors to compare contracted areas and areas served by public agencies.

Lowball bids are a common problem. Companies bid low to get the first contract, assuming they can jack up the price later. After a disastrous experience with one solid waste company, Phoenix learned to weed out the low bidder. "Quite frankly, the low bid is usually not a good bid," says Jensen. "They've done it at a loss, or too low a margin, and they're going to fail. So now we use 'the lowest responsible bid.' "

Another danger is that the private contractor will gradually develop a monopoly. Privatizing to a monopoly is not only senseless but extremely expensive. In services that require heavy equipment or a fleet of vehicles, some cities accept lowball bids, get rid of their own equipment, and then find themselves over a barrel when the contractor later raises its prices. When they turn to other private competitors, they sometimes run into an informal agreement not to compete on price—a recurring problem in road construction. Hence Phoenix always keeps at least two of its garbage districts in public hands—so it will always have the capacity to compete.

Finally, there is the danger of fraud. As Paul Starr has written, "Contracting is the locus classicus of the political pay off." During the heyday of Boss Tweed, contracting was often rife with corruption—one reason the Progressives turned most service delivery over to public bureaucracies. In some places, the problem still exists: Marion Barry's administration in Washington, D.C., was known to steer contracts to Barry's political supporters—and, in some cases, girlfriends. Many of the abuses that surfaced during the federal Housing and Urban Development scandal in 1989 involved developers who used their political connections to obtain contracts.

The solution is fairly simple. Corruption is difficult when a contracting system meets four criteria: the bidding is truly competitive; the competition is based on hard information about cost and quality of performance; the contractors are monitored carefully; and a relatively nonpolitical body is set up to perform these tasks. If an agency like the city auditor's office in Phoenix exists, with the capacity to evaluate competitors based on hard data—and if that information is public—politicians have trouble steering contracts to their cronies.

Despite all the difficulties, contracting can save significant sums, particularly if public providers are inefficient. It works best, says Harvard's John Donahue, author of *The Privatization Decision*, when public agencies can define precisely what they want done, generate competition for the job, evaluate a contractor's performance, and replace or penalize those who fail to achieve expected performance levels.

Overall, most public agencies appear pleased with their contractors' performance. A 1989 survey by the National Commission for Employment Policy found that 72 percent of local officials rated the quality of their contracted services "very favorable," 10 percent "slightly favorable," 13 percent "slightly unfavorable," and 5 percent "very unfavorable." The same study found that contracting saved local governments 15 to 30 percent.

Public versus Public Competition

Contracting is difficult enough that governments sometimes prefer to pursue the same results by stimulating competition between their own organizations. As noted earlier, public organizations in competitive environments often perform just as well as private organizations. Some places now use competition between public schools—a subject we will return to in a moment. Phoenix constantly compares the cost, efficiency, and effectiveness of many city services with those offered by other cities. "If you can draw good comparisons, even if it's not actual competition, that puts the pressure on," says City Auditor Jim Flanagan. "You'll behave differently if in fact the service you provide is looked at in that manner."

CREATING COMPETITION
FOR INTERNAL GOVERNMENT SERVICES

Most of the examples listed above involve services provided to the public. But many government agencies do not serve the public; they serve other government agencies. They include printing, accounting, and purchasing offices, telecommunications and data processing services, vehicle fleets, repair operations, and dozens of others. Normally, the idea of having to compete never crosses their employees' minds. Even their customers rarely imagine going to outside competitors: it never occurs to the police chief to send his cars down to Jiffy Lube, rather than the city maintenance shop.

When public managers do exercise such options, remarkable things begin to happen. E. S. Savas tells a story from Yugoslavia, of all places. It seems that the city fathers of Ljubljana solicited bids for some city planning work not only from their own planning office, but also from the planning agency of Zagreb. "An American observer there at the time remarked that he had never seen city employees anywhere work as hard as Ljubljana's city planners, who wanted desperately to avoid the humiliation of having their own city's work contracted out to their professional and regional rivals."

American governments are beginning to use similar techniques. When Sandra Hale took over Minnesota's Department of Administration in 1983, she found morale low and dissatisfaction widespread. The department was known, satirically, by its initials: DOA. Its customers—managers in other departments—thought its services were shoddy, its prices too high, and its procedures hopelessly out of date. When they bought personal computers, they still had to fill out forms and jump through hoops left over from the days when computers cost $100,000. Central Stores had never even stocked Post-it Notes.

Hale hired a management consultant who had experience in state government, Babak Armajani, as her deputy. He surveyed the agency's customers, then began working with its units to improve their performance. He helped the Public Documents Center, which was running a deficit, shift to market prices, pro-

mote its products, and look for a profit. Soon sales had increased by 17 percent and the center was turning a $111,000
annual profit. He watched how Central Stores responded when
the department lifted its procurement ceiling of $50 and let
other agencies buy items costing less than $1,500 on their own.
Suddenly, Central Stores had new competition—so its managers began changing their policies. (They stocked Post-it Notes,
for one.) Observing these changes, Hale's management team decided to inject marketplace dynamics—competition, profit, and
the like—into the rest of the department.

First the department had to sort out each of its bureau's
proper roles. Some played both a service and a regulatory role:
for instance, the Information Management Bureau provided
mainframe computer services, but also controlled who could
buy a computer and who could not. "This was a disaster," said
Deputy Commissioner Jeff Zlonis. "There was a clear conflict
of interest, because some employees were telling agencies
whether they could have a PC, while earning their livelihood by
selling mainframe services." So first Hale and Armajani separated service from control, creating two different information
bureaus. The new Information Policy Office was a "steering"
operation, setting policy about who could buy what kind of
computers, with what common standards. The new Inter-
Technology Group was a service operation, selling computer
services such as data processing, voice mail, and electronic
mail. It was a classic divestiture of rowing from steering.

About half of the service budget was already in what the department called revolving funds, under which service bureaus
charged their customers directly and relied entirely on income
they generated. Hale and Armajani made virtually all service
bureaus revolving funds, then divided them between those that
should remain monopolies and those that should be forced to
compete.

This was the key breakthrough. Activities that were judged better off as monopolies, such as those in which the economies of
scale favored one provider, or the legislature wanted every agency
to buy the same service, were called utilities. Their rates were set
through negotiation with their customers—in comparison with

the rates of other providers, both public and private. Other bureaus, dubbed marketplace activities, were opened up to competition: data entry, Central Stores, micrographics services, and
management consulting. Suddenly their customers—other state
agencies—could buy from them or from anyone else. This was a
shock to many employees.

But, says Sandra Hale,

> our customers took us seriously. It wasn't long before we
> knew that services like typewriter repair and systems design
> and programming didn't and couldn't have competitive
> rates. So they went out of business. On the other hand, our
> micrographics services, Central Stores, and management
> consulting were very competitive with private-sector vendors.
> In fact, they became growth businesses.

Between 1987 and 1990, the InterTechnology Group's sales
grew from $35 million to $60 million a year. Its computer rates
fell by 20 percent, its telecommunications rates by 17 percent.
The Management Consulting Group virtually tripled its volume. Meanwhile, many delivery and turnaround times were cut
by more than half. Overall, reports Hale, the cost of utilities and
marketplace operations rose less than 1 percent per year from
1986 through 1990, while inflation averaged 4.7 percent a year
and the state general fund increased by 5.7 percent a year. In
1991, the revolving funds *cut* their costs by 4.5 percent, saving
the state $3.6 million.

All these results could have been achieved simply with good
management. There is no genius to stocking Post-it Notes, eliminating obsolete bureaus, and cutting costs. The problem is,
public agencies don't always do such things, because they have
no incentives to do them. The genius of enterprise management—as Minnesota called its strategy—is that it forces managers to act. Competition does not wait for good management:
if managers cannot keep costs down and improve quality, their
customers go elsewhere and they go out of business. Competition is the permanent force for innovation that government
normally lacks.

PUBLIC EDUCATION: A CASE STUDY

To most people, competition between garbage collection firms seems only natural. Why would anyone prefer monopoly? Competition in road construction, in health care, even in public transit, seems like nothing more than common sense. And forcing department of administration bureaucrats to compete for a living—what a refreshing idea!

But turn the conversation to education and all bets are off. Most of us went to public schools. Most of us have an image of the public school stamped indelibly on our psyches. It never occurs to us that public schools could be different. We assume that schools are synonymous with buildings, and that children are *assigned* to buildings. Students don't choose; parents don't choose; and schools don't compete for their customers. The sky is blue, and the public school is a monopoly.

And yet, as Peter Drucker pointed out several years ago,

America is the only major developed country in which there is no competition within the school system. The French have two parallel systems above the elementary grades, a public one and a Catholic one, both paid for by the state. So do the Italians. Germany has the Gymnasium, *the college-preparatory school for a fairly small elite. In Japan, schools are graded by the performance of their students on the university entrance exams. The teachers of high-ranking schools are recognized, promoted, and paid accordingly. The American public school, by contrast, has a near-monopoly—no performance standards and little competition either within the system or from the outside.*

Writing in 1988, Drucker noted that this pattern was changing. He described Minnesota's decision to move toward choice and competition in education, as East Harlem had before it. Since 1988, at least seven other states have followed Minnesota's lead, offering their students the option of attending school in a different district: Iowa, Arkansas, Ohio, Nebraska, Idaho, Utah, and Massachusetts. (Vermont and Maine have long allowed school districts to give students vouchers for use in private schools.) California, Washington, and Colorado have opened up limited choice, particularly for those in high school. And dozens of cities now offer choice, including Rochester, New York; Montclair, New Jersey; Seattle; and San Jose.

Unfortunately, many of these systems give parents a choice of schools, but don't really force schools to compete. Inferior schools that fail to attract many students still get filled up—with the children of parents who aren't paying attention. Such systems are usually an improvement over traditional assignment systems, because they let parents choose the style of education they prefer, and they let principals and teachers experiment with different methods. But they lack the power to force improvement that competition delivers.

When it comes to the effects of competition, education is no different from any other service industry. As Governor Tommy Thompson of Wisconsin explains:

> *Competition breeds accountability. Under the concept of parental choice, schools will be held accountable for their students' performance. Schools providing a high quality education would flourish, the same way as a business that improves its quality for its consumers. Schools failing to meet the needs of their students would not be able to compete, and in effect would go out of business.*

John Chubb and Terry Moe, authors of a Brookings Institution book called *Politics, Markets and America's Schools*, studied data on 500 high schools around the nation to discover what factors most influenced student performance. The greatest influence was, of course, the aptitude the student brought to school—something determined largely by family background. But the second most important influence was the school itself. Yet the traditional factors we often emphasize—teacher salaries, per pupil expenditures, class size, graduation requirements—had no impact on school performance. Instead the keys were parental control, the clarity of the school's mission, strong leadership, and the degree of freedom and respect offered the teachers (in our terms: community ownership, a mission-driven organization, and decentralized authority). To develop these attributes, Chubb and Moe found, schools needed autonomy from external control—from administrators, unions, and school boards. "The more freedom that the school was granted to chart its own course," they discovered, "the more likely it was to become effectively organized":

> The real issue in school reform, then, is: how do you provide autonomy and still hold schools accountable? After all, you can't just turn over the keys of the school to the teacher and principals and be sure that they're going to be held accountable. . . .
>
> The only empirically and logically compelling way in which autonomy and accountability can be maintained is to move to a different system of accountability. You need a system that holds schools accountable not from the top down, but through the market process, through the competitive process. You need a system that holds schools accountable by giving them autonomy—and by observing how well the schools succeed in winning the support of parents and students.

After John Chubb delivered the remarks quoted above, Robert Wagner, Jr., then president of the New York City Board of Education, questioned him. East Harlem's District 4 had indeed used competition to produce successful schools, he noted. But District 13 had done it in the opposite way: through strong, autocratic leadership. Perhaps the issue is "one of leadership rather than choice." Chubb's answer should be tacked up on the wall of every school district in America:

> You can get effective schools through other means—such as the force of powerful leadership. But if we have to rely on the development of truly unusual leaders in order to save our schools, our prospects simply aren't going to be very good. The current system is simply not set up to encourage that kind of leadership. A system of competition and choice, on the other hand, automatically provides the incentives for schools to do what is right.

This is the key. Leaders can urge schools to improve; legislatures can order schools to improve; outstanding principals and superintendents can force schools to improve. But only competition can motivate *all* schools to improve—because only competition for customers creates real consequences and real pressure for change when schools fail. Only competition forces principals and teachers—constantly—to make the difficult changes necessary to meet the needs of their students. This was the fundamental insight that drove a small group of activists in Minnesota to thrust public school choice onto the national agenda.

The Minnesota Experience

District 4 developed its choice system incrementally. It was a quiet process, invisible to those beyond the borders of East Harlem. Minnesota, the first state to institute statewide choice, was a different story altogether. The first state to publicly debate the issue of competition in public education, Minnesota triggered the national debate about choice. As such, the Minnesota story reveals a great deal about both the ideological issues and the practical realities of competition in public education.

The story begins in the late 1970s, when the Citizens League, a combination citizens' organization and think tank, created a task force to examine the results of court-ordered desegregation. Minnesota had long prided itself on its excellent public schools. But to its surprise, the task force surfaced growing complaints. Regardless of race or class, what people were most disturbed about was the declining quality of their schools. So the league set up a second task force, to examine the quality issue. Again they were surprised. "To put it in terms of our departed prophet Garrison Keillor," says former Citizens League Director Curtis Johnson, "we were just a little above average. Not bad, but not nearly so deserving of the smugness that was so prevalent."

Seven years before the nation began hearing about choice, the task force opted for radical change. "Everybody always wants to go after the symptoms," explains Ted Kolderie, Johnson's predecessor at the Citizens League. "But what you've got to ask yourself over and over and over again is, 'What is causing the system to behave like that?' You've got to find what is causing those symptoms to appear, and then go fix the cause."

The league's report shocked the community—both because it said Minnesota's schools were woefully inadequate and because it called for some system of competition, whether through vouchers or choice of public schools. In response, the Minnesota Business Partnership, made up of the Twin Cities' 80 largest corporations, decided to commission its own study. A massive, intensive look at the schools, it came to the same conclusions. After the Business Partnership report came out, Kolderie, Johnson, Joe Nathan (who had written a book that endorsed choice), former Republican governor Al Quie, and several others began meeting to formulate a strategy.

In 1984, they convinced John Brandl, a state senator, to introduce a bill to give low-income students vouchers they could use at any school, public or private. The system was obviously failing those kids, they argued, so why not start with them?

The bill failed. But late that year, Governor Perpich decided he needed an education reform agenda. When his top aides brought him the ideas of Johnson, Kolderie, Nathan, and their group, he jumped at them. Where other governors would have seen only political pitfalls, Perpich instinctively saw truth. On the eve of the legislative session, at a Citizens League breakfast, he unveiled a proposal to let Minnesota children attend school in any district they chose. It sent shock waves through the education establishment.

After furious debate, the legislature defeated the bill. But it overlooked a separate clause in the education bill, drafted by a legislator, which allowed juniors and seniors to take their state education dollars to a college and finish high school while earning dual credits. Buried within a long bill, the measure survived. Suddenly 16- and 17-year-olds in Minnesota public schools had a choice.

In the program's first year, only about 3,600 students—two percent of those eligible—took advantage of it. Some enrolled in college; others took only one or two college courses. But they and their parents loved it. A survey of those participating during the first two years found that 95 percent were satisfied or very satisfied, 90 percent said they had learned more through the program than if they had taken only high school courses, and 87 percent of parents reported that their children spent more time studying for their college courses than they did for high school courses. Not all participants were the elite: 60 percent were B, C, or D students. More than half of those participating received As or Bs in their college courses.

In 1986, the education establishment tried to gut the program. But the cat was out of the bag. When its supporters organized hearings, Curtis Johnson says, "parents swarmed the capitol":

> They wouldn't let it happen. Student after student showed up to say, "This transformed my life. I was bored, I didn't care about school, I wasn't even going to go to college, and this just made me come alive." Parents showed up to say, "I couldn't get my kid to study, and now I can't stop him."

By 1987, 5,700 students were participating (about 5 percent of those eligible statewide; 10 percent in Minneapolis). Roughly a quarter were attending college full-time. Faced with very real competition for their students—and, more significantly, for the dollars they brought—Minnesota's high schools responded. In three years, they quadrupled the number of advanced placement courses they offered. More than 50 high schools established cooperative courses with postsecondary schools, taught on the high school campus. Some schools used two-way television instruction.

In 1987, Perpich pushed through a second bill, allowing students aged 12 to 21 who were not succeeding in one school to attend another, as long as the shift did not have a negative impact on desegregation. The state advertised the program with the slogan: "Students on the verge of dropping out don't need a lecture, they need an alternative." In its first two years, 3,000 youngsters participated. *Half of them were dropouts returning to school.* Simply by allowing choice, in other words, Minnesota brought 1,500 dropouts back to school in just two years.

Minnesota subsequently opened the program to adult dropouts. Their options include Area Learning Centers and Alternative Programs, designed for those who want something other than the traditional high school. Some are run by private schools or firms, on contract with school districts. One is a new Minneapolis high school that meets in the evening. Once they entered these programs, the percentage of students expecting to graduate and enter college or vocational training more than doubled.

In 1988, the legislature finally passed Perpich's full choice program, freeing students to attend school in any other district, as long as the receiving district had room and the move did not harm desegregation efforts. All public dollars allocated for the student now followed him or her to the other district. Parents must transport the student to the district boundary of the school he or she attends, but if the family is low income, the state will pay for public transportation.

The first year in which all districts had to participate was 1990–1991. That fall, 6,134 students applied to leave their district. Another 6,000 chose the college option, while almost 8,000 enrolled in Area Learning Centers, 3,000 chose public Alternative Programs, and 750 chose private Alternative Programs that contracted with school districts. In all, nearly 24,000 of Minnesota's 720,000 students exercised a choice. Perhaps 30,000 more exercised their choice options *within* individual districts.

Altogether, it is safe to assume that 5 to 10 percent of Minnesota's public school students chose to change schools in one way or another. Hence, even in the program's first full year, schools faced a very real threat of losing students. "It changes the conversation in the boardroom," says Curtis Johnson. "Instead of arguing for 45 minutes about which lawn mower to buy, suddenly they're asking, 'Are we providing anything that anybody would want to come to, by their choice?'"

One district reopened a school it had closed, because so many students left the district in response to the closing. Another, which had tried to stop its juniors and seniors from taking the

college route, finally turned around and created an entire package of advanced placement and college-in-the-school programs.
"As soon as our people saw those kids walking out the door and
we couldn't stop it," an administrator confided to Ted Kolderie,
"we decided we had to do something ourselves."

In a suburban district with a long history of stonewalling parental demands and defeating property tax increases, 200 students signed up to leave. The superintendent personally
interviewed all 200 families, and voters passed a tax increase by
70 percent. The district developed a coherent strategy to compete with its neighboring suburbs, focused on the use of technology in the classroom.

In 1991, Kolderie, Johnson, and their allies pushed a bill
through the legislature that allows groups of teachers to create
new public schools. In truly competitive markets, they reasoned, much of the significant competition comes from new
firms that have discovered a better way to please their customers. This is particularly important in education, because many
parents do not want their children traveling great distances to
school. Hence their true choices are limited unless new schools
spring up in their area.

"School choice alone won't change a closed system," explains
Kolderie; "what's needed is to open the system to enterprising
people who want to start innovative new schools." In some
places, like East Harlem, district leaders make sure this happens. But in many places, Kolderie points out, "the district's
ability and willingness to start new schools is bound to be limited . . . by its desire not to threaten the other schools it owns."
The answer, Kolderie concludes, is a system under which districts and states can charter new schools created by teachers,
parents, or private organizations. The Minnesota bill, a political compromise, is only a pilot program. It allows only eight
charter schools, created only by teachers and chartered only by
school boards. But it is a beginning.

Minnesota's choice system has other limits. It mandates competition between districts, but not competition *within* each district. (The state's large districts offer significant degrees of
choice, however, and smaller districts normally have only one

junior high and one high school.) It mandates choice, but not choices: it creates pressure for schools to diversify their programs and teaching styles, but does not mandate the decentralization of authority that would facilitate such changes. And it does not force school districts to open and close schools, as District 4 does in East Harlem. Schools that excel and attract more students rarely grow or clone themselves. Poorly performing schools are rarely closed and reopened under new management.

Still, Minnesota's system is a revolution in public education. In a few short years, it has convinced a majority of Minnesotans of its virtues. When Governor Perpich first proposed choice, in 1985, only about a third of those surveyed supported the idea. By 1989, 60 percent did. Even more revealing, in a poll taken by the Minnesota Education Association, 60 percent of teachers supported choice.

The Equity Issue

Perhaps the greatest objection to competition between schools is based on a concern for equity. A pure competitive marketplace—an unrestricted voucher system, for instance—would be certain to produce inequitable outcomes, because the affluent would add money to their vouchers and buy the best education they could afford. Most others would be unable to do this, and the education market would segregate by income group.

We believe this would be a mistake. Our public schools exist to provide education, but they also exist to bring children from all walks of life together. This mixing of social classes and races is extremely important in a democracy; without it, we lose our capacity to understand and empathize with those who are different from us. When that happens, it is not long before our society loses its ability to care for those who need help. We become a collection of individuals, not a community.

Any marketplace can be structured in different ways by government rules, of course. Verne Johnson, another leader of the Minnesota reform movement, puts it well:

I am not for laissez-faire. I am for controlled competition. Public policy absolutely must control what kind of

*competition takes place, and public policy and financing
must take care of those who don't have enough money.
Deregulating everything means that the people with
money win and the rest of them lose, and we can't have
that. Secondly, you can't have destructive competition;
you have to have informed consumers, for example, and
government has to set that up. Within those parameters,
the more that you can energize market forces like competition, the better you are.*

In a voucher system, schools accepting vouchers could be for-
bidden from charging tuition beyond the voucher and required
to achieve some degree of racial balance. But given the risks
that the political process would create a voucher system without
such controls, equity will be easier to maintain in a public
school system.

Even public choice systems must be carefully structured to
ensure equity, of course. Parents need reliable information
about the quality of each school, and particular efforts must be
made to get that information to low-income, poorly educated
parents. Students need free transportation. Integration must be
preserved—something many districts do by setting a bottom
line for the percentage of minority students in each school.

Some who oppose public school choice fear that low-income
students, whose parents may be less able to make informed
choices or less committed to quality education, will be left behind in failing, shrinking inner-city schools as better students
flee. This is precisely what happens under the old system, of
course: those with financial resources flee to private schools or
the suburbs, while those without remain trapped.

Choice advocates in East Harlem and Minnesota argue that
their approach has exactly the opposite effect: competition
forces failing schools to improve—or forces the district to
change their management. "We're not really working for the 2
percent or the 5 percent who leave," says Verne Johnson.
"We're working for the 95 percent who are still there, to energize and revitalize the system." East Harlem offers living proof.
Competition *has* revitalized the system. Failing schools *are* im-

proved, and failing management *is* replaced. Students in inferior schools are not left behind, they are rescued.

The same thing happens in almost any marketplace, if competitors have to compete for their funds. In higher education, for example, the worst students end up in the schools with the lowest standards, but those schools don't necessarily degenerate. Because they face competition—and because they could go bankrupt—they strive constantly to improve. (This is not the case with public institutions that are guaranteed a certain number of students or a certain amount of financial support, however. True competition means competition for students *and* funds.)

Even the auto industry demonstrates the power of competition to improve the low end. During the 1950s and 1960s, when GM, Ford, and Chrysler faced little foreign competition and tacitly divided up the American market to avoid antitrust prosecution, low-end cars did deteriorate. The Big Three had little financial incentive to pursue new customers at the low end, so the Falcon and the Comet degenerated into the Pinto and the Vega. But once the Japanese invaded, with real alternatives that took away real customers, Detroit responded. Today, the low-end consumer enjoys more choices, better quality, and lower prices (in inflation-adjusted dollars) than ever before.

Some critics fear that schools in competition will pander to children in order to attract more students—perhaps teaching with the television or spending half the day on sports. In a system still "steered" by the state and by local school boards, however, basic standards make such behavior very difficult. Such fears are exaggerated in any case: When District 4 in East Harlem opened a "sports school," which used sports as a lure but offered rigorous academics, most of East Harlem's poor minority parents would not let their children attend for fear they would not get a good education. The district finally had to change the school's name.

Another common argument is that the poor will not make their choices based on good information about the schools. All choice advocates agree that an aggressive information system—something beyond mailings of written material—is necessary.

In places like East Harlem and Cambridge, Massachusetts, both of which have many low-income families, such systems clearly work. "Critics say choice cannot work in inner-city schools because parents lack the necessary education to make informed choices," notes Sy Fliegel, one of the pioneers of choice in East Harlem:

> *They are wrong. Inner-city minority parents are no less concerned than their middle-class counterparts to see their children educated in stimulating, orderly, vigorous schools and no less capable of choosing those schools when information is made available to them. . . . Schooling often represents the only avenue of escape from a much more desperate situation.*
>
> *We provide parents with reading and math scores and high school placements. Our parents and our kids know who the best teachers are and which are the best schools. They make selections based on experience, word of mouth, and public information about the schools.*

In East Harlem, choice has extended opportunities normally reserved for middle-class whites to poor black and Hispanic children. If we drop our ideological blinders and look squarely at reality, it becomes clear that choice, properly designed, will not threaten equity but *increase* it. "Choice exists now," explains Ted Kolderie. "You can go to private school, or you can move your place of residence to another district—and people in fact do this all the time. You can even go to a lot of public schools without moving, if you're willing to pay tuition. So choice exists, but it's related to your family income."

This is the argument Kolderie, Perpich, and their allies ultimately used to bring Minnesota's teachers' unions around. "We said, 'Those who can afford it already have choice,' " recalls Curtis Johnson. " 'So you want to deny the extension of it to the poor, is that right?' " It was an argument that carried the day.

MANAGING COMPETITION

As the discussion above makes clear, competition must be carefully structured and managed, if it is to work. Just as in education, unregulated markets generate inequity. Organizations selling services, whether job training or transportation or day care, tend to "cream" off the most profitable business: those who need the least training; those bus routes most heavily traveled; those parents who can pay for day care.

This is exactly what happens in health care today. For-profit hospitals turn away patients who have no insurance, sending them to overcrowded public hospitals. The consequences of this practice, known as patient dumping, can be severe. In one six-month study of a public hospital in Dallas, 77 percent of those patients transferred in from other hospitals had no insurance. In other words, private hospitals routinely turned away patients without insurance, sending them to a public hospital that would take them. Eleven of them died on the way in.

A different form of inequity can threaten those who work for competitive service providers. Careful studies indicate that wages paid by governments and private contractors are, on average, fairly comparable. But some studies suggest that contractors offer fewer benefits, such as health insurance. Governments also tend to be more aggressive than private contractors about hiring and promoting minorities and women.

Competition that is structured carefully, however, can produce more equitable results than service delivery by a public monopoly. Contractors can be required to provide comparable wages and benefits and to promote affirmative action, for example. This is important, if the values we embrace through our governments are not to be lost when those governments use competitive contracts.

Contractors can also be required to serve all segments of the market, to keep from creaming off the most profitable customers. During the National Science Foundation study on garbage collection, E. S. Savas found that competition actually heightened the equity of service delivery—because public agencies were, in effect, creaming. When city forces encountered delays and did not want to pay overtime, they would simply skip some areas that day—often the poorest areas, because they had the least political clout. With a contractor that didn't happen, because the contractor had no choice but to fulfill his contract. "It's a job to be done, rather than a set of neighborhoods to be differentially placated, depending upon their political strength," Savas says.

If not carefully structured, markets that look competitive can also succumb to monopolistic power. In both contracting and procurement systems, for example, some projects are so massive that for all practical purposes it is impossible to switch providers once the job has begun. Defense contractors who build submarines and ships enjoy this protection; it explains why they get away with endless cost overruns and seem impervious to sanctions. A similar problem is emerging with private corporations that contract to operate prisons, many of which demand 20- to 30-year contracts. "There is some reason to fear that instead of being competitive like the trash collection industry," John D. Donahue wrote in *The Privatization Decision*, prison management "will be competitive like the nuclear-submarine industry—which is to say, not at all."

Even when private firms do not have monopolies, they at times develop enough political power to stifle competition. In mass transit, private bus companies spend considerable sums to influence legislatures, to get and keep their contracts. In garbage collection, large private firms use their power to lobby against policies that would reduce the volume of garbage, such as recycling and source reduction. Even in day care, private firms try to restrict the competition.

This pattern suggests that governments would be wise to deny firms with which they do large volumes of business the right to lobby or make campaign contributions. Such prohibitions may have constitutional problems when applied by law to all private firms, but they can certainly be written into specific contracts. If a company wants the public sector's business, it simply agrees to forgo any effort to influence public policy in related areas. The conflict of interest is obvious.

None of this is to say that public monopolies don't require the same careful oversight. The postmasters sent enormous volumes of free mail to lobby Congress for a rate hike in 1990. School principals in Chicago sued to eliminate the reform program that took away their lifetime job security. A public employee union in Michigan sued to block the state from contracting out job training for welfare recipients. Rural Metro, a private firm that operates fire departments in some 30 communities, has been threatened so often by unions that it will no longer bid against a unionized fire department. The threat usually goes something like this: "If you come in here, we're going to raise money from every union in the country and make trouble in *your* backyard." Unions may have less money to spend than large corporations, but public employees vote at twice the rates of the general public.

Competition is here to stay, regardless of what our governments do. In today's fast-moving marketplace, the private sector is rapidly taking market share away from public organizations. Public schools are losing ground to private schools. The Postal Service is losing ground to Federal Express and UPS. Public police forces are losing ground to private security firms, which now employ two-thirds of all security personnel in the nation.

We can ignore this trend and continue with business as usual, watching fewer and fewer people use public institutions. We can sit idly by as a vicious cycle unwinds in which the less people depend on government the less they are willing to finance it, the less they finance it the worse it gets, and the worse it gets the less they depend on it. Or we can wake up—as entrepreneurial leaders from Phoenix to East Harlem to Minnesota have—and embrace competition as a tool to revitalize our public institutions.

The choice is not quite as stark as it would be in a competitive marketplace: compete or die. But it is stark enough. Our public sector can learn to compete, or it can stagnate and shrink, until the only customers who use public services are those who cannot afford an alternative.

– 4 –

Mission-Driven Government: Transforming Rule-Driven Organizations

Never tell people how to do things Tell them what you want them to achieve and they will surprise you with their ingenuity
—General George S. Patton

Public housing is one of the most centralized, bureaucratic, dysfunctional systems in American government. The federal Department of Housing and Urban Development controls virtually everything a local housing authority does. "The HUD office we have here is almost obsessed with this book of regulations they've got," says Andrea Duncan, executive director of the Housing Authority of Louisville. "If you deviate from that by the slightest bit, they've got to write you up. If a specification says the screw should be three-quarters of an inch long, and the contractor put in half-inch screws, they want them all taken out and changed."

Being entrepreneurial types, Duncan and her colleagues figured out a way around HUD's rules: They created a nonprofit subsidiary, Louisville Housing Services, which can do things the housing authority can't dream of doing. It can spend money on awards dinners for housing authority employees, run a scholarship program for kids in public housing, even develop

new housing. "We established it just to get out of the HUD regulations, to be able to move a little faster," says Duncan.

Louisville Housing Services' first big project was the sale of a
100-unit complex to public housing residents. Its second project was construction of 36 new units, which it sold to more public housing residents. It borrowed the money (using the income
from the first 100 mortgages as a partial loan guarantee), built
new condominiums in just five months, and sold them for
$32,000 to $36,000.

"I'm still working on a development program with HUD we
started two years ago," Duncan told us, by way of contrast:

*We've got the buildings there, all we have to do is rehab
them. We have made no progress, because the buildings have
lead paint, and HUD cannot decide what to do, how to go
about the lead-based paint removal, because they didn't budget for it and there's not enough money. They won't let us go
ahead until they get clearance, and they can't get clearance
until it goes through region, and up to Washington, and
back down again. I mean it's crazy. These buildings are vacant. Meanwhile, over here at our subsidiary, we not only
put a deal together, we've got people living in the units, and
it's time to go on to the next deal. There's no comparison.*

The punch line? Louisville Housing Services has *no* employees. It is run by a half-time consultant, who contracts with
private firms or hires housing authority employees in their off-
hours when he needs something done.

We have seen the same pattern hundreds of times over the
past decade: public entrepreneurs who are frustrated by their
huge, rule-driven bureaucracies simply go offshore, creating
smaller, mission-driven organizations. This is one reason why
public authorities and special districts are the fastest growing
forms of government organization today.

Massachusetts has at least a dozen quasi-public corporations
to do economic development and job training. Tampa General
Hospital created a subsidiary to combat infant mortality. St.
Paul and Minneapolis created a nonprofit corporation to

finance low-income housing. In its first ten years, it helped more than 1,700 families buy homes, helped finance more than 2,000 rental or cooperative units, helped create more than 1,000 units for people threatened by homelessness, and spun off a development corporation that has since helped build or renovate more than 1,800 units. And it had only *one employee*.

That employee, Tom Fulton, first articulated for us the concept of mission-driven government. It was late one Friday afternoon, in his office in Minneapolis. We had come to hear about his Family Housing Fund, and Fulton had regaled us with tales of the inertia and waste he encountered when dealing with federal and state bureaucracies—the 35-page manuals of regulations and 20-page legal opinions. "You know," he said, "we don't even have an application form. That doesn't mean we don't know what we want: we have a two-page list of criteria, and when someone approaches us for a loan, I go through them. We don't have a thousand rules; we fast forward to the distilled essentials of the deal. *Our organization is mission-driven rather than rule-driven*."

Fulton meant that the guiding force behind everything the Family Housing Fund did was its mission—its *fundamental purpose*. This may sound like common sense, but in government it is rare. Most public organizations are driven not by their missions, but by their rules and their budgets. They have a rule for everything that could conceivably go wrong and a line item for every subcategory of spending in every unit of every department. The glue that holds public bureaucracies together, in other words, is like epoxy: it comes in two separate tubes. One holds rules, the other line items. Mix them together and you get cement.

Entrepreneurial governments dispense with both tubes. They get rid of the old rule books and dissolve the line items. They define their fundamental missions, then develop budget systems and rules that free their employees to pursue those missions.

Some rules are necessary to run any organization. But as James Q. Wilson writes, "The United States relies on rules to control the exercise of official judgment to a greater extent than any other industrialized democracy." Wilson ascribes this tendency to our system of checks and balances, which makes each power center so weak that everyone falls back on rules to control what everyone else can do. But the tendency escalated dramatically during the Progressive Era, when reformers were struggling to control Boss Tweed and his cronies. To control the 5 percent who were dishonest, the Progressives created the red tape that so frustrates the other 95 percent.

To this day, whenever things go wrong, politicians respond with a blizzard of new rules. A business would fire the individuals responsible, but governments keep the offenders on and punish everyone else by wrapping them up in red tape. They close the barn door after the horse has escaped—locking in all the cowhands.

We embrace our rules and red tape to prevent bad things from happening, of course. But those same rules prevent good things from happening. They slow government to a snail's pace. They make it impossible to respond to rapidly changing environments. They build wasted time and effort into the very fabric of the organization.

When the Federal Aviation Administration needed to recruit, train, and move air traffic controllers quickly in the 1980s, civil service procedures made it impossible. When air traffic controllers needed even the simplest pieces of equipment, the procurement process took 9 to 12 months.

When the Massachusetts Revenue Department decided it could generate $100 million in new revenues if it had 40 more auditors, it took a year just to create the positions.

When Massachusetts enacted a series of controls after construction scandals in the 1970s, public construction slowed to a crawl and its price skyrocketed. The reformers legislated an absence of even the appearance of wrongdoing "at a price of no product," said former Boston Redevelopment Director Frank Logue. "They have created a process which makes cowards out of everyone."

The U.S. Postal Service has a rule book the size of a collegiate dictionary. The New York City school system has a rule book the size of *two* collegiate dictionaries. Principals in New York cannot tell school custodians when to open and close their schools—much less discipline or fire them. They cannot even fire teachers, in practice. And the Board of Education cannot fire or transfer a principal, once that principal has put in three years at a school.

"We have created a bureaucratic monster that functions essentially as a special-interest state," says Andrew Stein, president of the city council. "It is a state in which every powerful group's prerogatives are protected, everyone's special claims are honored—the custodians, the principals, the 110 Livingston Street bureaucrats, the board of examiners. Everyone, that is, except the children."

All this has an insidious effect on employees. "It's suffocating, entangling," says Tom Fulton. "It's like Gulliver, being tied down." Unable to do what they know is right, fearful of punishment if they are found to be ignoring the rules, many public employees simply give up. They forget their agency's mission and settle for following its rules. They write memos upon memos, in the time-honored tradition known as "covering your ass."

Fernando Noriega, director of the mission-driven Community Redevelopment Agency in Tampa, Florida, sums it up perfectly: "What's happened in the public sector has been a massive attempt to demotivate the employees, by not letting them exercise their minds—by telling them exactly what they have to do and when they have to do it and how they have to do it."

This impulse to control is embedded in virtually every set of rules by which government operates: the budget system, the personnel system, the procurement system, even the accounting system. Every rule was originally laid down with the best of intentions. But the cumulative effect is gridlock.

The price we pay is staggering. Rule-driven government may prevent some corruption, but at a price of monumental waste. Who can put a price tag on the employees who have given up? Who can put a price tag on the bureaucracies that grow ever larger, because they are so locked up by rules and line items that they cannot do anything new without adding more people and more resources?

Those who rail against "waste, fraud, and abuse" should
think twice the next time a politician tells them we have to control the bureaucrats, so they don't waste our money. The very
control mechanisms those politicians support make waste—
staggering, monumental waste—inevitable.

THE ADVANTAGES OF
MISSION-DRIVEN GOVERNMENT

Mission-driven organizations turn their employees free to pursue the organization's mission with the most effective methods
they can find. This has obvious advantages.

*Mission-driven organizations are more efficient than
rule-driven organizations,* for one. Louisville Housing Services
employs only one half-time consultant. The Family Housing
Fund had only one employee for 10 years; now it has three. St.
Paul, Visalia, Phoenix, Indianapolis—all are well below average in employees per capita. As Morton H. Halperin noted long
ago, bureaucracies are often happy to trade less money for
greater control.

*Mission-driven organizations are also more effective than rule-
driven organizations: they produce better results.* Look at the
contrast between Louisville Housing Services, or the Family
Housing Fund, and HUD. Or consider education. All the research shows that administrative autonomy and clear goals are
critical to the success of schools. As East Harlem's Sy Fliegel puts
it, "Every school that is successful has a mission, has a dream."

*Mission-driven organizations are more innovative than rule-
driven organizations.* Rule-driven organizations stifle innovation, because there is always some rule that stands in the way.
Stuart Butler and Anna Kondratas describe a classic example in
their book *Out of the Poverty Trap.* When a Philadelphia youth
gang decided to go straight, its leaders approached the city with
a proposal to rid the streets of abandoned cars. Who, after all,
knew more about stripping cars than their members? City administrators were very interested, but one thing stood in the

way: city rules required that the youths be insured—and who would pay for the insurance? Frustrated, the gang went back to the streets.

Mission-driven organizations are more flexible than rule-driven organizations. If an agency performs a function that is simple, patterned, and repetitive, its operations can effectively be structured by rules. Even today, McDonald's restaurants are run according to extremely precise rules. But less and less of what government does is simple, patterned, and repetitive.

To take advantage of the unanticipated, organizations must have flexible rules and budgets. Visalia bought a swimming pool at half price because its employees were unencumbered by line item budgets. Teachers in East Harlem are able to run effective schools because they have permission to break the rules. "I'll tell you something," says East Harlem's Michael Friedman, pointing to a six-inch-thick book called *Standard Operating Procedures, Board of Education, City of New York.* "If you had to follow that book, you could not run any one of these schools. You could not do the special things that we do."

Mission-driven organizations have higher morale than rule-driven organizations. A visitor to East Harlem's schools cannot miss the esprit de corps, among both students and teachers. A visitor to the Latimer administration in St. Paul quickly noticed the same thing. It was, quite simply, one of the *happiest* organizations we have ever encountered. And why not? A recent recruit told us: "I was hired to come up with new ideas, I was given a lot of slack and I was told not to worry about stepping on toes. They said, 'People won't hold it against you during your honeymoon, and that may be the only way you'll get some of your ideas done.' "

SCRAPING THE BARNACLES
OFF THE SHIP OF STATE

How do we create mission-driven governments? The first task is to scrape off the dead weight of accumulated rules, regulations, and obsolete activities. Many people understand the need to deregulate the private sector, but few apply the same thinking to the public sector. Even the Reagan administration fought to control the bureaucrats, not to deregulate them.

Government needs some rules, of course. The ship of state needs a coat or two of paint; if we take it down to bare metal, it will rust. The problem is, most governments have acquired several dozen coats of paint and layer upon layer of barnacles. The goal of deregulation is to get back to the one or two layers of protection we really need—so the ship can *move* again.

Visalia decided that two regulations had to be eliminated for every new one signed. Washington State gave its Schools for the 21st Century waivers to any rules that stood in their way. Bob Stone's Model Installations program gave waivers to base commanders. "Once they've had the heady experience of challenging and defeating stupid regulations," Stone said, "they're never the same."

Entrepreneurial leaders do away not only with obsolete regulations, but with obsolete programs. Every year, a typical business is forced to winnow out some of its products or services, because they no longer sell. But in government, managers have no incentive to winnow out their product mix. They simply add more and more services and regulations until finally a fiscal crisis or tax revolt forces a massive cutback—which is typically executed with all the subtlety of a meat ax.

In 1803, the British created a detachment to stand on the cliffs of Dover and watch for Napoleon. In 1927, they finally quit funding it.

In 1939, Minnesota prohibited line agencies from buying items that cost more than $50 without approval from Central Purchasing. In the mid–1980s, it finally raised the limit, to $1,500.

A century ago, states required manufacturers to sterilize the horsehair in mattresses and display tags showing they were properly inspected and licensed. (You know the tags; they say: "Do Not Remove Under Penalty of Law.") Fifty years ago, mattress manufacturers quit using horsehair. In 1990, one state finally repealed its law.

In 1935, Franklin Roosevelt created the Rural Electrification Administration to bring electricity to rural America. Its work, as former director Harold Hunter says, "was done a long, long,

long time ago." Today, it hands out low-interest loans to massive telecommunications firms—at a $1.2 billion-a-year cost to the taxpayer.

To slough off the obsolete, governments have tried a variety of methods:

Sunset laws set a date on which a program or regulation will die unless it is reauthorized—thus forcing a review. Colorado passed the first sunset law in 1976; by 1983, 35 states had one kind or another. Florida has gone the furthest: it sunsets all regulations, all trust funds, and all advisory committees, commissions, councils, and boards. (If that seems like overkill, think again: California spends $1.9 billion a year on 400 advisory commissions, boards, and councils.)

Unfortunately, sunset laws have not fulfilled their promise. Unless governments measure the results of their activities and regulations, sunset review committees have trouble knowing whether they're worth keeping. When Common Cause surveyed states that had sunset laws in 1982, 46 percent said inadequate measurement of agency performance created significant problems. If results were measured, however, think what effect it might have if every activity of government required a periodic vote of confidence to continue.

Review commissions examine government regulations or activities to weed out the obsolete. Again, Florida has gone the furthest. Every 20 years, a Constitutional Revisions Commission is appointed to review and change the state constitution. Every 10 years, a Taxation and Budget Reform Commission is called together to review the state's tax, budget, and planning systems; its revenue needs; and its efficiency and productivity. The commission has the power to propose statutory changes to the legislature and to put constitutional changes on the ballot.

Zero-based budgets require agencies to justify every element of their budget every year. A good idea in theory, they have proven in practice to be too cumbersome, too time-consuming, too fraught with paperwork, and too easy for managers to manipulate. In most places, they have died of their own weight.

Phoenix has developed a successful modification: it asks every manager to submit a prioritized list of cuts every year that add up to 10 percent of his or her budget. The city council ranks them and votes to eliminate the most expendable. Governor Branstad in Iowa has proposed a complete budget review for each department every five years, in which every program would disappear unless the legislature authorized it again.

CREATING A MISSION-DRIVEN BUDGET SYSTEM

Government's rules are aggregated into systems—budget systems, personnel systems, purchasing systems, accounting systems. The real payoff comes when governments deregulate these systems, because they create the basic incentives that drive employees. If leaders tell their employees to focus on their mission, but the budget and personnel systems tell them to follow the rules and spend within the line items, the employees will listen to the systems. The leaders' mission will vanish like a mirage.

Few people outside government pay any attention to budget systems. But budgets control everything an agency does. They are onerous and omnipresent, useless and demeaning. They suck enormous quantities of time away from real work. They trap managers in yesterday's priorities, which quickly become tomorrow's waste.

At the root of these problems lies a villain. Most public budgets fence agency money into dozens of separate accounts, called line items. This was originally done to control the bureaucrats—to hem them in on all sides, so they could not spend one penny more than the council or legislature mandated on each item of government. But once again, our attempt to prevent bad management made good management impossible.

If you started a business, you would ask your bookkeeper to track how much you spent on travel, supplies, personnel, and so on. But you surely wouldn't let the bookkeeper control how much you spent under each account. The same is true of family budgets: you may set aside so much for groceries, so much for the mortgage, and so much for car payments every month. But if the washing machine breaks, you find the money to fix it, and if manufacturers offer rebates on new cars, you seize the opportunity.

Public managers cannot do this. Their funds are fenced within line items that are often absurdly narrow. In one branch of the military, base managers have 26 different accounts for housing repairs alone! A typical manager of a city department has 30–40 line items for every program or division. In most cities and many states, legislatures not only dictate line items, they tell each unit how many full-time employees it can have.

Theoretically, a manager can request permission from the finance office or the legislature to move funds across the fences. But this is risky, because more often than not the answer is: "We're glad to know you don't need so much in this account, and we'll take back the surplus. But we're sorry, money's tight, we can't let you move it to the other account."

As a consequence, managers usually stick with the line items they have. This creates incredibly perverse consequences. At one military base, one housing area had no sidewalks. The commander had no line item to build sidewalks, but he did have an account to repair them. So he repaired the sidewalks in the other two areas, but left residents of the third to walk in the mud. In welfare departments, money for job training, job placement, and the like is in separate line items from welfare grant money. Spending more on training and placement normally saves money on welfare grants. But when times get tight, states cut their training and placement accounts. The welfare account—which is an entitlement, driven by the number of people who apply for welfare—then skyrockets.

By fencing money into line items, in other words, we waste billions of dollars every year.

But it gets worse. As we explained in the Introduction, if managers do not spend their entire budgets by the end of the fiscal year, they lose the money they have saved and they get less next year. Most public managers know where they could trim 10 to 15 percent of their budget. But why go through the pain of transferring or laying people off, if you can't use the money for something more important? Especially if your savings are going to be handed to some other manager who overspent his budget! Who in their right mind would save any money, under these circumstances?

Smart public managers spend every penny of every line item, whether they need to or not. This explains why public organizations get so bloated: *our budget systems actually encourage every public manager to waste money.*

Fairfield's Expenditure Control Budget

In 1979, the northern California city of Fairfield invented a solution. As is so often the case, it sprang from the mind of an outsider, who was unencumbered by the knowledge that "it's always been done this way." Fairfield's assistant finance director was an immigrant from the Philippines, where he had been a banker. He could not believe how Fairfield budgeted. He suggested to City Manager Gale Wilson that Fairfield budget the way his bank did in the Philippines, roughly the way a family budgets: it sets up accounts for various major expenditures, but if something breaks down or an opportunity comes along, it shifts money from one account to another.

Wilson understood the argument but doubted that the city council would accept it. Then, in 1978, Proposition 13 put a drastic hole in Fairfield's budget. Now, Wilson decided, he could get permission to change. He proposed a general fund budget that eliminated line items and allowed departments to keep what they didn't spend. Each department's budget was determined by a formula: it got the same amount as last year, increased to account for inflation and growth in the city's population. (The city manager could adjust these amounts, and when revenues fell short and the city council failed to act, an automatic across-the-board cut kicked in.)

The new system assumed that departments would maintain the same level and mix of services, at a minimum. If the council wanted a major new initiative, it would appropriate additional money. Managers still used line items to track their expenditures, but the council never saw them or voted on them. They became an accounting device to help managers, not a control device to hem them in.

Ted Gaebler, who convinced Visalia to adopt the system six months later, suggested to Wilson that the idea would spread faster if they gave it a politically appealing name. So they called it the Expenditure Control Budget.

The new system transformed the way managers thought about their money. In the past, if the police chief needed more officers, he asked for more money. If the manager or city council said no, he blamed them. It was never his fault. No one expected him to comb through the budget he already had, to find savings.

Now the dynamics changed. "Spend it or lose it" gave way to "save it and invest it." The contrast was glaring. Chuck Huchel, chief of public safety, saw it every day. His city budget came the new way, but his police department hustled a fair number of federal grants, which came the old way. "It's amazing," he said, "the same people behave differently with the two streams of money:

> With the federal grants, we prepare a budget in advance, and we put on all the bells and whistles, all the frills—we try to anticipate everything we might need. When we get an authorization, we spend everything that's on the list, whether we need to or not. People don't say, "Oh I can save some money here, or I can use it another way now," because it's in the plan. You don't have incentives to make the cost savings, because if you don't spend it you give it back.
>
> With the city money, they know that any savings they make can be applied to other programs or other equipment. So you say, "Hey, I don't actually need this to make the program work, so I'm not going to spend it." Plus they get creative about saving money. We needed a weather covering over a gas pump, to protect people from the rain when they were gassing up their vehicles. The architectural design to make it like a gas station came to around $30,000. We thought that was outrageous. So somebody said, "What

*about these bus stop covers—the glass-enclosed ones?" We
checked, and they cost $2,500. We put one of those up, and it
works fine.*

The results speak for themselves. By 1981, California had
named Fairfield one of its four most fiscally sound cities. By
1991, the city's departments had spent $6.1 million less than
they were appropriated. The General Fund, then $30.2 million,
had spent $28.8 million less than its revenues. This allowed the
city to take care of several unfunded liabilities, to salt away an
unrestricted reserve as a hedge against recession, and to build a
$20 million Intergovernmental Service Loan Fund, which
makes start-up loans to new capital projects, such as a theater
and a sports complex.

The new budget system also proved itself when sales and
property tax revenues plummeted during the 1991 recession.
First the city decided to draw down half of its $10 million in
reserves over the next three years, to limit the spending cuts
required. When the state then transferred several revenue
sources to the counties—deepening the city's fiscal hole—Fairfield simply changed its budget formula for the next three years.
From July 1, 1991, through June 30, 1994, departments will
receive no increase for inflation or population growth.

"When I came here from Sacramento, my instinctive reaction was that this system was crazy," said Finance Director Bob
Leland, who previously worked in the state finance office. "It
was totally alien to what I had experienced. But I got converted
in a hurry. I wouldn't trade it now."

Over the past 10 years, perhaps a dozen other cities have
adopted the Expenditure Control Budget, including Scotts
Valley, Kingsburg, and Porterville, in California; Chandler,
Arizona; and Las Vegas, New Mexico. Dade County, Florida,
uses a similar system, which it calls Operational Budgeting.
Other cities have dropped their line items without allowing
departments to keep any of their savings. At the state level,
Arizona got rid of line items for several years under Governor Bruce Babbitt, with great success. And other states use

lump-sum budgets—or few line items—in some agencies and departments.

Even the Defense Department has experimented with mission-driven budgeting, as we explained in the Introduction to this book. After he read about Visalia's use of the Expenditure Control Budget, Bob Stone developed his Unified Budget Test, which allowed six bases to swap money between line items and one of the six to keep its savings. Eight air force bases still use a unified budget, and the army has reduced or eliminated many of its budget restrictions. (Unfortunately, base commanders in both branches are still subject to the spend-it-or-lose-it rule.) A few other federal agencies, including the U.S. Forest Service and the Bureau of Indian Affairs, have also moved toward unified budgets.

The shift is under way even in other nations. Sweden, Canada, Britain, Denmark, and Australia now budget by broad policy categories, and Canada allows those in charge of each category—called an "envelope"—to keep and reuse their savings.

The Strengths of Mission-Driven Budgeting

Fundamentally, the Expenditure Control Budget empowers organizations to pursue their missions, unencumbered by yesterday's spending categories. That is why we call it a mission-driven budget. Its advantages are overwhelming:

Mission-driven budgets give every employee an incentive to save money. Everyone begins to look at things differently: Do we really need the air conditioning on all day? Could we find a better deal on word processors? In Visalia, when the mechanics decided they needed better tools, even they began to search for savings. For years, one of the shop's heaters had blown hot air outdoors. It had been a standing joke. Now they shut it off, repaired several other heaters, and cut small doors in the shop's huge vehicle doors, so they could close them during the winter. Within 18 months, they had reduced energy consumption by 30 percent. They used the savings to buy new tools.

Mission-driven budgets free up resources to test new ideas. Peters and Waterman note that entrepreneurial managers constantly bootleg resources—"squirreling away a little bit of money, a little bit of manpower"—to carry on new experiments. Mission-driven budgets give public managers the capacity to do that.

Mission-driven budgets give managers the autonomy they need to respond to changing circumstances. Line item budgets trap resources into old patterns. In Fairfield and Visalia, managers constantly shift their resources to meet new needs and phase out obsolete activities. This autonomy not only fosters responsive government, it builds morale and unleashes creativity.

Mission-driven budgets create a predictable environment. Managers know what their budget will be six months before the fiscal year begins. They don't spend months sweating over a budget, negotiating with the finance department, carefully balancing three dozen accounts—only to watch part-time legislators who know nothing about their area cut it up at the last minute, on a political whim. Nothing is more frustrating to a public servant. Nothing creates more cynicism within the ranks.

Mission-driven budgets simplify the budget process enormously. For people inside government, budget season is six months of hell. In traditional systems, managers come up with their wish lists six to eight months ahead of time, to submit to the finance office. (In the Department of Defense, they submit requests *three years* ahead.) The finance department spends months whacking away at their wish lists. Finally, it sends a mammoth budget to the council or legislature. (The 1990 federal budget was 1,376 pages long. San Francisco's is literally two feet thick. Visalia's is *two pages* long.) Legislative committees then pore over thousands of line items to make their own cuts and additions.

After months of toil and turmoil—in which legislators have to say yes or no hundreds of separate times to dozens of powerful interest groups—a budget finally emerges. Then, within weeks, the departments begin submitting budget amendments to cover unanticipated expenses—eating up more legislative time. "Here [in Fairfield] it's sort of magical," says Leland. "You tell people what they've got, and they stay within it. They manage for the long haul."

Mission-driven budgets save millions of dollars on auditors and budget officers. No one has to spend months whacking away at departmental budget requests. No one has to spend all year checking to see that managers don't overspend any of their line items. Fairfield has just one budget analyst in its finance department.

Finally, mission-driven budgets free legislatures to focus on the important issues. It is a truism in government that the amount of money in a line item is inversely related to the amount of time the legislature spends debating it. Legislators, city council members, and school board members are often lawyers or small-business people. They're familiar with decisions about buying computers and hiring secretaries. They feel useful when they can help make such decisions. But nothing has prepared them to deal with the larger policy issues: AIDS, or crime, or poor schools. So they feel less comfortable in that arena.

Mission-driven budgets relieve legislators of micromanagement decisions, freeing them to focus on the larger problems they were elected to solve. Once they have that luxury, they usually learn to enjoy it. Of all the city councils that have adopted the Expenditure Control Budget, we've never found one that would go back.

TRANSFORMING A RULE-DRIVEN PERSONNEL SYSTEM

The only thing more destructive than a line item budget system is a personnel system built around civil service. Most personnel systems in American government are derivatives of the federal Civil Service Act of 1883, passed after a disappointed job seeker assassinated President Garfield. A typical Progressive reform, civil service was a well-intended effort to control specific abuses: patronage hiring and political manipulation of public employees. In most places, it accomplished its goals. But like a howitzer brought out to shoot ants, it left us with other problems. Designed for a government of clerks, civil service became a straitjacket in an era of knowledge workers.

Fifty years ago, governments were not unionized. Nor had the courts outlawed most patronage hiring and firing and protected most employees from wrongful discharge. In other words, most of what civil service procedures were established to prevent has since been ruled illegal or made impossible by collective bargaining agreements. Yet the control mentality lives on, creating a gridlock that turns public management into the art of the impossible.

Several years ago the Massachusetts Taxpayers Foundation, a nonprofit watchdog group, surveyed state managers in Massachusetts. "No issue . . . evoked such a consistent and intense response as civil service hiring procedures," it reported. "Managers uniformly find that it hinders rather than helps them hire suitable employees, and with some bitterness cite civil service as the most serious impediment to accomplishing their mission." The Foundation labeled civil service "a nightmare," "a scandal," and "an unmitigated disaster."

In business, personnel is a *support* function, to help managers manage more effectively. In government, it is a *control* function—and managers bitterly resent it. Civil service rules are so complex that most managers find them impenetrable. The federal personnel manual, to cite but one example, is 6,000 pages long. Consider just a few of the major problems:

Hiring. Managers in civil service systems cannot hire like normal managers: advertise a position, take résumés, interview people, and talk to references. They have to hire most employees from lists of those who have taken written civil service exams. Often they have to take the top scorer, or one of the top three scorers—regardless of whether that person is motivated or otherwise qualified. (In San Francisco, if two applicants tie for the top score, the one with the highest social security number gets the job.)

The hiring process usually takes forever. When E. S. Savas studied New York City's system during the 1970s, he found that the higher people scored on the civil service exams, the less likely they were to be hired, because they had the savvy to find other jobs in the seven months that normally passed between testing and hiring.

Our favorite horror story comes from Michigan, where the Treasury Department, which invests $20 billion in state pension funds, is expected to hire *venture capitalists* from those who score well on the civil service exam.

Classification. Civil service jobs are classified on a graded scale, and pay within each classification is determined by longevity, not performance. Personnel departments spend thousands upon thousands of useless hours deciding whether such-and-such a job is a GS-12 or a GS-13, telling managers they cannot pay the salary they want to because the classification doesn't allow it, and blocking their efforts to reclassify people. Even when classification changes are approved, the process takes forever. In Massachusetts, where local governments have to get approval from the state, it can take two years.

Promotion. When people hit the top of their pay range, they cannot earn a raise without earning a promotion into a new type of work. But promotions are controlled by the personnel department, not the manager. They seldom have anything to do with performance. In a typical line job—in a police department, or data processing office—managers have to promote from among those already in the proper career track who have scored highest on the promotional exam.

Firing. There's an old saying: "Government workers are like headless nails: you can get them in, but you can't get them out." Federal employees cannot be fired until a manager has spent months (if not years) carefully documenting poor performance and the employee has then exhausted three appeals processes— the first two of which alone take an average of 224 days. State and local governments have their own versions of this scenario. The process is so time consuming and difficult that few managers ever fire anyone. (James Q. Wilson estimates that in one recent year, fewer than two-tenths of 1 percent of federal civil service employees were fired.) Instead managers tolerate incompetents, transfer them, or bump them upstairs.

Layoffs. When governments reduce their numbers through layoffs, civil service employees with seniority can bump those with lesser seniority. Middle managers can bump secretaries who can bump mail room clerks. In the Reagan cutbacks of 1981, a secretary at the Department of Energy who had worked her way up to running a program—and was proud of it—was bumped back to secretary. When New Jersey laid off 1,000 employees in 1991, 20,000 people received notices that they might be bumped.

Typically, layoffs comb out the young, eager employees and leave behind the deadwood—in jobs they neither know nor want. For a manager, says Rutgers University political scientist Alan Rosenthal, this is "like playing Russian roulette with five chambers loaded." In scientific agencies, one former director told us, bumping replaces "highly trained experts with people who have no experience or knowledge of the area. It maximizes seniority, and it maximizes destruction."

The result is a system in which managers cannot manage, deadwood is kept on, and morale goes through the floor. When a consulting firm surveyed St. Paul's employees, even the nonmanagerial people—whom the system was created to protect—were fed up. While their unions defended the system—particularly pay and promotion by seniority—67 percent of employees favored pay based on performance and 96 percent said performance should be considered in making promotions. Several years later, we asked the personnel director how much civil service limited the creativity of the bureaucracy, even after a series of reforms. His answer: "How high over 100 percent can I go?"

At the federal level, things may be even worse. Federal employees we know describe colleagues who spend their days reading magazines, planning sailing trips, or buying and selling stocks. Scott Shuger, who interviewed several dozen federal employees for the *Washington Monthly*, found that most estimated the number of "useless personnel" in their offices at 25 to 50 percent.

The waste in this system is mind-boggling. With 17.5 million civilian government employees (roughly 15 million of them full-time), our public payroll approaches $500 billion a year. Benefits add another $100 billion or so. One study found statistical evidence not only that civil service increased spending, but that the increases were "positively associated with the length of time Civil Service has been in effect." No one can say how much lower our personnel costs could be with a rational system, but 20 percent is not an outlandish guess.

Some governments—particularly at the local level—have taken action. Mayor Latimer pushed through some changes in St. Paul, although nothing close to what he wanted. Iowa now allows managers to hire from among dozens of people who receive one of the top six numerical scores on a general aptitude test. It also lets managers bypass seniority during layoffs, with the permission of the Personnel Department. San Francisco is attempting to reform its system.

The most dramatic move has come in Florida, where Governor Lawton Chiles convinced the legislature to sunset the civil service system, while turning two departments free to invent a replacement. If the legislature has not reauthorized the system by June 30, 1992, or authorized a new one, it will disappear.

At the federal level, the Civil Service Reform Act of 1978 held some promise, but the Reagan administration did little to exploit it. The one exception was the so-called China Lake Experiment, a demonstration project authorized by the act.

The China Lake Experiment revolutionized the personnel system at the Naval Weapons Center in China Lake, California, and the Naval Ocean Systems Center in San Diego. It classified all jobs in just five career paths (professional, technical, specialist, administrative, and clerical). It folded all 18 GS (General Schedule) grades into four, five, or six pay bands within each path. It allowed managers to pay market salaries to recruit people, to increase the pay of outstanding employees without having to reclassify them, and to give bonuses and salary increases based on performance. It automatically moved employees who received repeated marginal performance evaluations down to the next pay band. And it limited bumping to one career path and based it primarily on performance ratings, not seniority.

The experiment, which continues, is widely considered a roaring success. Personnel officers, who no longer have to spend all their time dealing with arcane classification issues, can now actually help managers manage. Turnover rates have declined, particularly for those employees considered by managers the best performers. Managers who previously complained that they could not keep their most skilled people have been able to improve the quality of their skilled employees. In 1987 surveys, more than 80 percent of the employees who responded preferred the new system to the old, and 70 percent even supported performance pay.

The federal Office of Personnel Management was pleased enough with the results to draft legislation permitting other agencies to adopt the same basic system. Unfortunately, the Reagan administration decided that it had to be "cost neutral"—meaning that any pay increases or bonuses had to be paid by reducing staff or pay elsewhere. In part for this reason, in part because several public employees unions opposed any merit pay, Congress yawned.

Still, the China Lake Experiment shows the way toward a modern personnel system, by demonstrating the success of:

- broad classifications and pay bands;
- market salaries;
- performance-based pay; and
- promotion and layoffs by performance rather than seniority.

Other important elements would include:

- hiring systems that allow managers to hire the most qualified people (within legal and affirmative action guidelines);
- aggressive recruitment of the best people; and
- streamlining of the appeals process for employees who are fired.

The task is less to reform civil service than to define the appropriate personnel system for a modern government and create it. When we ask entrepreneurial public managers what they would do with civil service, most simply say, "Scrap it and start over." Indeed, some of the most entrepreneurial public organizations we know—including Visalia, the Housing Authority of Louisville, and many public authorities and quasi-public corporations—get along just fine without civil service. Even 50 years ago, leaders who were bent on creating mission-driven organizations—such as the Social Security Administration and the FBI—got their agencies exempted from the system. Texas has managed to survive without a civil service system all along.

Like the steam engine, civil service was a valuable breakthrough in its day. But that day has long since passed. We obviously need some protection against patronage hiring and firing. But it is time to listen to our public entrepreneurs and replace a civil service system designed for the nineteenth century with a personnel system designed for the twenty-first.

BUILDING MISSION-DRIVEN ORGANIZATIONS

As organizations scrape off the barnacles of line-item budgeting, civil service, and obsolete rules and programs, their next task is to define their mission and build around it. A ship freed of barnacles is not yet a ship on course to its destination. Public entrepreneurs use a number of basic strategies to build mission-driven organizations.

Creating a Mission Statement

Clarity of mission may be the single most important asset for a government organization. Increasingly, public agencies seek that clarity by constructing mission statements. "The role of a mission statement," explains Police Chief David Couper of Madison, Wisconsin, "is to focus on the purpose of the organization, to call attention to what is important, and to set organizational goals to align practices with values."

The experience of hashing out the fundamental purpose of an organization—debating all the different assumptions and views

---

held by its members and agreeing on one basic mission—can be a powerful one. When it is done right, a mission statement can drive an entire organization, from top to bottom. It can help people at all levels decide what they should do and what they should stop doing.

Chunking and Hiving

Public organizations work best when they have *one* clear mission. Unfortunately, governments tend to load several different—and often conflicting—missions on each agency as the years go by. In 1989, Representatives Lee Hamilton and Benjamin Gilman reported that Congress had given the Agency for International Development (AID) 33 objectives, 75 priorities, and 288 reporting requirements. Among its 33 missions: to win friends in the developing world, to feed the hungry, to counter initiatives of the Soviet Union, to dispose of U.S. agricultural surpluses, to build democratic institutions, and to strengthen the American land grant college system and the historically black colleges and universities. No wonder AID had failed in its primary mission: to stimulate economic development in the Third World.

In a world of niche markets, the problem becomes even more intense. Historically, most public institutions have been designed to serve mass markets: the schools to educate all children, the Postal Service to deliver all the mail. Today we need institutions whose mission is to serve one niche. Doug Ross, who ran the Michigan Department of Commerce during the 1980s, confronted this reality head on. He split off the agency's development functions from its regulatory functions, creating a 400-person Development Department within the department. He then split the Development Department into 10 action teams—one focusing on capital markets, another on manufacturing technology, another on small business. He gave each one great autonomy—in fact, he spun off several as separate organizations—and he encouraged each one to develop its own mission statement.

Peters and Waterman called this chunking (breaking large organizations up into small groups) and hiving (spinning off new teams and organizations).

Organizing by Mission Rather Than by Turf

Missions do not respect turf lines. In his book *Neighborhood Services*, John Mudd, a former New York City official, put it this way: "If a rat is found in an apartment, it is a housing inspection responsibility; if it runs into a restaurant, the health department has jurisdiction; if it goes outside and dies in an alley, public works takes over." Similarly, if a poor woman needs health care, she must sign up with Medicaid; if she needs money, she must visit the welfare department; if she needs a job, she must find her way through a maze of training and placement programs; if she needs housing, she must negotiate a similar maze. Improving the lives of the poor is the core mission of none of these agencies or programs. Each simply provides a discrete service.

Organizations built around turf rather than mission tend to be schizophrenic. Commerce departments that handle matters related to business—rather than to a particular mission—must simultaneously regulate existing businesses and try to recruit new businesses. Welfare departments that handle the welfare turf—rather than a mission of helping the poor—often urge people to get jobs with one hand, while stripping those who succeed of their health coverage with the other.

The solution is to reorganize around mission, not turf. When George Latimer became mayor of St. Paul, five organizations dealt with planning and development: the Port Authority, the Housing and Redevelopment Authority, the Office of City Planning, the Community Development Office, and the Planning Commission. All five charged off in different directions. Latimer pushed through a reorganization that left three agencies, each focused on a specific mission and each extraordinarily effective in pursuing that mission.

Creating a Culture around the Mission

To imprint the mission of an organization on its members, leaders build a culture around it. They articulate their values and model the behavior they want.

Bob Stone has been trying to do this in the Department of Defense for 10 years. Stone was an early disciple of *In Search of*

Excellence. He had his eight staff directors read the book, then took them off for a one-day retreat to talk about it. There they decided their primary value was not productivity or efficiency or austerity, but excellence. Stone decided to hold a contest to see who could come up with a motto that would best capture that value. The winner was "Excellent Installations—The Foundation of Defense." To this day it is printed on all office stationery and publications.

One of the corporate leaders profiled by Peters and Waterman, Ren McPherson of the Dana Corporation, had substituted a one-page statement of philosophy for 22.5 inches of policy manuals. Stone and his staff decided to write a values statement patterned after McPherson's. They called it their Principles of Excellent Installations (see next page).

Soon someone suggested that Stone put a condensed version of this statement on a wallet-size "gold card." He and his staff have recruited more than 20,000 military people, including most of the highest brass in the Pentagon, to sign the principles and carry the card.

Stone addresses every Naval Commanders Course (a three-week course for new base commanders) on the gospel of excellent installations. The Army Chief of Staff, General Vuono, created an Army Communities of Excellence program based on the principles of excellence. Every army base commander, every division commander, and every infantryman who is picked for command is imbued with the value of excellence. Army bases compete for $10 million in prizes each year, based on how well they embody that value.

Stone is normally a fairly modest person. But when we asked him what influence he thought the principles had had, he said:

I think they've changed the way most influential people in the military think about military installations. They've been copied in all sorts of places. I got a visit a couple of weeks ago from the people from the Naval Audit Service, and they were complaining about this damn guy in the Marine Corps who kept insisting that it was okay to build new marine barracks, even though the existing barracks met minimum adequacy standards.

Department of Defense

Principles of
EXCELLENT INSTALLATIONS

These principles guide all members of the Excellent Installations Team.

Purpose

To provide for our customers-the soldiers, sailors, marines, and airmen who defend America—excellent places to work and live, and excellent base services

Serve Our Customers

We are here only to serve our customers and their families.

Know our customers and their desires

Get out and talk and listen to them in their workplaces, homes, and communities

Tell the American people, the Congress, and our bosses, what our customers need, using real-life stories that people can relate to

Show unjustifiable overcommitment to improving facilities and services for our customers

Manage for Excellence

The hundreds of thousands of people—in and out of uniform—who work at Defense installations are our most important asset.

Provide them with freedom and incentives to unleash their drive and entrepreneurial genius

Discourage conformity, uniformity, and centralization because they stifle innovation

Push responsibility and authority as far down into the organization as possible—and that's a lot further than most people think

Promote competition by providing installations people lots of information on how people at other installations are doing at similar jobs, then celebrate the winners

Encourage installation commanders to take charge, use all the authority available to them, demand relief from stifling over-regulation, and exercise an innovative spirit

Pay for Excellence

Defense cannot afford less than excellence. There is no such thing as a bad investment in excellent facilities for our people, because excellent facilities engender pride—the fuel of human accomplishment.

Protect our installations from deterioration Every year replace at least 2% of our physical plant, and do more repair and maintenance than the year before

Encourage and enable the troops to improve their own facilities They get better facilities far sooner and a greater feeling of pride and ownership

Foster the Excellent Installation Approach

Keep fighting the natural tendency of large organizations to ration authority, to over-centralize, and to over-regulate.

Help anyone who is trying to promote the excellent installation idea.

Find examples of what the excellent installation approach has accomplished and hold them up as models for others

EXCELLENT INSTALLATIONS — THE FOUNDATION OF DEFENSE

They said, "We told him he was wasting money. And he just kept saying, 'Bob Stone says it's okay.' He says we're not supposed to have minimum adequacy standards." They wanted to know how they could nail this son of a bitch. I told 'em, "He's right, that's official DOD policy—our policy is to provide excellent barracks, not minimum barracks."

Stone's decade-long campaign demonstrates several of the basic techniques used by hundreds of smaller public organizations: retreats, group competitions, awards, and values statements. Other leaders use stories, myths, and metaphors to communicate their values. George Latimer used slogans—"The Self-Reliant City," "The Homegrown Economy"—and symbols. When energy conservation became his priority in the late 1970s, he created an Energy Commission open to anyone in the city who wanted to join, then shut down city hall for three days to send every city employee willing to volunteer—plus hundreds of community volunteers—out into the neighborhoods, to help teach people how to weatherize their homes. This three-day celebration of Latimer's values—volunteerism, activism, and conservation—was an extremely powerful symbol.

Creating Permission to Fail

"What's the one thing I could promise anybody about combat?" Commandant A. M. Gray of the Marine Corps asked his commanders in a 1987 speech. "Uncertainty. How do people deal with uncertainty? How do you get people to have initiative, boldness and to act?"

"You learn it in an outfit where you're allowed to do things. You learn it in an outfit where you're allowed to make mistakes."

Entrepreneurs are people who fail many times. Tom Peters and Robert Waterman told managers to make sure their organizations generated a reasonable number of mistakes—because if they weren't failing occasionally, they weren't trying hard enough to succeed. Florida's *State Management Guide* makes a similar point: "If a department or program director does not have the opportunity to do things wrong, authority is lacking to do them right."

Visalia invented an award for the year's most spectacular failure. It was called the Nugmeyer Award—after Joanna Nugent and Roy Springmeyer, who came up with the idea. Ted Gaebler won it one year for proposing, on television, to give back a portion of the city's surplus by paying all citizens a "dividend"— without consulting beforehand with the city council. The message to city employees was clear: It's okay to make mistakes; we'll laugh along with you.

A NEW ACCOUNTABILITY SYSTEM

It is hard to imagine anyone actively choosing a civil service system today, or comparing a traditional line item budget to a mission-driven budget and opting for the former. These systems live on not because anyone likes them, but because they're like the furniture: they've been in place so long we assume they belong there.

There are three principal obstacles to the spread of mission-driven budget and personnel systems. The first is the mind-set just described: "We've always done it this way." The second is the desire by some elected officials to retain control over the pork barrel, through line items. And the third is the usual shortage of trust between legislatures and executives. Even those legislators who are willing to forgo the pork barrel often have doubts about giving the executive more leeway. "What happens if the managers don't perform?" they ask. "What if they steal the money, or use half of it for travel? What if they hire all their campaign workers? We're elected to control things like that."

The Supreme Court has ruled virtually all patronage hiring and firing unconstitutional, and a modern personnel system would establish some limits of its own. As for spending, auditors still audit for corruption under mission-driven budgets. No public entrepreneur wants to give anyone permission to defraud the taxpayer. The question is: Should we roll out the howitzer every time corruption appears?

Peter Drucker long ago pointed out that "control of the last 10 percent of phenomena always costs more than control of the first 90 percent." If it costs far more to eliminate corruption than we save by doing so, is it worth the expense? If by making corruption virtually impossible we also make quality performance virtually impossible, have we done a good thing? If by tying everyone up in rules we so demoralize public employees that they give up, is it worth the enormous cost we bear in deadweight?

There is another way. Entrepreneurial governments rely on information about the results of government spending—the cost and quality of government programs—to detect fraud and abuse. A century ago, it was relatively easy to hide corruption. With today's information technologies, it is harder. By carefully measuring results, entrepreneurial organizations can minimize the need for rules.

This is the trade-off necessary to get permission to scrape off the barnacles. It is the answer to the legislator's first question: "What if the managers don't perform?" To be successful in politicized environments, where trust is minimal, mission-driven governments need to marry their budget systems to performance measures. If legislators are to stop holding managers accountable for following hundreds of rules and spending every penny of every line item, they will need another standard. As we will see in the next chapter, entrepreneurial governments hold them accountable for their results.

– 5 –

Results-Oriented Government: Funding Outcomes, Not Inputs

> *What I've noticed about bureaucratic programs is that for all their rules and red tape, they keep very little track of what actually happens to the people they're serving If that's built in from the beginning—if you keep track of the results—you can dispense with a lot of red tape.*
>
> —Tom Fulton, President of the Minneapolis/
> St. Paul Family Housing Fund

Several years ago, the Illinois Department of Public Aid decided to reexamine the way it reimbursed nursing homes for Medicaid patients. It paid according to the level of care provided: for severely ill residents who needed more care, the state paid more; for those who needed less care, it paid less. This seemed entirely logical and fair, but when state analysts finally looked at the results, they were horrified. The overriding goal of state policy was to keep the elderly as independent as possible, so as to minimize costs. Yet the percentage of nursing home residents who were bedridden was rising steadily.

Apparently, by paying more for bedridden patients, the state had given nursing homes a financial incentive to *keep* them bedridden—and a disincentive to get them up, involve them in physical activities, and help them function independently. Because the funding formula focused on inputs but ignored outcomes, it had produced the exact opposite of the state's intentions.

To its credit, the Department of Public Aid quickly changed its system. It developed a set of performance measures that rated patient satisfaction, community and family participation, and the quality of the nursing home environment. Nursing care managers now visit each institution periodically and rate them, much the way the Michelin Guides rate restaurants. The higher they rate, the higher their reimbursement level: a six-star rating is worth $100,000 a year more than a one-star rating. The state also publishes the ratings, so consumers can choose between nursing homes based on their quality. Illinois nursing homes, in other words, now compete for their customers based on their performance.

Unfortunately, the new system is still the exception. Traditional bureaucratic governments act just as Illinois did before its study. They focus on inputs, not outcomes. They fund schools based on how many children enroll; welfare based on how many poor people are eligible; police departments based on police estimates of manpower needed to fight crime. They pay little attention to outcomes—to *results*. It doesn't matter how well the children do in one school versus another, how many poor people get off welfare into stable jobs, how much the crime rate falls or how secure the public feels. In fact, schools, welfare departments, and police departments typically get *more money* when they fail: when children do poorly, welfare rolls swell, or the crime rate rises.

Entrepreneurial governments seek to change these rewards and incentives. Public entrepreneurs know that when institutions are funded according to inputs, they have little reason to strive for better performance. But when they are funded according to outcomes, they become obsessive about performance.

Because they don't measure results, bureaucratic governments rarely achieve them. They spend ever more on public education, yet test scores and dropout rates barely budge. They spend ever more on job training for welfare recipients, yet welfare rolls continue to grow. They spend ever more on police and prisons, yet crime rates continue to rise.

With so little information about results, bureaucratic governments reward their employees based on other things: their longevity, the size of budget and staff they manage, their level of authority. So their employees assiduously protect their jobs and build their empires, pursuing larger budgets, larger staffs, and more authority.

Why did we ever do it this way? In part, we have Boss Tweed to thank. In their battle against public corruption, the Progressives slapped controls on everything they could. Unfortunately, that meant controls on inputs. At the time, it was not easy to measure results. There were no computers, no calculators, and little experience with performance measurement, even in business. Most tasks entrusted to governments were also fairly straightforward, so performance tended to take care of itself. When government picked up the garbage, delivered the water, and constructed the roads and bridges, the results of its activities were clear to all.

This legacy has endured because the ultimate test in government is not performance, but reelection. Private organizations focus on results because they will go out of business if the key numbers go negative. But governments don't go out of business. Failure in government is not failure to achieve results, it is failure to secure reelection. As one state legislator put it, "Pleasing the voters is our performance evaluation."

Politics focuses on perceptions and ideology, not performance. In ordinary times, politicians get reelected based on how the voters and interest groups *perceive* them, not on how well their government provides services. Even department heads at the federal and state levels are more politicians than managers. "You learn very quickly that you do not go down in history as a good or bad Secretary in terms of how well you ran the place," wrote Michael Blumenthal, after his stint in President Carter's cabinet. In Washington, "you can be successful if you appear to be successful."

But we are no longer in ordinary times. Today's citizens refuse to pay higher taxes for services whose prices skyrocket while their quality declines. "You're seeing it everywhere," says James R. Fountain, Jr., assistant research director at the Governmental Accounting Standards Board: "a growing frustration among taxpayers that they don't know what they're getting for their money."

As a result, words like *accountability, performance,* and *results* have begun to ring through the halls of government. Luckily, we now have the technology needed to make such words mean something. We can generate, analyze, and communicate a thousand times more information than we could just a generation ago, for a fraction of the cost. Fountain's organization, which sets the accounting standards followed by most state and local governments, is in fact redefining "generally accepted accounting standards" to include performance measurement. It hopes to release its first performance accounting standards, for general adoption, by the mid-1990s.

In an equally telling sign of the times, President Bush and the nation's governors have adopted a set of national education goals for the year 2000, with specific objectives such as a 90 percent graduation rate and first-in-the-world ranking in math and science achievement. They are developing benchmarks by which to measure each school's or state's progress toward those goals.

Not everything government does generates results that can be measured. How would we measure the performance of diplomats in the State Department, for instance? But in an astonishing variety of public activities, entrepreneurial leaders are developing new ways to measure and reward outcomes:

- The federal Job Training Partnership Act created a system that operates almost entirely on performance contracts: training vendors are paid according to how many people they place in jobs—not how many people they enroll in training.

- At least nine states now tie their funding for vocational education to job placement rates. In Arkansas and Florida, for instance, an adult program that repeatedly fails to place 70 percent of its graduates in jobs loses its state funding.

- At the Housing Authority of Louisville, if rent collections fall below 97 percent, or turnaround time for vacant apartments exceeds 14 days, or the "site appearance" falls below a graded standard, the managers are warned. If the problem persists, they are replaced.

- In Illinois's Cook County, the nation's second largest, the courts are experimenting with report cards for judges, based on ratings from jurors, witnesses, and lawyers. Several states use similar systems.

- Six states are testing performance standards for entire courts, developed by the National Center for State Courts and the U.S. Department of Justice. They use customer surveys, focus groups, analysis of case files, and other methods to measure things like how accessible the courts are, how affordable justice is, how swiftly courts handle cases, how impartial court decisions are, and how effective courts are in enforcing their orders.

- Governments are shifting the way they fund highway construction. In the past, they specified the inputs they expected from contractors: so many inches of material A, topped by so many inches of material B. Today, they increasingly specify the number of years the highway is expected to last and hold the contractor accountable if it fails. Some offer performance bonuses for contractors who beat their deadlines; a Minnesota firm earned itself an extra $1 million by completing a stretch of Interstate 94 a year early.

- Some states even sign performance agreements with utilities that operate nuclear power plants. Boston Edison pays a penalty if its Pilgrim plant operates at full capacity less than 60 percent of the year, but earns up to $15 million extra if it operates at full tilt more than 76 percent of the year.

THE PERFORMANCE LEADER: SUNNYVALE, CALIFORNIA

To see the full power of performance measurement, one has only to visit Sunnyvale, California, a city of 120,000 in the heart of the Silicon Valley. It is only fitting that Sunnyvale should lead the performance revolution. As the home of thousands of computer jocks, Sunnyvale has a culture steeped in information technology. Few other places on earth would be so receptive to the use of performance measures. But where Sunnyvale pioneered, other cities and states have begun to follow.

Sunnyvale's managers measure the quantity, quality, and cost of every service they deliver. Because the city council has this information, it no longer votes on line items: it votes on service levels. It does not tell the Department of Public Works: "We want to spend $1 million reconstructing highway A, $500,000 repairing roads B, C, and D, and $250,000 filling potholes throughout the city." Instead it defines the results it wants. Using a classification system developed by the city, it says, "We want every road surface now at level A maintained at that level; every road surface now at level B brought up to level A within X years; and every surface at level C brought up to level A within Y years." The department tells the council exactly how much that will cost, depending on the numbers used for X and Y, and the council decides how much to spend to achieve the results it wants, and how fast.

Sunnyvale uses literally thousands of measures. In each program area, the city articulates a set of "goals," a set of "community condition indicators," a set of "objectives," and a set of "performance indicators." Goals are fairly self-explanatory: "Provide a safe and secure environment for people and property in the community"; "Control the number and severity of fires and hazardous materials incidents and provide protection for the lives, welfare and environment of people within the community."

"Community condition indicators" give the city information about the current quality of life. For example:

- the number of days in which ozone standards are exceeded;

- the number of traffic accidents per million vehicle miles;

- the number of persons receiving Aid for Dependent Children; and

- the number of persons at or below the poverty line.

"Objectives" set the specific targets for each unit of city government. In street landscaping, for instance, one objective is to "maintain trees and shrubs in a healthy state with a loss factor of no more than five percent." In public safety, one objective is to keep the city "within the lowest 25 percent of Part 1 crimes for cities of comparable size, at a cost of $74.37 per capita." And in transportation, one objective is to "achieve a ratio of 3.42 accidents per million miles traveled."

"Performance indicators" provide specific measures of service quality, which reveal how well each unit is doing in meeting its objectives. They include numbers such as:

- the percentage of trees needing replacement that are replaced within two months;
- the percentage of job trainees who get jobs, their average wage at placement, and the satisfaction level of their employers;
- the percentage of participants in a recreation program who rank it "good" or above; and
- the number of complaints about recreation facilities.

Not all of Sunnyvale's measures are equally useful. Managers constantly refine them, eliminating those judged inadequate or not worth what they cost to collect. But enough of the measures are solid that Sunnyvale's city council can predict quite accurately the results it will achieve depending on how it allocates its resources. In other words, by measuring results, Sunnyvale gives its decision makers the information they need to make intelligent decisions. They can tell success from failure. They can see where increased spending will produce the results they want. And they can predict the results of any spending cut.

"In a normal political process, most decision makers never spend much time talking about the results they want from the money they spend," says City Manager Tom Lewcock. "With this system, for the first time they understand what the money is actually buying, and they can say yes or no."

Because the council has control over outcomes, it has gladly eliminated many of the rules and budget line items that hamstring most public managers. "Our council does not know how many people work for the city, nor do they really care," says Lewcock:

> They do not focus on line items. There is no approval process for hiring people around here; management does it. The essential thing the council does is set policy: what level of service, how many units are going to be produced, and at what unit cost. What they have done is give us freedom over the management of city affairs, in return for them getting true policy control.
>
> Our council feels so good that they are in fact the policy leaders that they don't feel it's a risk at all to let managers manage. To me, that's the big secret that has allowed us to be risk-takers and to do things without always having to check the political implications.

Because Sunnyvale can measure the results of each unit's work, it can also reward managers based on whether they succeed or fail. If a unit exceeds its service objectives for quality and productivity, its manager is eligible for a bonus of up to 10 percent of his or her salary. "This puts them in an environment where it is to their advantage to find productivity improvements," says Lewcock.

This system generates tremendous productivity. The city keeps a four-part Municipal Performance Index, which measures both its efficiency and its effectiveness over time. Between 1985 and 1990, the city's average cost per unit of service went down 20 percent, after factoring out inflation. (In other words, its productivity increased by roughly 4 percent a year.) In 1990, when it compared its own costs to those of similar size and type cities, Sunnyvale found that it used 35 to 45 percent fewer people to deliver most services. Its employees were paid more, but its operating budget was still near the low end of comparable cities, and its per capita taxes were lower than those of any comparable city in its sample.

THE POWER OF PERFORMANCE
MEASUREMENT

Organizations that measure the results of their work—even if they do not link funding or rewards to those results—find that the information transforms them.

What Gets Measured Gets Done

"All you have to do is measure something and people respond," says John Pratt, a former director of Massachusetts' welfare department. In 1979, Massachusetts had a 23 percent error rate, the highest of any industrial state. (Cases in "error" were those lacking the documentation required to support the level of grant awarded.)

> When we began measuring error rates statewide, nothing happened. But as soon as we published the rates for each office, things changed. Because now the finger was pointed at managers: everyone knew if their office had a high rate. It only took 12 months to cut it down to 12 percent. Six months later, when we published error rates for each supervisor, it fell to 8 percent.

During New York City's fiscal crisis in the 1970s, an independent foundation developed a method to measure the cleanliness of streets, called Scorecard. It then sent out volunteers every month to rate each of 6,000 streets. The sanitation department had always focused on inputs: How many trucks were assigned to each district? How many men were needed on each truck? Now it began to look at the Scorecard information, which rated outcomes: How clean was each street? Using this information, it reassigned its street cleaners and began to reward crews that made the greatest improvements. By 1986, the percentage of streets rated "filthy" had declined from 43 to 4 percent. Nearly 75 percent were rated "acceptably clean."

The foundation, called the Fund for the City of New York, went on to develop outcome measures for parks maintenance, job training and placement, foster care, home care services, school maintenance, and other programs. "In large institutions, public and private, things are counted, and whatever *is* counted, counts," said then Executive Director Greg Farrell. "What is counted shapes and influences the behavior of the organization. It helps make public policy practicable, gets it out in the field, on the ground. And it leaves a trail."

The simple act of defining measures is extremely enlightening to many organizations. Typically, public agencies are not entirely clear about their goals, or are in fact aiming at the wrong goals. When they have to define the outcomes they want and the appropriate benchmarks to measure those outcomes, this confusion is forced into the open. People begin to ask the right questions, to redefine the problem they are trying to solve, and to diagnose that problem anew. "When the measurement process starts," says Stan Spanbauer, president of Fox Valley Technical College in Wisconsin, "people immediately begin to think about the goals of the organization."

If You Don't Measure Results, You Can't Tell Success from Failure

The majority of legislators and public executives have no idea which programs they fund are successful and which are failing. When they cut budgets, they have no idea whether they are cutting muscle or fat. Lacking objective information on outcomes, they make their decisions largely on political considerations. Large, powerful organizations—whether public agencies or private contractors—make the most noise and have the best connections, so they escape relatively unscathed. Smaller, more entrepreneurial organizations take the hits.

Likewise, when political leaders decide to increase their efforts in any area, they often have no idea where to put the new money. When the Bush administration declared war on drugs, it had no idea what worked. So it poured most of its money down the same holes the Reagan administration had already poured $21 billion—interdiction, investigation, and prosecution. Yet as the *Wall Street Journal* reported, eight years of effort on that front had "hardly put a dent in the drug traffic." One of the few evaluations the *Journal* could find, done by the Rand Corporation, had concluded that $5.72 billion spent on Coast Guard cutters, Customs Service jets, and radar-equipped blimps had done little more than raise the price of illegal drugs by 4 percent. As for drug treatment, an administrator of the Alcohol, Drug Abuse and Mental Health Administration, which spent nearly $2 billion in 1989, admitted to the *Journal* that his agency didn't even monitor the results. Congressman Charles Rangel of New York summed it up well: "We're spending blindly. We don't know what we've bought."

Police forces make this mistake all the time. Research proves that doubling the number of patrol cars on the streets has no effect on the level of serious crime—or on public anxiety about crime. Yet when crime rates rise, the police buy more squad cars.

One sage summed up this approach with these words: "Inasmuch as we have lost sight of our objectives, we are going to redouble our efforts."

If You Can't See Success, You Can't Reward It

By rewarding successful managers, Sunnyvale has increased its productivity by 4 percent a year. By rewarding successful schools, School District 4 has revolutionized education in East Harlem.

Rewarding success works even in places where most governments have given up. When the Housing Authority of Louisville sold a public housing development to former tenants, they kept the place in better condition than most condominiums, filed far fewer insurance claims for damages, and paid their mortgages on time just like any other group of homeowners. When the Federal National Mortgage Association began rewarding A and B students at a Washington, D.C., school with mentors, summer jobs, and money for college tuition, the number of A and B students rose from 33 to 130. When wealthy New Orleans oilman Patrick F. Taylor guaranteed college tuition for 180 7th and 8th graders—most of whom had already failed two or more grades—only 11 dropped out of high school. In an average American school, roughly 50 of 180 would drop out; among those who had already failed two grades, at least half would call it quits before graduation. In 1989, the state copied Taylor's effort; within two years more than 1,300 Taylor Plan students were in Louisiana colleges and five other states had adopted similar tuition guarantees.

If You Can't Reward Success, You're Probably Rewarding Failure

Rewarding success may be common sense, but that doesn't make it common practice. In education, we normally reward failure. "If you're failing, you qualify for aid," explains East Harlem's Sy Fliegel. "If you're doing well, then you lose the aid." In public safety, we also reward failure: when the crime rate rises, we give the police more money. If they continue to fail, we give them even more. In public housing, we reward failure: under federal funding formulas, the better a local housing authority performs, the less money it gets from HUD.

Rewarding failure creates bizarre incentives. It encourages school principals to accept the status quo. It encourages police departments to ignore the root causes of crime and simply to chase criminals. It discourages housing authorities from working to improve their operations.

Our tendency to reward failure has literally crippled our efforts to help the poor. Most of the money we spend on the poor—welfare, food stamps, Medicaid, public housing, housing vouchers, child care vouchers—rewards failure, because it goes only to those who remain poor.

If a welfare recipient saves enough to buy a car so she can look for work, her grant is reduced. If she finds a job, she not only loses her welfare check, she loses her Medicaid coverage (after a year), her food stamps are reduced, and if she lives in public housing, her rent often triples. One study, done in Louisville, showed that a public housing resident with two preschool

children had to earn $9 an hour in 1989 just to break even with
her total welfare package. And Louisville is not an expensive
place to live; elsewhere the figure would be higher.

Under these circumstances, why would a single mother with
two or three children ever leave welfare? This explains why
even our most effective efforts to move people into jobs seem
never to shrink the welfare rolls.

Not only do we punish those who get off welfare, we require
little of those who stay on. In fact, we call programs like welfare
"entitlements" precisely because people are "entitled" to them,
regardless of how they behave. The combination of rewarding
failure and expecting nothing in return for benefits breeds dependency—undermining people's motivation to improve their lives.

Healthy relationships are built on mutual obligations. If we
expect nothing from people, we usually get it. But if we expect
effort in return for what we give, we usually get that. Louisville
Housing Services is extremely strict about mortgage payments
from the former public housing tenants who buy its condominiums. "If you raise the expectations," says Director David Flei-
schaker, "people will jump through the hoops."

Increasingly, governments are beginning to build demands for
performance into their poverty programs. The federal Family
Support Act of 1988 required many welfare recipients to participate in education, training, or work. Minnesota's Learnfare initiative requires teenage mothers of school age to attend school if
they want welfare. Wisconsin's Learnfare program penalizes welfare families when their teenage children miss three days of
school without a written excuse. Arkansas requires the social security numbers of both parents when birth certificates are issued,
then uses that information to track down absent fathers and demand parental support for welfare children.

If You Can't See Success, You Can't Learn From It

Entrepreneurial public organizations are learning organizations. They constantly try new things, find out what works and
what doesn't, and learn from the experience. But if an organiza-

tion doesn't measure results and can't identify success when it happens, can it learn from success? Without feedback on outcomes, innovation is often stillborn.

The greatest opportunities for innovation in business, Peter Drucker counsels, are "unexpected successes." When a product or service takes off unexpectedly, there are inevitably important lessons to be learned. The same principle applies to government, as the following story demonstrates.

During the 1970s, the Ford Foundation created the Manpower Demonstration Research Corporation, to test a Swedish concept called "supported work." The idea was to create a sheltered work environment—usually a subsidized business set up specifically for this purpose—for ex-convicts, ex-addicts, high school dropouts, and long-term welfare recipients. Over the course of the year, while working, the participants would receive counseling, training, and other support services. At the end of the year, they would get help finding "real" jobs. The corporation set up a dozen supported-work experiments around the country and carefully measured their results against those of a control group. (With 10,000 participants, it was the largest control group experiment ever done on an urban program.)

The Massachusetts entry was called Transitional Employment Enterprises (TEE). It emerged as the most successful of the dozen experiments, largely because it stumbled on a different way of doing business. While trying to place its participants in jobs with the Massachusetts Department of Public Welfare, TEE argued that they could outperform Kelly Services. Fortuitously, an errant computer destroyed thousands of welfare files, and the department—in crisis—took TEE up on the idea. It hired TEE workers to re-create its written files, and lo and behold, they *were* better than Kelly Services. Once its crisis was over, the department convinced Blue Cross/Blue Shield, which handled Medicaid processing for the state, to hire TEE workers as temporaries. They were so productive that the company began hiring them for permanent jobs.

Suddenly, TEE found itself running a placement service for Blue Cross/Blue Shield. But because of its supported-work philosophy, it continued to provide support services for its people after they started their jobs—helping with their personal problems, helping them learn the ropes at work, and helping their managers supervise them. Only after they had successfully performed on the job for four to six months did the company have to hire and pay them; until then they remained on TEE's payroll.

The combination worked so well that TEE decided to market itself to Boston businesses as a placement service for low-end jobs. The results were extraordinary: 90 percent of those hired stayed with the company for at least a year; 83 percent for at least two years.

It was a classic unexpected success. And because all results were measured, it did not go unnoticed. TEE used its data to convince the Massachusetts legislature to spend $6 million a year funding 21 supported-work corporations around the state. Since then, TEE and its successor, a for-profit firm called America Works, have placed thousands of people in jobs, in four different states. Today, America Works is completely performance funded. States do not pay it a dime until a welfare recipient has been on the job for four months; they do not pay in full until the person has stayed another three months. In other words, the states pay only for results.

If You Can't Recognize Failure, You Can't Correct It

People often wonder why government programs live on for decades after they have become obsolete: why a state keeps inspecting meat long after the federal government begins duplicating its work; why HUD keeps a large urban renewal staff long after most cities have quit doing much urban renewal; why California has 400 commissions that spend almost $2 billion a year.

The answer, at least in part, is that no one outside the bureaucracy can tell if these offices and commissions do anything worthwhile, because no one measures the results of their work. In a 1990 article, the *Washington Monthly* told the sad story of Community Mental Health Centers—an initiative launched in

1963 by President Kennedy to create community centers so the mentally ill could be moved out of hospitals (or "deinstitutionalized"). Kennedy thought he was pushing control of services out of the bureaucracy, into the community. In his message to Congress, he announced that "reliance on the cold mercy of custodial isolation will be supplanted by the open warmth of community concern and capability."

Unfortunately, no one bothered to track the results. The National Institute of Mental Health handed out millions of dollars to firms that promised to build and staff Community Mental Health Centers and to serve all residents in the area for 20 years. But the institute rarely bothered to check whether the recipients followed through. Many converted to private, for-profit status and provided care only to those who could pay; others focused on psychotherapy for the worried well rather than care for the mentally ill. When the General Accounting Office finally forced the institute to hire a contractor to visit centers, in the late 1980s, it found that only 46 percent were fulfilling their commitments. Meanwhile, perhaps a million mentally ill Americans wandered the streets, sleeping in cardboard boxes or homeless shelters.

The same story can be told about many public programs. Consider public housing and welfare, which between them cost us roughly $30 billion per year. Both systems were created during the 1930s to accomplish specific missions. Welfare (AFDC) was designed to provide an income for widows with children. Public housing was created to give temporary housing to the unemployed during the Depression, as we saw in chapter 2. Both programs worked quite well for a time. But when the postwar economic boom brought many of their recipients into the work force and replaced them with uneducated black sharecroppers from the South, both programs faced an entirely different clientele. Yet both kept operating exactly as they had before. Not surprisingly, they soon found themselves in deep crisis. Had each program defined its intended outcomes and measured whether they were being achieved, policy makers would have known by 1960 that they had a massive failure brewing. Had their funding been tied to outcomes—how many

welfare recipients left the rolls for jobs, how long each family
stayed in public housing, the crime rate at each public housing
development—the funding would have shifted gradually to
those innovators who devised new strategies to deal with the
new clientele. But by 1990—*30 years later*—that process had
barely begun.

If You Can Demonstrate Results, You Can Win Public Support

Many governors point out that even today's antitax electorate
has supported tax increases for education—if linked to some
form of accountability for performance. Civic leaders in Phoenix, long a hotbed of antitax fervor, believe their voters passed
$1 billion in bond issues in 1988—probably the largest munici-
pal bond approval in American history—because the city had a
reputation for sound management, certified by the bond rating
agencies. But such claims are largely anecdotal.

In 1990, an organization called Florida TaxWatch came
about as close as one can to proving the connection between
documentation of results and public support. Although normally not eager to raise taxes, the organization had joined several prominent business groups to back an increase in the
gasoline tax, to fund highway construction—one of the hottest
issues facing the legislature. When it commissioned a poll of
628 registered voters to measure support, it found that 57 percent described the state's transportation system as "fair" or
"poor." Yet when asked if the legislature should increase the gas
tax by 4 cents per gallon to pay for improvements, only 43 percent said yes. Why? Because two-thirds of those with an opinion
believed the state wasted more than 20 percent of every tax dollar it collected. So Florida TaxWatch rephrased its question:
"Would you favor a four-cent gas tax hike if the legislature
made sure the increase would take effect only if the Florida Department of Transportation (DOT) improves its performance?"
Now 59 percent said yes. (Of those who said no, nearly half
chose, as their reason, that "state government can't be trusted
to spend money without wasting most of it.")

"Funding tied to performance by the Florida DOT will be accepted by a significant majority of Floridians, funding with no such assurances will not," Florida TaxWatch concluded. "It is as simple as that." With its data in hand, it proposed a gas tax increase that would be rescinded unless the DOT hit specified performance benchmarks. The legislature amended the bill slightly, but passed it overwhelmingly. When spending is conditioned on results, it suggested, voters—and politicians—will respond.

PUTTING PERFORMANCE MEASURES TO WORK

Many people in government resist the idea of performance measurement because they have seen it done poorly. When the Job Training Partnership Act passed in 1982, for instance, it mandated performance-based contracts with training providers. But many of the original contracts encouraged providers to train those who were the most job-ready, because they rewarded providers on the basis of how many trainees they placed. This encouraged providers to cream off the easiest to serve, and led to severe criticism.

Performance measurement in education has been criticized for other reasons—principally because it relies on standardized tests, which do not necessarily reflect anything but rote learning. Critics also fear that standardized tests will force all schools to teach the same subjects in the same way—robbing them of the flexibility to try different methods. But such criticisms have pushed many states to refine their tests. Maine's tests now include a writing sample and focus increasingly on problem solving. California and Massachusetts are moving in similar directions. Vermont is testing a statewide assessment that includes an exam, a single piece of work chosen by the student, and collections of a student's work, called portfolios. Connecticut is assessing high school students in math and science based on team-oriented projects that take up to a semester of work.

This pattern—adoption of crude performance measures, followed by protest and pressure to improve the measures, followed by the development of more sophisticated measures—is common wherever performance is measured. It explains why so many public organizations have discovered that even a poor start is better than no start, and even crude measures are better than no measures. All organizations make mistakes at first. But, over time, they are usually forced to correct them.

For those readers interested in a detailed discussion of the art of performance measurement, we recommend appendix B. For those less interested in such details, the more important question is: Once the appropriate measures are in place, how do governments use the information they provide to improve their performance? There are at least three common answers. Some organizations link pay to performance. Others use performance information primarily as a management tool, with which to continually improve their operations. And still others tie their spending to results. The most entrepreneurial attempt to do all three.

Paying for Performance

The most common strategy is performance pay: some kind of merit or bonus system for high performing individuals and/or groups. Phoenix, Sunnyvale, Visalia, and many other organizations use this practice.

The traditional approach goes by the name Management by Objectives, or MBO. Although it covers a variety of specific plans, the term usually describes a system in which managers sit down with their superiors every year and negotiate a list of objectives. A manager who reaches or exceeds his or her objectives is eligible for either a bonus or a merit increase in salary.

Unfortunately, this is probably the least effective approach. Its most glaring flaw is the fact that the objectives rarely have anything to do with the organization's key results: the quantity, quality, and cost of its services. "In a lot of these systems you just sit down and say, 'Now what do we plan to do this year?' " explains City Manager Tom Lewcock of Sunnyvale. "So you come up with artificial stuff that has no relationship to anything." Such systems can easily degenerate into subjectivity and favoritism. To avoid this problem, many managers simply award equal merit increases or bonuses to everyone—the standard practice in the federal merit system. Those who try to reward particular individuals sow resentment and distrust throughout their ranks.

Managers under typical MBO systems also tend to set their objectives artificially low, so they can be sure to meet them. Others meet their artificial objectives by sacrificing the organization's more fundamental objective: service quality. "In the Michigan Modernization Service I was told to serve 250 customers a year," says John Cleveland, the organization's former director. "You know what? I met that quota, but I met it by sacrificing quality, and by defining it as the number of customers in the door. So I ended up with an enormous backlog, and it took 7.5 months to serve the typical customer. That happens all the time."

James Q. Wilson describes a classic example of "gaming the numbers" in his book *Bureaucracy*. Under J. Edgar Hoover, FBI agents were under pressure to produce ever-rising numbers of arrests, recoveries of stolen goods, and so on. To meet their goals, they began to ask local police departments for lists of stolen cars that had been found—so they could claim them as recoveries. To increase the numbers of fugitives they apprehended, they began concentrating on military deserters, who were far easier to find than normal criminals. By the 1970s, U.S. attorneys were declining to prosecute 60 percent of the cases the FBI presented, often because they were so trivial.

Finally, strict MBO systems can create internal conflict within the organization. Each department focuses obsessively on meeting its objectives, while ignoring the impact on other departments or on the ultimate goal—customer satisfaction. Each manager worries about hitting his or her numbers, rather than solving the underlying problems that get in the way of customer satisfaction. Few are willing to take the risk of pursuing major new opportunities that are not covered by their stated objectives.

Sunnyvale avoids most of these problems by using actual levels of service quantity, cost, and quality—some of which are measured by surveying customer satisfaction—as its objectives. When managers surpass these levels, they are rewarded with bonuses, and the new level becomes their expected base. Hence managers stay focused on the organization's fundamental purpose. And rather than setting their annual objectives artificially low, they push them ever higher—because that's how they earn bonuses.

Sunnyvale does experience one flaw of MBO systems, however: the fact that they motivate through fear. "The number-one problem with a system like this is it puts all sorts of pressures on people that they're not used to dealing with," says Lewcock. "It doesn't feel real good. That is a very natural human reaction, and I understand it. When people are feeling stressed around those kinds of things, they are not necessarily performing to their ultimate."

One solution is to reward groups rather than—or in addition to—individuals. Visalia used bonuses to reward groups more often than individuals, on the theory that individual rewards encourage people to hoard information and compete with one another, while group rewards encourage people to share information and work together. Visalia also allowed groups that improved productivity to keep 30 percent of the savings (or new revenues) they generated. Lewcock would like to use group rewards in Sunnyvale, but in the past has been rebuffed by the unions.

The idea of rewarding groups is also gaining steam in the bitter debate over merit pay for teachers. Most teachers have resisted individual merit pay, understanding that because it would inevitably be based on subjective judgments, it would create resentment between teachers and hurt morale. The Urban Institute's Harry Hatry, who has reviewed a variety of merit pay plans, has concluded that combinations of individual and group incentives work better.

Al Shanker, president of the American Federation of Teachers, has proposed a five-year national competition to pick "merit schools," whose teachers would receive financial bonuses starting at $15,000. This would make great sense, if tied to parental choice. Under a system of choice, schools would be evaluated not by subjective criteria, but by actual customer satisfaction. Schools that attracted the most applicants would be rewarded with bonuses. (The community's socioeconomic background would have to be factored in, of course; schools in ghettos could not compete on a level field with schools in wealthy suburbs.) "If the Soviet Union can begin to accept the importance of financial incentives to productivity," says Shanker, "it's time for public education to do the same."

Managing for Performance

Sunnyvale's approach is clearly an advance over the traditional government practice of ignoring results and using no financial incentives. It is also superior to traditional MBO systems. In the hierarchy of management practice, in other words, Management by Results is more effective than both Management by Guesswork and Management by Objectives. But even Management by Results can be improved.

One approach used by an increasing number of governments is Total Quality Management—the management philosophy developed principally by W. Edwards Deming. Deming argues that once we learn about poor performance (or "quality," the term he uses), we do not necessarily know what is causing it. It might well be factors outside the control of the workers and the manager—like students' family backgrounds. As one Rochester teacher put it, in rejecting a contract that proposed merit pay, "I give the same effort to every class, but the results don't always match. I don't think I should be accountable alone. These kids come in here with an awful lot of baggage."

In Deming's view, only 15 percent of the problems in most organizations are caused by the workers and managers involved. The other 85 percent stem from the broader systems within which these people work—the education system, the budget system, the personnel system, and so on. Performance pay gives people an incentive to improve performance, but it does not give them the authority or the tools to change the systems that lie behind their problems.

Deming's approach uses performance data to pinpoint problems, then gives employees tools they can use to analyze them, isolate their root causes, develop solutions, and implement them. Under quality management, explains Peter R. Scholtes, author of a quality text called *The Team Handbook*, "numerical measures . . . guide the search for better performance, and are recognized as a means rather than an end. They lead the way to a deeper understanding of the organization, and are not used as criteria for judging individuals."

Deming also points out that organizations can solve their problems most effectively if the employees get involved in crafting the solutions. The employees know the system best, and they know where the problems lurk. Even if a manager can diagnose the problem, without employee buy-in it is difficult to solve it. Hence Total Quality Management uses teams of employees— often known as quality circles—to tackle most problems in the workplace.

Total Quality Management, or TQM, has been embraced by public organizations at all levels. The federal government has even set up the Federal Quality Institute to propagate the faith. In practice, however, most of these organizations implement only a part of the Deming approach. Many fail to track the results of their work, for instance, or to define exactly what results constitute quality performance. Very few focus on the basic systems that drive their organizations, so they remain in the realm of 15 percent solutions, rather than transforming their organizations. When organizations do use TQM as it is intended, however, it is an extremely powerful tool. When John Cleveland brought it to the Michigan Modernization Service, his first project brought the time it took to serve each customer down from 7.5 to less than 3 months. When Madison, Wisconsin, embraced TQM, it saved millions of dollars—in everything from refuse collection to motor vehicle repair. We will return to Madison's story, and to the subject of Total Quality Management, in the next chapter.

Budgeting for Results

Management by Results and Total Quality Management are both effective means to force organizations to act on the performance information they receive. But in government, the most important lever—the system that drives behavior most powerfully—is the budget. Most managers work in government, after all, not to enrich themselves but to have some positive impact on their community. That opportunity is available only to the degree that they can get control over resources. How do they get that control? Through the budget system. Results-oriented organizations find that they ultimately need to develop budget systems that fund outcomes rather than inputs.

There are several ways to do this, depending on the service and organization involved. The first is simply by adding output and/or outcome measures to a mission-driven budget. (An *output* is a measure of the volume of something actually produced; an *outcome* is a measure of the quality. For more on this distinction, see appendix B.) This gives managers and legislators the information they need to reward excellence or intervene when performance falls short, whether by replacing people, adding resources, or stimulating efforts to improve.

The second variation is Sunnyvale's approach: to actually budget for the service level desired—to "buy" a defined level of quantity and quality. With services that have clear and tangible results, such as street maintenance and job training, this is not difficult. If a legislature or city council budgets for the training and job placement of 1,000 people, for instance, payment can be made contingent on successful job placement. If the department in charge places only 900 people, it gets only 90 percent of its money.

With other services, it is difficult to buy outcomes, but possible to buy outputs. In health care, for example, governments would find it impractical to fund only successful outcomes. But they could—in fact, they already do—fund outputs. Medicare pays $X for each kidney dialysis, $Y for a double heart bypass. In such cases, one can still attempt to measure the outcome. When it falls short, those in charge (or those involved) can investigate and take corrective action.

ENTREPRENEURIAL APPROACHES TO BUDGETING

Budget Type	Definition	Examples
1. Mission-Driven Budgeting	See chapter 4.	See chapter 4.
2. Output Budgeting	A budget system that focuses on the output of services, i.e., the volume produced.	
Budget for Mission, Define and Measure Outputs	Budget system defines the mission and the outputs desired, measures them, but does not tie dollars spent to volume of outputs.	$X per supply depot, with data gathered on number of boxes shipped, cost per box, etc. $X per job training center, with data gathered on number of people trained, number placed in jobs, cost per trainee, etc.
Pay per Output	Budget allocates $X for each output produced. Producers get funds only when they produce the output desired.	$X per box shipped. $X per soldier recruited. $X per person trained.
3. Outcome Budgeting	A budget system that focuses on the outcomes of the funded activity, i.e., the quality, or effectiveness, of services produced.	
Budget for Mission, Define and Measure Outcomes	Budget system defines the mission and the outcomes desired, but does not link dollars spent to quality of outcomes.	$X per supply depot, with data gathered on number of boxes shipped and percentage of shipments rated acceptable by recipients; $X per job

Budget Type	Definition	Examples
		training organization, with data gathered on percentage of trainees who get jobs, job retention rate, employer satisfaction, employee satisfaction, etc.
Pay per Outcome	Budget allocates $X for each outcome produced. Producers get funds only when they produce desired outcomes.	$X per trainee who gets job and holds it at least 90 days. $X per soldier trained to expected level of competence.
4. Customer-driven Budgeting	See chapter 6.	See chapter 6.

The table above summarizes the different types of budgets discussed here (and in other chapters). They are not mutually exclusive: one government can use all methods, each for the programs to which they best apply.

Many cities now use one or more of the budget techniques described in the chart, and both Florida and Oregon have begun working to develop some form of outcome-oriented budget. Even the Defense Department is experimenting with the concept, which it calls a Unit Cost Budget. The philosophy is the same as Sunnyvale's: figure out how much it costs to deliver a unit of service (to recruit a soldier, to train a sailor, to sell an item at a commissary), and then budget for the service level desired. The experiment began because the Defense Logistics Agency (DLA), under pressure to contract out its supply depots, felt it had to cut its costs to stave off the threat. Interestingly, its approach was heavily influenced by Total Quality Management, which much of the Defense Department has embraced.

As it turned out, the supply depots were the perfect place to start, because their desired outcome was so clear: the successful shipment of some item of supply. In essence, the DLA decided that each box received by a supply depot would be worth $X, each box shipped would be worth $Y. (It experimented with different figures at different depots, using the historical costs at each depot.) The depots received all their funds this way; all line items disappeared. The more boxes a depot received or shipped, the more money it received.

Each depot had a productivity increase target of 10 percent a year for two years, then 3 percent a year thereafter. Beyond that, they could reinvest any surplus they generated during the fiscal year. (Anything left over at the end of the year would return to the DLA, however.) Depot managers were free to spend their funds as they saw fit: if they needed to hire an extra person, they did so; if they needed extra equipment, they bought it. As long as they could perform the same service for 3 percent (or 10 percent) less than the year before, they could manage their money as they thought best.

At one supply depot, the DLA let the employees split up half of all savings beyond the 3 percent goal. According to Joan Freeman, who ran the unit cost budgeting team:

> That gave us an installation full of budget analysts, because everybody was looking at their process. It pushed them to look at the way they worked and ask: "Is there a better way?" It caused managers to be more involved with their employees. Before they made an investment they would notify their employees to see if they had some ideas, or whether this equipment would help them, or whether they had some knowledge of it. Management still made the decisions, but it gave employees an opportunity to speak out that they never had before.

The Unit Cost Budget also allowed the DLA, for the first time, to get a handle on its true costs, to compare costs at different installations, and to pinpoint problems. Although "we didn't always hit our productivity goal," says Freeman, "it gave us a point of discussion, in explaining why we didn't meet it. For example, some of the facilities out there were in terrible shape, and we had neglected them for years." So "we made the decision to upgrade the facilities, to get a productivity increase in the future."

When Don Shycoff, who spearheaded the effort, moved to the Defense comptroller's office, he convinced the comptroller to try Unit Cost Budgeting for all "support" activities. By 1991, the system—now called the Defense Business Operations Fund—was operating for all Defense supply depots and inventory control points. By 1992, the comptroller's office hoped to have it in place for all depot maintenance, commissaries, military training, military recruiting, and medical care.

Similar trends are visible in other nations. In November 1989, Bob Stone's colleague Gerald Kauvar hosted a 14-nation conference on defense budgeting. All 14 nations agreed that "a modern defense resource management system must include:

- "knowledge of full costs;
- a unified [i.e., non-line-item] budget;
- decentralized control of dollars and personnel, both military and civilian;
- freedom from unnecessary regulatory burden (internally and externally imposed); and
- accountability for mission results."

Translated into our terms, this means that a modern budget system must be mission-driven, decentralized, and results oriented. France, Great Britain, and the Netherlands have already moved their defense budgets in this direction. Great Britain, Denmark, Sweden, Canada, Australia, and New Zealand are all shifting toward mission-driven, results-oriented budgets for their entire national governments, using many of the same mechanisms developed here.

One other powerful method exists to focus public organizations on their results—a method that takes us into the next chapter. One might call it Customer-Driven Budgeting: putting money into customers' hands and forcing service providers to earn their keep by pleasing those customers. The desired outcome of most services, after all, is a satisfied customer. And how better to get that outcome than to make service agencies dependent on their customers for their very survival?

– 6 –

Customer-Driven Government: Meeting the Needs of the Customer, Not the Bureaucracy

Quality is determined only by customers.
—David Couper, Chief of Police, Madison, Wisconsin

When was the last time you felt like a valued customer at your children's school? How about your motor vehicles office? Your city hall?

Few people in government ever use the word *customer*. Most public organizations don't even know who their customers are. When Bob Stone took his Defense Installations staff on retreat to discuss *In Search of Excellence*, their first task was to define their customers. The results were a big surprise, even to Stone. "We had thought of our customers as the secretary of defense, or the Congress, or the American taxpayer," he says. "But we figured out that the people we were supposed to serve were the troops—the soldier, sailor, airman, or marine who defended America. It was something none of us had thought of before."

Democratic governments exist to serve their citizens. Businesses exist to make profits. And yet it is business that searches obsessively for new ways to please the American people. Most

American governments are customer-blind, while McDonald's and Frito-Lay are customer-driven. This may be the ultimate indictment of bureaucratic government.

Why is it this way? Simple. *Most public agencies don't get their funds from their customers.* Businesses do. If a business pleases its customers, sales increase; if someone else pleases its customers more, sales decline. So businesses in competitive environments learn to pay enormous attention to their customers. Public agencies get most of their funding from legislatures, city councils, and elected boards. And most of their "customers" are captive: short of moving, they have few alternatives to the services their governments provide. So managers in the public sector learn to ignore them. The customers public managers aim to please are the executive and the legislature—because that's where they get their funding. Elected officials, in turn, are driven by their constituents—in most cases, by organized interest groups. So while businesses strive to please customers, government agencies strive to please interest groups.

The real customers of the Department of Transportation have not been drivers and mass transit riders, but highway builders and public transit systems. The real customers of the Department of Housing and Urban Development have not been poor urban dwellers, but real estate developers. If this sounds like an overstatement, consider the comment made by David Forsberg, then New England regional chief for HUD, after Jack Kemp changed HUD's focus: "I can't tell you what a help it's been to be able to say, 'HUD's constituency is low- and moderate-income people.' You can say, 'HUD is not here to service the developers and industry groups.' "

The greatest irritant most people experience in their dealings with government is the arrogance of the bureaucracy. People today expect to be valued as customers—even by government.

In 1950, nearly two-thirds of Americans who had jobs did unskilled labor, while one-third worked with their minds. Today that ratio is reversed. The result is a generation of citizens who have very different expectations from those held by their industrial-era mothers and fathers. Our parents stood in line for hours at the Registry of Motor Vehicles with a shrug: that was simply the way the world worked. We stand in the same lines and fume. Our parents accepted the public schools as a given, something they could not change. We organize committees, demand new programs, raise funds, and volunteer to teach special units—and if that doesn't work, we send our kids to private schools.

Many of us ignore government, assuming that we are too busy to waste our time on such a hopeless cause. But when we do brush up against the public sector—when our children enter school, or the state decides to build an incinerator in our community—we refuse to be passive. We want *proof* that the incinerator will be safe. We want to *choose* which school our children will attend. We welcome help with child care, but we will choose where and by whom that care is given, thank you. We need help with health care expenses—but the last thing we want is a public health system in which we have no choice of physician or hospital.

As we become a society dominated by knowledge workers, we are also breaking into subcultures—each with its own values and life-style, each watching different things on television, each shopping at different kinds of stores, each driving different kinds of cars. We have been transformed from a mass society with a broad and fairly homogeneous middle class to a mosaic society with great cultural diversity, even within the middle class. We have come to expect products and services customized to our own styles and tastes, from television networks to restaurants to beer.

And yet traditional public institutions still offer one-size-fits-all services. Traditional education systems still deliver a "brand X" education. Traditional housing authorities still offer an identical apartment in a cluster of identical high rises. Traditional public libraries still offer only books, newspapers, and magazines. When consumers accustomed to choices confront public institutions that offer standardized services, they increasingly go elsewhere.

To cope with these massive changes, entrepreneurial governments have begun to transform themselves. They have begun to listen carefully to their customers, through customer surveys, focus groups, and a wide variety of other methods. They have begun to offer their customers choices—of schools, of recreation facilities, even of police services. And they have begun to put their customers in the driver's seat, by putting resources directly in their hands and letting them choose their service providers.

This takes competition a step further: rather than government managers choosing service providers in a competitive bidding process, it lets each *citizen* choose his or her service provider. It establishes accountability to customers. "I can't think of a better mechanism for accountability than parental choice," says Sy Fliegel, of East Harlem's District 4. "If you begin to see that youngsters are not coming to your school, that is the highest form of evaluation."

To make their public institutions as customer-driven as businesses, in other words, entrepreneurial governments have learned to finance them like businesses. If schools lose money every time a student departs—as in Minnesota—do teachers and administrators act differently? Of course. If motor vehicle offices were paid only when they processed driver's licenses or registrations—so the more they processed, the more money they received—would their employees act differently? You bet. With the consequences of attracting customers so clear, the scramble to cut waiting times would be intense. We might even find offices staying open evenings and Saturdays, operating drive-by windows, and advertising the shortest waiting lines in town!

GETTING CLOSE TO THE CUSTOMER

All the management experts, from Peters and Waterman to Drucker and Deming, dwell on the importance of listening to one's customers. They counsel managers to expose their employees directly to their customers. Hewlett-Packard asks customers to make presentations describing their needs to its engineers. All senior managers at Xerox spend one day a month taking phone calls from customers. "There is simply no substitute for direct access," says former Xerox CEO David Kearns. "It keeps managers informed, it keeps them in touch, it keeps them honest."

Drucker even describes nonprofit organizations that act this way. One of them, Willowcreek Community Church in South Barrington, Illinois, is one of the nation's largest churches, with 13,000 parishioners. Bill Hybels founded it in the mid-1970s, when he was still in his early twenties. He picked a growing community with relatively few churchgoers and went door to door, asking, "Why don't you go to church?"

> Then he designed a church to answer the potential custom-
> ers' needs: for instance, it offers full services on Wednesday
> evenings because many working parents need Sunday to
> spend with their children. . . . The pastor's sermon is taped
> while it is being delivered and instantly reproduced so that
> parishioners can pick up a cassette when they leave the
> building because he was told again and again, "I need to
> listen when I drive home or drive to work so that I can build
> the message into my life."

There is no reason public organizations cannot act this way; religion is at least as hidebound as government. Fortunately, some do:

- The Duval County School Board, in Florida, surveyed its community and discovered a pressing need for day care for latchkey children, before and after school. So the district launched a Community Schools program that keeps most schools open from 7:00 A.M. to 5:45 P.M. School is free, but parents pay $20 a week for the full child-care service.

- The Dallas Parks and Recreation Department operates a full-service recreation center 24 hours a day, for people who work odd shifts. It has volleyball, softball, concerts, and art shows around the clock. A side benefit, according to the Dallas Police Force: reduced crime rates.

- The California Department of Motor Vehicles is test-marketing self-service, computerized terminals at which drivers can renew their licenses as easily as they get cash from a bank card machine. If those who use the terminals say they like them, on a customer survey, the state hopes to expand their use to vehicle registration and put them in supermarkets and shopping malls.

- The Rochester, New York, public schools have developed a Home-Based Guidance program, in which each teacher becomes a mentor for 20 students. Throughout the students' years at the school, it is the teacher's job to keep track of them, to get to know their parents, to visit their homes, to stay in touch over the summer.

Perhaps our favorite practitioner of customer-oriented government was Lee White, who retired recently from her job as head librarian in Oakland, California. Librarians are normally thought of as shy and retiring. Not Lee White. One of the first things she did when she took over was to survey her customers. The survey told her that the libraries were neglecting two important groups: children and ethnic minorities.

To bring children into the libraries, White pushed her librarians to stock videotapes. "That took a long time," she sighs. "I finally had to give them some of my own money to do it." Then she created a public library channel on cable TV. Next came a summer reading club with a big prize: any child who proved he or she had read 10 books got a free trip to see the Oakland A's. (Once a month White also brought an A's ballplayer—Jose Canseco was the biggest draw—into the library.) Five thousand kids signed up.

To bring in minorities, White created Latino and Asian collections—the latter in nine languages. She developed Asian cassettes, particularly for Hmong refugees, who do not have a written language. She sent an American Indian bookmobile around the community.

For other adults she set up a literacy project with 800 volunteers; a Lawyers in the Library program, in which volunteer lawyers dispensed free legal advice; a free income tax preparation service; and a books-on-tape library. White even tried to keep one branch open until midnight and to put a laundromat in another. The city staff nixed the latter idea because it didn't want to compete with private laundromats!

THE TOTAL QUALITY METHOD

In 1984, the mayor of Madison, Wisconsin, Joseph Sensenbrenner, attended a lecture by W. Edwards Deming. Like many cities, Madison was in a severe fiscal squeeze. Federal aid had been cut sharply. Property taxes were at record levels. "Budget hearings were becoming an annual nightmare," Sensenbrenner says. "The people of Madison did not want their services cut or their taxes raised. In their view, city services were in a steady decline already, even as they paid more for them."

Sensenbrenner sums up the plaint of the modern public official in four words: "I felt boxed in."

Deming's approach sounded like a way out of the box. Deming urges organizations constantly to ask their customers what they want, then to shape their entire service and production processes to produce it. In effect, Total Quality Management stands the traditional organizational chart on its head: it says that the customers are the most important people for an organization; those who serve customers directly are next; and management is there to serve those who serve customers.

"This is the single most difficult thing about Total Quality Management," says John Cleveland, one of several managers who introduced it to the Michigan Commerce Department. "Every question becomes: 'How does this add value to the customer?' There's a period of intense ignorance you have to go through, because you don't know much about your customers—because no one talks to their customers." By forcing organizations to listen, TQM has been extremely effective at changing their cultures.

Consider the Police Department, one of six departments in Madison—known as Transformation Departments—that have fully embraced the new gospel. In 1987, it began mailing a survey to every 50th person it encountered, whether a victim of crime, a witness, a complainant, or a criminal. (It is now up to every 35th person.) Every month, more than 200 people receive the survey, which comes with a postage-paid, self-addressed return envelope. It asks them to rate the officers they encountered on seven factors: concern; helpfulness; knowledge; quality of service; professional conduct; how well they solved the problem; and whether they put the person at ease. They can rate an officer "excellent," "good," "fair," "poor," or "very poor." An open-ended question asks: "How can we improve the quality of our service in the future?"

Forty percent of the recipients return the survey—a figure the department reached only after Chief David Couper started including a handwritten note explaining that he personally reads every survey. Couper publishes the results in the departmental newsletter and sends positive comments along to the officers who receive them. On a scale in which 3 is "fair" and 4 is "good," the department has increased its average rating from 3.8 to 4.3.

In its Experimental Police District, which we will describe in chapter 9, responses to the departmental customer survey go directly to the officer involved—as a kind of personal feedback system. Mary Anne Wycoff, who did an evaluation for the National Institute of Justice, relates the kind of impact that feedback has had:

> Fairly early after they began getting the customer reports, one officer got one back that was quite critical. He read it out loud to his colleagues, quite sarcastically, expecting them to agree that it was ridiculous. And there was dead silence. It was clear that the group did not necessarily agree with him. That kind of change in peer relations can have a big impact on people. That officer was very surprised.

In 1991, Couper created an employee project team to develop methods to find out what services the customers in each of the city's districts most wanted: traffic enforcement, noise control,

control over street violence, and so on. Couper ticks off what he calls "the important questions": "What are the important customer needs in your district? How did you find out what they are? What methods did you use? What are you doing to address those customer-identified problems? And how do you know when you've been successful?" If it can answer those questions, Madison will have a police department that offers customized rather than standardized services, then measures the results.

Perhaps the most thoroughly customer-driven public institution we have ever encountered is Fox Valley Technical College, a junior college that serves 45,000 part- and full-time students in Appleton, Wisconsin. In 1985, a local paper company suggested that Fox Valley offer training in quality and productivity for area businesses. After the college president, Stanley Spanbauer, and his colleagues looked into TQM, they decided to create a Quality First program for their own employees. Since then, they have restructured virtually their entire operation around the needs of their customers.

To identify those needs, they do an annual Student Satisfaction Survey, which asks a representative sample of 650 students to rate teaching effectiveness, different instructional methods (labs, lectures, group discussions, work experience, computer-based instruction), and student services such as admissions, counseling, and the library. Each division of the school receives its own results, which allow it to pinpoint problems and take appropriate action.

One problem, for instance, was course cancellations. Every year, Fox Valley had to cancel 16 percent of the classes listed in its catalog, because not enough students signed up. "You can get some real dissatisfied customers that way," says Spanbauer. "But once we pinpointed the departments where we were having the greatest problems, it improved markedly, because it was pure and simple a lack of good planning."

Fox Valley also surveys its business customers, which contract for training courses and economic development services. It has roughly 1,200 separate contracts with business, industry, and government every year, far more than any other technical college in Wisconsin. Using a computerized system its people developed, it can tell businesses that request training within a matter of hours whether the curriculum already exists; if not, how long it will take to develop; how much it will cost; and when the course can begin.

Fox Valley tracks the job placement rate of graduates carefully, to see if its courses are in fact preparing them for jobs that are in demand. Ninety-three percent of 1988–1989 graduates surveyed found jobs within six months; of those, 87 percent did so in areas directly related to their course work.

To force its instructors to take seriously the requirement of preparing their students for success in the job market, Fox Valley decided in 1990 to offer students a guarantee. If a graduate cannot find a job in an area related to his or her training within six months, the college guarantees up to six free credits of additional instruction (two or three courses), plus support services such as counseling, career development, or help with interviewing techniques. The school also guarantees training courses for business customers: if a business is not satisfied, it will repeat a course for free, with a new instructor.

"I just figure it tightens up the front end," says Spanbauer. "You begin to look at students more carefully in terms of counseling them before they go into a program. And the faculty will ensure that what they teach is relevant, because they know that a major criterion is whether or not the student gets a job."

As it listened to its customers, Fox Valley realized that the traditional academic calendar was frustrating to many of them. People did not need training only in September and February, and businesses did not hire only in January and June. So the school switched to a Perpetual Enrollment/Graduation calendar. Courses are taught in three-week modules, and every course has at least three entry points and three exit points each year. In some courses students can enroll daily. Most instruction is individualized: students move through their course work at their own pace. Fox Valley instructors use at least 150 different "computer-assisted instruction" programs, and students have access to 1,600 computer terminals. As Spanbauer put it in his 1987 book, *Quality First in Education . . . Why Not?*, "Why do educators in traditional schools continue to insist, by their actions, that all students are the same, learn at the same rate, and learn best in the same manner?"

Since Fox Valley has little control over the quality of previous education its students have received, it has also concentrated on counseling and remedial programs to bring its customers up to speed. For those having trouble, the school developed an 18-hour counseling course, called "College Survival Skills," that deals with things like time management and study habits. Testing the course with an experimental group and a control group, Fox Valley found that it decreased the dropout rate by 22 percent. As a result, several departments now require it.

Total Quality Management stresses the constant measurement and improvement of quality. As one more tool to do this, Fox Valley developed a kind of quality checklist. It lists Indicators of Excellence in seven key areas: Goal Setting, Quality Based Management, Customer Service, Human Resources, Curriculum and Instruction, Use of Technology, and Marketing. Under Customer Service, for example, the indicators ask whether:

- customers are satisfied with the unit's products and/or services;
- service unit customers have an opportunity to evaluate services;
- customer service and satisfaction in service units are continuously monitored, evaluated, measured, and used as a basis for constant improvement;
- students evaluate each of their courses; and
- evaluations are used as a basis for improving curriculum and instructional delivery.

All 62 instructional programs, plus service departments like accounting and the food service, are expected to use these indicators to do self-audits, to identify areas in which they need to improve. At least once every seven years, each one is audited by a team of six outside experts. Between major audits, a computerized quick-check system flags any programs whose basic

LISTENING TO THE VOICE
OF THE CUSTOMER

As the examples cited in this chapter make clear, there are dozens of different ways to listen to the voice of the customer:

Customer Surveys. In addition to the organizations described in the text, we have seen customer surveys used by Phoenix, Sunnyvale, and Orlando, Florida; by the Massachusetts Bay Transportation Authority, the Housing Authority of Louisville, the Michigan Commerce Department, and the New York Department of Labor; by court systems in Michigan, Washington State, and Los Angeles; and by the Naperville, Illinois, police department.

Customer Follow-up. Fox Valley Technical College and the Michigan Modernization Service have surveyed their customers six months, a year, or two years after they were served to see whether the service actually yielded the desired results. Fox Valley even plans a follow-up survey after five years.

Community Surveys. These are even more common than customer surveys. Every year, many cities—including Visalia, Sunnyvale, Fairfield, St. Petersburg, Dayton, and Dallas—survey their residents to see what they like and dislike about their city and their government. The International City Managers Association has even published a how-to book called *Citizen Surveys.*

Customer Contact. Police Chief David Couper of Madison spends one month of every year in the field, working as a frontline police officer. Florida TaxWatch has recommended that "every state employee who does not have direct contact with the public should spend a minimum of two days a year in direct contact service." Minnesota's STEP program (see chapter 9) urged managers to sit in the service areas of their offices to talk with customers, and to ask frontline employees what they heard from customers and how service could be improved.

Customer Contact Reports. Madison's Experimental Police District gives customer feedback directly to the employee who served the customer.

Customer Councils. Several housing authorities, including Louisville's, use resident councils to stay in touch with their customers. The Michigan Modernization Service used a customer council to give it feedback, particularly on new ideas.

Focus Groups. Common in industry and in political campaigns, focus groups bring customers together to discuss a product, service, or issue. The consulting firm Jobs for the Future discovered through focus groups that people in Indiana reacted negatively to the phrase *job training program,* because it implied there was something wrong with them. They preferred *career development opportunities,* because it implied respect for their potential.

Customer Interviews. Michigan's Literacy Task Force interviewed 130 people—both providers and customers—to find out what kind of adult education and job training system Michigan needed. It discovered that social problems—issues of motivation, attitude, and expectations—were a greater obstacle than lack of programs. And it learned that many Michigan workers saw "going back to school" as a traumatic idea and associated visiting government service offices with receiving welfare or unemployment—"something successful people just don't do."

Electronic Mail. In Santa Monica, California, citizens can use the city's Public Electronic Network to communicate directly with any department. Staff members are expected to respond to any request within 24 hours. Citizens can hook up through their own computers, or they can use public terminals located throughout the city.

Customer Service Training. Many governments, including Madison, Phoenix, Wisconsin, and Arkansas, now offer customer service training to their employees. San Antonio has developed an interesting wrinkle: its Yes, It Is My Problem initiative encourages city employees to solve citizens' problems in one phone call, rather than bouncing them from agency to agency.

Test Marketing. Customer-oriented governments test new services to see if people like them before imposing them on everyone. The Phoenix Department of Public Works tested its one-person, automatic side-loading trucks with 90 homes; when it found 96 percent liked the service, it adopted the system citywide. The Minnesota Department of Natural Resources tested the use of credit cards in one park before accepting them statewide.

Quality Guarantees. At least a dozen community colleges in Michigan guarantee their training to industry. West Virginia's

Guaranteed Work Force Program retrains employees at no cost, to employer specifications, if employers are not satisfied. Many high schools in Colorado and West Virginia guarantee qualifying graduates to employers; if the graduate has problems with some basic skill needed on the job, the high school will bring him or her up to speed for free.

Inspectors. The New York City Taxi Commission sends inspectors out as undercover passengers to police the behavior of New York's taxi drivers. Private firms routinely send professional service raters out to check the quality of their banks, supermarkets, and restaurants. An entire industry has grown up to provide this service on contract.

Ombudsmen. Some customer-driven governments create an ombudsman, so citizens have someone they can call who will work with the offending department to straighten out the problem. Peter Drucker calls ombudsmen "the hygiene of organizations—or at least their toothbrush." Sweden, which invented the idea, even has a national ombudsman—as do the rest of the Scandinavian countries and most of the British Commonwealth. In the United States, at least 15 states, cities, and counties had ombudsmen by 1988.

Complaint Tracking Systems. Many cities have systems that track responses to inquiries and complaints, to improve the city's response time. With Phoenix's computerized system, city council members can see whether citizens in their district are getting the answers they need from city departments.

800 Numbers. Governor Donald Schaeffer in Maryland set up a red-tape telephone hotline on which citizens can report cases of bureaucratic mismanagement. The Michigan Commerce Department uses 800 numbers to make it easy for businesses to call. The Georgia Public Service Commission set up 800 numbers so all residents could call their county officials for free.

Suggestion Boxes or Forms. The open-ended question asked by the Madison Police Department's customer survey is in effect a suggestion box. Fox Valley Tech has 23 suggestion boxes on its campus. The Michigan Treasury Department puts a suggestion box right on its tax forms.

numbers—enrollments, dropouts, job placement rates, costs, student-teacher ratios, and so on—suggest problems. If the problems look real, the school calls in an audit team.

In the public sector, unlike business, most institutions have multiple sets of customers. Since it exists not just to educate and train individuals but to strengthen the local community and economy, for instance, Fox Valley has at least three sets of customers: students, businesses, and the community. Many of its service departments, like purchasing and accounting, also have internal customers: the departments that use their services. So Fox Valley also conducts detailed surveys of the community and of its own employees. Although we are dealing primarily with external customers in this chapter, much of what we have described also applies to internal customers.

PUTTING CUSTOMERS
IN THE DRIVER'S SEAT

The single best way to make public service providers respond to the needs of their customers is to put resources in the customers' hands and let them choose. All the listening techniques listed above are important, but if the customers do not have a choice of providers—schools, training programs, motor vehicle offices—they remain dependent on the goodwill of the provider. The providers are in the driver's seat, and customers can only hope they drive where the customer wants to go. When the customers control the resources, on the other hand, *they* choose the destination and the route.

Most customers know what is important to them. For one it might be a school with a good national reputation. For another it might be a school whose graduates get well-paid jobs. For a third it might be a school close to home. If the customers have access to all the relevant information and they vote with their feet by deserting one school, no one can argue that that school is providing quality education.

Putting resources directly in customers' hands may at first sound like a radical idea, but it is not. In fact, it is not even a

new idea. Vouchers, cash grants, and funding systems that allocate a set dollar amount for each customer served have been
around for decades.

Food stamps are vouchers. The $2 billion WIC program (the
Special Supplemental Food Program for Women, Infants and
Children) uses vouchers. Many states, including California,
Massachusetts, Connecticut, and parts of Minnesota, provide
vouchers or their equivalents to low-income people for child
care. HUD funds housing vouchers. Our largest housing subsidy—the mortgage interest tax deduction—is the equivalent of
a voucher. Pell grants, the primary form of federal financial aid,
are like vouchers: their recipients can use them at any accredited college. In fact, most of our higher education system is
customer-driven, and it is widely considered the best in the
world. If it works so well for 18- to 25-year-olds, why not 5- to
18-year-olds?

Perhaps the best contrast between a system that funds individuals and one that funds institutions occurred after World
War II, when our soldiers came home. To pay for their college
educations, Congress passed the GI bill—perhaps the most successful social program in American history. Congress didn't
fund GI colleges; it let every GI pick an accredited university,
college, or technical school and offered to pay for it. With this
act, Congress turned millions of battle-scarred young men into
the educated backbone of a 30-year economic boom.

In health care, Congress took the more traditional route. It
built GI hospitals, and it assigned veterans to specific hospitals.
One system let customers choose their institution, hence promoting competition; the other system assigned customers to institutions that could take them for granted, because they were
monopolies. Which worked better, the GI bill or veterans'
hospitals?

The advantages of the GI bill approach are obvious. *First, customer-driven systems force service providers to be accountable to
their customers*. Because customers can take their business elsewhere, providers must constantly seek feedback on their needs
and then do what is necessary to meet them. "There are two ways
for accountability to come about," explains sociologist James

Coleman, for three decades one of our leading authorities on education. "One way is from the top down, which is a bureaucratic mode of authority. The other way is from the bottom up—for there to be accountability to parents and children. I think everything that we've seen suggests that the second is a more effective mode of accountability than the first."

Second, customer-driven systems depoliticize the choice-of-provider decision. Even in competitive service delivery systems, public agencies usually contract with various providers (e.g., for training) or allocate budgets between various providers (e.g., between public colleges). Too often, politics interferes with these decisions. The providers with the largest constituencies get the most money, simply because they can bring the most political pressure to bear during budget time. Every college, every real estate developer, every large human service provider, has its constituency—many of which include heavyweight campaign contributors and workers. Few politicians get elected because service providers do a good job, but many politicians get defeated because a constituency rebels—so the politicians usually listen. But when the customers control the resources, no legislature can protect inferior providers from the verdicts rendered by those customers.

Third, customer-driven systems stimulate more innovation. When providers have to compete, they constantly look for ways to cut their costs and increase their quality, as we explained in chapter 3. But when they get their funds from their customers, rather than from a legislature, they also have far greater incentives to *invest* in innovation.

James Q. Wilson, in his book *Bureaucracy*, compares the plight of a Registry of Motor Vehicles manager who wants to improve service with that of a McDonald's franchise manager. If the registry manager wants to invest in new equipment or more clerks, he has to convince the legislature. But individual legislators will not benefit if lines get shorter and customers are happier at one registry (or even at all registries). So why should they pay the political price of raising taxes or fees—or taking money away from some other agency—to spend more at the registry? The McDonald's franchise, in contrast, will earn more if its lines get shorter and its service faster. So its manager can easily justify the investment, and its owners will eagerly make the investment. Unfortunately, Wilson omits the punch line: if registries received their funds according to how many customers they served, like McDonald's restaurants do, they might act like McDonald's.

Fourth, customer-driven systems give people choices between different kinds of services. Standardization was very important to the Progressives, because the political machines of the day often dispensed services unevenly. Those of the right religion, or those who voted the right way, or those who worked for the local ward captain, were treated well. Others were left to fend for themselves—or worse, persecuted.

Even today, many still have an ingrained feeling that public agencies should give everyone the same kind of service, because there is one right way to do things—to run a school, to hand out welfare, or to run an army. One reason educational choice has not spread faster, says education professor Mary Anne Raywid, "is that it challenges one of education's most deep-seated and broadly pursued assumptions: that there must be a right answer to questions of educational practice, and that all other answers can thus only be inferior."

We don't think this way about private goods or services, of course. No one wants Apple to produce exactly the same kind of computers as IBM. Even 50 years ago, when Henry Ford said, "You can buy a car in any color, as long as it's black," his attitude almost destroyed Ford Motor Company. Today the same attitude is destroying American education and American government. *People don't want standardized services anymore.*

Can you imagine requiring that all Medicaid and Medicare recipients go to public hospitals? Or requiring all commuters to use the same form of transportation? And yet we require virtually all children who attend public school to endure the same basic style of education—even though we know different children learn in different ways. Perhaps Joe Nathan said it best, in *Public Schools By Choice*: "We believe that true equality of opportunities *demands* that different kinds of programs be

available. We think providing identical programs to all students
guarantees unequal results."

Do you know anyone who doesn't want to choose the school
his or her children attend? Of course not. People may oppose
choice in principle, but if they can afford it, everyone either
chooses a neighborhood with good schools, sends their children
to private schools, or uses a public school of choice. Even those
who oppose choice in principle are fast disappearing. Gallup
polls show that the percentage of adults who believe parents
should be able to choose the public school their children attend
increased from 12 percent in 1980 to 62 percent in 1990. Support is highest among young adults (age 19 to 29) and racial
minorities, at 72 percent. Even a majority of teachers said that
choice would help their students in a 1989 poll.

*Fifth, customer-driven systems waste less, because they match
supply to demand.* The type and volume of most public services
are determined not by what customers want—by their demand—but by law. And legislatures create laws in response to
the demands not of individuals, but of constituencies. Consequently, those laws tend to dictate impartial treatment and
equal service to all members of the targeted group. This is a
natural impulse, and it often ensures a basic fairness in public
systems. But it has perverse side effects. Some customers may
not want the standardized service; many may need other things
far more. But if the law exists, the money is spent.

Poor women may need training, housing, child care, and
Head Start, but our laws make it far easier for them to get food
stamps and welfare. (Think of the waste in that equation—of
both human potential and taxpayers' dollars.) Dislocated workers may want health insurance, but the programs we fund are
more apt to pay for job-search clubs. Systems that put resources
in customers' hands allow them to buy what they want, rather
than what the legislature or city council thinks they need. Hence
they tend to satisfy their customers while wasting far less.

*Sixth, customer-driven systems empower customers to make
choices, and empowered customers are more committed customers.* Education research shows that students are more commit-

ted to education in schools they have chosen. Schools of choice have lower dropout rates, fewer discipline problems, better student attitudes, and higher teacher satisfaction. The same applies to virtually any other service: housing, training, health care, even recreation.

The differences can be dramatic. In 1982, American Express set up the Academy of Finance in New York, for potential high school dropouts. It combined schoolwork with job experience, and it promised each student a summer internship in the financial world. These students were failing in the standard system, but having chosen a school that made real-world sense to them, they took it very seriously. "They did their schoolwork; they showed up for work on time; they wore suits and ties," says Louis V. Gerstner, Jr., then president of American Express. "Ninety percent of the first class went on to college."

Finally, customer-driven systems create greater opportunities for equity. When governments fund programs or institutions directly, equity becomes difficult to enforce. If we do enforce it, limiting use to the poor, we create separate institutions that not only deteriorate but develop a stigma. Think only of public housing or public health clinics, and you will understand the problem. "Separate but equal" is virtually impossible, if all those using the separate institution are poor.

If we do not limit the program or institution to the poor, we have no way of ensuring equity. Often we produce just the opposite, because the affluent become the most intense users of the service. Think of how we fund public universities: we use state tax revenues collected from everyone to subsidize higher education primarily for the middle and upper middle class. Studies done in Wisconsin and California have shown that their fine public university systems actually promote inequality, because those who attend them come from more affluent families, on average, than those who do not.

When governments fund individuals rather than institutions, it is much easier to promote equity. They can simply equalize the funding for each individual—or even increase it for those with less income. This also removes the stigma of subsidies for the poor by allowing them to participate in the mainstream—to attend any school, live in any apartment building within their means, use any health clinic.

Customer-driven systems will *not* promote equity if information about the cost and quality of different providers is not accessible to all customers. Even public schools, for instance, will act like businesses when forced to compete for their students and dollars; they will manipulate test scores, produce slick brochures, and put on the best marketing campaign they can muster. Government's responsibility is to make sure all families, no matter what their income or education levels, have accurate information about the quality of the schools and the satisfaction levels of their customers, and to police the marketplace for fraud.

Two other caveats: First, what we have discussed in this section applies to service delivery, not regulation. In regulatory activities, the primary customers are not individuals but the community at large. Second, customer-driven systems require head-to-head competition between service providers. If there are few competing service providers and new competitors face significant barriers to entry, customers will encounter the problems of monopoly. And if the economics are such that direct competition on each route would be inefficient—as in garbage collection—a city can choose between competitors, but it makes no sense to allow individual customers a choice.

TURNING AGENCY-DRIVEN GOVERNMENT ON ITS HEAD

As powerful as it is to put resources in customers' hands, it is not always enough. If the service providers are public, or publicly funded, entrepreneurial governments often find that they face one more step: they must transform their existing bureaucracies. If the Veterans Administration suddenly shifted to vouchers, its hospitals would have to undergo profound and wrenching changes.

Traditional public systems—even those that put resources in people's hands—are designed for the convenience of administrators and service providers, not customers. Medicare is so complex that many of the elderly have to hire private firms to help them navigate the jungle of paperwork, forms, and claims. Our social welfare systems are so fragmented that many poor families have to wait in line at five different offices and fill out 10 different forms. In 1989, the assistant secretary for health testified that there were 93 federal programs administered by 20 different agencies related to the reduction of infant mortality.

To understand what happens when a system works for the convenience of its agencies rather than its customers, consider the story of Youngstown, Ohio, as told by Terry Buss and Roger Vaughan in their remarkable book *On the Rebound.* During the late 1970s and early 1980s, 25 steel plants closed in the Youngstown region. Forty thousand steelworkers lost their jobs. As might be expected, the existing service delivery infrastructure geared up to help them. None were in the habit of asking their customers what they needed, but that didn't stop them. With federal and state money flowing, each mustered all the data it could to prove that the dislocated steelworkers needed just what it had to offer: psychological counseling, or job training, or financial counseling.

Buss and his colleagues at Youngstown State University went back later and asked a scientific sample of the 4,000 workers laid off from Youngstown Sheet and Tube what they needed and which services had been of value. Only 20 percent, it turned out, had used retraining programs. Vaughan explains why:

> *The Job Training Partnership Act (JTPA) was originally intended to help disadvantaged people, poor people. Then it was extended to deal with the problem of worker displacement, because it passed in 1982, when displaced workers were a prime issue. So it was that displaced steelworkers in Youngstown were sent to sessions where they were told how to show up for work on time, what the work environment was like, and what employers expected of you. Not surprisingly, they were furious.*

Other programs trained people for steelworking, welding, and small-engine repair, areas in which there were no jobs available. Overall, only 37 percent of those "retrained" found work. *Those who avoided the training programs actually had better luck finding jobs.* "The only program that worked was when JTPA dollars were turned over to the Steelworkers Union, and they trained their own to help their own," says Vaughan. "They actually had steelworkers helping steelworkers."

The mental health system was even worse. To get more funding, one community mental health center demonstrated an increased demand from dislocated workers. But when Buss's researchers looked at its files, they found that it had listed every family member of an unemployed person as a separate case. "We were led to believe that displaced workers suffered psychological trauma from the loss of jobs," says Vaughan.

But in Youngstown, the homicide rate went down. Divorce went down. Child abuse cases went down. All the pathologies that we in our minds believe are associated with unemployment went down. They spent millions on mental health programs in Youngstown, and we were able to trace 33 steelworkers who used them.

The one service the steelworkers most often said they wanted, when Buss and his colleagues asked, was health insurance. But there was no health insurance agency in town, so no one stepped in to meet that need.

Transforming an agency-driven system like this would require more than putting resources in customers' hands. A job training voucher, a mental health voucher, and a financial counseling voucher would have been big improvements. But what dislocated workers really needed was some form of resource that would let them decide their own needs.

Perhaps the most dramatic effort at this kind of transformation took place in Michigan during the 1980s. In 1983, Governor Blanchard asked a newspaper publisher, Philip Power, to chair his Job Training Coordinating Council. Power spent several years trying to understand the state's job training infrastructure—essentially the same one that had served Youngstown so poorly. He found it incredibly confusing, because it seemed to have no rationality. "I kept asking people who was the expert, who was the genius who could come in and tell us how this system worked," he smiles. "And the governor's staff would say, 'There isn't any.' So then we went to lots of conferences, but we didn't find anything there either." Finally, at one conference, Power complained to a federal official about the poor quality of JTPA's management information system. "He said, 'It's not a management information system. It wasn't designed for that. It was developed for filling out the federal forms required.'

"I guess that's when I got angry."

In frustration, Power did what any business person would do when confronted with a business he or she doesn't understand: he took an inventory. "I said, 'Let's just see what we've got.' "

The results were "absolutely astonishing." Michigan had 70 distinct job training or adult education programs, funded by $800 million a year. They ranged from JTPA programs to welfare training programs to summer youth programs to adult basic education. Each had been legislated into existence separately. Most were invisible to the average citizen. Most were hard to access; in fact, you had to be "disadvantaged" or unemployed, or to have done something wrong, to get at much of the money. Many customers who qualified got bounced from one office to another, where they filled out one form after another—until finally they gave up.

Some of the money came from Washington, some from state government, some from local government. Nine state departments or agencies had jurisdiction over at least one of the 70 programs. No one knew which were effective and which were not, because few collected any performance data. It was, in effect, a nonsystem: 70 categorical pots of money with no coherence, no user-friendliness, little performance data, and little management. People in government often talk about "funding streams," but these were puddles: funds could not flow from one to another as needs shifted. They were driven by legislation and organized for the convenience of public agencies—not driven by demand and organized for the convenience of customers.

"That inventory tore my head off," says Power. "The top managers in state government were stunned. This was an absolutely invisible $800 million. We had all thought we had a money problem—but we didn't have a money problem, we had a management problem."

Gradually, Power and his colleagues developed a plan to turn the 70 programs into a coherent Human Investment System. They started by creating a steering organization at the top, the Human Investment Fund Board, which included the directors of the nine state agencies and representatives of key business, labor, and education organizations. They pulled the frontline agency and provider organizations at the local level together into Core Groups, to adopt identical one-page intake forms, hook into the same computers, and begin acting like different intake points for the same system. They set the Core Groups to work defining performance targets and measures for the entire system. They mapped out a set of Opportunity Stores—offices with common logos and bold colors, like those of any other service franchise—which would be sprinkled in shopping malls, community colleges, and main streets all across Michigan, to act as the visible "front doors" of the system. They set up Opportunity Directories: kiosks with automatic teller machines, like those used by banks, which customers could use to electronically browse through the training and education options available in their geographic and interest area. And they created an Opportunity Line—an 800 number anyone could call to get information about training and education services.

Finally, in a master stroke, they invented an Opportunity Card: a "smart" credit card, with a computer chip, which would go to every Michigan citizen of working age. Citizens would have a social security card for retirement, a driver's license for transportation, and an Opportunity Card for lifelong education and training. They could bring their card to any Opportunity Store, where a counselor would insert it in his or her computer, read the data from the person's last entry into the Human Investment System, and advise them about how and where to find the training or education they wanted. If they were interested in learning computer-aided design, the counselor would tell them which programs existed in the area, how much they cost, what percentage of their graduates had found jobs and at what salary levels.

The counselor would then electronically graze the 70 categorical pots of money. An unemployed or poor person might qualify for funding from one or more pots. That information would be put onto the smart card, and the customer could then use it to buy services from any vendor in the state: a training program, a community college, a private technical school, even a university.

As this system matured, Power and his colleagues reasoned, information about customer demand and vendor performance would build up in the data base. Gradually, it would become clear which training vendors placed 90 percent of their graduates in jobs and which placed only 40 percent, which community college programs sent their graduates off to solid jobs and which did not, which adult education programs significantly raised their students' reading levels and which did not. It would also become clear which of the 70 pots of money were in high demand and which were irrelevant.

As this information built up, Power believed, both customers and service providers would pressure the legislature to eliminate some of the pots, expand others, and revise the rest. Ultimately, the legislature might realize that an effective lifelong learning system would not have 70 pots of money, but one—and that every citizen of Michigan below a certain income level ought to have access to it. At that point, the Opportunity Card would become a true voucher. Power and his colleagues dreamed of $500 a year in education and training credit piling up on each worker's card, so they could buy the retraining and job placement they needed throughout their careers.

The result would be a truly customer-driven system. Customers would know exactly where to go for information about the quality and availability of various services, and they could choose the service they preferred. All vendors—public programs, private schools, community colleges, for-profit firms—would have to compete for their dollars by providing quality training or education. The market would respond to the needs of the customers. Businesses could even use the system to select contractors for training they needed, or to handle the retraining funds they set aside for those they laid off.

There was only one thing wrong with Power's vision. It required the full backing of a governor, and Power's governor lost an election while the system was still under development. Continuity of leadership is critical in transforming public systems. (This is another huge difference between business and government: political successors are often more adversarial than business successors.) Because Opportunity Cards were not yet widely available during the 1990 campaign, in which Governor Blanchard sought a third term, his opponent ridiculed the idea as a public relations gimmick. During speeches, he would invariably ask the audience, "Does anyone here have an Opportunity Card?" When he won, he quickly dismantled the system. It was such an important breakthrough, however, that other states immediately began to look into it.

USER-FRIENDLINESS, TRANSPARENCY, AND HOLISM

Power and his colleagues believed a customer-driven system should be "user-friendly": customers "should not be faced with a confusing maze of fragmented programs, conflicting eligibility requirements, and multiple forms to fill out." They also felt it should be "transparent": customers should be able to sort through their options without having to sort through the complex bureaucracy behind them.

Think of our public systems as an infrastructure—like sewers, water pipes, and electrical lines—and the idea of transparency becomes clear. Customers don't care how infrastructure systems work; they don't want to know what goes on underground. They just want the lights and faucet and phone to work. User-friendly, transparent systems are designed to hide the underground pipes and wiring, but to give customers all the information they need about the lights and faucet and phone.

Customer-driven systems also allow individuals to meet their needs in a holistic way, without applying to half a dozen different programs. Michigan's Opportunity Card and Stores were designed to help customers buy any kind of education, training, or placement services they needed, without visiting half a dozen offices. Multiservice shelters for the homeless—which bring an array of services together under one roof—offer yet another example.

A recent *Governing* magazine article about at-risk youth illustrated the importance of a holistic approach. It described a girl who was on welfare, was pregnant, and had a juvenile record. Through her contacts with corrections and social welfare agencies, she had more than half a dozen different caseworkers. The system was so fragmented that while each agency was performing a discrete service, no one was dealing with her real emotional needs. "The kid has all these people providing services, and everybody's doing their own thing and Tasha's not getting better," one caseworker said. "We need to have one person who says, 'Now look, let's talk about a plan of action for Tasha.'"

Even the AFL-CIO has begun to protest fragmented, user-hostile systems. In a publication called *Making Government Work,* its Public Employees Department recommended restructuring service delivery systems to create one-stop shopping, single intake systems, case management, and the like. It held up models such as New York State's merger of Job Service and Unemployment Insurance offices into Community Service Centers, in which the unemployed can sign up for unemployment insurance and food stamps and receive information about education, training, child care, and jobs—even during the evening. The idea, it said, is to "serve people, not funding streams."

A time will come when people won't believe that a pregnant high school girl in America once had more than half a dozen different caseworkers. A time will come when people won't believe that the poor in America once had to visit 18 different offices to get all the benefits to which they were entitled. And a time will come when people won't believe that parents in

America once could not choose the public schools their children attended.

By the evidence piling up across this land, that time will come sooner than most of us think. In a world in which cable television systems have 50 channels, banks let their customers do business by phone, and even department stores have begun to customize their services for the individual, bureaucratic, unresponsive, one-size-fits-all government cannot last.

—7—

Enterprising Government: Earning Rather Than Spending

The tax revolt . . . is here to stay. We have to guarantee future revenues by creating new revenue sources.
—Gale Wilson, former city manager, Fairfield, California

In 1990, Ace-Federal Reporters, Inc., offered to pay the Federal Energy Regulatory Commission (FERC) for the privilege of transcribing its hearings. Ace had discovered, over the previous eight years, that it could make whopping profits by selling transcripts to the thousands of law firms that argued before FERC every year. When FERC rebid the contract in 1990, three of Ace's competitors offered to perform the service for free. But Ace went them one better: it volunteered to pay $1.25 million.

FERC turned down the offer. As FERC officials explained, they couldn't keep the money. They would have to turn it over to the U.S. Treasury, and they would have to hire a clerk to set up the account and monitor the contract. To FERC, in other words, it was an expense, not a source of revenue. Who needed it?

Ace sued, of course. "I never thought I'd see the day that I'd have to sue the government to force them to take money," its lawyer mused.

This is a particularly glaring example, but similar stories unfold every day of the year, in virtually every government in America. Our budget systems drive people to spend money, not to make it. And our employees oblige. We have 15 million trained spenders in American government, but few people who are trained to make money. In most governments, few people outside of the finance and revenue departments even think about revenues. No one thinks about *profits*.

The typical public employee, in fact, resents the fact that he or she occasionally has to worry about revenues—because budgets fall short or taxpayers revolt. The police, the librarians, the social workers—most believe they are doing God's work, and the public should be grateful. They are often justified in this opinion. But can you imagine the creativity they would turn loose if they thought as much about how to *make* money as they do about how to *spend* it?

Many readers remember the 1984 Olympics. Eight years earlier, in Montreal, the Olympics had rolled up a $1 billion public debt—a debt Canadians will still be paying off in the year 2000. But the Los Angeles Olympic Organizing Committee, formed about the time Proposition 13 passed in California, understood that the citizens of Los Angeles were not about to pay $1 billion to subsidize the Olympics. So they spent three years convincing the International Olympic Committee that they could break the pattern of 85 years and finance the Olympics without public money.

The Olympic Committee finally agreed, and the organizers went to work. They recycled old facilities. They drummed up corporate sponsors. They recruited 50,000 volunteers—not just to park cars, but to organize transportation, to feed thousands of people from 118 countries, and to help with a sophisticated antiterrorist system. The organizing committee, led by civic entrepreneur Peter Ueberroth, painted a vision that included not only spending money but making money. And the 1984 Olympics turned a profit of $225 million.

Pressed hard by the tax revolts of the 1970s and 1980s and the fiscal crisis of the early 1990s, entrepreneurial governments are increasingly following Ueberroth's example. They are searching for nontax revenues. They are measuring their return on investment. They are recycling their money, finding the 15 or 20 percent that can be redirected. Some are even running for-profit enterprises.

- The Milwaukee Metropolitan Sewerage District transforms 60,000 tons of sewage sludge into fertilizer every year and sells it—generating $7.5 million in revenue.

- Phoenix earns $750,000 a year by siphoning off the methane gas generated by a large wastewater treatment plant and selling it to the city of Mesa, for home heating and cooking.

- Chicago turned a $2 million annual cost into a $2 million source of revenue by contracting with a private company to tow away abandoned cars. The city once spent $24 per car to tow cars; now a private company pays $25 a car for the privilege.

- The St. Louis County Police developed a system that allows officers to call in their reports, rather than write them up. The department then licensed the software to a private company—earning $25,000 every time it sells to another police department.

- The Washington State ferry system generated $1 million a year in new revenues during the early 1980s by rebidding its food service contract; more than $150,000 a year by bidding out a contract to sell advertising in the terminal building; and another $150,000 a year by letting a contract to operate duty-free shops on its two international boats.

- Paulding County, Georgia, built a 244-bed prison, when it needed only 60 extra beds, so it could charge other jurisdictions $35 a night to handle their overflow. In the jail's first year of business, it brought in $1.4 million, $200,000 more than its operating costs.

- Enterprising police departments in California are earning money by renting out motel rooms as weekend jails. The courts often let those convicted of drunk driving serve their time on weekends. So some police departments reserve blocks of cheap motel rooms, pay someone to sit outside and make sure everyone stays in their room, and rent the rooms to convicted drivers as jail cells at $75 a night.

TURNING THE PROFIT MOTIVE
TO PUBLIC USE

In the early 1970s, Ted Gaebler worked in Columbia, Maryland, the "new town" built by developer James Rouse, of Boston's Quincy Market and Baltimore's Inner Harbor fame. Columbia was created by a private corporation, not a public organization. It was Rouse's first experiment in the use of business practices to solve public problems.

Gaebler learned many lessons at Rouse's knee, but perhaps the most fundamental was the power of the profit motive. Gaebler and his colleagues would often be stymied by some problem, gnashing their teeth and getting nowhere. Rouse would walk in and ask, "How could we profit from solving this problem?" That question invariably unleashed tremendous creativity.

Seven years later, Gaebler became city manager of Visalia. Sixty days after he took the reins, Proposition 13 eliminated 25 percent of the city's tax revenues. So Gaebler began asking Rouse's question. When the school district needed $1.4 million to build a new school, Gaebler asked what it could put on the table. Months later, after a complex series of land purchases and negotiations, it completed a four-parcel swap and sale that left the district with $1.2 million and a prime site for its new school and the city with commercial property worth more than $1.5 million.

"Other cities do a project and see what the expense is," said John Biane, then Visalia's real estate manager. "We do a project and figure out how much money we can make."

The word *profit* is anathema to traditional governments, of course. When a public entrepreneur in Rhode Island began marketing a state software program to the private sector—pulling in $275,000 a year for the state—his superiors gave him no encouragement or extra staff, because they did not consider making money to be their job. Frustrated, he left state government and launched a private company—and the state disbanded its marketing effort. When Minnesota's Department of

Administration negotiated a deal with IBM to develop six "expert systems" pioneered by its InterTechnology Group, the state attorney general announced that it had to limit its royalties, because it was a nonprofit organization.

We can no longer afford this attitude, in an age of fierce resistance to taxes. This is not to say that most public services should be sold for a profit—most shouldn't. But think of all the public services that benefit individuals: the golf courses, the tennis courts, the marinas. Typically, the taxpayers subsidize those services. Average working people subsidize the affluent to play golf and tennis or moor their boats. Why not turn such services into profit centers?

When Ted Gaebler arrived in Visalia, the city was charging men's recreational softball teams $25 per season. Gaebler asked his staff how much the softball program cost the city—for umpires, equipment, park maintenance, and so on. No one knew. They put an intern on it, and in traditional governmental fashion an answer came back three years later. Softball cost the city $140 per team, per season.

No one had ever voted to subsidize the men's softball league, so Gaebler asked his staff to recommend a new fee. Three weeks later they came back with a figure: $90. "Where did you get that?" he asked. "Well," they answered, "we think that's what the traffic will bear." Gaebler decided to pose James Rouse's question.

The occasion he chose was a public hearing on softball fees, in the recreation building. It was a hot July night, and 300 angry ballplayers showed up. To begin the meeting, Gaebler walked to a blackboard at the front of the room, erased the figure $90, and wrote down $400. An hour later, 300 people walked away happy to pay a $400 fee. Why? Because they had decided to recruit team sponsors, who would pay the $400. Ballplayers no longer had to pay a fee, merchants got cheap advertising and loyal customers, and the city earned $260 per team, per season. It was pure profit—which the city invested in girls' softball and recreation for senior citizens.

Within a year or two the city had a new problem: it had 300 teams, and they were overflowing the portable toilets. Again in traditional government fashion, the finance director assured the recreation director that if she wrote up a request she could get portable toilets tacked onto the end of the five-year capital improvement plan. If she could then get a state matching grant, in six or seven years the city could buy her some new toilets.

"I don't think you understand," the recreation director responded. "These people are killing our trees *today*."

Having caught a whiff of the entrepreneurial spirit, she suggested a solution: why not take $85,000 out of the savings her department had built up (under its new budget system) and invest in 12 flush toilets? To pay for the water and sewer systems needed, she would put a concession stand on the front end and lease it out to the highest bidder. A&W Root Beer won the concession, and in 31 months its contract repaid the city's investment. From then on, it generated pure profit—$24,000 a year or more. The ballplayers got not only their toilets, but the opportunity to buy soft drinks, beer, and hot dogs. A&W earned a profit, but so did the city. Where were the losers in that story?

Fairfield, the city that invented the mission-driven budget, was even more aggressive. In 1976, a developer approached then city manager Gale Wilson for permission to develop a small shopping center. Wilson and his staff believed that Fairfield—which sits astride Highway 80, halfway between San Francisco and Sacramento—would grow into a perfect location for a large regional mall. (Fairfield had 51,700 people in 1976; today it has 80,000.) So they created a Redevelopment Authority, which bought 90 acres of land for $3.6 million, sold 48 to the developer for a $2 million profit, and built a new highway interchange. The developer put in a "super regional mall" with more than a million square feet and five large department stores. As part of the agreement, Fairfield negotiated a piece of the action: 10 to 17 percent of net cash flow for 65 years. When Proposition 13 limited the city's take from property taxes, Wilson negotiated a 55-cent-per-acre assessment for off-site improvements—roads, sewers, and the like—for 25 years. It now brings in between $400,000 and $500,000 a year and covers the cost of the bonds floated to pay for the improvements.

After the mall opened, in 1985, the city began leasing and selling off its other parcels. Overall, according to Fairfield's calculations, its investment of $8 million in land purchases and relocation costs had generated, by mid-1991, $6.4 million in sales, $9.4 million in increased property taxes, and $15.4 million in sales taxes. The profit-sharing agreement is generating $120,000 a year, and ground leases from the second major parcel developed, the Gateway Plaza, will kick in soon. The city still owns about 35 acres, which it intends to sell or lease as the market can absorb them.

Fairfield has since taken a similar approach to its other development projects. When a developer tried to build a large residential development just outside city limits, for instance, the city backed a county proposition that made it difficult to develop land outside a city, then proposed a deal that convinced the developer to build in Fairfield. The city built a public golf course around which the developer could build, then allowed him to increase the number of homes in the project from 800 to 1,200. The only catch: the developer had to donate land for the golf course and a public school, build a public road into the project, and put in the storm drainage system.

The city used revenue from the course and clubhouse to pay off the $7 million it borrowed to build the course. The result: The developer got higher value building lots, because they surrounded a golf course, and the city built its first public golf course with no subsidy from the taxpayers.

The project worked so well, in fact, that the city then negotiated a similar deal with another developer—in which the developer not only donated land but built a reservoir. As we write, Fairfield is studying the option of selling the first course and investing the profit of $20 to $25 million in some other amenity, such as a sports complex. "We intervened in the market by creating more value," explains City Manager Charlie Long. "The golf course created higher home prices because it created more value, and we then take that increment of profit and put it in the public sector to pay for more amenities."

Lest you think this kind of entrepreneurship can happen only in California, Cincinnati earns 17 percent of the profits from a hotel and office complex in the city center, for which the city assembled the land and arranged the financing; San Antonio is a partner in several real estate projects, including a Sheraton hotel; and the Metropolitan Area Transit Authority in Washington, D.C., has developed lucrative real estate above and around some of its subway stations. Orlando, Florida, even struck a deal in which a developer built a new city hall.

Orlando Mayor Bill Frederick, first elected in 1980 in the wake of a nationwide tax revolt, understood that his citizens wanted lower taxes. (He pushed property taxes down by 29 percent over the next decade.) He knew that if he wanted to accomplish anything, he would have "to look to new solutions—especially when it comes to finances."

"If Orlando had taken 5 percent of its General Fund revenue in 1980 and used it to finance a 30-year series of bonds," he explains, "we could have built only $30 million worth of capital projects." Instead Orlando used a series of profit-making authorities and funds to build nearly $2.5 billion worth of facilities—an expanded airport, a new basketball arena, wastewater treatment plants, a performing arts center—with virtually no subsidy from local taxpayers.

The crowning achievement was city hall. To avoid dipping into general revenues, the city used seven acres around the old city hall as a lure—asking developers to compete for the right to develop the land. The winner, Lincoln Property Company, agreed to build a $32.5 million, 246,000-square-foot, state-of-the-art city hall, complete with its own closed-circuit television system. In exchange, it got the right to build two office towers adjacent to city hall. Ground rents from the towers will pay off the city's construction bonds.

In addition, the city will receive 20 percent of the net proceeds from office and retail rents over a set income level, plus 20 percent of the proceeds from any sale or refinancing. (If Lincoln fails to build city hall to the city's satisfaction, or fails to begin paying ground rents on the first office tower in 1992 and the second in 1996, it will forfeit a $750,000 deposit.) The city expects the project's revenues to pay off its 30-year bonds in 10 to 12 years.

After 75 years, the entire project will revert to city ownership. "I know 75 years seems like a long time," says Lew Oliver, the city's project manager. "But Rockefeller Center is 65 years old and it is some of the hottest property in New York." Oliver estimates that the Orlando project will be worth $3 billion by 2070—by which time the city will already have collected some $700 million in ground rents.

RAISING MONEY BY CHARGING FEES

Making profits through development deals is one of the more aggressive methods used by enterprising governments. It is also riskier than many of the alternatives. Fairfield has made money hand over fist from its mall, but it lost roughly $500,000 from a series of energy investments when the price of oil collapsed.

Perhaps the safest way to raise nontax revenue is simply to charge fees to those who use public services. User fees have become ever more popular as resistance to tax increases has mounted. Sunnyvale generates 37 percent of its operating budget from fees, another 3 percent from franchises and concessions. The average local government (not counting school districts) raises more than 25 percent of its revenues from user fees. They are particularly common for garbage collection, water and sewer services, recreation facilities, parking, health services, police services at special events, building inspections, and zoning services.

The public clearly prefers this approach. "All of our public-opinion polls indicate that when you confront citizens with their preference for raising revenue—user fees, property tax, local sales tax, local income tax—user fees win hands down," says John Shannon, former executive director of the Advisory Commission on Intergovernmental Relations, in Washington. "That's what's kept this [user fee] movement skipping right along."

And why not? What is fairer than a system in which those who benefit from a service and can afford to pay for it do so, while those who don't benefit don't have to pay? What is fair about subsidizing Little League but not youth soccer—as Visalia discovered it was doing? What is fair about subsidizing golf while cutting more important public services, as Dayton discovered it was doing?

User fees are not always appropriate, of course. They work under three conditions: when the service is primarily a "private good," benefiting the individuals who use it; when those who don't pay for it can be excluded from enjoying its benefits; and when fees can be collected efficiently. "Collective goods," which benefit society at large, should not be charged in full to paying customers. Mass transit, for instance, benefits everyone—whether they use it or not—by limiting traffic congestion and pollution. If it were priced to cover its costs in full, fewer people would use it and the society would lose much of this collective benefit.

Even user fees charged for private goods have some drawbacks. If it costs $1 to use a public swimming pool or $2 to use the tennis courts, for example, poor children will not have the same access as others. To solve this problem, some governments forgo certain user fees; others provide free season passes, vouchers, or their equivalent to poor families; still others give recreation staff the authority to admit poor children for free. This approach equalizes the customers, without spending enormous amounts to subsidize everyone. "It defies logic to give services free to high-income folk because you're worried about low-income folk," says John Mikesell of Indiana University, an expert on state and local taxes and fees. "That gives welfare to the rich."

Other user fees actually make public systems more progressive. When governments pay for water and sewer systems out of general tax receipts, the poor often subsidize the rich, who use far more water. Even when this is not the case, user fees for a service not heavily used by the poor, like highways, can be used to subsidize a service more accessible to the poor, like mass transit. In such cases, the impact is clearly progressive.

User fees have two advantages: they raise money, and they lower demand for public services. Both help balance public budgets.

When consumers do not have to pay the full price of a service, they often consume far more of it than they otherwise would. Norm King, city manager of Moreno Valley, California, compares the dynamic to a restaurant dinner in which the diners agree beforehand to split the bill. When he knows the bill will be evenly shared, he says, "I have the filet mignon." When he pays his own bill, on the other hand, "I may well have the chicken, and not the filet mignon."

When Minnesota's Department of Administration required some of its services to charge their full costs, it learned these lessons. Demand for long-distance telephone service fell by half, because suddenly departments had to pay for what they used. On the other hand, it was now clear that those who chose to buy valued their services. The Management Analysis Division, which sells management consulting, grew rapidly. "Since we've been charging the involved parties have taken more seriously our recommendations and are much more committed to carrying them out," says Terry Bock, who runs the unit.

SPENDING MONEY TO SAVE MONEY: INVESTING FOR A RETURN

A third characteristic we have seen in enterprising governments is an "investment" perspective—a habit of gauging the return on their spending as if it were an investment. This is not a way to make money; it is a way to save money. By measuring their return on investment, they understand when spending money will save them money.

Businesses focus on both sides of the balance sheet: spending and earning, debits and credits. They don't care as much about the spending side as the earning side: they will spend whatever is necessary to maximize their returns. But governments look only at the spending side of the ledger. Ignoring returns, they concentrate only on minimizing costs. Frequently they refuse even to consider significant investments that would generate significant returns—simply because of the cost. They postpone spending on road repair until the road has to be rebuilt, at three times the cost of simple resurfacing. They ignore the minor expense of health care for pregnant women, but pay the massive expenses of premature babies.

A few politicians have begun to throw around the word *investment* to justify their spending—as in "This appropriation for our schools will be an investment in our future." But few really think like investors. The average tax auditor in the Los Angeles Clerk's office generates 140 times his or her salary in increased tax collections. But during the 1991 recession, Los Angeles hired no additional auditors. "Politically, when you're laying off cops and firemen, you can't hire auditors," a city official explained. An entrepreneurial city wouldn't lay off the cops and firemen: it would train a few of them as auditors and quickly make enough money to keep the rest on.

Careful studies have estimated the return on investment for every dollar spent on Head Start at close to $5 over the life of the student—in lower welfare costs, education costs, and crime costs, and higher tax revenues from earnings. But we still spend enough to provide Head Start to only a third of all poor children.

Welfare spending tells a similar story. Studies have demonstrated that welfare-to-work programs produce their greatest financial return by investing in women who need help the most: those who have been on welfare the longest. It takes far more money to buy the education, training, and other support they need to get permanently off welfare, but the return is significant—because without the intervention, they are virtually guaranteed to stay on the rolls. Many of these investments pay themselves back—through welfare savings—only in the second or third year. But when Robert Stumberg of the National Center for Policy Alternatives reviewed state welfare programs, he found only three or four that even measured their return beyond the current budget year.

"I keep coming back to trying to rationalize economic returns," Stumberg says. "Convincing people to spend more money now, or serve fewer people now, on the grounds that you shouldn't be trying to reduce cost per capita in a one- or two-year period. You should be trying to think like an investor, and maximize your long-term return."

Stumberg argues that we should give teeth to politically popular terms such as "investment" and "partnerships" by giving them the kind of serious content they have in the private sector. Partnerships are used in business all the time, he points out—but they are structured by contracts, and they specify a return on investment. What we need is a form of accounting that measures return on investment, as businesses do. Stumberg suggests an "economic impact statement":

Say you've got a budget proposal to invest $5 million in a low-income housing project this year by subsidizing the rehab of the building. You convert that investment into a per-unit cost in the context of its 30-year life, and you compare that to alternative investment scenarios. That cost might translate into something like $40,000 per housing unit, in present dollar terms. But then when you add in down-the-road costs your 30-year public expense for that property is going to look more like $150,000. In contrast, you might be able to make a $50,000 investment now, which would only require $20,000 more over the 30-year cycle. That would tell you the politicians are about to vote on something that would be twice as expensive as the alternative.

In Florida, managers in the Department of Health and Rehabilitative Services are working to develop a system that will measure return on investment. Several states have required specific returns from their investments in economic development—no doubt because those involved in economic development are often accustomed to thinking like investors. Kansas enacted a venture capital tax credit for investors in new venture capital firms, provided that those firms invested at least 60 percent of their money in Kansas businesses. The legislation required an annual analysis of the fiscal rate of return generated by the tax credit. Iowa set up a customized job training program for industry that recouped its investments through a corporate tax increment assessed on increases in property value or income taxes paid by the firm's workers.

Perhaps our favorite illustration of an investment mentality comes from a far less likely source, however: the decision by Santa Clara, California, to buy an amusement park.

Santa Clara is a city of 93,000 that borders both San Jose and Sunnyvale in California's Silicon Valley. In 1976, the Marriott Corporation opened a theme park called Great America, on undeveloped land in north Santa Clara. It quickly proved profitable, but during the late 1970s the Silicon Valley explosion occurred and the land skyrocketed in value.

In 1983, City Manager Don Von Raesfeld heard rumors that Marriott was planning to sell the land. He and the mayor asked Marriott to grant the city the right of first refusal. Perhaps fearing that the city would seize the park under its power of eminent domain or use its zoning powers to block development of the land, Marriott eventually agreed. Von Raesfeld and his colleagues believe that it did so only to defuse political opposition, never dreaming that the city might exercise the option. After all, how many cities—particularly of Santa Clara's size—would be willing to spend close to $90 million for an amusement park? To Marriott's surprise, Santa Clara was.

The key was the city's investment perspective. Under Von Raesfeld's leadership, Santa Clara's Redevelopment Agency and its publicly owned utilities were already run with a private sector, return-on-investment mentality. In purchasing Great America, the city council was simply continuing the tradition. It was willing to spend $88.5 million because it knew that expenditure would save it a tremendous amount of money down the road.

The goal was not profit, but traffic control. Traffic in the area was already horrendous, particularly when the high-technology firms let out every afternoon. If Marriott's 200 acres were turned into office and industrial buildings, it would get even worse. "We wanted the park to be maintained, because it was the best traffic mitigator that there was," says Von Raesfeld. "We could spend all kinds of money, equal to what we were paying for the park, and never be able to adequately mitigate 200 acres of intense industrial development."

Still, the decision was not an easy one. Some, including newspaper editorialists, argued that the city had no business competing with the private sector. "It was a terrible split, an emotional split, that was played up in the San Jose *Mercury News* for almost a year," remembers Jennifer Sparacino, who succeeded Von Raesfeld when he retired. "We had bad press, we had a lawsuit. It was a very wrenching decision."

At 11:11 P.M. on January 31, 1984, 49 minutes before its right of first refusal expired, the city council voted four to three to buy the park. At the same time, they put a nonbinding referendum on the June ballot, asking whether the Redevelopment Agency should preserve the theme park, as long as it did not require any of the city's general funds. Seventy-six percent of the voters said yes. In June 1985, after a lawsuit, Santa Clara finally closed the deal—becoming the only city in America to own a theme park.

The city then contracted with Kings Entertainment Corporation, which runs several large amusement parks around the country, to operate the park for five years, with a right to purchase after that period. In 1989, it sold Kings the park facilities—but not the land. (This time it put a right of first refusal into the sale contract, should Kings Entertainment ever decide to sell.) Kings agreed to pay $5.3 million a year for at least 50 years to lease the land. (When gross revenues top $56 million—as they already have—5 percent of everything above that amount also goes to the city.) The city came out of the deal with $42 million in debt left over from the 1984 purchase, which should be repaid by Kings' lease payments in 15 years. At that point, the city will have an income of at least $5.3 million a year, ownership of 200 valuable acres, and a continuing solution to its traffic worries. This was clearly a deal made by investors, not spenders.

TURNING MANAGERS
INTO ENTREPRENEURS

If managers cannot keep any of their earnings, they are not likely to pursue them. If managers' budgets are supplied regardless of whether their departments earn anything, they are not likely to spend time trying to make money. If we want public managers to think like entrepreneurs, in other words, we have to give them incentives to do so. There are a number of ways to do this:

Shared Savings and Earnings

As we explained in chapter 4, traditional budget systems contain no incentive for managers to save money or make money. Consequently, they act like the people at FERC did when offered $1.25 million: "What, me make money?"

Mission-driven budgets solve this problem by allowing departments to keep all or part of any funds they save or earn. Fairfield, Visalia, St. Paul, Phoenix, Dade County, Los Angeles County, and Minnesota all practice some version of shared savings. (Dade County and Los Angeles County call it profit sharing.) Even the Department of Defense has endorsed the concept. Its Directive for Installation Management says: "Unless prohibited by law, a share of any resources saved or earned at an installation should be made available to the installation commander to improve the operations and working and living conditions at the installation."

Politicians and green-eyeshade budget officers will often try to recapture any savings or earnings by appropriating less in the next fiscal year. Hence budget formulas are necessary to protect managers from raids on their hard-earned profits. In Fairfield, unless the city council votes to change service levels or the budget goes into deficit, a department normally receives the same amount as the year before, adjusted for inflation and community growth. Visalia does the same, although it gives departments only half the inflation increase.

The shared earnings principle can also be applied to individual pay. In Visalia and Phoenix, employees receive a percentage of any savings or earnings that result from their ideas. (Phoenix typically gets 1,000 suggestions a year and saves $2 million annually by implementing them.) Some cities pay a few of their managers on commission. And governments often pay those who manage public investments, such as pension funds, based on the performance of their investment portfolios.

Some places even extend the principle to contractors. Under Mayor Henry Cisneros, San Antonio contracted with a private law firm to collect its taxes. "They get a percentage of what they collect," Cisneros explained. "As a result, they have a tremendous incentive to collect taxes, and they do things we couldn't do in terms of the legal process." In California, a firm called Municipal Resource Consultants (MRC) does tax audits for more than 100 local governments, collecting 25 to 35 percent of any new revenues it turns up.

Innovation Capital

In the private sector, businesses routinely raise capital to pursue attractive investments. "Typically, innovative companies have two separate budgets: an operating budget and an innovation budget," says Peter Drucker. "Top management spends as much time and attention on the fifty pages of the innovation budget as on the five hundred of the operating budget—and usually more."

In most governments, managers can raise innovation capital only by securing an extra appropriation from the council or legislature—a very difficult process. We all understand that "it takes money to make money," but in government we seldom act on that premise.

A mission-driven budget provides a partial solution, because it allows managers to accumulate savings, which they can use as seed capital. Riverside, California, set up a $100,000 seed fund, controlled by the department heads, to make small loans for new initiatives. Governor Lawton Chiles of Florida tried a slightly different version in 1991: to balance the budget he asked all agencies to eliminate 5 percent of their spending, but he then offered half of that amount back to agencies that developed plans to invest it to increase productivity or effectiveness.

Gifford Pinchot III advocated something similar for large private corporations in *Intrapreneuring*, his book on entrepreneurs within large corporations:

Perhaps the most tangible form of business freedom is the power to spend money on new ideas without having to ask for permission. . . .

Given that the basic motivation of the intrapreneur is the drive to realize a vision in his or her own way, failing to

provide the freedom to do so is a fundamental failing in re-
ward systems. Intrapreneurs should be able to build up
"freedom credit" on the basis of past successes—that is,
something akin to the capital that entrepreneurs earn.

Pinchot called his solution "intracapital." Some corporations already provide it, he noted. Ore-Ida chooses five "fellows" every two years and gives each one a $50,000 annual budget to fund other employees in the exploration of new ideas. Texas Instruments awards "wild hare" grants to intrapreneurs; it also gives some managers the authority to award "IDEA grants" of up to $25,000 for the development of prototypes.

In government, the simplest approach might be a loan pool against which managers could borrow automatically, up to a certain limit. To ensure political accountability, they might need executive approval to borrow up to a higher limit, and legislative approval beyond. Such a fund would put more control in the hands of managers—a worthy goal in itself. But by requiring repayment, it would also force managers to think like investors. They could secure investment capital, in other words, only if they had some prospect of generating a return. If that return failed to materialize, they would have to dip into their own budgets to repay the loan.

A government could capitalize such a fund without any cost to the taxpayer, simply by selling revenue bonds. If they were marketed correctly—as "innovation bonds," or "restructuring bonds"—business leaders might buy them to demonstrate their support for better government. Other citizens might also, if the bonds were sold in small units. Local governments have already begun to sell tax-exempt "mini-bonds" in denominations as low as $100.

Enterprise Funds

If we want public employees to become "revenue conscious," we need incentives that encourage them to make money as well as to spend it. Guaranteed incomes create all the wrong incentives. A manager with a hefty budget supplied entirely by the legislature will act much like a teenager with a hefty allowance.

Neither will beat the bushes for new ways to earn or save money.

Babak Armajani, who helped Governor Perpich reinvent government in Minnesota, discovered this as he watched how differently the Department of Administration's "revolving funds"—which had to earn all their income—acted from the rest of the department:

> *I noticed that general fund activities employed as many people as the legislature's staffing limits permitted, whereas revolving fund activities usually employed fewer people than they were allowed. In my conversations with revolving fund managers, I got the sense that their time horizon was different from that of general fund managers. If managers of a revolving fund could invest in something that had a pay-back of three years, they were inclined to go with the project. Beyond this, revolving fund people, with some exceptions, just seemed a lot more upbeat and creative, and there was definitely a lot better morale.*

While Minnesota uses the term *revolving funds,* most governments call self-supporting units *enterprise funds.* (If they are structurally independent, they are usually called public authorities.) Enterprise funds are quite common today; most local governments operate at least one or two. Orlando has seven: refuse collection, a parking fund, a stormwater utility, the golf course, the wastewater system, the Centroplex Fund (which manages a stadium, arena, exposition hall, and performing arts center), and the Civic Facilities Authority, which manages several stadiums. Adding enterprise fund earnings to other profits and fees, Orlando actually collects 30 percent more in earnings than it does in taxes. (If we counted the Greater Orlando Airport Authority, an independent public authority, earnings would absolutely dwarf taxes. It has built one of the fastest growing and highest quality airports in the country *with no subsidies from local taxpayers.* Most of its expenses are covered by airline gate fees.)

Enterprise funds, like user fees, are not appropriate for all services. It would be ludicrous to require a police department, which provides a collective good, to charge for all of its services.

Yet it is equally ludicrous for a city to ask its taxpayers to subsidize a private good such as golf. Other activities, like job training, produce both private and collective benefits; hence governments often provide them a partial subsidy.

Several years ago, Pensacola, Florida, developed a useful way to classify public services. It divided them into two categories: "general government functions," which "generate virtually no revenue"; and "public enterprise functions," which do generate revenue. It divided public enterprise functions into three categories:

- activities designed to create profit;
- activities structured to break even but return no profit;
- activities which can partially, but not completely, support themselves.

Profit Centers

The first two categories of enterprise funds, those expected to break even or make a profit, put public managers in much the same position as business managers. When he was mayor of Tampa, Bob Martinez ran Tampa's water and sewer services, solid waste collection, public marinas, and golf courses as enterprise funds. "They're a business," he said. "The departments are so organized that you could conceivably sell them."

Enterprise funds like Tampa's create powerful incentives to make money. We have seen the phenomenon many times. The San Francisco suburb of San Bruno owns its cable television system, for instance. David Thomas, who runs it, is a typical entrepreneur. He has pride of ownership. He is mission-driven. He plans ahead. He strives to please his customers. He is aware of his competitors—and he beats the pants off them. In 1991, San Bruno charged its 11,200 subscribers $12.55 for a 31-channel package.

Private cable companies in the county charged an average of $19.57 for the comparable package. Yet even at San Bruno's low price, the system generated enough money to upgrade all its hardware—cables, boxes, everything—every 10 years, without borrowing a dime. (This is after it returns 5 percent of gross revenues to the city.) "We don't use the word *profit*," Thomas smiles, "but we do use the term retained earnings."

We saw the same mind-set in Santa Clara. Like San Bruno's cable company, Santa Clara's publicly owned electric utility returns 5 percent of gross revenues to the city, but still charges 30 to 40 percent less than its private competitor does in surrounding communities. Thirty years ago, it spearheaded a group of other municipal utilities to form the Northern California Power Agency, which then built a large, 200-megawatt geothermal energy project, as well as the last major dam in California. When tax credits favored wind energy, the utility bought 2,600 acres and leased them out to private companies to build windmills.

Santa Clara's Water and Sewer Utility created a solar division—in effect, the nation's first solar utility. It provides hot water units for apartment buildings and swimming pools. The utility buys, installs, and maintains the equipment, charging the customer a monthly fee for six months of the year to cover the costs.

When the city's housing market became extremely tight, Santa Clara's Redevelopment Agency leased the existing city golf course to developers, who are putting in 2,000 apartment units; used the lease revenues to pay for a new golf and tennis club built over the city's old landfill; and put in wells to tap the natural gas generated by the buried garbage. The new course anchors the Santa Clara Trade and Convention Center (built next to Great America), which includes a 240,000-square-foot convention center, a 502-room hotel, and an office building. "One of our major goals was to create a long-term revenue stream for the city," says City Manager Jennifer Sparacino, "and it is definitely accomplishing that." Despite problems filling up the office building, the entire deal is already generating a positive return.

The private sector often complains about public enterprise, arguing that government should not compete with business. And many public leaders buy the argument. Lewis V. Pond, city manager of San Bruno, wants to sell the cable system. "We can't make money," he told us, "because we're a government." But where is it written that government should handle only lemons, while business gets all the profit centers? As Don Von Raesfeld said during the Great America debate, "It's been awfully interesting to me in my career as a city manager here that the people are always willing to push on to government losers in this country. The winners are always to be preserved to the private enterprise system."

In reality, there are several good reasons why government *should* sometimes compete with the private sector. Some services are natural monopolies. It is inefficient to string two or three sets of electrical lines and or bury two or three sets of gas lines in a city, for example. In such cases, governments can grant a private monopoly and regulate its prices, or they can create a public monopoly. The latter option often delivers a better deal to the public. For 100 years, publicly owned utilities have sold electricity at lower prices than their private counterparts. Today, publicly owned cable television systems do the same.

In other areas, where there is insufficient private competition, public enterprise can act as a competitive yardstick, forcing private firms to lower their prices and pursue greater efficiency. The Phoenix Department of Public Works does this by competing in garbage collection.

Finally, there are some occasions on which the private sector chooses to abandon a profitable business. Marriott sold Great America even though it was profitable, because industrial development would have been *more* profitable. (Being private, Marriott could ignore the public costs, which would have been enormous.) The Mets dropped a minor league franchise they owned in Visalia not because it was unprofitable, but because they decided to limit their farm system to the eastern United States. When no private buyers turned up, Visalia did just what Santa Clara did. It took over the franchise, proved it could make money for six years, and sold it to local owners for a profit.

Identifying the True Cost of Services

This may strike many readers as odd, but most governments have no idea how much it costs to deliver the services they offer.

Even if they can give you a budget figure for each service, it typically excludes "indirect costs," such as administrative overhead, capital costs, and employee fringe benefits. One study of 68 cities found their true costs to be 30 percent higher than their budgeted costs. Doug Ayres, who owns a company that helps California governments determine their true costs, says that only 4 percent of local governments know the direct cost of each service they provide, only 2 percent know the total cost of each service they provide, and only 10 percent can even tell you what services they provide!

Obviously, public managers cannot think like investors or pursue profits if they don't know their true costs. How can one measure the return on an investment if one doesn't even know how much that investment costs? How can one pursue a profit if one doesn't know how much one is spending? How can one even establish an appropriate subsidy if one doesn't know the cost of a service?

Governments all over America are unintentionally subsidizing softball teams, golfers, developers, and corporations—because they can't tell if their charges cover their costs. Once they expose the true cost of their subsidies, elected officials often decide that some are inappropriate. A dramatic example occurred in New Zealand, when the Labor Government turned its postal service into a publicly owned corporation—the equivalent of a public authority. On discovering how many of its 1,200 post offices were subsidized, the board decided to close almost half of them. Because Parliament expected an uproar, it voted a $42 million subsidy to keep them operating. Now that the subsidy was out in the open for all to see, however, support melted away. Members of Parliament had to ask themselves: Is it more important to spend $42 million keeping tiny post offices open, or should we spend it on education, or highways? Six months later, New Zealand Post closed 432 post offices.

Sunnyvale, Phoenix, Visalia, and Fox Valley Community College all have systems that define the true cost of their services. This can become extremely cumbersome and expensive if it requires workers to document their time on each job and departments to hire extra accountants. More efficient are costing systems in which accountants go in retroactively to figure out what the real costs were for each service, then use that information to project the costs for the next year.

An enterprising government exposes its subsidies to public light, relies on public pressure to do away with them—and then finds ways to make money from the services involved. It raises its greens fees for golf. It asks softball teams to get sponsors. It limits its tax subsidies. If it gets truly creative, it might even charge those convicted of drunk driving for the cost of processing the arrest, as San Jose does; or charge those whose malfunctioning security systems set off false alarms, as Baton Rouge does; or charge motorists who run into city-owned trees, as Fairfield does.

Such practices may not yet be widespread. But ask yourself: Are they not more consistent with American values than subsidizing the affluent to play golf and use marinas?

And is there anything more American than enterprise?

— 8 —

Anticipatory Government: Prevention Rather Than Cure

For centuries we were taught to worship our ancestors and to be true to our traditions, and it was good that we did so. But now, given the novelty and quantity of the challenges rushing at us from the future, we need to do something we have never had to do before, and which I fear we may not be able to do now: we must worship our descendants; we must love our grandchildren more than we love ourselves.
— Jim Dator, University of Hawaii futurist

Traditional bureaucratic governments focus on supplying services to combat problems. To deal with illness, they fund health care services. To deal with crime, they fund more police. To combat fires, they buy more fire trucks.

There was a time when our governments focused more on prevention: on building water and sewer systems, to prevent disease; on enacting building codes, to prevent fire; on inspecting milk, meat, and restaurants, to prevent illness; on research that would lead to vaccines and other medical cures, to stamp out disease.

But as they developed more capacity to deliver services, their attention shifted. As fire departments professionalized, they developed the art of fire suppression, not prevention. As police departments professionalized, they concentrated on chasing down criminals, not helping communities prevent crime. Even environmental agencies, while quick to acknowledge the superiority of prevention, somehow found themselves spending most of their money cleaning up pollution.

The bureaucratic model brought with it a preoccupation with service delivery—with *rowing*. And organizations that focus their best energies on rowing rarely do much steering. They develop tunnel vision. Because they are programmed to think of government as service delivery by professionals and bureaucrats, they wait until a problem becomes a crisis, then offer new services to those affected—the homeless on the street, school dropouts, drug users. Hence we spend enormous amounts treating symptoms—with more police, more jails, more welfare payments, and higher Medicaid outlays—while prevention strategies go begging. Consider:

- Homicide is the leading cause of death for black males between the ages of 15 and 34. Since 1986, gunshot wounds to children age 16 and under have increased by 300 percent in major urban areas. Deaths from gunshot wounds have soared among black youths, while leaths from other forms of violence have remained .evel. Yet we do almost nothing to prevent the ownership of guns.

- Every year American industry produces more than two tons of hazardous wastes for every man, woman, and child in the nation. Industry could cut this amount in half in five years, according to the Congressional Office of Technology Assessment. Yet the Environmental Protection Agency spends 99 percent of its budget *managing* pollution, not preventing it.

- The United States ranks 20th in the world in infant mortality—ahead only of Greece among the industrialized democracies. According to the National Commission to Prevent Infant Mortality, the average hospital cost for low-birth-weight babies is $500,000—at least 250 times the average cost of medical care during pregnancy. Careful medical studies prove that preventive care during pregnancy saves money: estimates range from $2 to $10 for every $1 invested. Yet 20 million women and infants in America still have no health insurance.

- In 1991 the federal debt reached $3.6 trillion—$14,000 for every man, woman, and child in America. Every year we spend $200 billion in federal taxes simply to pay *interest* on that debt. This amounts to $3,000 in additional taxes for the average family of four. If current trends continue, by the year 2000 the average family of four will have to pay more than $5,000 a year in taxes—*simply to pay interest on the debt.*

These statistics present an appalling indictment of our governments. Our ship of state is like a massive ocean liner, with all the luxuries above decks but no radar, no navigation systems, and no preventive maintenance below. "Instead of anticipating the problems and opportunities of the future, we lurch from crisis to crisis," wrote Alvin Toffler in *Future Shock*. "Our political system is 'Future-blind.' "

Our culture has become equally future-blind. With the pervasive influence of television—particularly television advertising—the old ethic of hard work, savings, and self-denial has given way to a new ethic of instant gratification. We buy now and pay later—consuming more and saving less than any other people on earth. In Washington, we borrow $1 of every $5 we spend—not for one year, but year after year. The Reagan and Bush administrations tripled the national debt in a decade, transforming America from the world's greatest lender to its greatest debtor.

In an age when change comes with frightening rapidity, future-blindness is a deadly flaw. "We've all seen companies that were exceptionally well run or cities that were well run—that did everything just right—and suddenly the environment changed around them and they fell apart," says Bill Donaldson, a city manager renowned for his entrepreneurial leadership in Scottsdale, Arizona; Tacoma, Washington; and Cincinnati, Ohio.

In today's global village, events in Japan or Kuwait can suddenly turn our world upside down. Ask the Rust Belt states, which saw entire industries die in the early 1980s. Or ask the oil states, which saw their tax revenues drop through the floor when the price of oil collapsed. "For a long time, government could be somnolent," says political scientist John Bryson. "But now we're sleeping on waterbeds—and we're not alone in the bed. When anybody moves in the bed, we wake up."

Fortunately, the pendulum appears finally to be swinging the other way. New governors in three of our largest states—California, Florida, and Illinois—have made prevention a central theme of their administrations. States, cities, and counties are increasingly banning the sale of unnecessary pollutants: ozone-depleting chemicals, polystyrene foam cups, nonrecyclable plastic packaging. States are shifting dollars from high-technology medicine designed to prolong life for the already feeble to preventive medicine designed to give newborns a healthy start.

"How much better to provide prenatal care to assure 50 or 60 healthy newborns than to pay for neonatal care for one unhealthy baby," says Governor Pete Wilson of California. "How much better to prevent pregnant women from using drugs, than to suffer an epidemic of drug babies."

Anticipatory governments do two fundamental things: they use an ounce of prevention, rather than a pound of cure; and they do everything possible to build foresight into their decision making.

In a political environment, in which interest groups are constantly pressing public leaders to make short-term decisions, neither is easy. Hence anticipatory governments have been forced to change the incentives that drive their leaders. They have developed budget systems that force politicians to look at the 10-year implications of all spending decisions. They have developed accounting methods that force politicians to maintain the programs and infrastructure they build. And they have begun to attack the electoral process—with its political action committees, campaign contributions, and 30-second sound bites—that produces future-blind politicians. We will come back to these efforts later in the chapter.

PREVENTION: SOLVING PROBLEMS RATHER THAN DELIVERING SERVICES

"To paraphrase the late economist Ernst Schumacher, the smart person solves problems, the genius avoids them. Preventing disease is easier and cheaper than treating it. Preventing crime is easier and cheaper than treating it." So wrote David Morris, founder of the Institute for Local Self-Reliance, in his 1983 paper for the city of St. Paul, "The Homegrown Economy."

Santa Clara demonstrated this mentality when it fought to preserve its Great America theme park—to prevent future traffic problems.

San Jose demonstrated this mentality when it inspected every piece of infrastructure it owned and set up a schedule for maintenance, renovation, and reconstruction. The idea was to do each piece of work at the moment when it could reestablish maximum useful life at the most cost-effective price.

New Jersey demonstrated this mentality when it sought to prevent homelessness by intervening *before* people lost their homes—with one-time loans, security deposits, or rent payments. According to state officials, the effort helped more than 15,000 households in its first six years—at one-thirtieth the cost of putting them in welfare hotels.

Fire Prevention

Perhaps the sharpest contrast between reactive and preventive government can be found in a place few would think to look: our nation's fire departments. Most cities spend a fortune on their fire departments—often 20 percent of their entire general fund. Yet the United States has a terrible record. According to the National Fire Protection Association, we have the highest fatality rate from fire in the industrial world. Why? Because we spend most of our money *responding* to fires, not *preventing* them.

Many poorer cultures ingrain the value of fire prevention in their citizenry, because fires can be so disastrous. In Europe, many nations fine citizens for carelessness or negligence with fire; others condition fire insurance, which is mandatory, on compliance with strict fire and building codes; still others allow insurance companies to reimburse owners for only part of their losses from fire, so they have incentives to prevent it.

We have our building codes, but we rely primarily on massive response once a fire has begun. "We're a throwaway society," says Palm Springs Fire Chief Tom Robertson, past president of the California Association of Fire Chiefs. "We're so impressed with our U.S.A. technology that we think we can solve every problem after the fact."

Our fire departments have powerful incentives to keep things that way. If they were actually to prevent fires—by emphasizing building inspections, code enforcement, burning bans, sprinkler systems, and the like—they would need fewer fire fighters. (Fresno, California, required sprinklers in all downtown buildings decades ago; as the city doubled and redoubled in population, the fire department remained the same size.) Needless to say, few fire departments want to shrink.

If a fire department were given a lump sum budget and allowed to keep any savings, these incentives would change. Suddenly prevention would benefit the department, because it would save money. This is precisely what happens in Scottsdale, Arizona, which since 1948 has contracted with a private company to operate its fire department.

The company, Rural Metro, was founded by a newspaper reporter who lived on the outskirts of Phoenix and had no fire protection. He and his neighbors bought a fire truck to protect their area, but the neighbors got cold feet. To make the payments on the truck, he began to sell fire protection to individual homeowners. Scottsdale, then a small desert town, decided to sign up. Today, Rural Metro operates fire departments and/or ambulance services in 50 communities with 5 million residents, spread through Arizona, Texas, Tennessee, Florida, and Oregon. A for-profit company, it is owned by its 1,475 employees.

Rural Metro expands by offering superior quality for a lower price. Hence it has a tremendous incentive to prevent fires. "Most fire people talk about, 'It took us three minutes to get here,' " says Bob Edwards, who runs Rural Metro's Scottsdale operation. "But of course the place burned for 25 minutes, and it was a total loss. We talk about fire prevention more than fire protection."

Edwards worked for six years to convince Scottsdale to pass an ordinance requiring sprinkler systems in every new building constructed—the first in the nation to include all new residential buildings. Effective as of January 1986, it has reduced fire losses, insurance rates, and fire department costs. It even saves 23 percent on infrastructure costs—because the city needs smaller water pipes, storage systems, water pumps and the like. Passed when only a third of the city's land was developed, it will save $7 million in infrastructure costs by the time the city is fully built out, according to city estimates. "You also save fire department growth," says Edwards. "When you have sprinklers, you don't have to have an army to fight the fire, because when you get there, it's going to be a small fire or it's going to be out."

Rural Metro works closely with developers. Although they are not city employees, two of its fire protection engineers are stationed at city hall, in the division that checks building plans. "We work with the developer from the beginning," says Edwards. "A building cannot open without our approval."

Rural Metro has also made Scottsdale the only city in the state to use "gray" water—treated wastewater—in its firefighting system. The result of all this innovation: Scottsdale's fire department costs just over half the national average for a city its size. It has safer buildings, too: between 1986 and 1991, while the assessed value of property in Scottsdale shot up by 86 percent, fire losses decreased by 15 percent.

Rural Metro is driven by the profit motive, a particularly powerful incentive in an employee-owned company. Fairfield's Public Safety Department (which includes both police and fire) does not make a profit, but it does get a lump sum budget and it is allowed to keep its savings. Hence it has some of Rural Metro's incentives. Not surprisingly, it has assigned a dozen people to work on prevention. The fire division members do everything from code enforcement and safety checks on new developments to installation of sprinkler systems and smoke alarms for senior citizens and the handicapped. Fairfield's fire division costs were the sixth lowest of 65 Bay Area cities when the city last surveyed them. Yet it had a better insurance rating than all but two other cities in its county.

Other forms of prevention have emerged even in cities like Boston and New York, which have cut arson rates by studying fire patterns, vacancy rates, and tax arrearages, then intervening in areas where arson appeared likely. Several cities in California are operating a Cooperative Home Insurance Program, in which homeowners are eligible for lower insurance rates (from a private company) if they pass a comprehensive safety inspection. Homeowners get a financial incentive to take preventive measures, and the city gets a financial dividend from the insurance company if losses are low enough.

Health Care

During the 1970s, the U.S. Surgeon General estimated that 50 percent of illness was related to behavior, 20 percent to the environment, 20 percent to genetics, and 10 percent to medical care. Cigarette smoking causes cancer. Fatty diets cause heart disease. Air pollution causes $40 billion a year in health care costs. Stress costs business more than $150 billion a year, according to some estimates. A research team at the University of Louisville summed it up this way: "Our mode of life itself, the way we live, is emerging as today's principal cause of illness."

Yet we respond to illness primarily with medical care. In 1983, we spent 7 times as much on medical care as on environmental controls and 20 times as much on medical care as on self-care medication, fitness equipment, and nutrition, according to the Congressional Office of Technology Assessment.

As the industrial era has given way to the information age, people have begun to pay more attention to the maintenance of health. Americans have begun jogging, doing aerobics, and pumping iron. Many have quit smoking and changed their diets. Companies have given their employees incentives to join health clubs, and health maintenance organizations (HMOs) have done the same with their patients.

Our governments have also tried to change our behavior. Health warnings on cigarette packages have had some impact. The federal government has banned smoking on airplanes. Many jurisdictions have required nonsmoking areas in restaurants or banned smoking in public buildings. California has required health warnings on all alcoholic beverages and in all premises that sell alcohol.

Other governments have begun to shift their health care spending ever so slightly from remediation to prevention. The federal government in 1990 mandated broader Medicaid coverage for pregnant women, infants, and children under six. Several states have recently put new money into preventive services for low-income pregnant women and their babies.

The boldest moves have come in Oregon, which halted Medicaid funding for transplants in 1987, using the money instead to expand care for pregnant mothers. The state then asked for federal waivers to eliminate Medicaid funding for other high-technology procedures, so it could afford to expand coverage to 80,000 poor people now ineligible for welfare. "We had to ask: Is our objective to guarantee all Oregonians access to health care or to keep all Oregonians healthy?" said Dr. John Kitzhaber, the physician-senator behind Oregon's effort. "We decided our objective was to keep all Oregonians healthy."

Environmental Protection

Prevention has made its greatest strides in the environmental arena. *Governing* magazine summed the situation up this way in 1991:

> *At present, federal and state regulations—and consequently, most technology development—focus on "waste destruction and separation." The intent is to treat the pollutants to reduce the level emitted into the atmosphere by a smokestack, tailpipe or water discharge system.*
>
> *Meanwhile, there is a growing trend toward "pollution prevention" and "waste reduction." This entails reducing production of pollution at the source, through recycling, use of materials that pollute less and reliance on "cleaner" energy sources.*

Prevention has scored some notable victories already: the mandatory bottle deposit laws passed by 10 states; the federal ban on lead in paint and gasoline; and federal bans on other toxic chemicals. In addition:

- Vermont banned the sale of new cars that use ozone-depleting chemicals in their air-conditioning units.

- Nearly 30 jurisdictions have banned polystyrene (Styrofoam) or other plastic packaging, including Minnesota, Maine, and Vermont.

- California in 1990 enacted a plan requiring drastic cuts in air pollution from automobiles.

- Massachusetts in 1989 required companies that produce toxic wastes to reduce their production; the state provides technical assistance, which is funded by a tax on firms that use toxic materials.

- By 1990, 10 states and dozens of cities, including New York City, had implemented mandatory recycling plans.

- New York, California, Connecticut, and Wisconsin have passed laws or negotiated agreements requiring newspaper publishers to use a certain percentage of recycled paper.

- Ohio's Solid Waste Management Advisory Council, a statewide steering organization, has adopted a comprehensive plan that calls for a 25 percent reduction in landfilled waste in five years through recycling and prevention.

- Suffolk County, New York, banned nonrecyclable plastic, polystyrene, and polyvinyl chloride packaging unless it enters the county as part of an existing package. It took the action after its infamous garbage barge could not find a home in 1987 and the state ordered it to close its landfills by 1990.

So many governments have jumped on the prevention bandwagon that industry has mobilized to curb production of pollutants on a voluntary basis—to head off more draconian measures. Dupont, Procter & Gamble, and other large oil, chemical, and consumer product corporations have formed the Council for Solid Waste Solutions, which has committed to a goal of recycling 25 percent of all plastic bottles by 1995. McDonald's has stopped selling food in polystyrene containers. Dow Chemical has launched a Waste Reduction Always Pays (WRAP) program, which taps employees' ideas to curb the company's use of toxic chemicals. In its first year alone, an investment of $3 million eliminated 57 million pounds of pollutants and generated a return on investment of 84 percent, according to Dow.

GOVERNING WITH FORESIGHT: ANTICIPATING THE FUTURE

Some governments are not only trying to prevent problems, they are working to anticipate the future—to give themselves radar. This is extremely difficult in today's short-term political environment. But it is also extremely important, given the pace of change and the tremendous pressure on politicians to sell out the future.

It is said that there are three types of people in the world: those who make things happen; those who watch things happen; and those who don't know what hit them. This is equally true of governments. Unfortunately, most of our governments don't know what hit them.

When the National Conference of State Legislatures asked legislative leaders several years ago what state governments needed to improve the most, the virtually unanimous answer was their capacity to grapple with long-range problems. "We in government react to crisis," says Andrea Duncan, who runs the Housing Authority of Louisville. "We wait until there's a mess on our hands and then say, 'Now what do we do?' instead of thinking, 'Okay, what's coming down the road? Let's plan for this and anticipate it.' "

The problem has its roots, in part, in the demassification of American society. During the industrial era, our political system evolved to respond to the needs of a mass society. Power was shared between large blocks—principally business, labor, and agriculture. Each had its representative organizations: the Chamber of Commerce, the AFL-CIO, the Farm Bureau. Political campaigns were financed by such groups, and political consensus was brokered between such organizations. But today our mass society has fractured into thousands of pieces. "Instead of a few widely voiced, class-based slogans calling, say, for jobs or housing or social security, the political decision-maker today faces a clamor of competing, often contradictory demands from" single interest groups, Alvin Toffler wrote more than a decade ago. "Designed to respond to mass movements, mass opinion, mass media, and large flows of relatively simple information, the system is now struggling against a tidal wave of de-massified mini-movements, de-massified opinions, increasingly de-massified communications media, and torrents of specialized data pouring in through fast-multiplying channels."

Toffler argued that we needed political systems capable of sifting through this noise to find the common interest—processes that could bring together many different constituencies to hammer out a collective vision of the future. At the end of his 1970 book, *Future Shock*, he coined a phrase for his solution: "Anticipatory democracy."

Futures Commissions

In the last 20 years, anticipatory processes have become increasingly common. The simplest technique, in a political environment, is the Futures Commission—a process through which citizens analyze trends, develop alternative scenarios of the future, and establish recommendations and goals for the community. Futures commissions are often created by communities that have experienced some form of trauma, such as economic collapse.

The first big futures project, in fact, took place in Dallas after the shock of President Kennedy's assassination. Suddenly characterized by the national media as "the hate capital of the nation," Dallas found itself under attack for its ultraconservatism, its business-dominated power structure, and its resistance to civil rights. To counter this image, the mayor resigned to run against a conservative incumbent congressman, and the business-dominated Charter Citizens Association nominated an activist businessman named Erik Jonsson for mayor.

Jonsson proposed a Goals for Dallas program—"a systematic process of determining what was to be done, how we were to do it, when we were going to do it, and what tools and resources were available." The idea was to move city government out of its short-term posture. "When I came to city hall," Jonsson later explained, "I found that essentially we were living on a one-year basis. You presented to the council a one-year budget on August 15. On October 1 you accepted or rejected the final budget . . . and that was what you did in the succeeding year. That was no way to run a railroad or a city."

Goals for Dallas began in 1965, when Jonsson appointed a one-year planning committee of 26 influential citizens. They spent nine months developing a set of 98 goals in 12 general areas. They then held a series of neighborhood meetings, revising the goals in between each round. After they published their final goals, they organized 12 committees to push the relevant public and private agencies to fulfill them. By 1972, the city had achieved nearly 27 percent of the goals and made "substantial progress" toward 43 percent more. More than 100,000 citizens had participated in the process.

It is impossible to establish cause and effect with any precision, but significant bond referenda passed in 1967 and 1972, to redevelop downtown Dallas, improve the flood control system, build an airport, and so on. Other goals that were achieved included a vast increase in green space and a major expansion of the community college system. The entire process had a significant impact on city government. "Goals for Dallas was to some degree responsible for the more sophisticated city budget, the better information system, and the overall improved management system," said then city manager George Schrader. "The city . . . was forced to make these improvements in order to respond to the goals set by the citizens."

At least 170 other governments have followed in Dallas' footsteps, according to the Institute for Alternative Futures—including the Carter administration in Georgia. As experience has built up, futures projects have become quite sophisticated.

"Alternatives for Washington," initiated by Governor Evans in 1974, used conferences; a Delphi survey (a series of question-naires, each building on feedback from the previous one); a se-ries of television programs depicting alternative scenarios for Washington's future; a statewide questionnaire that laid out a dozen different scenarios and asked people to choose their pref-erence; opinion surveys asking for feedback on specific ques-tions; cost/benefit study teams; and town meetings.

Perhaps the most successful futures project was conducted by the Florida House of Representatives. The Speaker's chair in Florida rotates every two years. In 1985, Jon Mills convinced his predecessor to let him chair the Speaker's Advisory Com-mittee on the Future, made up of 45 citizens and 7 House mem-bers. Under Mills's leadership, the committee spent two years developing a set of long-term issues and goals, then published what it called *The Sunrise Report*.

When Mills became Speaker, in late 1986, he had an agenda ready. In a move many observers thought suicidal because it created a public scorecard, he released close to 30 legislative initiatives the committee recommended before each session. Yet he was able to shepherd more than 80 percent through to passage. They included a series of environmental laws, a wel-fare reform initiative called Project Independence, a low-income housing program, and the Taxation and Budget Reform Commission described in chapter 4.

Strategic Planning

It is one thing to anticipate the future; it is quite another to make decisions based on foresight. An increasing number of public institutions have attempted to do so, using a private sec-tor discipline known as strategic planning. In essence, strategic planning is the process of examining an organization's or com-munity's current situation and future trajectory, setting goals, developing a strategy to achieve those goals, and measuring the results. Different strategic planning processes have different wrinkles, but most involve a number of basic steps:

- *analysis* of the situation, both internal and external;
- *diagnosis*, or identification of the key issues facing the organization;
- definition of the organization's fundamental *mission*;
- articulation of the organization's basic *goals*;
- creation of a *vision*: what success looks like;
- development of a *strategy* to realize the vision and goals;
- development of a *timetable* for that strategy;
- measurement and evaluation of *results*.

In government, one other element is necessary: a *consensus*. A government has more stakeholders than a business, and most of them vote. To change anything important, many of those stakeholders must agree. This is the piece most private sector versions of strategic planning miss, according to John Bryson, author of *Strategic Planning for Public and Nonprofit Organizations.*

The Fund for the City of New York operates an exchange program with Tokyo. "When we take our guys to Japan, they come away awed by the degree to which the Japanese take planning seriously," Greg Farrell, its former executive director, told us. "They're talking about the twenty-first century all the time." The Tokyo Metropolitan Government begins with a long-range planning process, guided by its vision of what Tokyo should look like in the twenty-first century. It then develops ten-year plans for both operational and capital projects, with specific goals and costs. From these flow three- to four-year administrative and fiscal plans, which are developed in great detail. Finally comes the annual budget-making process, which conforms to the three- to four-year plan.

Sunnyvale, California, uses a system much like this. Phoenix, Fairfield, the Housing Authority of Louisville, the Madison Police Department, and Fox Valley Technical College all do strategic planning. Oklahoma has even created a public-private steering organization called Oklahoma Futures, which develops a five-year strategic plan for the entire state economy. The plan lays out goals for dozens of organizations, public and private.

Strategic planning is not something done once, to develop a plan, but a process that is regularly repeated. The important element is not a plan, but *planning.* By creating consensus around a vision of the future, an organization or community builds a sense of where it is going among all its members. This allows everyone—not just leaders—to understand what direction they need to take. It helps them seize unexpected opportunities and deal with unexpected crises, without waiting for word from the top.

Strategic planning does not promise that decisions will be correct; only that they will be made with foresight. The best laid plans go awry—particularly in government, where leaders may go through the motions of planning but still make decisions in response to political pressures. Part of the value of strategic planning is that it helps an organization recognize and correct its mistakes.

Strategic planning systems can of course deteriorate into meaningless exercises. During his last year as Florida governor, Bob Graham pushed an ambitious system of long-range planning through the Florida legislature, involving a State Comprehensive Plan, 10-Year Functional Plans for each agency, and regional plans prepared by Regional Planning Councils. Unfortunately, when Graham left office Governor Martinez ignored the system, and it quickly degenerated into makework. When this happens, strategic plans not only waste enormous time and money, they can become actual barriers to innovation.

At its best, however, strategic planning permeates the culture of an organization, creating an almost intuitive sense of where it is going and what is important. John Bryson uses the analogy of hockey great Wayne Gretzky, whose sense of strategy is highly refined but purely intuitive: "I skate to where I think the puck will be." In an anticipatory organization, members work toward where they think the organization will be. "It is strategic *thinking* and *acting* that are important," says Bryson, "not strategic planning."

CHANGING THE INCENTIVES

Strategic planning is the antithesis of politics. It assumes a thoroughly rational environment—something that never exists in government. Even in the best of times, few politicians look beyond the next election. As a mayoral assistant in New York City once said, "Short-term planning is this afternoon's *New York Post.* Long-term planning is tomorrow morning's *New York Times.*"

Futures projects have the same problem. Even their most passionate advocates admit that few have changed the behavior of elected officials. "Indeed, there are not a few cynics who say that legislatures and future planning mix like oil and water," says Neal Peirce, the nation's leading columnist on state and local government. "The reasoning is that legislators' lives revolve around the election cycles. Politics forces them to be preoccupied with district or regional problems, to go for fast, short-term payoffs instead of thinking and acting long-term."

During the 1970s, the Congressional Clearinghouse on the Future worked hard to introduce foresight into the U.S. Congress. Judging by the record of the 1980s, the effort failed. As early as 1978, its leader, Congressman Charlie Rose, diagnosed the problem:

> *Congress as a representative body doesn't act, it reacts. Members of Congress respond to their constituents' wishes and whims. We seek quick-fix solutions to problems because short-term results are more likely to keep us in office than the early and costly attempts to anticipate emerging problems.*

Even prevention is a hard sell in a political environment. Where leaders have embraced it, they have usually been driven by unavoidable financial or political pressures: toxic wastes found in drinking water; landfills that have closed; or a Medicaid system whose cost doubles every five years.

Prevention is not nearly as attractive to politicians as is a visible response to crisis. Prevention is quiet, but politicians who mount all-out attacks on symptoms generate great publicity. Prevention is also threatening to industry, because it requires difficult changes in production practices. It is subversive to companies that sell remediation—which explains why solid waste companies often block efforts to reduce the volume of garbage. And it is even threatening within public bureaucracies, because it renders some of the professional problem solvers—like social workers and fire fighters—obsolete.

When political parties were stronger, they could at times overcome such pressures. A president could define a coherent, long-term platform and use party discipline both to force legislators to come along and to give them political cover when they did so. ("I know my constituents don't like it, but I did it for my president.") In parliamentary systems, this is still the case. But in the United States, our political parties are so weak that legislators operate largely as individuals, raising their own money and rising or falling on their own reputation and voting record. Hence they have virtually no incentive to look beyond the short-term interests of their constituents. And in an electoral system dominated by money, that often means the short-term interests of their largest campaign contributors.

There are ways to build in foresight, despite the political environment. In Florida, the legislature came along because House Speaker Jon Mills lead the effort. Elsewhere strong governors or mayors have forced foresight on legislatures or councils. But if we depend on extraordinary leadership, anticipatory government will remain the exception. To make it the rule, we must change the incentives that drive decision makers. Entrepreneurial governments have attempted to do this in several ways: by changing budget systems, changing accounting systems, creating regional governments, and reforming the electoral system.

Long-Term Budgeting

Most American governments use one-year budgets; a few budget for two years at a time. In either case, their leaders act with information only about the short-term impact of their decisions. Typically, they have no idea what will happen to spending or revenues beyond the first or second year. In today's world, this is the equivalent of flying a 747 through the fog with no instruments.

It does not have to be this way. Sunnyvale, California, projects all revenues and costs, in both its operating and capital budgets, over the next 10 years. When the city council is considering a new initiative or a change in service levels, it sees the impact not for 1 year, but for 10. If it is debating whether to repair a road this year or to wait, it sees that the cost will triple if it waits four years. If it is deciding whether to buy land for a park, it sees what it will cost to staff and maintain the park for 10 years.

This process makes the long-term costs of decisions painfully clear to the press and the public. Skeptics often argue that it is impossible to predict spending and revenues with any accuracy 10 years ahead. They are right. But the point is not to make projections that are 100 percent accurate. Through trial and error, Sunnyvale has become quite sophisticated in its projections, but it does not pretend to predict the future. The point is simply to *flag problems that loom ahead.* Any dip in revenues—regardless of how accurately one can pinpoint the severity—is worth knowing about in advance. Likewise any increase in costs.

The 10-year projections let "us begin to make policy changes before we reach the edge of the financial cliff," says former mayor John Mercer. Mercer finds it "incredible" that most cities budget on a one-year basis: "There is no way that they can tell whether a new program can be supported over the long term."

Sunnyvale has married its budget system to a long-range planning system. The city council and its advisory commissions develop long-range plans for every element of the budget: transportation, recreation, law enforcement, and so on. The council then devotes the off year of its two-year budget cycle to long-term planning. The year begins with a daylong workshop, at which the council sets priorities for the coming year. In advance, the staff flags anything in the city's long-range plans that has not yet been addressed. The staff and advisory commissions also make recommendations, in one-page position papers. At its workshop, the council ranks the items, from highest priority to lowest.

The staff then comes back at a second meeting with estimates of what it will cost to achieve each of the council's priorities. The council builds its calendar for the year around its priority issues, examining them one by one. By the end of the year, it is ready to insert its new priorities into the biennial budget.

This system allows Sunnyvale's leaders to be proactive rather than reactive. City managers are normally quite cynical about politicians, but Tom Lewcock, Sunnyvale's city manager, says he has had a revelation:

> In the right environment, all of the myths about how elected officials behave have come falling down for me. They don't have to be short-range thinkers, they can be long-range thinkers. They don't have to be people who say, "I know this is more important than that, but we're going to spend our time on that, because I've got constituents on my back." They don't have to be any of those things.

Lewcock can cite endless examples. One year the council designated the issue of open space as one of its priorities. It began with a study, which stumbled on an eye-opening statistic: because of demographic change, half the city's schools had closed or were going to close over the coming decade. This would create problems, because most parks were located next to schools and depended on the use of their athletic fields, tennis courts, and other facilities. The question was, how could the city afford to buy the closed schools, particularly after Proposition 13 had eliminated two-thirds of its property tax base?

The council developed a plan, listing those schools it felt the city had to have and those it could do without. It then said to the school district: if you sell anything, please sell these. "Ten years later, after many schools have been sold to developers, we have not lost one school we wanted to keep," says Lewcock. "We now have a stronger park system, and we have a $10 million reserve fund in our budget for acquisition of any remaining sites that become vacant." The 10-year budget was instrumental, because once the council adopted its open space plan, the budget included costs for park acquisition 10 years out. As a result, "money that otherwise looked like surplus got put into this reserve fund for open space."

Another example dealt with street maintenance. The city did a study showing what it had to invest each year to keep the streets from deteriorating to the point where costs would skyrocket. But after Proposition 13, the council was not eager to spend the extra $400,000–$500,000 a year required. Once the information was overlaid on the 10-year budget, however, the high expense of bringing the streets back to good condition if the city didn't allocate the new maintenance money became obvious. "What it clearly showed was we would literally be going broke, if we didn't spend the money now," says Lewcock.

> The mayor said, "If we don't do it now we'll never be able to afford it, so the decision is to maintain the roads the right way, or to let the road system fall apart. It's as black and white as that." And the council made a unanimous decision to spend the money. Managers tell councils this kind of thing all the time, but you had to put it into a frame that shocked them—that got them to say, "Yes, we understand this."

In 1988, the 10-year budget flagged a shortfall looming about five years out, because of a slowdown in population growth. The council commissioned a yearlong study of the problem, which looked at revenue and spending forecasts for 20 years. It concluded that while problems would emerge by the fifth year, they would become severe after 10 years. Sunnyvale was starting with large reserves, and its total budget was only $125 million. But by the year 2010, it would have a $150 million deficit. To head off the problem, the city needed to come up with $3.5 million a year in new revenues or spending cuts—between 5 and 10 percent of its operating budget. While the council absorbed this shock, the 1990 recession hit—knocking revenues down another $1.5 million a year.

In response, the staff combed through the 10-year budget for savings. It recommended, and the council passed, several fee increases, cancellation of several planned capital improvements, and a few other changes. "These are relatively cheap and painless items," says Lewcock.

> But they closed a $5 million annual gap. The thing is, without our system of projections, no one could have even identified a problem. We didn't have a deficit. We had plenty of reserves. . . . You wouldn't see any problem in a one- or two-year budget. But we were able to peer into the future and see trouble coming. Getting our council to focus on a problem that begins to get serious 10 years out, and then take action today—I still can't quite believe we did that.

The secret, Lewcock says, is to recast the information on which politicians make decisions. "One of the keys in government is to take things that aren't politically acceptable in the normal context and change the context—to create a different way for the decision makers to look at them." When you do that, "the very same issue often turns out to be politically acceptable."

Minnesota is the state-level equivalent of Sunnyvale. It uses a two-year budget, but projects all costs and revenues out four years. (Nebraska also projects spending decisions out four years.) Whenever a legislative committee considers a policy change, the finance department provides a "fiscal note" that details the four-year implications of the change. "This forces the legislature to confront the long-term implications of what they're doing," says former finance commissioner Peter Hutchinson. "They talk about it all the time—and when they don't, the governor does." Since the state began making four-year budget projections, in the late 1980s, the legislature has in effect balanced its budgets for four years, rather than two. "We used to produce budgets that were wildly out of balance in the second biennium," says Hutchinson. "That doesn't happen anymore."

Many states now do long-term revenue projections, and both California and Florida prepare serious spending forecasts. Fairfield, Dallas, San Antonio, and Ft. Worth also prepare long-range expenditure forecasts. In Washington, both the Office of

Management and Budget and the Congressional Budget Office publish five-year projections of spending and revenues, by major category. (All these forecasts project spending as it would unfold without any policy changes.)

All these measures are helpful in flagging future problems and trends. But if they are not built into the budget, they do not force decision makers to confront the long-term consequences of their actions—or allow the press to see those consequences. When a governor's staff proposes a budget item or a legislator votes on an appropriation, no one sees a 10-year spending projection—unless a fiscal note provides it. (Congress separates appropriations bills from the budget process, so its forecasts have even less impact on individual appropriations.) As a result, legislators act in blissful ignorance, claiming to have made responsible decisions. Only later, when the next forecast shows the 5- or 10-year trend, is it clear whether they were penny wise but pound foolish. "If you don't put the financial projections into the actual decision-making context," says Lewcock, "they're not very useful."

This is obviously easier in a relatively rational environment like Sunnyvale than in a highly politicized city or state. It requires that politicians trust the objectivity of the forecasts, then agree to take them seriously. Often elected officials prefer to ignore bad news, so they question the accuracy of the numbers. To make long-term budgeting work, each community will have to figure out its own solution to this problem. Florida uses a consensus process involving staff from both houses and the governor's office: until they all agree, no forecast can be made. Other communities might have to hire a prestigious economic forecasting firm to create the necessary authority and neutrality. Whatever the method, trust is critical.

Cross-Departmental Budgeting

Sunnyvale's system not only flags the future implications of today's spending decisions, it flags the impact of a decision made regarding one department on all other departments. Minnesota's fiscal notes include the impact on other departments *and* other jurisdictions, such as local governments and school districts.

Typically, governments cut spending in one department or line item to save money, only to find that it drives spending up in another department or line item—or at another level of government. Faced with a severe deficit, Massachusetts enacted sharp cuts in child care and rent subsidies in its fiscal 1992 budget. Everyone knew that would drive up spending on welfare and homeless shelters. The *Boston Globe* found single mothers who would be forced back on welfare if they lost the child-care subsidy and splashed their pictures across the paper. But because legislators did not have to vote on budget items that specified how much each cut would cost other departments, they closed their eyes and slashed the budgets. If governors and legislatures were forced to deal with the cross-departmental implications of all spending decisions, this would be more difficult.

The flip side is also true: if budgets showed the cross-departmental impact, governments might invest more in prevention. In her book on successful antipoverty programs, Lisbeth Schorr asked why governments "more readily appropriate money to repair a disaster than to prevent one." One answer, she concluded, was that expenditures for prevention typically came out of one department's budget, while the savings accrued to another's. So no department had an incentive to invest in prevention.

Contingency or "Rainy Day" Funds

The simplest and most widespread form of long-term budgeting is the reserve fund, which cushions the blow when recession hits. Many cities require that 3 to 5 percent of all revenues be held in a contingency fund, as an automatic protection against the tendency of politicians to spend every dime. After the 1982 recession virtually bankrupted them, many states adopted the practice. By 1989, 28 states required what they call "rainy day" funds—although few were as large as 5 percent of general revenues, the figure recommended by the National Conference of State Legislatures.

Oklahoma, which suffered a disastrous plunge in revenues when the price of oil collapsed, created one of the most stringent set of rules. Its legislature can appropriate no more than 95 percent of estimated tax revenues each year. If the remaining 5 percent come in, they go into an interest-bearing account to meet future shortfalls. Anything above 100 percent goes into a separate rainy day fund, for emergencies.

Accounting for the Long Haul

In any institution, people pay attention to what is counted. The budget is one method of counting; the accounting system is another. And in government, accounting systems give the long term short shrift.

Businesses and governments practice very different forms of accounting. Businesses use "accrual accounting," in which any future obligation incurred (a debt, a commitment to pay a pension) is counted as an expense. Governments normally use cash accounting, in which expenses are not counted until money is actually paid (or a slightly different version called modified accrual accounting.) Hence governments can rack up enormous future obligations—far beyond their capacity to pay—and their accounts will look perfectly balanced. Government accounting, in other words, is future-blind.

Why would governments do their books in such shortsighted fashion? As with so many of our public systems, the answer takes us back to the Progressive Era, when we last reinvented our governments. Herman Leonard described the process in his book *Checks Unbalanced: The Quiet Side of Public Spending.* "The profession [of public accounting] developed in response to a rising level of public alarm about government corruption in the early years of this century," he explained. The focus was on "control" systems, to make it difficult to steal. Because fraud usually dealt with current transactions, not future obligations, the focus remained almost entirely on the short term.

The results were perverse. Since pension commitments were not transactions, they were not counted as current expenditures. Consequently, many governments ignored their responsibilities to build up reserves adequate to meet future obligations. Nor were tax credits and deductions or loan subsidies counted as spending items, since they too were not transactions. But perhaps the worst problem was the treatment of physical assets like roads, waterways, buildings, and machinery.

Physical assets are investments: when a government builds a highway or dam, it is creating something of value, almost like a savings account. As that dam ages and wears out, its value declines—because without expensive repair, it will ultimately give way. This use is a form of spending; in business it is called depreciation. But as Leonard points out, "our accounting systems hardly notice." Since they were designed to track cash transactions, they don't record the declining value of a physical asset:

> At all levels of government, accounting records almost entirely ignore what assets are owned, their state of repair, and their value. These systems therefore imply that it costs nothing to use existing assets. Indeed, they suggest the opposite: by cataloging the costs of maintenance as a current expense, they make it seem cheaper to use up assets than to keep them in good repair.

In this way, public accounting reinforces the politician's natural preference for building impressive new structures that will win votes, rather than spending money on maintaining existing structures. (Leonard quotes E. S. Savas: "Have you ever seen a politician presiding over a ribbon-cutting for an old sewer line that was repaired?") Our accounting systems also allow politicians to cut spending for maintenance during budget crises—as they often do—without appearing to incur any expense. In reality, they are building up tremendous future expenses. Under accrual accounting, these would show up as current expenditures, in the form of depreciation. But under cash accounting, depreciation is invisible.

Not surprisingly, as we reinvent our governments for the first time since the Progressive Era, a concerted effort is now under way to shift governments to a form of accrual accounting. (At least one other country, New Zealand, has already made the shift.)

During the late 1970s, after New York City and Cleveland nearly went bankrupt, Congress began to discuss ways to impose better accounting standards on state and local governments. Fearing action from Washington, the National Governors Association and eight similar bodies created the Governmental Accounting Standards Board (GASB), to do the job themselves. The majority of state and local governments are required by their constitutions or charters to use Generally Accepted Accounting Practices. Since GASB defines these standards for the public sector, the majority of governments have little choice but to comply with its guidelines.

During the 1980s, GASB released new pension standards, and in 1990 it released standards that require governments to adopt a form of accrual accounting, beginning in July 1994. As GASB Chairman James F. Antonio told *Governing* magazine, "The whole thrust is to make governments aware not just of current liabilities but what they're facing down the road." A member of GASB's Advisory Council put it more bluntly: "Elected officials don't think of a crisis until the bridge collapses. Well, accrual accounting makes you aware of any potential crisis. It allows you to plan and program responsibly."

GASB's standards deal with future financial obligations such as pensions and legal claims, but because so many governments rebelled at the threat of being held to private sector depreciation standards, they exclude depreciation. GASB is still wrestling with the depreciation issue, trying to find a public sector equivalent to business depreciation that makes sense. The goal is something like "life-cycle costing": some accounting measure that will show a failure to maintain a physical asset as a form of current spending, so even if politicians forgo maintenance they will incur a cost in the budget. With one stroke, this would eliminate the incentive to defer maintenance.

Most governments use capital budgets to finance their long-term assets. They require balanced operating budgets, but they borrow to finance expenditures whose benefits will be long term—just as families do when they buy houses and cars. The federal government, however, does not have a capital budget. It makes absolutely no distinction between spending on welfare

checks and spending on an asset that has continuing value, like
a highway. It simply borrows indiscriminately—so debt has no
relationship to investment. The American people have no way
of limiting their federal borrowing to genuine investments in
their future.

The federal government also ignores GASB standards. But
the budget director and the comptroller general have put together the Federal Accounting Standards Advisory Board,
which is working on accrual accounting standards. Like other
elements of the shift from bureaucratic to entrepreneurial government, the trend appears irreversible. In a world of inexora-
ble change, governments that remain future-blind are simply
taking too big a risk.

Regional Government

To turn foresight into prevention, governments need jurisdiction to deal with the problem in question. "I find that the most
significant and complex problems are those questions of the future that do not stop at a city border," says George Latimer.
"Consequently, their solutions must be regional rather than
municipal."

In many ways, we have outgrown our governments. The
building blocks of our economy today are regional economies,
which radiate out from a city or group of cities: the Greater
Boston region, the Greater Chicago region, the Greater Los Angeles region. Each region has integrated needs—for public
transit, for water and sewer systems, for solid waste treatment,
for economic development. But few have integrated governments. County governments once played this role, but many
regions have outgrown their counties.

In the 1960s, the federal government pushed local governments to create voluntary "councils of governments," but most
had so little authority that they were ineffective. It also mandated regional land use planning councils, which were equally
ineffective.

Americans have always preferred ad hoc, pragmatic solutions
to sweeping "good government" reforms. This is precisely how

they are handling the regional problem. Rather than creating regional governments, most areas have created regional bodies to handle specific functions: a regional transit authority, a regional water authority, a regional planning authority.

More than 20 cities have merged with their county to create a more effective regional government—as Indianapolis did. Since 1985, eight states—led by Florida and Vermont—have mandated regional land use planning organizations to manage growth. And in other areas strong regional bodies have sprung up on their own, such as the Cape Cod Commission.

Minnesota, the land of rational government, is one of the only places that has created a true regional government. In the mid-1960s, the Citizens League recommended a Metropolitan Council with enough power, in then director Ted Kolderie's words, "to guide the growth of the entire [Twin Cities] metropolitan area." In 1967, the Minnesota legislature created such a council and gave it power to review and suspend local government projects that affected the entire region. In some areas it has been effective: in forcing solutions to the region's solid waste problems; in developing a regional park system; in routing freeways; and in structuring mass transit. In other areas it has been less effective.

Despite its mixed record, some argue that the Metropolitan Council has been the Twin Cities' most important innovation. "Individual governments can be superb entrepreneurs," says John Bryson, "but if no one is looking out for the region as a whole, it can still go to hell."

Clearly, different regions are choosing different paths. But equally clearly, most areas are under pressure to find some way to get their hands around the new problems of the metropolitan region.

Changing the Political System

This book is about governance, not politics. But as governments struggle to lengthen the time horizons of their officials, they quickly discover that much of the problem stems from the short-term incentives built into the electoral process. As the

1990s dawned, a movement to change those incentives gathered steam.

In Florida, former U.S. senator Lawton Chiles ran for governor calling for election finance reform, to limit the influence of special interest lobbies on elected leaders. In his first months in office, he pushed a bill through the legislature limiting campaign contributions to $500 per candidate for each contested election and creating partial public financing for gubernatorial and cabinet-level races. The Minnesota legislature passed a bill combining public financing for candidates for the U.S. Congress with voluntary spending limits for those who accept public money. New Hampshire passed a law limiting spending for congressional races. And national campaign finance reform began to work its way through the U.S. Congress.

Meanwhile, California, Oklahoma, and Colorado passed referenda limiting the terms of their elected officials. Limiting the number of times an official could run for reelection, supporters argued, would limit their tendency to sacrifice long-term wisdom on the alter of short-term reelection. We already do this, of course, with the president and many governors.

Perhaps the most effective efforts have not been those that have changed the electoral process, but those that have created powerful constituencies for the future. Over the past 20 years, hundreds of civic leadership coalitions, with names like BUILD Baltimore, the Greater Indianapolis Progress Committee, and Confluence St. Louis, have sprung into being. In essence, they act as keepers of the long-term agenda. By focusing on major issues that loom ahead, they create a forum for anticipatory thinking. By engaging as political activists and lobbyists, they then turn that agenda into government policy. Where political parties and elected leaders have failed to respond to new realities, these organizations have become virtually the only way a community can get a handle on its long-term problems.

No one would argue that these efforts take us far enough. During the Progressive Era, the American people reinvented virtually their entire political system—introducing the initiative, referendum and recall, direct election of U.S. senators, the enfranchisement of women, voter registration, the council-manager form of government, and many other reforms. As the current wave of reinvention matures, they will no doubt do the same. Alvin Toffler said it well in *Anticipatory Democracy*:

> *I fail to see how it is possible for us to have a technological revolution, a social revolution, an information revolution, moral, sexual and epistemological revolutions, and not a political revolution as well. . . . Simply put, the political technology of the industrial age is no longer appropriate technology for the new civilization taking form around us. Our politics are obsolete.*

– 9 –

Decentralized Government: From Hierarchy to Participation and Teamwork

There is nothing that can replace the special intelligence that a worker has about the workplace No matter how smart a boss is or how great a leader, he/she will fail miserably in tapping the potential of employees by working against employees instead of with them
—Ronald Contino, former deputy commissioner,
New York City Sanitation Department

Fifty years ago centralized institutions were indispensable. Information technologies were primitive, communication between different locations was slow, and the public work force was relatively uneducated. We had little alternative but to bring all our public health employees together in one hospital, all our public works employees together in one organization, all our bank regulators together in one or two huge institutions, so information could be gathered and orders dispensed efficiently. There was plenty of time for information to flow up the chain of command and decisions to flow back down.

But today information is virtually limitless, communication between remote locations is instantaneous, many public employees are well educated, and conditions change with blinding speed. There is no time to wait for information to go up the chain of command and decisions to come down. Consider the school principal who discovers students wearing beepers to stay in contact with their superiors in the drug trade. In a centralized system, the principal asks the school board to promulgate a regulation about beepers. By the time a decision comes down, six months later, the students are carrying mobile phones—if not guns.

In today's world, things simply work better if those working in public organizations—schools, public housing developments, parks, training programs—have the authority to make many of their own decisions.

In the information age, "the pressure for accelerated decision-making slams up hard against the increased complexity and unfamiliarity of the environment about which the decisions must be made," Alvin Toffler wrote in *Anticipatory Democracy*. The result is "crushing decisional overload—in short, political future shock." Toffler described two possible responses:

One way is to attempt to further strengthen the center of government, adding more and yet more politicians, bureaucrats, experts, and computers in the desperate hope of outrunning the acceleration of complexity; the other is to begin reducing the decision load by sharing it with more people, allowing more decisions to be made "down below" or at the "periphery" instead of concentrating them at the already stressed and malfunctioning center.

Traditional leaders instinctively reach for the first alternative. When fiscal crisis erupts, they consolidate agencies and centralize control. When savings and loans fail, they create a superagency in Washington. When drug traffic escalates, they appoint a national drug czar. But this instinct increasingly leads to failure. Centralized controls and consolidated agencies generate *more* waste, not less. The Resolution Trust Corporation falls further and further behind the complexity of the marketplace. Our drug czar watches in impotence as shooting wars between drug gangs erupt in city after city.

Entrepreneurial leaders instinctively reach for the decentralized approach. They move many decisions to "the periphery," as we have already described—into the hands of customers, communities, and nongovernmental organizations. They push others "down below," by flattening their hierarchies and giving authority to their employees.

Decentralized institutions have a number of advantages.

First, they are far more flexible than centralized institutions; they can respond quickly to changing circumstances and customers' needs. Doug Ross, former director of the Michigan Commerce Department, offers the perfect illustration. "The only way we could serve our businesses in a rapidly changing marketplace was by decentralizing authority," he told us. "I couldn't know as much about any of our programs as the people who were out in the field, dealing day in and day out with businesses. If the decisions had to come up the chain of command to me, I had to learn enough to make them, and then they had to go back down, we could never respond quickly enough to the needs of our customers."

Second, decentralized institutions are more effective than centralized institutions. Frontline workers are closest to most problems and opportunities: they know what actually happens, hour by hour and day by day. Often they can craft the best solutions—if they have the support of those who run the organization. This gives participatory organizations a tremendous advantage. Ronald Contino, who used participatory management to turn around the New York City Sanitation Department's Bureau of Motor Equipment (BME), puts it well: "On the basis of proven experience, I regard the BME worker as our most valuable resource, who has more capability to improve the organization as an entity and solve its problems than barrels of management specialists bearing very profound ideas about what should be done in the workplace. Armed with the employee involvement programs that we have put in place, the worker has an overriding advantage: it is *his/her* workplace."

Third, decentralized institutions are far more innovative than centralized institutions. The policy experts at Harvard's Kennedy School of Government discovered this in their work on the Ford Foundation's Innovation Awards. Their biggest surprise, they testify, was the discovery that innovation does not usually happen because someone at the top has a good blueprint. Often, it happens because good ideas bubble up from employees who actually do the work and deal with the customers.

Fourth, decentralized institutions generate higher morale, more commitment, and greater productivity. When managers entrust employees with important decisions, they signal their respect for those employees. This is particularly important in organizations of knowledge workers. If we are to tap the skills and commitment of development specialists, teachers, and environmental protection officers, we cannot treat them like industrial workers on an assembly line. Employers of all kinds have learned the same thing: to make effective use of knowledge workers, they must give them authority to make decisions. Management fads come and go, as all public employees know. But participation is not a fad; it is all around us, in virtually every industry.

Harlan Cleveland, former dean of the Humphrey Institute at the University of Minnesota, wrote a fascinating book about managing in a knowledge economy called *The Knowledge Executive.* "In the old days when only a few people were well educated and 'in the know,' leadership of the uninformed was likely to be organized in vertical structures of command and control," he said. "Leadership of the informed is different: it results in the necessary action only if exercised mainly by persuasion, bringing into consultation those who are going to have to do something to make the decision work." Authority, in other words, is increasingly "delegated upward." "Collegial not command structures become the more natural basis for organization. Not 'command and control' but 'conferring and networking' become the mandatory modes for getting things done." Cleveland called this "the twilight of hierarchy."

While the rest of society has rushed headlong away from hierarchy—whether through the student movements of the 1960s or the women's movement that began during the 1970s or the entrepreneurial movement of the 1980s—most governments have held tight to the reins. Their message to employees has not changed: Follow orders. Don't use your heads, don't think for yourself, don't take independent action. If something goes wrong that is not strictly your responsibility, ignore it. If you absolutely have to make your own decision, choose safety. Never, ever, take a risk.

This message is enormously destructive. For decades it has cowed public employees, left them docile, passive, and bitter. In traditional, hierarchical organizations, they may complain, but they can barely conceive of taking control into their own hands.

The resulting inertia carries an enormous price tag. "Seeing the waste, some call for *more* centralized controls," says Gifford Pinchot III. "But the waste is not being created by inadequate controls. *It is being created by removing the sense and fact of control from the only people close enough to the problem to do something about it*" (emphasis added).

To return control to those who work down where the rubber meets the road, entrepreneurial leaders pursue a variety of strategies. They use participatory management, to decentralize decision making; they encourage teamwork, to overcome the rigid barriers that separate people in hierarchical institutions; they create institutional "champions," to protect those within the organization who use their new authority to innovate; and they invest in their employees, to ensure that they have the skills and morale to make the most of their new authority. Entrepreneurial leaders also decentralize authority *between* governmental organizations—pushing decisions down from Washington to the states and from state governments to local governments. We will discuss each of these five strategies later in this chapter.

Governments that want to be accountable to their citizens cannot simply turn their employees free, of course. Voters demand some accountability. Hence organizations that decentralize authority also find that they have to articulate their missions, create internal cultures around their core values, and measure results. Accountability for inputs gives way to accountability for outcomes, and authoritarian cultures give way to the kind of "loose-tight" cultures described by Peters and Waterman in *In Search of Excellence*, in which shared values and missions take the place of rules and regulations as the glue that keeps employees moving in the same direction.

THE WORLD ACCORDING TO CREECH

Perhaps the starkest example of decentralization we came across occurred in the nation's largest and most centralized bureaucracy: the Department of Defense. According to military historian Martin van Creveld, successful armies have always decentralized authority. But during the 1960s, the U.S. military lost sight of this lesson. Defense Secretary Robert McNamara, who came to the Pentagon from the helm of the industrial-era Ford Motor Company, was a devotee of centralized systems. Enthralled by the idea of efficiency through centralized control and systems planning, his whiz kids churned out cost-benefit analyses and new regulations faster than the field commanders could follow them. Authority gravitated upward, and those on the field felt their ability to make decisions slip away.

As the military bogged down in Vietnam, the urge to centralize intensified. Ultimately, President Johnson took personal control of the war. He ordered bombing runs and battlefield campaigns from the White House. His people at the Pentagon pored over aerial photos and pinpointed targets 10,000 miles away. Generals at headquarters in Vietnam commanded frontline troops over the radio. And the U.S. military paid the price.

Fortunately, our leaders learned from defeat. When they expelled Iraq from Kuwait in 1991, they used a very different approach. President Bush, who stressed repeatedly that he would not repeat the mistakes of Vietnam, gave General Norman Schwarzkopf only two missions: expel Iraq from Kuwait and destroy the fighting power of Iraq's Republican Guards. He told the military what he wanted done, but he let them figure out how best to do it. General Schwarzkopf took the same attitude with his battlefield commanders.

One of those responsible for this philosophical shift was General W. L. (Bill) Creech—a man who remains a legend within the U.S. Air Force, even in retirement. In 1978, Creech took over the Tactical Air Command (TAC), a $40 billion, 115,000 person, 3,800 aircraft operation. On any given day, nearly half of its planes could not fly because of mechanical problems. The number of training sorties flown by its pilots had dropped 7.8 percent a year for nearly a decade. Pilots who felt they needed 25 hours of flying time per month to stay combat ready were getting 15 or less. For every 100,000 hours flown, seven planes were crashing—many because of faulty maintenance. Pilots, mechanics, and technicians were leaving TAC in droves. "The U.S. military was coming apart," Creech later confided. "It was worse than you think."

Creech had worked in the Office of the Secretary of Defense during the mid-1960s, and he had seen McNamara's passion for centralization and standardization. He decided that passion was TAC's biggest problem. The air force used "a 'one size fits all' approach," he said in a 1983 speech. "A single maintenance organization was created that was supposed to fit organizations as disparate as [the Military Airlift Command], which does its maintenance on the road, to [the Strategic Air Command], which operates out of its main operating bases for alert, . . . to TAC, which deploys in squadron size packages all over the world. . . . *Everybody* does it *exactly* the same."

In addition, everything was centralized: maintenance, parts, planning, scheduling. "Control was at the top." Every single repair call had to go through the centralized maintenance shop, called Job Control—a process that slowed maintenance down to a crawl. Moving one F-15 part through the supply system, *Inc.* magazine reported, "required 243 entries on 13 forms, involving 22 people and 16 man hours for administration and record keeping."

Creech decided the cure was radical decentralization. During the days of centralization, the air force had put the mechanics and airplanes in a central pool, separating them from the squadrons—the 24-pilot teams, each with its own name, symbol, and fierce loyalties, that had entered American folklore during World War II. Creech reversed this. He assigned mechanics to squadrons, giving each mechanic the cap and patch of his own squadron—the Buccaneers or the Black Falcons. He assigned airplanes to squadrons, painting the squadron insignia—the same as the pilots and mechanics now wore—on their tails. (He even painted the name of the lead mechanic next to the pilot's name on the aircraft's nose.) He decentralized the supply operation, so spare parts were available right on the flight lines. And he let squadron commanders plan their own sortie schedules.

Creech lavished attention on his repair and supply people, improving their living quarters, investing in their training, and spending his own time giving them briefings. He had every building in the TAC command given a fresh coat of paint, and he invested in carpets and furniture and new barracks—on the theory "that if equipment is shabby looking, it affects your pride in your organization and your performance. . . . You either have a climate of professionalism, or one of deterioration and decay."

He also publicized results, embraced competition, and allowed squadrons and bases to concentrate on their missions. TAC set clear, measurable goals for each team. Creech encouraged bases to put charts of maintenance, supply, and sortie performance on the walls. Often they put the most vital statistics on big boards out in front of the unit, for the competition to see. TAC began giving out trophies and holding annual awards banquets to honor the best squadrons. "We actively stressed competition," Creech explained. "We instituted new goals and standards, but at the same time we gave the unit *control* over its own pace and schedules to meet its year-end goals."

"It was not long before a strong comradery grew up between pilots and their crew chiefs," according to *Inc.* "And pretty soon one squadron was working overtime to beat the other two squadrons in a wing, on everything from pilot performance to quality of maintenance."

The results speak for themselves:

- When Creech left TAC, 85 percent of its planes were rated mission capable, up from 58 percent when he arrived; he had taken TAC from the worst to the best of all air force commands.

- Fighter jets were averaging 29 hours a month of flying time, up from 17.

- TAC was capable of launching double the number of sorties it could when Creech arrived.

- The elapsed time between the order of a part and its delivery had dropped from 90 to 11 minutes.
- The crash rate had dropped from one every 13,000 flying hours to one every 50,000.
- And the reenlistment rate for first-term mechanics had nearly doubled.

TAC accomplished all of this with no new money, no more people, and a work force with less experience than the work force in place through the years of decline. "What was it primarily?" Creech asked. "We think it was *organization*. We think it was *decentralization*. We think it was getting *authority* down to the lowest level. We think it was acceptance of *responsibility* to go with that authority. We think it was a new spirit of *leadership* at many levels—making good things happen."

In any organization, Creech told *Inc.*, "there are lots of people just waiting for you to give them some responsibility, some sense of ownership, something they can take personal pride in. And it's amazing how, once you take those first steps, suddenly a thousand flowers bloom, and the organization takes off in ways that nobody could have predicted."

Traditional managers assume that if they decentralize authority they will have less control, he added. But the opposite is true.

When I left TAC, I had more control over it than my predecessors. I'd created leaders and helpers at all those various levels. Without that kind of network below you, you're a leader in name only.

It's not really that hard to run a large organization. You just have to think small about how to achieve your goals. There's a very finite limit to how much leadership you can exercise at the very top. You can't micromanage—people resent that. Things are achieved by individuals, by collections of twos and fives and twenties, not collections of 115,000.

General Creech retired in 1984, but his philosophy spread. While he was still at TAC, both the European and Pacific commands adopted many of his ideas. One of his disciples, General Larry D. Welch, succeeded him at TAC, then took his approach to the Strategic Air Command, and finally wound up as Air Force Chief of Staff. In 1990, a Welch protégé took over the air force's last centralized command, the Military Airlift Command, and began spreading the gospel according to Creech. And in the army, General Vuono's Communities of Excellence program is essentially modeled on what Creech did at Langley Air Force Base, TAC's showplace.

Creech was also instrumental in the success of Bob Stone's Model Installations initiative. When he was recruiting commanders, Stone says, a funny thing happened. "I briefed a bunch of generals, and they all said, very tensely, 'Have you shown this to Creech?' I'd say no. And a couple of them said, 'Well, I'd be interested in seeing what his reaction was.'" Once Creech came on board, 40 other commanders followed.

DECENTRALIZING PUBLIC
ORGANIZATIONS THROUGH
PARTICIPATORY MANAGEMENT

In his six years at TAC, Creech virtually doubled its productivity. He did so simply by recognizing human nature: people work harder and invest more of their creativity when they control their own work. Manufacturing businesses that embrace participatory management say it typically increases their productivity by 30 to 40 percent. Sometimes the increase is far higher. "The extra commitment of the self-motivated doesn't make just a 10 or 20 percent productivity difference," says Pinchot; "someone who is fully engaged in his or her chosen work can do in months what routine attendance to a task might not accomplish in years."

Participatory management is flourishing in entrepreneurial public organizations, from school districts to police departments. Consider the New York City Sanitation Department, a huge, sprawling organization that collects the garbage and sweeps the streets in a city of 7 million. In 1978, when Ronald

Contino was hired to manage the department's Bureau of Motor Equipment, it was a shambles. With more than 1,300 mechanics, welders, electricians, blacksmiths, and machinists, it was responsible for maintaining all Sanitation Department vehicles. Yet on any given day, it could keep only half of the city's 6,500 garbage trucks and street sweepers in operation.

Contino tapped the ideas of his employees through a top-level labor committee and a series of labor-management committees. Within three years, 85 percent of the garbage trucks were back in operation, and departmental innovations had saved more than $16 million. "This was possible because an environment had been created where each individual knew that he was being represented in the decision-making process, and that he had a direct 'pipeline to the top' to voice his very own concerns and desires," Contino says. "Changes in procedures were no longer viewed as orders generated by a distant elite, but rather as a product of teamwork and a universal desire to see the job improve."

Once the department was back on solid footing, Contino began handing day-to-day control over operations to line employees. He put a machinist in charge of his new Special Projects Division, which handled all new equipment orders. He had auto mechanics help write all specifications for new orders, test all new equipment when it first arrived, and staff the unit that negotiated and enforced warrantees. He created a Research and Development Group, composed entirely of auto mechanics, which has implemented at least 50 design improvements and licensed several to private companies, earning royalties for the city. An employee team even developed a new refuse wagon, a monstrous vehicle used to carry garbage from a wharf to a landfill. They call it "Our Baby."

Madison, Wisconsin, embraced participatory management as part of its Total Quality Management effort. (One of Deming's fundamental principles is employee involvement in decision making.) Madison's first quality team, in the Motor Equipment Division, saved $700,000 a year by creating a preventive maintenance program and reducing average vehicle downtime from nine days to three. Another employee group studied problems in solid waste, where waiting time at the Energy Recovery Plant was delaying drivers every afternoon. Management was planning to spend $1 million to double the size of the tipping floor, where the trucks unloaded. But by charting the traffic flow, the employees figured out that if drivers on the East Side simply started an hour earlier, the early afternoon traffic jam would disappear.

"That would never have happened if management had hired a consultant who said, 'Get the east side guys to start at six in the morning,' " says Tom Mosgaller, TQM coordinator for the city. "We would have had to bargain 'til hell froze over to get that. But because the employees came up with it, they owned it."

Madison has even shown how police departments can use participatory management. In the summer of 1986, Police Chief David Couper called a meeting to discuss the idea of a field laboratory, where the department could test new ideas. Over 50 members of the department showed up. They chose a 10-member planning team, which Mosgaller trained in quality management.

After intense discussions, the team recommended an Experimental Police District, with 38 members and jurisdiction over an area of 30,000 people. They interviewed all department employees to find out their concerns, then incorporated them into the management structure of the new district. This was the revolutionary step: *The employees elected their own captain and lieutenants. They developed their own staffing and work schedules. They designed and built their own district building.*

The Experimental Police District also surveyed its customers and adopted community-oriented policing (see chapter 2). To help carry out the community approach, detectives, officers, meter monitors, and clerical workers began meeting in teams. Cooperation between them increased dramatically. "They used to be stratified," says Mosgaller:

The great thing is what's happened to the meter monitors. We never used the meter monitors as the eyes and ears of the police force. They were just out there writing tickets. But they see things every day. And now they know what the

*detectives are looking for, so they can help. They're our best
information source— and they feel empowered.*

Today the Experimental Police District is an enthusiastic,
motivated organization. Absenteeism and workers' compensation claims have fallen sharply. In an employee survey taken
during the district's second year, more than 80 percent reported
higher job satisfaction than in their previous assignment, and
more than 60 percent believed they were more effective in solving crimes. The top five reasons they gave for choosing to work
in the district were "a more supportive management style," a
"less rigid structure," "greater input to decision-making,"
"more autonomy," and "a team atmosphere." The department
was so pleased with the results that in 1991 it created three
more decentralized districts, to cover the rest of the city. "I
think we've learned that effective working teams are 30 to 40
people," says Couper.

Participatory management is even spreading in public education. Traditionally, public school systems have been horribly
centralized. (Before its recent decentralization, Chicago had
500,000 public school students and 3,000 administrators; Chicago's Catholic school system, with 250,000 students, had *36*
administrators.) Yet study after study has proven that schools
in which principals and teachers have significant authority are
more successful than those in which the important decisions are
made by a central administration. So hundreds of school districts have begun to practice what educators call site management—pushing "decision-making authority down as much as
possible to the school level," as Arkansas Governor Bill Clinton
describes it, to "give the principals more authority [and] give
the teachers more authority."

Dade County, Florida, which encompasses Miami, has given
authority over most of its schools to teams of principals, teachers, and, sometimes, parents. In Dade County and in Rochester,
New York, each school now has a mission-driven budget. In
Chicago's first year of reform, it shifted $40 million from cen-
tral administration to the schools, cut 640 administration posi-

tions, and turned each school over to an elected council of parents, teachers, and community members.

Labor-Management Cooperation

Many public managers believe that unions are the greatest obstacle standing in the way of entrepreneurial government. Certainly unions resist changes that threaten their members' jobs—as any rational organization would. But most entrepreneurial managers tell us that unions have not been their primary obstacle. The real issue, they believe, is the quality of management. "Labor-management problems are simply a symptom of bad management," says John Cleveland, who ran the Michigan Modernization Service. "The issue in all organizations is the quality of the top managers. And traditionally, in political environments, the top appointees have no management experience. They don't stay around very long, and they don't pay much attention to management."

When the consulting firm Coopers & Lybrand conducted its Survey on Public Entrepreneurship, it found that local government executives said "governmental regulations," "institutional opposition," and "political opposition" were the greatest barriers to productivity improvements. "Organized labor opposition" ranked fourth out of six choices.

The rank and file are "anxious to help make changes," says Rob McGarrah of the American Federation of State, County and Municipal Employees (AFSCME). They understand what a poor job many public institutions do. If change means losing pay or giving up collective bargaining, they're not interested. "But if it's a question of new opportunities, our people are hungry for new opportunities."

Public sector unions are in much the same position their private sector counterparts were in when foreign competition decimated so many American industries. They can resist change—and watch their industry decline. Or they can work with management to restructure their organizations and regain the trust of their customers—the taxpaying public.

When Ron Contino took over the Bureau of Motor Equipment in New York City, labor-management relations were disastrous. So Contino decided his first move had to be a top-level labor committee, to prove to the work force that he was willing to share power. He asked the 20 union locals that represented his workers to nominate members. "I said, 'Give me the guy in your union hall that's always yelling about how lousy things are and how they've got to change,'" Contino remembers. "That's the guy I want."

Members of the Labor Committee were relieved of their other duties. They worked full-time on improving the organization: visiting work sites to ask their members how their jobs could be improved, bringing back formal suggestions, and meeting weekly with Contino and his top managers. In a year and a half, their ideas saved nearly $2 million. As employees realized their representatives had genuine power, they began coming forward with more suggestions. Having earned their trust, Contino then created labor-management committees throughout the organization. They helped develop the "profit center" and "contracting-in" initiatives described in chapter 3, which saved additional millions of dollars.

Many unions are ready for this kind of partnership. AFSCME now negotiates labor-management committees into many of its contracts. In Rochester and Dade County, the American Federation of Teachers has been a full partner in sweeping education reform efforts. And in Madison, the unions have been important allies in the Total Quality Management process.

No-Layoff Policies

Perhaps the best way to secure union cooperation is to adopt a policy of no layoffs. As noted in chapter 1, most governments lose 10 percent of their employees every year, so attrition often creates room for flexibility. Governments don't have to guarantee people the job they have, but they can guarantee *a* job, at comparable pay. Visalia did this. Phoenix guaranteed jobs, although not always comparable pay. District 4 in East Harlem has not laid off any teachers..

No one wants to innovate themselves out of a job. But when employees know they have job security, their attitude toward innovation changes dramatically. In Phoenix, several employees have even recommended that their positions be eliminated. Since Phoenix employees get to keep 10 percent of the first-year savings they generate through the city's suggestion program, these employees have not only moved to new jobs, but earned sizable bonuses in the process.

Flattening the Organizational Hierarchy

The most serious resistance to teamwork and participatory management often comes from middle managers, not unions. If employees are making decisions and solving problems, middle managers become superfluous. Too often they stand in the way of action, because their instinct, to justify their existence, is to intervene. As Peters and Waterman put it, middle management acts as a sponge. It stops ideas on their way down and stops ideas on their way up.

With today's computerized systems, managers also have so much information at their fingertips that they can supervise far more people than they once could. Their span of control is broader. If organizations keep all their layers of management— and all the middle managers continue to play their traditional roles—overcontrol quickly sets in. Hence participatory organizations find that they must eliminate layers and flatten their hierarchies. David Couper has eliminated the deputy chief layer between him and his captains. Phoenix eliminated 39 middle managers in one year, using an early retirement program. (It saved $1.5 million in the process.) Fox Valley Technical College has eliminated one vice president and six middle management positions over the past three years, simply by not replacing people when they retire.

THE TEAMWORK ORGANIZATION

Wherever we have found participatory organizations, we have found teamwork. Madison used quality circles; the Tactical Air

THE VARIETIES AND TECHNIQUES OF PARTICIPATORY MANAGEMENT

Participatory management varies in depth and quality. Some efforts are window-dressing; some are revolutionary. Some managers simply want more input from employees, but don't want to share power. Others view their employees as genuine partners who share responsibility for all aspects of the organization's productivity and quality of work life. The further organizations move along this path, the greater the payoff. There are almost an infinite number of devices they can use along the way:

Quality Circles are voluntary, temporary teams that use Deming's methods to improve work processes. They choose a problem or process to improve, then measure results, analyze data, pinpoint underlying causes, design and implement solutions, check the results, refine their solutions, and try again. In TQM lingo, they "Plan, Do, Check, Act."

Labor-Management Committees give managers and labor representatives a permanent forum in which to discuss their concerns. The Phoenix Department of Public Works, for instance, uses quality circles to attack specific problems, but it also has a labor-management committee to keep permanent lines of communication open on broader issues.

Employee Development Programs help employees develop their talents and capacities through training sessions, workshops, and the like. Organizations that provide such opportunities and follow up by promoting from within generate tremendous loyalty and commitment. At one point in Visalia, where city employees run the entire program, both the personnel director and the risk manager were former police officers. The airport manager was a former secretary.

Attitude Surveys give leaders more information about their employees' feelings than virtually any other technique. Both Phoenix and Fox Valley Technical College survey their employees every year. When an employee survey in the Madison Police Department revealed dissatisfaction with the way promotions were awarded, the chief asked a team of officers to create an entirely new system.

Employee Evaluation of Managers, although not yet widely used, is a powerful tool. Supervisors in the Madison Police Department developed a Four-Way Check, which solicits feedback from their employees, their peers, their bosses, and themselves.

Invention Policies help employees patent and develop new products or processes they invent. Visalia will put up the money to secure a patent, then either help with development, let the employee handle development, or help the employee license the invention to a private company. The state of Oregon and one of its employees owned the first patent for raised lane dividers on highways.

Innovation Champions encourage teams of employees to innovate and champion their efforts when they do. Minnesota's STEP program is described on pages 272–275, but Hawaii and Washington State have similar programs. In Washington's Teamwork Incentive Program, teams of employees that want to make changes in service delivery, reduce costs, or increase revenues apply to a productivity board. When their accomplishments are verified, they share 25 percent of the monetary gains. In its first seven years, the program saved the state $50 million.

Reward Programs are used to honor high achievers in virtually every entrepreneurial organization we have encountered. The National Forest Service's Groo Award is the most participatory award we have seen: every year each employee can give one other employee an award for outstanding performance. Fittingly, the award is named after its inventor, forestry technician Tyler Groo.

Command relied on squadrons; the Bureau of Motor Equipment used employee teams of all kinds. Visalia and St. Paul constantly created cross-departmental teams to develop new projects. East Harlem's schools were *run* by teams. This is no accident. When organizations push authority into the hands of employees, they quickly discover that to get a handle on major problems or decisions, those employees need to work together in teams.

Peters and Waterman described identical behavior in entrepreneurial companies. "Small groups are, quite simply, the basic organizational building blocks of excellent companies," they wrote:

> The action-oriented bits and pieces come under many labels—champions, teams, task forces, czars, project centers, skunk works, and quality circles—but they have one thing in common. They never show up on the formal organization chart and seldom in the corporate phone directory. They are nevertheless the most visible part of the adhocracy that keeps the company fluid.

Nearly 25 years ago, in *The Age of Discontinuity*, Peter Drucker explained why knowledge workers require teamwork organizations:

> Knowledge workers still need a superior. . . . But knowledge work itself knows no hierarchy, for there are no "higher" and "lower" knowledges. Knowledge is either relevant to a given task or irrelevant to it. The task decides, not the name, the age, or the budget of the discipline, or the rank of the individual plying it. . . .
> Knowledge, therefore, has to be organized as a team in which the task decides who is in charge, when, for what, and for how long.

In 1972, social psychologist Roger Harrison explained why entrepreneurial organizations rely so heavily on teams. Harrison divided organizations into four basic types:

- Those with a power orientation, including many traditional businesses, are autocratic and hierarchical.
- Those with a role orientation, such as traditional government bureaucracies, are carefully ordered by rules, procedures, and hierarchy.
- Those with a task orientation, like technology-oriented businesses, are extremely fluid and results-oriented.

■ And those with a person orientation, such as social groups, exist simply to serve the needs of their members.

Entrepreneurial organizations clearly fall into the task-oriented category. Because task-oriented organizations do whatever it takes to achieve results, Harrison explained, they typically change their structures and procedures as their tasks change. They constantly set up project teams and task forces. "These temporary systems can be activated quickly, provided with the necessary mix of skills and abilities, and disbanded again when the need is past. Their use provides what is, in effect, a continuously variable organization structure," Harrison wrote. As a result, "the task-oriented organization's greatest strength is dealing with complex and changing environments." In contrast, power- and role-oriented organizations have trouble dealing with change, because both "associate control with a *position* in the organization; neither provides for rapid and rational reassignment of appropriate *persons* to positions of influence."

Centralized, hierarchical organizations also divide themselves up into many layers and boxes. People begin to identify with their *unit*—their *turf.* Communication across units and between layers becomes difficult. This explains why innovative organizations so often use teams, according to Rosabeth Moss Kanter.

"The primary set of roadblocks to innovation result from segmentation," Kanter wrote in *The Change Masters*: "a structure finely divided into departments and levels, each with a tall fence around it and communication in and out restricted—indeed, carefully guarded." Even when one innovation succeeds, the innovation rarely spreads—because the communication between departments is so minimal and the fences so high.

In contrast, innovative organizations foster constant communication, so information flows quickly through their ranks. To do this, they regularly create new teams and new configurations, so nearly everyone comes into contact with nearly everyone else. In innovative organizations, Kanter says, "job charters are broad"; work assignments are "ambiguous, non-routine, and change-directed"; "job territories are intersecting"; and employees have enough "local autonomy" to "go ahead with large chunks of action without waiting for higher-level approval."

Madison illustrated Kanter's argument perfectly. When Mayor Sensenbrenner introduced TQM, he quickly discovered that the high walls between departments were among the greatest barriers to quality and innovation. His first quality team, at the Motor Equipment Division, isolated the city's policy of purchasing the cheapest (and therefore the lowest quality) parts as one of the underlying causes of vehicle maintenance problems. Sensenbrenner and the team decided to see if they could change the policy. First they visited the parts purchaser, who agreed that the policy was unwise but blamed central purchasing. So they visited central purchasing, whose staff again agreed with them, but said the city comptroller wouldn't let them change the policy. When they visited the comptroller, he also agreed— but said the city attorney would never approve a policy change. Finally, they visited the city attorney. What did he say? "Why, of course you can do that. . . . In fact, I assumed you were doing it all along."

"This," says Sensenbrenner, "was a stunning disclosure."

In addition to their capacity to innovate, to accomplish tasks, and to respond rapidly to changing environments, teamwork organizations display a series of other strengths:

- Cross-departmental teams bring different perspectives to bear on problems or opportunities, from different parts of the organization. People in isolated departments see only the local symptoms of a problem. Teams can see the whole problem.

- Team members who are confronted with different perspectives begin to think "outside the box" of their own department. When they take that habit back to their own office, they often dream up better ways to accomplish their goals.

- Teams break down turf walls, fostering collaboration across departments. "The issues no longer fit neatly within departmental lines, and organizations which don't realize that are going to endure a lot of frustration and relatively inadequate responses to changing times," says George Britton, a deputy city manager in Phoenix.

- Teams build lasting networks throughout an organization, because everyone gets to know like-minded people in other departments. Ideas and information flow more rapidly, and action becomes easier. To get anything significant done within a large organization, every entrepreneur needs an informal network of allies.

- Teams hold employees to high standards, acting as a more acceptable quality control mechanism than evaluations and orders from the top. In East Harlem, where small teams of teachers run most schools, teachers who don't perform "fall by the wayside on their own, because of the peer pressure that's put upon them within their own collegial group," says John Falco. "If you have one rotten apple in the bunch, it impacts the others. They put the pressure on. Those teachers see themselves; they come to me. They say, 'I can't make it here.' Many of them choose to go elsewhere, or to leave the system."

CREATING AN
INSTITUTIONAL CHAMPION FOR
BOTTOMS-UP INNOVATION

To be successful, participatory organizations must not only empower employees and teams, but protect them. Not all managers want their employees mucking around with decisions. Many of the participatory management efforts of the early 1980s failed, in fact, because managers did not support them. In Madison, managers were so unsupportive in the early years of quality management that at one point, every member of a quality team resigned.

Participatory management is also risky. It encourages employees to share information and confront underlying issues. In the fishbowl of city hall or the state capitol, where reporters are constantly looking for conflict and leaks, this invites negative publicity. "The wariness of this risk is one of the major fears that holds public managers back" from participatory efforts, according to Robert Krim, who runs the Boston Management Consortium, a public-private management consulting firm created by the city to help its departments.

Rudy Perpich, governor of Minnesota from 1976 to 1979 and 1983 to 1991, created an interesting solution: a kind of institutional "champion," designed to empower and protect entrepreneurs deep within the bureaucracy. Called Strive Toward Excellence in Performance (STEP), it was effective enough to win one of the Ford Foundation's first Innovation Awards.

STEP had an interesting history. During Perpich's first term, he had learned firsthand how much state employees resented edicts sent down from the top. To cut spending, he had created a Committee on Waste and Mismanagement. It had nickel-and-dimed employees in the worst way: forbidding them from buying new file cabinets, turning off every other overhead light, banning coffee-making machines from state offices. To this day, employees in Minnesota remember when the governor took away their coffee machines. In 1978, many of them took their revenge on election day, and Perpich went down to an unexpected defeat.

For the next four years, Perpich worked for the Control Data Corporation, in its Vienna office. There he learned something about managing knowledge workers. He particularly remembers the fury when American managers told their Austrian employees they could no longer keep wine in their office coolers.

When Perpich was reelected in 1982, Minnesota again faced drastic fiscal problems. His first impulse was to create a business group like the Grace Commission, which had combed through the federal government for waste, then submitted a gargantuan report that gathered dust on many shelves. Perpich planned to call it Strive Toward Efficiency and Productivity. Fortunately, he asked Dayton-Hudson Chairman William Andres to cochair the group.

Andres understood that productivity was not something that could be imposed from without. It had to be built in from below. "The way to get it is to empower the employees to do what's right," he told Peter Hutchinson, the vice president he assigned to the project. "When you help people figure out what's right—and empower people to do it—you get great results. You get results that are way beyond anything you could dream up in the big offices upstairs."

Hutchinson took this message to the working group that Sandra Hale, Perpich's commissioner of administration, had put together to design STEP. They proposed a bottoms-up, team-oriented approach—with a new name—and the governor agreed.

The program was simple. Perpich appointed a STEP board, which he and Andres cochaired. It solicited proposals from employees who had innovative ideas, and it chose the most promising as official STEP projects. It used criteria similar to those entrepreneurial governments were embracing all across America. STEP projects had to be proposed by a team, they could not require any new money, and they had to embody at least one of six principles: customer orientation, participatory management, decentralization of authority, performance measurement, new partnerships, or state-of-the-art technology.

The STEP seal of approval did four things. It gave people permission to innovate. It offered them technical assistance. It forced their bosses to sit up and listen. And it gave them protection when the inevitable flak hit.

One of the first STEP teams convinced the Department of Natural Resources to change its attitude toward its customers. During the mid-1980s, use of the state's 64 parks was declining and budget problems were nibbling away at the parks. A group of people within the department decided that they needed a marketing program. They applied for STEP status and won. First they asked park managers to brainstorm about what their customers wanted; soon managers were putting in children's play equipment in parks and electric hookups at campsites. Then they created the Passport Club—a kind of frequent-flyer program for park users, to lure them to outlying parks that were not heavily used. Next they began accepting credit cards, running advertising, and promoting park permits as Christmas gifts. Sales jumped 300 percent. Then they brought in a private company to improve their gift shops, and gift sales increased by 50 percent. Finally, they conducted a customer survey of 1,300 park users.

During the first year after the marketing strategy took effect, the number of park visitors jumped by 10 percent. Numbers like these got the department managers' attention; in 1987 they created a marketing coordinator position and hired the STEP team leader to fill it. They also set up their own Innovations Board, to keep an atmosphere of change alive in the department.

Another STEP project, in the agency that issues driver's licenses, cut waiting time for the public in half. Yet another helped the Department of Human Resources dig out from under a backlog of racial discrimination complaints against landlords, employers, and banks. This one demonstrated the role of STEP as a champion of innovation—a formal protector of entrepreneurs within the bureaucracy. When the department commissioner refused to give her staff the time needed to develop the new program, STEP's executive director threatened to tell the governor the project had failed because top management had not supported it. The next day, the commissioner relented.

The Perpich administration learned a number of valuable lessons from STEP, which it summarized in a book called *Managing Change: A Guide to Producing Innovation from Within*. One was that innovation often comes from the bottom up. "At least one-third of the (STEP) project managers are line employees, not middle or upper management," the book reported. Another was that projects run by teams do much better than those run by individuals. The lesson: "The Lone Ranger is not an appropriate role model." A third was that decentralization requires a firm commitment from the top. Without Perpich's full support, STEP would not have worked. Ironically, in centralized institutions and systems—whether state governments, school systems, or federal programs—those at the top must often change the rules before those at the bottom can innovate. Good ideas may bubble up from below, but in centralized systems those ideas are usually ignored. To empower employees to act on their ideas, policy makers must decentralize the locus of decision-making.

New mayors and governors, who so often create commissions to root out waste and increase productivity, could learn an enormous amount from STEP's success and Perpich's first-term failure. The contrast demonstrates one of our favorite maxims: efforts to improve productivity usually undermine both productivity and morale; efforts to improve morale by empowering employees usually heighten both morale and productivity.

INVESTING IN THE EMPLOYEE

Decentralization can work only if leaders are willing to invest in their employees. As General Creech said of his troops, "You can't treat them shabbily, and house them shabbily, and expect quality work in return." We found over and over again that entrepreneurial organizations paid their employees well and worked to improve the physical quality of their workplaces. In addition, they invested heavily in training.

No one wants poorly trained employees making important decisions, yet few governments spend much on training. Accurate statistics do not exist, but virtually everyone who has studied the situation believes that government spends far less on training than does business.

During the 1980s, Paul Volcker's National Commission on the Public Service estimated that the federal government spent roughly 1 percent of the civilian, nonpostal payroll for training, compared to 3 percent in Fortune 500 companies. In 1990, the Governor's Management Review Commission, in New Jersey, reported that the state spent only six one-hundredths of 1 percent of its $300 million management and supervisorial payroll on training or development. Western Electric, a major New Jersey corporation, spent 100 times that amount.

As they have moved into a globally competitive knowledge economy, in which constant updating of skills is virtually a prerequisite of survival, businesses have dramatically increased their investments in training. Entrepreneurial governments have learned the same lesson. Visalia was the first outside organization to send managers to Hewlett-Packard's management training program. Madison invests heavily in training. Phoenix provides 25 different courses for its employees every quarter. Like many governments, it also offers tuition reimbursement for employees who take courses at an accredited college.

Some unions even invest in training. According to Rob McGarrah, AFSCME often puts up money to get public agencies to provide training. AFSCME's District Council 37, in New York City, runs its own college. "Our members are hungry—almost desperate—for training," McGarrah says.

DECENTRALIZING THE FEDERAL SYSTEM

For many of our readers in the nation's capital, the issue of decentralization is synonymous with the issue of federalism. During the 1960s and 1970s, in a burst of national activism, we overcentralized many activities of government. Between 1963 and 1980, Congress created 387 new categorical grant programs—separate pots of federal money, tied up in federal rules and regulations, to pay for services delivered by state or local government. By 1977, they accounted for $1 of every $4 spent by state and local governments. Despite severe funding cuts and passage of a few consolidated block grants, 475 categorical grants still existed in 1991. And as the federal deficit widened, Congress increasingly turned to mandates—in essence, categorical programs *without* the funds.

We centralized responsibility for good reasons. During the industrial era, those in Washington had far more information and capacity than those in smaller state and local governments. And during the 1960s, many state and local governments were unwilling to do much of what the American people wanted done—particularly the hard work of racial integration. But 30 years later, many state and local governments are not only more effective than the federal government, but more progressive as well.

State leaders have been complaining bitterly about overregulation from Washington for 25 years, and local leaders increasingly complain about overregulation from state government. Ronald Reagan promised a "new federalism" but did little more than cut federal aid, leaving behind what some call "fend for yourself federalism." Clearly, it is time for an intelligent sorting out of federal, state, and local roles.

This is not the place for a full discussion of the solution; tomes have already been written on the subject. Let us simply suggest a rule of thumb, articulated by the National Conference of State Legislatures: unless there is an important reason to do otherwise, responsibility for addressing problems should lie with the lowest level of government possible.

The closer a government is to its citizens, polls show, the more they trust it. The closer it is, the more accountable its officials tend to be and the more likely they are to handcraft solutions rather than create one-size-fits-all programs.

Were we to adopt this rule of thumb, the federal government might have fewer employees and provide fewer direct services, but its role in steering American society would not decrease. In many areas, it would still have responsibility for providing funds and setting an overall policy framework, even if it delivered no services. These would include:

- Policy areas that transcend the capacities of state and local governments, such as international trade, macroeconomic policy, and much environmental and regulatory policy.

- Antipoverty policy, which requires investment in precisely those regions with the fewest financial resources. To equalize each area's ability to invest, the federal government must act.

- Social insurance programs like social security and unemployment compensation. If we want equal benefits

278   REINVENTING GOVERNMENT

throughout the country, we cannot expect rich and poor
states to shoulder the same burden.

■ Investments that are so costly that they require sizable
tax increases, which might discourage business from lo-
cating or staying in a city or state (one obvious example
is health care). States will avoid such responsibilities, for
fear of discouraging investment, unless the federal government bears much of the financial burden.

Even in many of these cases, however, programs can be designed to allow for significant flexibility at the state or local
level. The federal government can define the mission and the
outcomes it wants, but free lower governments to achieve those
outcomes as they see fit.

What we really need is a new model of grant program, built
around the principles of entrepreneurial government. Fortunately,
state governments have struggled with the same issue and come
up with some intriguing models. During the 1980s, Pennsylvania
Governor Richard Thornburgh and his policy chief, Walt Plosila,
designed one of the nation's most successful programs to stimulate
technological innovation and entrepreneurship. Called the Ben
Franklin Partnership, it was essentially a grant program for four
regional networks called Advanced Technology Centers. Each center made matching grants, called Challenge Grants, to small businesses, academic organizations and other organizations that
invested in technological innovation.

For our purposes, the key innovation was the method by
which the centers were funded. Every spring, each of the four
centers would submit a package of applications for Challenge
Grants. The state Ben Franklin board would rate each potential
grant according to a set of criteria: the project's potential for
commercial application, the number of jobs it would create, the
quantity of the private sector investment, and so on. It would
also rank each center's past results, on measures such as job
creation, corporate match, and the ability of grantees to attract
venture capital. Centers with higher average ratings would get
more money. They could then divide up their allocation as they
wished.

This funding formula forced centers to embrace the *mission* defined by the state—commercial development of technological innovations—and to push for the *results* the state wanted—private sector investment and job creation in Pennsylvania. But it left each center free to define its own methods.

Translated to the federal level, this approach would suggest broad Challenge Grants in a variety of policy areas. The federal government would set up broad criteria, based on factors such as need, quality of program, results, and state or local commitment. It would then make state or local governments compete for the grants. Several organizations, including the Committee on Federalism and National Purpose, the National Neighborhood Coalition, and the Heritage Foundation, have proposed mechanisms along this line. Congress has even debated a competitive grant program for antidrug strategies.

This approach would create incentives for state and local governments, but would leave the job of designing and running programs in their hands. By using performance criteria, Washington could exercise quality control without dictating program structure and content. And by making governments compete based on rational criteria, it could drive them toward the creation of entrepreneurial strategies. In this way, Challenge Grants could replace categorical grants and block grants as the heart of a genuine New Federalism.

– 10 –

Market-Oriented Government: Leveraging Change Through the Market

Instead of operating as mass suppliers of particular goods or services, . . . public agencies are functioning more as facilitators and brokers and seed capitalists in existing or incipient marketplaces. As the past decade has taught many of the leading private corporations, this more entrepreneurial role cannot be performed well by traditional command-style bureaucracies

—The Corporation for Enterprise Development

If you had set out to buy a home in 1930, you would have saved up 50 percent of the purchase price for a down payment and applied at your local bank for a five-year mortgage. That was how people bought houses in 1930, because that was how banks did business. During the New Deal, Franklin Roosevelt's Federal Housing Administration (FHA) pioneered a new form of mortgage, which required only 20 percent down and let the borrower repay over 30 years. Other government corporations created a secondary market so banks could resell these new loans. And the banking industry converted. Today we take our 30-year, 20 percent down payment mortgages for granted, because the federal government changed the marketplace. Ask yourself: would we be better off if FDR had created half a dozen low- and moderate-income housing programs?

In pioneering a new form of mortgage, the FHA was practicing a form of decentralization. But it was different from the decentralization we discussed in chapter 9; in fact, it might be more accurate to call it *uncentralization*. The FHA strategy let millions of individuals and banks make their own decisions, without commands from above or funding from government. Yet it accomplished a goal set by government.

What the FHA did, in essence, was structure the marketplace to fulfill a public purpose. This is a powerful and economical way for governments to accomplish their goals. By finding the incentives that can leverage millions of decisions, government can often accomplish far more than it can by funding administrative programs.

Think of the way some states have handled litter from bottles and cans. Rather than creating elaborate and expensive recycling programs, they have simply required buyers to pay a five-cent deposit on each bottle or can—to be returned when the bottle or can is returned. Anyone who lives in a state with a "bottle bill" can see the dramatic difference it makes: less broken glass in the parks, less litter on the streets, less garbage in the landfills. Those who don't live in bottle-bill states can read the studies documenting the effects: half a million fewer beverage containers on the streets of New York City every day; a 4 percent drop in landfill tonnage throughout New York State; broken glass prevalent in only 16 percent of Boston's parks.

American governments have always used market mechanisms to achieve their goals to one degree or another. We have long used tax incentives to influence individual and corporate spending. We have long used zoning to shape the growth of our communities. We have always set the rules of the marketplace—and often changed them when we wanted different outcomes.

But when confronted with a problem, most people in government instinctively reach for an administrative program. They believe their job is to "run things"—not to structure a marketplace. They share an unspoken assumption with a deputy mayor of Moscow described to us by E. S. Savas. An old guard Communist, he listened skeptically as Savas discussed the need for a variety of service delivery strategies in America's diverse and complex cities. Finally he announced, with great finality: "You cannot have each station master making up the railroad schedule! It's got to be centralized; somebody's got to control it."

In reality, of course, cities are not much like railroads. They don't have master schedules. They don't operate on one set of rails. They don't have one task. Cities are much more like markets: vast, complex aggregations of people and institutions, each constantly making decisions and each adjusting to the other's behavior based on the incentives and information available to them.

In a city, or state, or nation, managers cannot make up "the schedule" or "control" the decisions. They can manage administrative programs, which control specific activities. They could even manage a railroad. But to manage the entire polity, they must learn how to *steer*—as we stressed in chapter 1. And perhaps the most powerful method of steering is structuring the marketplace: creating incentives that move people in the direction the community wants to go, while letting them make most of the decisions themselves.

Think of the challenges facing our governments today: a health care system in crisis; an environment threatened as never before; a global economy in which American workers need dramatically better education and training throughout their careers; a changing family structure that makes quality child care virtually a necessity. Ask yourself if your governments have the capacity to solve these problems by raising taxes and spending more money. In today's fiscal and political climate, the answer is clear. Just as FDR's New Deal could not afford to build all the moderate-income housing Americans needed, our governments today cannot afford to supply all the health care, environmental protection, job training, and child care we need. The very thought is inconceivable.

If this is true, it means that government has no choice but to find a noncentralist approach. Our governments must consciously use their immense *leverage* to structure the market, so that millions of businesses and individuals have incentives to meet our health care, child care, job training, and environmental needs. Not surprisingly, this is precisely where they are heading:

- In health care, the debate about universal health care is really a debate about how to restructure the marketplace. No one recommends a British-style public health system, in which government administers the entire system and doctors and nurses are public employees.

- In environmental protection, the Clean Air Act of 1990 used a market mechanism known as emissions trading— a form of tax on pollution—to control acid rain. Environmental organizations have begun to advocate market-based regulatory strategies, such as "green taxes," and state governments have begun to pass them.

- In job training, several states are exploring variations of the Michigan Human Investment System. Rather than trying to fund more publicly administered job training programs, they are working to create functioning markets for job training, in which workers have the purchasing power and information they need.

- And in child care, when Congress passed its first major child-care bill, in 1990, the debate was between those who wanted Washington to fund day-care centers directly and those who wanted to use market mechanisms, like tax credits and vouchers, to give low-income families the power to make their own decisions. Needless to say, the latter view prevailed.

These trends have been spurred on by the collapse of communism in Eastern Europe, a development that has dramatized in living color the superiority of market systems over administrative systems. Since the fall of the Berlin Wall, market-oriented government seems almost to have been in the air. The trend has nothing to do with conservative calls to "leave it to the market," however. Structuring the market to achieve a public purpose is in fact the opposite of leaving matters to the "free market"—it is a form of *intervention* in the market.

(In reality, there is no such thing as a free market, if by that we mean a market free of government intervention. All legal markets are structured by rules, set down by governments. The only markets free of government regulation are black markets—and precisely because they operate outside government's authority, black markets are controlled through force and wracked by violence. Next time you hear someone condemn government and glorify the free market, ask him if he really means to hold the drug trade up as a model.)

Structuring the market is also the opposite of creating publicly administered bureaucracies to deliver services. It is a third way, an alternative to both the liberal call for administrative programs and the conservative call for government to stay out of the marketplace. It is a way of using public *leverage* to shape private decisions to achieve collective goals. It is a classic method of entrepreneurial governance: active government without bureaucratic government.

We are not saying that market mechanisms always work. Many collective goods provided by government, from parks to public safety, are not traded in markets. And many markets are deeply flawed. Government is often called on to act because a market has created severe social or economic problems. In the 1930s, government was called on because the market economy collapsed. Today government is called on because the market is moving us toward environmental catastrophe, while simultaneously leaving many of the poor and uneducated without jobs, homes, or hope. But as Franklin Roosevelt demonstrated 50 years ago, the most effective way to solve a problem generated by the market is often to *restructure* that market.

Market mechanisms have many advantages over administrative mechanisms. We have discussed some of them in previous chapters: markets are decentralized; they are (normally) competitive; they empower customers to make choices; and they link resources directly to results. Markets also respond quickly to rapid change. And as emphasized above, market restructuring allows government to achieve the *scale* necessary to solve serious problems. If a government can create incentives that affect millions of decisions made in the marketplace—rather than affecting only those activities for which the government pays—it can multiply its impact a thousandfold.

The trend toward market-oriented government, like the collapse of communism in Eastern Europe, is a direct product of the information age. With information expanding at a geometric rate and change breathing down our necks, we need systems that process information quickly, that build in feedback loops, and that move information out to millions of individuals—in the form of price signals—so they can adjust as reality changes. A group of mandarins sitting atop a hierarchical empire can no longer make effective decisions for all of us; they simply cannot cope with the volume of information or decisions they must handle. But a market can.

Markets are to social and economic activity what computers are to information: using prices as their primary mechanism, they send and receive signals almost instantaneously, processing millions of inputs efficiently and allowing millions of people to make decisions for themselves. Consider our higher education system: millions of students (and their parents) sift through volumes of information, compare prices, and finally choose their preferred schools. The colleges and universities do the same with student records, references, and applications. And a match occurs. Would some kind of administrative mechanism—such as the assignment of students to the college nearest their home—work better?

THE TROUBLE WITH GOVERNMENT BY PROGRAM

"When we think of 'government,' the word that automatically comes to mind is 'program,'" Philip Power and Jan Urban-Lurain wrote in Michigan's *Creating a Human Investment System*. "Ham and eggs; government and programs. We literally denominate government's workings in units of programs."

The word program of course covers much ground. Many "programs" are actually market mechanisms. But the vast majority are administrative mechanisms: monopolistic organizations, normally of public employees, that spend appropriated money to deliver a service. When we speak of programs here, this is what we mean.

Unfortunately, administrative programs have a series of flaws, when compared to markets:

Programs are driven by constituencies, not customers. As Power and Urban-Lurain explain:

> *Programs tend to be created in response to a constituency group-defined claim on resources, not in response to demand from individuals or labor markets. But mere membership in a constituency group does not entail one person's demand for something. As a result of this confusion, things—cash, goods, services—are regularly offered by programs to individuals who may not want or who are not prepared to use them effectively. The distribution of things provided by government responds to their supply, not to the demand for them by individuals.*

This is one reason why so many government programs, created with the best of intentions, fail so miserably to meet the real needs of those they are intended to help.

Programs are driven by politics, not policy. To create a program, political leaders must put together a coalition broad enough to pass a bill and fund an appropriation. Hence there is a constant pressure to make the program all things to all people. By the time a bill works its way through the legislative process, its original goals have often been watered down so far as to be meaningless, and it has often picked up a dozen other goals. Some may even be contradictory. One state development program had a goal of "new job creation" right alongside "the adoption of high technology means of production"—which often eliminates jobs.

Programs create "turf," which public agencies then defend at all costs. "We have all heard the cry of the bureaucratic jungle," says Philip Power: "*My* program; *my* money; *my* clients." Power and Urban-Lurain again hit the nail on the head:

Agencies come to assume that if they are not sole service providers for a client population, they will lose program funding; if they lose their money, they lose staff positions; if they lose staff, they lose status; if they lose status, they lose future funding. Therefore, bureaucracies naturally tend to spend their time and attention building and defending turf, not in managing well.

Programs tend to create fragmented service delivery systems. As we explained in chapter 6, when legislatures add new programs year after year, each with its own perfectly logical rationale, the result is an unintended hodgepodge of old and new. People have to visit a dozen different offices and apply to a dozen different programs to get the services for which they qualify. Each one has its own rules, its own forms, its own hoops through which people must jump. The system is neither transparent, nor holistic, nor user friendly.

Programs are not self-correcting. When government programs fail, their managers are often the last people to know, because they don't measure results. Typically, they use numbers to promote their program, not to manage it. But markets are self-correcting. Institutions that sell goods or services in competitive markets know when they are failing, and their very survival depends on their ability to correct those failures. Since markets involve millions of independent decisions—and every participant is constantly reevaluating their decisions—markets tend to correct errors fairly rapidly.

Programs rarely die. Except in dire fiscal crisis, most programs keep chugging along, year after year. Many politicians and administrators have broken their picks trying to eliminate an obsolete program that still has a constituency. While the general public remains oblivious, the program's beneficiaries fight tooth and nail to protect it. The politicians win no friends but wind up with a determined group of enemies, who retaliate on election day.

Programs rarely achieve the scale necessary to make a significant impact. To get a program enacted, politicians often accept appropriations they know are too low to do the job. Particularly if a program is successful, demand quickly outstrips funding. Head Start, long acclaimed as a success, still serves only a third of those eligible.

In a market, demand creates its own supply. Businesses selling in markets expand to meet whatever demand exists; government programs that receive appropriations through the political process do not. Few public organizations can grow by making money, so they ignore the search for new market niches, new services, and new customers. Even when they do get aggressive about meeting customer demand, they are often hamstrung by the legislative process. "If you've got a good new idea and the market for it is really large, you can't get to the market, because the political process controls your funding," says Peter Plastrik, former president of the Michigan Strategic Fund.

Plastrik and his colleagues in Michigan described administrative programs as "retailing," while they called market structuring "wholesaling." The Michigan Strategic Fund was designed to wholesale, by changing bank lending patterns and catalyzing the formation of new financial institutions. "Understanding that our $100 million is peanuts if you look at just the $16 billion of bank assets in the state alone," Plastrik said, "you quickly realize you can't buy success—you just can't do it. You don't have enough money." By wholesaling, the Strategic Fund *leveraged* success.

Finally, programs normally use commands, not incentives. Commands are sometimes necessary. But in today's world of knowledge workers and ever-expanding information, incentives are often more effective. This is particularly true when commands cannot be enforced, as is so often the case in public policy. Bureaucracies long ago refined the art of feigning compliance while ignoring commands they find disagreeable. Antony Jay and Jonathon Lynn captured this art brilliantly in their television satire for the British Broadcasting Company, "Yes, Minister." In one scene, a departmental minister tells his chief civil servant what he wants done, and the civil servant delivers an ambiguous answer. The minister presses, asking just what the civil servant meant:

Civil servant: *What I mean is that I am fully seized of your aims and, of course will do my utmost to see that they're put into practice. To that end, I recommend that we set up an interdepartmental committee with fairly broad terms of reference so that at the end of the day we'll be in a position to think through the various implications and arrive at a decision based on long-term considerations rather than rush prematurely into precipitate and possibly ill-conceived action which might well have unforeseen repercussions.*

Departmental minister: *You mean no?*

Civil servant: *Yes.*

Harry Truman once made the same point while contemplating Dwight Eisenhower's ascension to the White House. Eisenhower had been commander of the Allied forces during World War II. He was accustomed to giving orders and having them obeyed. But now he would command a civilian bureaucracy. "He'll sit behind that big desk and say, 'Do this' and 'do that,' " Truman remarked. "And do you know what will happen? Nothing."

In 1961, President Kennedy ordered U.S. missiles out of Turkey. More than a year later, during the Cuban missile crisis, he was stunned by Khrushchev's offer to remove Soviet missiles from Cuba if we took our missiles out of Turkey. As it turned out, the State Department had undertaken leisurely consultations with our allies about the withdrawal, then finally put together a five-year plan for dismantling the missiles. In the military, this is known as the "slow roll."

The same thing happens constantly in education. When many states ordered their top-down reforms in the 1980s, most school districts quickly reported compliance. But reformers who went out in the field found a far different picture. Newly required courses were simply old courses relabeled; required "remedial" services were minimal; required tests were administered, but some teachers were virtually teaching the test before it was given. (Ralph Tyler, a professor of education at Stanford and a leader in his field for 50 years, says this happens all the time, all over the world.) To make matters worse, the commands required teachers and principals to spend enormous amounts of time doing paperwork to document their supposed compliance. They created fierce resentment. As we saw in East Harlem and Minnesota, incentives work far better.

Even when commands can be enforced, they often create perverse side effects. When the courts ordered busing to desegregate the schools, for example, white families fled the urban public schools. Today school districts are increasingly using incentives, such as magnet schools and choice systems, to integrate their schools—with far greater success.

HOW GOVERNMENTS ARE
RESTRUCTURING THE MARKETPLACE

It may seem strange to argue that there are market-oriented alternatives to most administrative programs. But there are almost an infinite number of ways government can structure the market to achieve its ends. They are used all the time; many, like tax credits and user fees, are so common we barely notice them.

The six elements outlined in the box on the following page suggest six basic strategies to change the market. We have seen dozens of examples of virtually every one, already in use. Consider just a few of the highlights (for a discussion of market mechanisms not covered here, including procurement policy, public-private partnerships, loans, loan guarantees, and equity investments, see appendix A):

Setting the Rules of the Marketplace. Governments have done this since the day government was invented. Zoning laws set the rules for real estate development. Securities laws set the rules for the stock markets. Even something as simple as the market for taxicabs is regulated by public laws.

Governments constantly change the rules of the marketplace to solve problems. Consider just one example: automobile insurance. As rates have pushed steadily upward, states have tried a variety of market reforms to hold them in check. Some, like Massachusetts, have used command-and-control mechanisms,

WHAT IT TAKES TO MAKE
A MARKET WORK

To critique programs is not to argue that markets are always better. Some markets are deeply flawed. When a small number of firms dominate a market, true competition often disappears. When customers do not have adequate information, they are often victimized. Profiteers have preyed upon the poor and uneducated throughout our history—from the days when snake oil salesmen sold bogus medicines to more recent scandals in which shady mortgage companies have taken advantage of poor homeowners.

To work effectively and fairly, markets require a number of elements, outlined below. When a government is considering a market mechanism to solve a problem, it should see if these six elements exist. When they do not, it is usually possible to restructure the market to provide the missing elements. If not, it may be better to stay with an administrative mechanism.

Supply. There must be an adequate supply of the service—whether it is child care, home care for the elderly, low-income housing, or group homes for the mentally retarded. There should be enough suppliers to ensure competition.

Demand. Customers must have enough purchasing power to buy the product or service, and they must have a desire to exercise that purchasing power. In the job training market, for instance, many individual customers cannot afford to buy training. Many corporations are not motivated to buy training, because they often lose their trained workers to competitors.

Accessibility. Sellers must be easily accessible to buyers. Often this requires brokers, to carry out transactions. For example, buyers of stock do not meet sellers of stock; instead they use stockbrokers to make transactions. In services such as job training, brokers are rare. When they do exist, in the form of public programs, they are seldom visible or easily accessible to the public.

Information. When consumers do not have adequate information about the price, quality, and risks of a product or service, their decisions will be flawed. They will end up paying too much

for an inferior product—or worse, losing their home to an un-
scrupulous mortgage company.

Rules. These are normally established through government.

Policing. As in any activity, those who would prey on the uninformed need to know they may be caught and punished.

---

regulating insurance companies and setting their rates. (Done
in the name of the consumer, this ends up costing the consumer
dearly, because it eliminates competition.) Other states, including New York and Florida, have driven premiums down by limiting the consumer's ability to sue. (This is known as tort
reform.) Three states have driven rates down by adopting no-
fault systems, in which those injured are automatically reimbursed by their own insurance companies—thus eliminating
lawsuits to establish guilt. Eighteen others have opted for
watered-down no-fault laws, which have backfired. This process
of constant market restructuring will no doubt continue as long
as people drive cars.

Providing Information to Consumers. If consumers are able to
choose between competitive providers, government can force
fundamental changes simply by publishing information about
the quality of each provider. When the federal government began publishing the on-time records of airlines, it had a dramatic
impact—far greater than any regulatory command could have
achieved. When Arizona began to publish auto insurance, home
insurance, and hospital rates, it forced providers to compete
based on price. When California required companies to disclose
all toxic substances until the state ruled them safe, it not only
discouraged the use of toxics, but punished corporations for de-
laying the regulatory process.

Visalia used information to encourage energy efficiency. For a
fee, people selling their homes can now get an energy inspection
and a rating from the Board of Realtors. Sellers pay the fee to
add value to their homes by proving they are energy efficient.
Nearly a dozen states now operate similar systems. In San Fran-

cisco, such inspections are mandatory, and sellers are required to bring their homes or offices up to certain standards. The city's Public Utilities Commission estimates the measure saved $5 million in energy costs in its first five years, even before it was extended to commercial real estate.

Creating or Augmenting Demand. Governments create or change markets all the time by stimulating demand: giving people resources with which to buy services; requiring people to buy certain services; or simply encouraging their use. State vouchers (and their equivalent) have helped stimulate the emergence of functioning markets for child care. The GI bill created great demand for higher education, after World War II. San Francisco's energy law created demand for energy inspections.

Catalyzing Private Sector Suppliers. Governments constantly make deals with private corporations to augment the supply of some product or service. In 1988, the St. Paul Department of Planning and Economic Development convinced the First Bank to commit $94 million over five years to housing and economic development loans in poor communities. In 1990, the Federal Reserve Board pressured Massachusetts banks into promising $1 billion in loans to poor communities.

Some cities have even incorporated such deal making into their zoning processes. To prevent the deterioration of its downtown, Scottsdale created a series of incentives for businesses to supply infrastructure amenities—like parking garages and street improvements. Those that do so can get permission to increase their buildings' density, height, and other factors. Seattle, San Diego, and Tampa have all developed their own versions of this approach, called incentive zoning.

Creating Market Institutions to Fill Gaps in the Market. Often private investors leave portions of the market untouched because profits are too small, investors are ignorant of the profits to be earned, or prejudice clouds their vision. Typical market gaps include loans to small businesses, minority-owned businesses, and businesses owned by women. Today many state and local governments catalyze the formation of private or quasi-public corporations to fill these gaps. This is hardly unprecedented: early in American history, state governments helped organize and launch many private corporations. Many of Japan's largest businesses also began as government enterprises.

Catalyzing the Formation of New Market Sectors. Sometimes governments help create not just one corporation to expand the supply of a service, but an entire market sector. Consider health maintenance organizations (HMOs). The first group practice prepayment plan—the precursor of the modern HMO—was created by the Los Angeles Department of Water and Power in 1929. Four decades later, HMOs were still rare. Enamored of their advantages, Congress in 1973 passed the Health Maintenance Organization Act, to stimulate their creation. It volunteered federal funding to help establish private HMOs and mandated that employers who paid for health insurance give their employees the option of joining an HMO, if one existed in their area. States have also worked to stimulate the growth of HMOs. Today, thanks in part to governmental efforts, HMOs serve a significant share of the market.

In the 1980s, several state governments pursued similar strategies in economic development. Pennsylvania catalyzed the formation of a seed capital industry, which provides early stage venture capital. Michigan catalyzed both a seed capital industry and a new financial sector made up of business and industrial development corporations (BIDCOs), which specialize in providing long-term loans to smaller manufacturing firms.

Sharing the Risk of Expanding Supply with the Private Sector. Remember the story of Tampa's Community Redevelopment Agency, in chapter 1? It was a classic example of risk sharing. By guaranteeing bank loans for five years and subsidizing the labor of loan processing, Tampa convinced banks to make loans they would otherwise avoid. "We put the market together and presented it to the private lenders," says Community Redevelopment Director Fernando Noriega.

Risk-sharing is quite common. In the 1930s, the federal government shored up the banking system by providing insurance to depositors. The Small Business Administration has long guaranteed small-business and minority-business loans. The federal government virtually created a market for student loans by guaranteeing bank loans to college students.

And many cities have shared the risk of real estate deals with private developers.

Changing Public Investment Policy. Most governments invest significant amounts of capital: their pension funds, cash balances, and reserve funds. By choosing where to invest, they can have a significant impact on the supply of capital in different markets. In 1982, when the Michigan Treasury Department was allowed to invest up to 5 percent of its then $6 billion public pension fund in venture capital, it transformed Michigan from a state with virtually no venture capital to a state awash in venture capital. Other states quickly followed suit.

Dozens of state and local governments have also developed policies to put their cash balances in banks that pursue specific lending strategies. These are known as linked deposit programs, and they have been used for almost every purpose under the sun. Illinois used one to encourage minority-business loans, beginning in the late 1960s. Santa Monica, California, used one to encourage energy conservation loans a decade later. Ohio used one to encourage small-business loans during the difficult years of the early 1980s. And Boston announced one to encourage loans in minority communities in 1991.

Public money can be disinvested as well as invested. As South Africa discovered, divestiture can be a powerful tool. Public pension funds have created the Council of Institutional Investors, which discourages corporate activities such as "greenmail" and inflated management salaries by threatening divestiture.

Acting as a Broker for Buyers and Sellers. As we noted above, markets in which buyers cannot easily find sellers require brokers. Sometimes the public sector can play this role. Michigan's Opportunity Card and Opportunity Stores were designed to act as accessible, user-friendly brokers between buyers and sellers of adult education and training. Massachusetts' Bay State Skills Corporation (now copied by at least a dozen states) acts as a broker between businesses that need trained workers and sellers of training. It uses the lure of start-up capital—typically 100 percent the first year, 50 percent the second, and a small portion the third—to get corporations and educational institutions to create new training programs. Because its primary role is to bring together buyers and sellers, it funds training programs that buyers want—programs that respond to genuine market needs. As a result, those programs have extremely high job placement rates.

Pricing Activities through the Tax Code. The tax incentive is no doubt America's favorite method of leveraging change through the market. We use tax incentives to encourage people to buy houses and donate to charities, to encourage businesses to hire the poor and invest in research and development, and to encourage institutions to adopt not-for-profit status or employee stock ownership plans. Occasionally we even use taxes to discourage behavior that we are not ready to outlaw, such as smoking cigarettes and drinking alcohol. We could of course use the latter method far more widely. Think of all the things Americans would like to discourage but cannot bring themselves to ban: pornography, billboards, junk food, violence on television. A stiff tax might do the trick.

Pricing Activities through Impact Fees. An impact fee is a form of tax designed to impose the social cost generated by an activity, such as driving or building new subdivisions, directly on those who engage in the activity. The idea is simple: turn public costs into private costs, so people and institutions cannot shift the cost of their activities onto others. According to the Rand Corporation, cigarette taxes in America are now almost high enough to do this, but alcohol taxes are not.

Consider driving, which not only creates air pollution but requires expensive roads. Roads are a public as well as a private good—benefiting all Americans, whether they drive or not—so governments do not require motorists to pay their entire costs. Unfortunately, however, they barely require motorists to pay *any* of the costs. "One economist did a study that showed that for every new mile of freeway that's constructed in Los Angeles, the actual cost of construction if allocated only to those vehicles using that new freeway would be 13 cents per mile for the life of that freeway," said Norm King, manager of Moreno Valley, California, in a 1988 speech. "The amount being generated by the gas tax right now is about one cent per mile."

If a community built a new highway to ease commuter traffic, King pointed out, general taxpayers would subsidize more than 90 percent of the cost. "Now I wouldn't go out and ask any of you to pay for the gasoline I need to get to my work; but for some reason we have no qualms at all about asking our neighbors to pay for the cost of the freeway for us to get to work."

Impact fees have become common in high-growth areas like California, Florida, and the suburban counties around Washington, D.C. They are used to force developers to pay for the cost of roads, transit systems, sewers, water systems, and schools they make necessary when they build new developments. After Florida's 1985 Growth Management Act required that local governments have the money for all necessary infrastructure and services before approving new development, half of Florida's 67 counties adopted impact fees. By 1988, 58 percent of the communities that responded to a nationwide survey by the National Home Builders Association were using some form of impact fee—a number that had doubled in the previous five years.

Managing Demand through User Fees. A third variation on the pricing theme is the user fee, which can be used to manage demand for services. Traditional governments, which focus entirely on supplying services, have discovered that they can never outrun demand. They build new highways to fight congestion, and within years those highways are choked. They build new landfills, and within years they are filled.

"Our gut instinct is to provide more," says Norm King. "Our background has emphasized the supply side: how to build more freeways, how to build a bigger sewage treatment plant, how to build a new landfill." But with governments at every level stretched to their fiscal limits, this approach leads straight to bankruptcy. We have to "look at what we can do to manipulate the demand for that product downward so that we don't have to invest those funds in the first place."

To slow the use of landfills, governments now raise the price of garbage collection. To manage demand for highways, they raise tolls, develop special lanes for car pools, and give employers incentives to reduce rush-hour traffic by adopting flextime, car pools, and van pools for employees. They are even beginning to use peak load pricing, in which they charge more during peak travel hours. (Our telephone companies have long used peak load pricing for long-distance calls, and the airlines do the same with airfares.) The Washington, D.C., subway system charges more during rush hour, and the California Department of Transportation has negotiated franchise agreements with four private companies to build toll highways that will use peak load pricing. Singapore, Norway, and the Netherlands all use peak load pricing already. According to economist Steven A. Morrison, several studies have estimated its potential benefits at roughly $8 billion in the United States.

The principal objection raised against demand management is that user fees discriminate against the poor. But as we noted in chapter 7, that depends how the revenue generated by user fees is spent. If it were devoted to mass transit, it would benefit the poor. Another objection is the inefficiency and inconvenience of tollbooths. But the technology to charge drivers automatically, without tollbooths, is already in use in several places around the country. A laser system reads an electronic card installed in the cars of regular commuters and bills them according to the time of day.

Building Community. Changing the marketplace means more than restructuring the private, for-profit economy. It can also mean strengthening communities. For example, a handful of states award grants to community development corporations, which strengthen low-income communities by developing housing, creating jobs, enhancing public safety, and the like. Washington, D.C., has a condominium conversion law that gives tenants the right to buy their buildings when their landlords convert them to condominiums. Ft. Collins, Colorado, has created a zoning process in which developers must meet with and gain approval from community representatives before they get city approval for new developments. And of course the U.S. government funnels billions of dollars to churches and other community organizations every year, with its tax deduction for contributions to charitable organizations.

APPLYING MARKET-ORIENTED
THINKING TO GOVERNMENT'S
OTHER JOB: REGULATION

Most of our argument to this point has focused on the superiority of market mechanisms over administrative mechanisms. But administrative mechanisms are used primarily for service delivery. Regulation is another matter entirely. In the regulatory arena, traditional governments use command-and-control mechanisms: they lay down rules and order people to comply.

Environmental protection offers a perfect example. Ever since it created the Environmental Protection Agency (EPA), the federal government has relied primarily on a command-and-control strategy. Washington has tried a few market mechanisms: tax credits for energy conservation; several emissions trading experiments; a small tax on gas guzzlers. But the EPA has primarily set standards and dragged businesses or local governments to court for violating them. Often it has gone so far as to dictate the technology the business or government must use to comply with its standards.

This strategy has yielded some positive results. Air quality in most metropolitan areas has improved. The Great Lakes are much cleaner than they were in 1970, and many rivers have been cleaned up. Bans on toxic substances like DDT and PCBs have limited our exposure sharply.

But the command-and-control strategy has hardly been an unqualified success. Cities such as New York, Los Angeles, Boston, and Houston routinely exceed EPA standards for air quality—Los Angeles by 140 days a year. Half of all Americans still live in counties whose air is rated unhealthy by the American Lung Association. The EPA has regulated less than 20 toxic air or water pollutants, out of hundreds. And the entire effort has been extremely expensive. According to the EPA itself, by 1990 American corporations, governments, and individuals spent $115 billion a year to comply with federal environmental regulations. Studies suggest that other methods could have achieved the same results at 25 percent of the cost.

The command-and-control strategy has a number of drawbacks.

First, it does not change the underlying economic incentives driving firms or individuals. Because the EPA's commands run directly counter to economic incentives, businesses and firms often do their best to find some way around them, legal or illegal. A great deal of time and money goes into fighting and circumventing regulations, and illegal dumping increases.

Second, the command-and-control strategy relies on the threat of penalties—but in a political environment, many of those penalties can never be assessed. The original Clean Air Act, passed in 1970, ordered that air quality in cities meet EPA standards by 1987. By 1989, 96 cities still failed to comply. But what could the EPA do? Whenever it tried to impose penalties with real consequences, congressional representatives from the afflicted cities raised a storm.

Third, command-and-control regulation is a very slow process. It requires the EPA to establish unsafe levels of exposure to thousands of substances, with enough accuracy to stand up in court. EPA regulation tends to be an all-or-nothing matter. Since the consequences are so severe—requiring industry to scale back or eliminate its use of the substance in question—the stakes are very high. Hence industry drags virtually every decision through the courts, while often fighting in Congress as well. Not only does this take forever, it makes regulators extremely cautious about reaching their decisions, because they know they will be fiercely contested.

Fourth, regulations that specify the exact technology industry must use to control pollution discourage technological innovation. Most federal regulations require that industry adopt the "best available technology" when they install new plants and equipment. The EPA defines that technology, and businesses must use it. If they develop a better technology, they have to convince the EPA bureaucracy to redefine its standards—a costly, uncertain process at best. So, unlike competitive markets, EPA regulations discourage businesses from pursuing new technologies to solve their problems. They also discourage businesses from closing down their old, dirty plants and opening cleaner ones, because the best available technology is required primarily in new facilities and industries. Even the EPA's own Advisory Committee on Technology Innovation and Economics recently concluded that the regulatory system discourages the development of innovative pollution-control technology.

Fifth, because the command-and-control approach slaps the same requirements on industries all over the country, it is extremely expensive. No matter what the cost, it requires everyone to use the same technology and meet the same standards. This one-size-fits-all approach is tremendously wasteful, because it requires clean businesses to make the same investments as dirty businesses, rural businesses to make the same investments as urban businesses.

Sixth, the command-and-control approach forces EPA to focus primarily on large institutions, whether businesses or governments. After 20 years of effort in that arena, some environmentalists believe greater returns may now be found by concentrating on individuals and small businesses. But that is very difficult to do with the command-and-control approach. It is politically dangerous to order individuals and small businesses around, and enforcement is a nightmare.

Finally, command-and-control regulation has a tendency to focus on symptoms rather than causes. Regulations require specific technologies on cars, but ignore how much people drive. The EPA requires scrubbers in the smokestacks of coal-fired plants, but ignores what kind of coal the plants burn.

MARKET-BASED REGULATORY POLICY: INCENTIVES RATHER THAN COMMANDS

For 20 years, economists have been telling us there is a simple way around these problems. "When the EPA was created," James Q. Wilson writes, "economists who had studied the matter argued almost unanimously that the most efficient way to reduce pollution was to assess an effluent charge on polluters. The EPA ignored this advice and instead sued polluters in court."

As with other impact fees, the idea is to make sure that all of us, producers and consumers alike, face up to the full costs and consequences of our decisions—*when* we are making those decisions. This is done by building the cost imposed on society by the polluter into the cost of the product—whether gasoline, pesticides, electricity generated by burning coal, or products containing chlorofluorocarbons. When this is done, people have an incentive not to pollute. And businesses that don't spend money or time to reduce their pollution put themselves at a competitive disadvantage.

Economists refer to these social costs as "externalities." Peter Drucker points out that we have built externalities into the price of business before. "During the last century every developed country has converted industrial accidents from an externality into a direct cost of doing business," he says. "Every developed country has adopted workmen's compensation under which the employer pays an insurance premium based on its own accident experience, which makes the damage done by unsafe operations a direct cost of doing business."

Some substances are so harmful that they should simply be banned, Drucker adds. But this is not practical for every harmful activity. (Can you imagine a ban on driving, flying, dry cleaning, or barbecuing?) In such cases, impact fees, effluent fees, and other market incentives have many advantages. They create powerful economic incentives for everyone—businesses *and* individuals—to change their behavior, because they drive up the cost of activities that pollute. Consumers need no sophistication about which product is more environmentally damaging than another; they simply have to look at the price. If driving a heavily polluting car creates significant air pollution, it becomes expensive. If electricity from coal-fired plants creates acid rain, it becomes expensive. If disposing of plastic diapers fills up landfills, they become expensive.

Not only does this approach give everyone clear price signals about the cost of pollution, it lets them decide how best to respond. If they want to keep driving the dirty, gas-guzzling car, they can. But if they want to drive an energy-efficient, clean car, they will save money. If they want to stick with expensive electricity, they can. But if they want to put solar panels on their roof, they will save money.

If pollution became a significant expense, industries would do what they could to avoid it—developing cleaner technologies, changing the fuels they burned, recycling materials, and conserving energy. The profit motive is a powerful incentive to innovate. A system of "green taxes," as they are becoming known, would turn loose the creativity of corporate America to find cleaner ways to live, work, and produce.

Green taxes also encourage people to address the root cause of the problem, rather than dealing with its symptoms. In the past we forced coal-fired plants to install scrubbers. The price incentive would drive them to find the cleanest and least expensive way to produce—perhaps by switching to a cleaner fuel. In the past we forced auto manufacturers to install catalytic converters. Emission charges or green taxes on gasoline would drive everyone to find the cleanest form of transportation that was practical.

Green taxes might also avoid some of the drawn-out legal battles that come with all-or-nothing regulation, because the stakes would be lower. They would give governments more flexibility: by raising or lowering the fee, they could vary the pressure. They would be far cheaper, because they would achieve their goals more efficiently. And they would generate public revenue, which could be used both to clean up pollution and to invest in activities that prevent it, such as mass transit.

Market incentives appear to be the wave of the future. During the late 1980s, they finally began to attract significant attention. Watching Western Europe debate green taxes, several environmental organizations endorsed the idea. (European nations have always had very high gasoline taxes, which have helped limit their air pollution significantly. Now they are beginning to apply the same idea to other products.)

States and cities also began to experiment. Iowa, Minnesota, and Oregon taxed agricultural pesticides and fertilizers, then devoted some of the revenues to groundwater protection. Florida passed a tax on nonrecycled paper and a law requiring disposal fees on certain containers if 50 percent of them were not recycled by October 1992. Oregon and New Jersey created investment tax credits for the purchase of recycling equipment. California's South Coast Air Quality Management District persuaded the EPA to exempt it from "best-available-technology" language so it could use new technologies as they developed. And Seattle got an enormous amount of attention by creating a voluntary recycling program that used price as its lever—charging $14 for every garbage can not separated for recycling. By 1990, Seattle was recycling 37 percent of its trash, more than any other city in the nation.

In Washington, the Clean Air Act of 1990 stimulated interest in market-based strategies, because it included an emissions trading program to control acid rain. Emissions trading is a market mechanism that acts like a green tax: polluters can pay to pollute or innovate to save money. The EPA first tried it during the 1970s. It gave credits to firms that reduced air pollution below the level set by law, and allowed them to trade the credits between different sources of pollution within the firm or sell them to firms in the same general location. The idea was to encourage businesses to meet EPA's goals, but to let them figure out the most innovative and economical way to do so. If they could reduce one source of pollution economically, they could use the credits generated to offset others that were more expensive. This stimulated only a limited market in emissions trading, but is still estimated to have saved business between $5 billion and $12 billion.

In 1982, the EPA extended the idea to lead in gasoline. If refiners produced gasoline with lead content below EPA requirements, they earned credits, which they could sell to other refiners that were still above required levels. This produced a lively market in credits, partly because buyers and sellers had far greater access to one another in the relatively homogeneous refining industry. The EPA estimated that the trading program saved 20 percent of the cost of reducing lead in gasoline.

In 1990, acid rain was the most contentious environmental issue facing Congress. The Bush administration recommended and Congress passed an emissions trading system, in which coal-burning electric power plants essentially receive credits for the amount of sulfur dioxide emissions they are allowed. They can use any means to reduce their emissions, and if they emit less than they are allowed, they can sell their credits to other plants. Paul Portney of Resources for the Future, a research organization that helped pioneer the concept of market incentives, estimates that this will reduce the cost of compliance from $8 billion a year to $4 billion.

By 1991, proponents of market-based environmental regulation found themselves suddenly in the mainstream. The press began writing about green taxes and other market incentives, members of Congress began introducing bills, and the environmental community swung cautiously behind the idea. In 1988, Harvard's Robert Stavins published a study, with Senators Timothy Wirth and John Heinz, which outlined 36 market-based approaches to environmental problems. In January 1991, he told *Fortune* magazine: "Two years ago, we were complaining that no one listened to us. Now it's almost as if night had turned to day."

THE EMERGENCE OF
SMARTER MARKETS

Market-based strategies like those just described are possible only because the information age has radically increased our ability to measure pollution and quantify its impact. Only in the past decade, for example, have we developed continuous emissions monitors that are capable of measuring the sulfur emissions from a power plant, or electronic systems that can record which car is passing and at what time, without a tollbooth. Businesses are even developing systems that can measure the exhaust pollution from cars as they pass. Technology like this makes it possible to use market mechanisms in ways we could barely dream of just a decade ago.

The Institute for Alternative Futures, led by futurist Clement Bezold, labels this trend the emergence of "smarter markets"—markets in which buyers and sellers have access to vastly more information than they previously did. One result, Bezold points

out, is that consumers are beginning to "consciously vote their
values with their dollars." "Socially responsible" investment
firms now invest their clients' money only in corporations that
meet certain criteria. The Council on Economic Priorities has
published a book that rates corporations and their products according to nine values. Environmentalist Denis Hayes, the orig-
inator of Earth Day, has launched an organization to certify
products that are environmentally sound. It will sell an official
Green Seal to companies, to display on those products. "Our
objective is to help American consumers vote with their pocket-
books on environmental issues," says Hayes. "We expect the
Green Seal to become a catalyst for sweeping change in consumer purchasing habits."

Some products already come with stickers that indicate their
energy efficiency: cars, hot water heaters, furnaces, refrigera-
tors, and air conditioners. Nearly a dozen states have established voluntary energy rating systems for houses, as Visalia
did. In the Washington, D.C., area, a sophisticated consumer
organization rates the region's health plans according to customer satisfaction, price, and other factors, for public comparison in *The Washington Consumer Checkbook*. And health care
researchers are beginning to develop further yardsticks with
which to measure the quality of various health care providers.

With computer technology, it has become possible not only to
develop such information, but to make it readily available to
large numbers of people. Think of the Michigan Human Investment System and Opportunity Card: they were attempts to create a smarter market in job training, using "smart" credit cards,
electronic information kiosks, and a computer system with data
on the performance of every job training or adult education
provider in the state. By facilitating the emergence of smarter
markets such as this, governments can empower citizens to
shape the marketplace according to their own needs and values.

RESTRUCTURING MARKETS *WITHIN*
THE PUBLIC SECTOR

Markets exist not only in the private sector; they also exist
within the public sector. When they do, we normally call them

systems: the education system, the job training system, the mental health system. But they are markets, just as surely as the financial system, the banking system, and the health care system are markets. If we applied market-oriented thinking to our public systems, we could accomplish a great deal.

Unfortunately, few people think about government this way. Even business people drop their market mind-set when they work with government. Norm King tells a story about the Palm Springs City Council, whose business members could not understand the idea of lowering demand for water by raising its price:

> The irony is that our often conservative, local business people, whose very livelihood is dependent upon understanding the laws of supply and demand, do not understand how supply and demand concepts work in a government situation or could work in a government situation. So you have five people, all of them local business people, all of them depending upon supply and demand in their own occupations, resisting the idea that consumption would go down if the user was charged the full cost of water consumed. What we have is a very interesting dichotomy. As capitalists, we believe that the laws of supply and demand work well in the private sector but we disbelieve their validity in the public sector. This in spite of the fact that properly implemented pricing systems will promote the conservation of many government resources.

Ted Kolderie describes a similar phenomenon in the education reform movement. He points out that institutions work when they create the right incentives. Yet business leaders rarely focus on the incentives built into the education system. Instead they create "partnerships" and sponsor projects. "Business's involvement today is roughly the equivalent of doing your daughter's homework," Kolderie says. "It is a kindness, but a misdirected kindness." It consists of:

> Donating computers. Giving science teachers summer training. Recognizing outstanding teachers. Motivating students to graduate by promising them a college education. Helping

pass a law extending the school year or toughening teachers' tests. It is hard to criticize such efforts. . . . [But] the test is always whether these efforts change the system. . . .

Business should be tougher. When approached for support, executives should ask the central question: "If these things are so important, why aren't they important enough for the system to do itself? Why are they done only when we finance them?" . . .

If business were thinking strategically, it would be helping to see that the schools get opportunities and incentives to innovate on their own.

We have argued throughout this book that the key to reinventing government is changing the incentives that drive public institutions. This is simply another way of saying that the key is *changing the markets that operate within the public sector.* In education, this might mean moving to a competitive market in which customers have choices and key stakeholders (parents and teachers) have genuine control. In job training, it might mean injecting information about the quality of all training providers into the system, putting resources directly into customers' hands, providing them with accessible brokers, and empowering them to choose between competing providers. In unemployment insurance, it might mean creating a financial incentive for corporations to retrain employees rather than lay them off, or creating an incentive for those collecting unemployment to seek retraining—something that is still discouraged in many states.

The idea is to apply the same analysis one would to a private market: to ask, What's wrong with this market? What is missing? Demand? Information? Competition? What elements of the market need to be improved to make it work effectively? What other public systems have to change to make this possible? Budget systems? Personnel systems? Accounting systems? This is precisely the kind of thinking Philip Power and his colleagues in Michigan applied to job training, and Ted Kolderie and his colleagues in Minnesota applied to education.

Some would call this a systems approach. A few governments use such an approach. Those that embrace Total Quality Management, for instance, learn that 85 percent of the problems in a typical operation stem from the systems, only 15 percent from the people. But most public sector TQM projects focus on very minor systems, the ones that are easiest to change: the schedule for garbage truck drivers; the way the city's fleet is purchased. Changing these is important, but the real challenge is whether TQM can address the big systems: budget, personnel, and accounting, or education, job training, and unemployment insurance. Tom Mosgaller, Madison's TQM coordinator, believes TQM will run its course if it deals only with the micro systems. "It's valuable that you improve queuing [of garbage trucks] and back injuries," he says, "but it doesn't transform the culture. If you don't move it up into those fundamental infrastructures, after a while the unions and the employees will say, 'Come on guys, cut the crap.' "

BALANCING MARKETS AND COMMUNITY

Much of what we have discussed in this book could be summed up under the rubric of market-oriented government: not only systems change, but competition, customer choice, accountability for results, and of course public enterprise. But market mechanisms are only half the equation. Markets are impersonal. Markets are unforgiving. Even the most carefully structured markets tend to create inequitable outcomes. That is why we have also stressed the other half of the equation: the empowerment of communities. To complement the efficiency and effectiveness of market mechanisms, we need the warmth and caring of families and neighborhoods and communities. As entrepreneurial governments move away from administrative bureaucracies, they need to embrace both markets *and* community.

In Washington, this would be called moving right and left at the same time. The political media are quick to label "conservative" those who embrace markets and "liberal" those who empower communities. But these ideas have little to do with traditional notions of liberalism or conservatism. They do not address the goals of government; they address its methods. They can be used to implement any agenda. They can help a community or nation wage war on poverty, if that is its priority, or lower taxes and cut spending, if that is its priority. *Reinventing Government* addresses *how* governments work, not *what* governments do. And regardless of what we want them to do, don't we deserve governments that *work* again?

–11–

Putting It All Together

[*From 1875 through the 1930s social*] *innovation took the form of creating new public-service institutions. . . The next twenty or thirty years will be very different. The need for social innovation may be even greater, but it will very largely have to be social innovation within the existing public-service institution To build entrepreneurial management into the existing public-service institution may thus be the foremost political task of this generation*

—Peter Drucker, *Innovation and Entrepreneurship*

Our map is complete. It is now yours to use. We hope that you find it a helpful guide in the process of changing *your* governments. Used almost as a checklist, the ten principles offer a powerful conceptual tool. One can run any public organization or system—or any of society's problems—through the list, and the process will suggest a radically different approach from that which government would traditionally take. This is the checklist's ultimate value: the power to unleash new ways of thinking—and acting.

To illustrate, let us offer a simple exercise. What would happen if we took three of the most intractable problems American society faces and ran them through the list? What would our health care, education, and criminal justice systems look like, organized according to the ten principles of entrepreneurial governance? We provide this exercise not to propose definitive solutions to these problems, for we are not experts in education, health care, or criminal justice. We simply intend to demonstrate the power of the ten principles when used as an analytic tool.

CREATING AN EFFECTIVE
HEALTH CARE SYSTEM

Health care looms as the next big crisis. In 1991, we spent $750 billion on health care—*12 percent* of our gross national product. This was more than double the share of 30 years ago. (Canada spent only 8.5 percent of GNP on health care, West Germany 8 percent. Yet both had lower infant mortality rates and longer life expectancies, and their people were far more satisfied with their systems than Americans were.) Our spending is growing so fast that without fundamental changes it will double by the year 2000, according to Secretary of Health and Human Services Louis Sullivan.

Meanwhile, an estimated 34 million people have no health insurance at all. Insurance firms are refusing to cover many people, hospitals are going bankrupt, and each sector of the market is desperately trying to shift its costs to others. Doctors complain bitterly about mindless overregulation by governments and insurance companies that are trying to control costs. And the situation is clearly coming to a boil: in a recent national survey, 89 percent of Americans said our health care system needed "fundamental" change.

New technologies that have radically prolonged average life spans have increased the cost of health care throughout the developed world. But inflation has been highest in the United States, because our health care system is so poorly structured. It is reactive, not preventive: it is built to treat disease, not to preserve health. It is extremely hierarchical, with too many functions reserved for highly trained, highly paid physicians and too few for physicians' assistants, nurse practitioners, and nurses. Our public programs, like Medicare and Medicaid, are overly centralized and rule-driven, with virtually all regulations set in Washington and waivers needed for any experimentation. They are funded primarily based on inputs, not outcomes, and they rarely promote price competition between service providers. Customers almost never receive enough information about performance to make informed choices among doctors, hospitals, and insurance plans, so the system is shaped not by the choices customers make, but by the preferences of providers (hospitals, physicians, insurance companies, health maintenance organizations, Medicaid, and Medicare).

Perhaps most fundamental, our governments have abdicated a steering role in health care. Policy is made largely by the private sector—insurance companies, hospitals, HMOs, and the medical profession. Government simply reacts. It rarely tries to shape the health care marketplace. It simply pays the bills that come its way—for the poor, the elderly, and public employees.

In an entrepreneurial health care system, government would play a steering role. It would set the rules—perhaps creating a mechanism for negotiating limits on health care costs, requiring that all Americans have health insurance, and providing funding at least for the unemployed and poor. But it would not try to row. It would leave the practice of medicine in private hands.

An entrepreneurial system would encourage competition, particularly through prepaid plans, which allow consumers to shop for the best price. It would allow customers to choose their doctors and hospitals. It would measure and publicize results—customer surveys, medical outcomes, and the like—so customers could choose based not only on price but on quality. It would create strong incentives for preventive care, in part by encouraging prepaid arrangements, under which insurers benefit by preventing disease, and in part by encouraging preventive behavior (perhaps by making activities like smoking and drinking more expensive).

An entrepreneurial government would preserve the decentralized nature of our system, with many different health care institutions, but would push for less hierarchy, so more of the routine medical care could be provided by less expensive nurse practitioners, midwives, physicians' assistants, and nurses. It would encourage enterprising behavior by health care institutions, making them survive in a competitive (although carefully structured) marketplace. And it would structure that marketplace to meet social needs. Simply by requiring that insurers and prepaid plans take all comers, for example, it could end the current practice of competing for the business of low-risk patients and dumping the rest on the public sector.

This kind of system would share some features of the Canadian model, but its closest—although not identical—parallel is in Germany (actually, in the former West Germany). The German government steers the system, which consists of more than 1,000 insurance companies (most of which are nonprofits, much like Blue Cross/Blue Shield), but pays for less than 14 percent of the care. (Government in the United States does little steering but pays for more than 40 percent of all health care.) The German government requires that everyone have health insurance, but subsidizes only the unemployed and self-employed. Premiums are paid through payroll deductions, split 50–50 between employer and employee. Consumers choose their doctors and their insurance company, but the government sets uniform payment rules and procedures, as well as limits on overall costs. Doctors' rates are set through negotiation with the insurance funds.

The German system is the best in the world, in the opinion of many experts. Germans spend just over half as much as we do, per capita, on health care. They devote only 8 percent of GNP to health care, compared to our 12 percent. They hold medical inflation in check better than any other developed nation. Yet everyone has health insurance, and they enjoy far more liberal benefits than Americans.

REINVENTING PUBLIC EDUCATION

Traditional public education is a classic example of the bureaucratic model. It is centralized, top-down, and rule-driven; each school is a monopoly; customers have little choice; and no one's job depends on their performance. It is a system that guarantees stability, not change.

Public education's customers—children, families, and employers—have changed dramatically over the past 50 years. Yet most schools look just like they did 50 years ago. We still require most children to attend the school closest to their home, as we did in the days of the horse and buggy. We still organize school calendars as if children were needed on the farm all summer. We still schedule the day as if Mom will be home at 3 P.M. We still put each student through the same 12-year program, grade by grade. We still measure students' progress in course credits, using a system designed in 1910. And we still put teachers in front of rows of children, primarily to talk.

"We know based on research that people remember about 10 percent of what they hear, 20 percent of what they see, 40 percent of what they discuss and 90 percent of what they do," says Adam Urbanski, vice president of the American Federation of Teachers. "But we still largely use one teaching style: 'I talk, you listen and you learn.' "

In 1983, with the publication of *A Nation at Risk*, our leaders announced what most Americans already knew: the old system was failing us. During the 1980s, they tried all the conventional medicine. They increased total spending on public education by 29 percent, after inflation. They passed major education reform bills in 47 states, most of which accepted the old model but commanded it to speed up—by requiring more courses, more tests, and more time in school.

Critics dubbed this the "more-longer-harder" strategy of education reform. Like most command-and-control strategies, it failed. Dropout rates were higher in 1990 than they had been in 1980. Scores on the two major college entrance exams (the SAT and ACT) rose only about 1.5 percent between 1982 and 1987, then leveled off or dropped. In tests used to compare student achievement in advanced industrial nations, we were in worse shape in 1990 than in 1980.

By the late 1980s, many education reformers had given up on traditional answers. A consensus began to emerge around the idea of restructuring. In September 1989, at their Education Summit, the president and the governors adopted restructuring as their agenda, endorsing a number of the principles of entrepreneurial governance: "greater choice for parents and students"; "a system of accountability that focuses on results, rather than on compliance with rules and regulations"; "decentralization of authority and decision-making responsibility to the school site"; a personnel system "that provides real rewards for success with students" and "real consequences for failure";

and "active, sustained parental and business community involvement."

What would a school system restructured according to these and the other five principles look like?

State governments and school boards would steer the system but let others row. They would set minimum standards, measure performance, enforce goals such as racial integration and social equity, and establish the financing mechanisms necessary to achieve their standards and goals. But the school districts would not *operate* the schools. Public schools would be run—on something like a contract or voucher basis—by many different organizations: teachers, colleges, even community organizations. It would be relatively easy to create a new public school. Teachers would work for the school, not the school district. Steering would be separate from rowing.

Parents would have a great deal of control over their children's schools—as in New Haven or Chicago. Schools would have to compete to attract students, and each school's funding might depend on the number of students it could attract. Yet each school would be relatively free to define and pursue its own mission. Most authority would be at the school level, and district or statewide rules would be kept to a minimum. Those who ran each school would have to meet very basic state and school board standards for curriculum, length of school day, and so on. But they would have far greater freedom to create the kind of school they felt would best meet the needs of their customers. Each school would develop its own budget, based on the number of students it attracted, and would retain any funds it did not spend. It would decide how much to pay its teachers, whether to provide performance bonuses, whom to hire, and whom to fire. Tenure would be eliminated or radically redefined.

The state would measure and publicize many different kinds of results: test scores; evaluations of students' other work; parent, student, and teacher satisfaction surveys; honors won by students (both academic and nonacademic); dropout rates; college placement rates; perhaps even evaluations by neutral panels of expert observers. The system's primary customers—parents—would use this information to choose the schools their children attended. By measuring performance but letting parents choose, school boards and state departments of education would avoid the subjective task of rating schools. They would let parents decide which schools were best for their children.

Schools would seek to prevent problems rather than constantly trying to remediate failure. Hence they might begin to work with families to solve problems at home, before children arrived at school unprepared. They might work with communities to attack the problems that were undermining the success of their students, whether drug use, violence, or lack of connection to the world of work. They might sponsor preschool programs and Head Start centers.

Schools would be encouraged to earn more money by attracting more students, starting another school, or providing new services. Have you ever wondered why most public schools have not offered nursery school, or before- and after-school care—or simply rented space to other organizations to do so? Were they allowed to keep their revenues, they no doubt would. Have you ever wondered why a new industry of private learning centers has sprung up to sell remedial education, after school, but the public schools don't compete for the business? If they could earn revenue by doing so, perhaps they would. Blue Hills Regional Technical School, a high school in Canton, Massachusetts, has recruited adults to receive training alongside its high school students—because it can charge $2,500 per adult in tuition. When demographics cut down the pool of customers from which it drew, the school acted like any business would: it went looking for other customers. Its staff loves the idea, because the serious attitude of the older trainees rubs off on the high-schoolers.

Finally, our state governments and local school boards would solve problems that arose by changing the rules and incentives of the system they had created. If racial segregation were a concern, for example, they might require a certain percentage of minority students in every school, as some districts do. If schools in poor communities began to close, so poor students lost their neighborhood schools, they might create financial incentives for teachers to create new public schools in those neighborhoods, or change the funding formula to award more money to schools with large numbers of disadvantaged students.

Together, these changes would create a system in which parents could choose what they wanted for their children and schools would have no alternative but to provide it, if they wanted to survive. Schools would have great freedom, but they would be directly accountable to parents. Incentives would replace commands.

The problem with education is not that we don't know what works. We do. The research is clear, and there is remarkable consensus among education specialists. The problem is that many schools won't—or can't—do what works. Twenty years ago companies were writing computer software that could teach reading, math, even writing—yet only a tiny percentage of all schools now teach that way. Business has embraced computer technologies, radically changing its training methods, but our public schools have not.

Institutional change is painful, and in our current education system, this pain can be avoided. *No one has to change. No one has to do better.* Public education is "the only industry we have where if you do a good job, nothing good happens to you, and if you do a bad job, nothing bad happens to you," says David Kearns, former CEO of Xerox, now an undersecretary of education. We can spend all the money we want, but if we do not change this fact, we will not get better schools. Indeed, 150 different studies have agreed that there is no correlation between spending on education and how much students learn.

Is the kind of system outlined above utopian? Well, private schools are run according to most of these principles. The parochial school system operated by the Roman Catholic church embodies most of them—and produces far better results for far less money than comparable public school systems. Even the president of one of the two major teachers' unions wants to turn schools free from most school board regulations, let teachers run them, pay them according to the performance of their students, let them fire incompetent colleagues, let parents have choice of public schools, and waive any union contract provisions that stand in the way. "It's no surprise that our school system doesn't improve," says Albert Shanker, president of the American Federation of Teachers. "It more resembles the communist economy than our own market economy."

RETHINKING OUR APPROACH TO CRIME

Perhaps the only public system in worse shape than education and health care is criminal justice. Since 1960, violent crime has increased 12 times faster than our population. Our murder, rape, and robbery rates are the highest in the world. Our courts and prisons are so full that criminals know real punishment is unlikely. Yet the system is bankrupting state and county governments. While the prison population more than doubled in the 1980s, total state corrections spending more than *tripled*.

Again, the problems stem in part from an outmoded way of approaching the problem. Radical change is afoot in a few places, but for the most part our criminal justice system is made up of large, rule-bound, reactive bureaucracies: police departments, court systems, and prison systems.

Our governments do not play a catalytic role, trying to work with other sectors of society to strengthen families and communities and thus prevent crime. They simply hire more public employees to staff the assembly line: more cops, more court officials, more prison guards. No one steers, because the system in any geographic region is fragmented into many different fiefdoms: dozens of police departments, several different court systems, and three different corrections systems (federal, state, and local).

Our governments rarely give communities and citizens any control over public safety; they leave that to the professionals (the police). They rarely offer their customers any choices (mediation services, alternative dispute resolution forums, community courts, environmental courts, "emergency room" treatment for pressing cases, restitution for victims). They rarely let the police or courts or prisons define a mission and go after it; they tie them up in rules and red tape. They rarely use competition: Unlike large corporations, governments don't let security companies compete to provide their police protection. And they rarely tie police, court, or prison funding to outcomes such as arrest rates, conviction rates, recidivism rates, or customer satisfaction surveys. They just shovel more money in as the inputs—the number of crimes, the number of cases, the number of inmates—rise.

Consider an alternative suggested by our ten principles. The system would be managed, at the state and local levels, by steering organizations—call them Public Safety Coordinating Councils. The state council would fund local coordinating councils, perhaps at the county level. These councils would bring together representatives of all the providers (the county sheriffs, state attorneys, U.S. district attorneys, public defenders, police chiefs) and some of the customers (the civic coalitions, neighborhood organizations, superintendents of schools). The councils would steer their local systems, but would not row.

The state council would fund local councils on a competitive basis. They would receive most of their funding based on demographics and need, but they would compete for bonuses based on the strategies they chose and their performance. Funding formulas would encourage them, for instance, to do strategic planning, to invest in prevention, to survey their customers, to empower communities through community-oriented policing, and to convince participating agencies to adopt mission-driven budgets and personnel systems. No one would have to do these things, but the incentives would be clear. The state council would measure all the results it could—crime rates, recidivism rates, response times, court performance—and award extra funding to those who performed best.

Local councils would in turn use many different mechanisms to achieve their goals—contracts, vouchers, seed capital, partnerships. They might invest in community organizations, push public housing authorities to adopt resident management, and contract with organizations that work with troubled families. They might seek to change the marketplace by offering partial insurance to banks that invest in high-crime areas. They might even encourage their cities to ask different police departments to compete for the contract to offer their police protection, as some of the "contract cities" in southern California do.

This kind of approach, which embodies most of our principles, would be a revolutionary change. Yet it is not too far from what the Governor's Commission for Government by the People recommended to Florida Governor Lawton Chiles in October 1991.

A NEW PARADIGM

What we are describing is nothing less than a shift in the basic model of governance used in America. This shift is under way all around us, but because we are not looking for it—because we assume that all governments have to be big, centralized, and bureaucratic—we seldom see it. We are blind to the new realities, because they do not fit our preconceptions.

University of Minnesota political scientist John Bryson put it well, when we interviewed him several years ago:

In the past, we let markets work until they failed; then we responded with public bureaucracies. We're struggling to figure out a new way, somewhere between markets and public bureaucracy. So far, there's no theory guiding it. People don't have a real clear idea of why past practices aren't working, or what a new model might be. So they can't learn from success or failure: there is no theoretical framework people can use to integrate their experiences.

What we need most if this revolution is to succeed, in other words, is a new framework for understanding government, a new way of thinking about government—in short, a new *paradigm*.

Historian Thomas Kuhn introduced the notion of a paradigm three decades ago, in a book called *The Structure of Scientific Revolutions*. As Kuhn defined it, a scientific paradigm was a set of assumptions about reality—an accepted model or pattern— that explained the world better than any other set of assumptions. It could be as all-encompassing as Newtonian physics or as specific as the notion that life exists only on earth. Each scientific paradigm had its own set of rules and illuminated its own set of facts. As long as it explained most observed phenomena and solved the problems most people want solved, it remained dominant. But as new phenomena began to contradict it, the paradigm succumbed to increasing doubt. As these anomalies multiplied, it was thrown into crisis. Finally, someone articulated a new paradigm—such as Einstein's quantum mechanics—and a broad shift took place.

Kuhn argued that human beings deal with social reality in much the same way—"that something like a paradigm is prerequisite to perception itself." His book described almost perfectly what is happening to our view of government today.

Each of us has a mental image of government, a set of assumptions that guide our perceptions. From the 1930s to the 1960s, what might be called the New Deal paradigm reigned supreme. During the 1960s and 1970s, anomalies began to appear. Many supporters of New Deal government were blind to them, because of their paradigm. Others—particularly the young and those who found themselves paying for New Deal government but not directly benefiting—felt the anomalies acutely. When they rejected the New Deal paradigm, the young turned to radical doctrines, while those on the right reached back to the previous paradigm of a free market society and a laissez-faire state. Barry Goldwater articulated this view in 1964, and by 1980 it had triumphed in the election of Ronald Reagan.

But many practitioners, particularly in state and local government, needed something more than a nineteenth century paradigm if they were to deal with the new realities. They had little choice: they *had* to grapple with the tax revolt, the sad state of public education, the runaway costs of prisons and Medicaid. Washington remained mired in an ideological stalemate between one party still wedded to the New Deal paradigm and another wedded to the laissez-faire paradigm, but visionary state and local leaders gradually began to adjust, developing new practices and new vocabularies. Suddenly, the field of government was brimming with new catch phrases: "public-private partnerships," "alternative service delivery," "contracting out," "empowerment," "Total Quality Management," "participatory management," "privatization," "load shedding." All the symptoms of what Kuhn called a paradigm crisis appeared: the traditional rules blurred, experimentation spread rapidly, and practices once so accepted that they were simply part of the woodwork (civil service, line-item budgets, teacher tenure) were called into question.

As we entered this period, our national leaders seemed almost bewildered, as if they had been outrun by reality. National politics appeared increasingly incomprehensible. People wanted problems solved that the old paradigms simply did not address. The parties debated issues (the flag, prison furloughs, patriotism) that had little to do with voters' primary concerns. Hence voter turnout plunged, and some of the best candidates left office or refused to run in the first place—just as scientists often abandon their fields during paradigm crises.

In the void, politicians turned to negative campaigning. Things were so confusing, so much in flux, that they found it risky to tell voters exactly what they stood for. Instead they told them how bad their opponents were. This produced a further revulsion toward politics—and by association, toward government.

Without a new paradigm, the parties had little choice but to cling to the old. Kuhn is explicit on this point: "A scientific theory is declared invalid only if an alternate candidate is available to take its place." With no new approach to offer, the politicians could only stand on the edge of the void and hope someone came up with something before the voters got fed up and gave them a shove.

In this situation, traditional party politics became almost irrelevant. A few years ago Ted Kolderie related a conversation in which former Minnesota governor Elmer Andersen, when asked to name a few people who had the capacity to be governor someday, replied, " 'You know, I don't think that's really the right question.' "

"At a time when the public is clear with itself about its situation, and about where it wants to go, elected officials are very important," Andersen said.

Then they know the job they have to do, and they are able to get that job done—disagreeing marginally, of course, about how and how rapidly.

But we are now in a time when the public is quite unclear about its situation, and about where it wants to go. So, inevitably and understandably, elected officials hesitate. They have to wait for that consensus to develop. And the job of developing that new consensus is a job that has to be done by others.

"In Gov. Andersen's terms," Kolderie concluded, "the real question today is who is putting together some new understanding of the problems, and some new ideas for action, to which the elected officials will, in time, respond."

Those who are putting together "some new understanding" tend not to be those who have been in politics or government for a long time. "Almost always the men who achieve these fundamental inventions of a new paradigm have been either very young or very new to the field whose paradigm they change," Kuhn tells us. " . . . being little committed by prior practice to the traditional rules of normal science, [they] are particularly likely to see that those rules no longer define a playable game and to conceive another set that can replace them."

As we have traveled the country talking to public entrepreneurs, we have been struck by this reality again and again. The men and women who are piecing together a new way of doing government are relatively new to public service. Many are young; many had previous careers, as journalists or business people or social activists. When they entered government, they could see the anomalies fresh.

These new leaders are not making their revolution through the conventional channels of political parties. Indeed, conventional politics stands in their way. Many of the changes they are making involve more rational approaches—but politics is not a rational business. Politicians often make decisions based not on what will produce the best results, but on what will get them reelected. Because they are rewarded for delivering pieces of the pie to constituency groups, they show little interest in reinventing the pie. Because they respond to vested interests that have organized to protect what they already have, they tend to ignore the unorganized interests who would benefit from change. The media reinforces these tendencies by reporting the drama of politics—the conflicts, the horse races, the scandals—more than the substance of government. The result is an environment in which substantive change is risky and politicians are punished more for trying something and failing than for running a mediocre or ineffective government.

Because crisis often leaves them no choice, entrepreneurial leaders find ways to overcome these obstacles—just as their Progressive forebears did when they imposed the rationality of bureaucracy on the political machines. Some have developed quite sophisticated strategies to overcome the political and bureaucratic obstacles (a subject that will have to wait for another book). We have identified, in the box on the following pages, a few of the elements that make their success possible—including crisis, leadership, vision, and trust. When enough of these elements are present, even the most politicized environment will give way. And once the dike is breached, change will come like a tidal wave. We are not so naive as to suggest that the process is easy. But we do believe it is *inevitable*—just as the transition from machine rule to Progressive government was inevitable.

One can see how the process works by looking at education, the public system that has moved farthest toward a paradigm shift. The public grumbled about the schools for ten years before our leaders officially declared a crisis, in 1983. It then took five years of old-paradigm failure before a group of visionary leaders in Minnesota—a state with a healthy civic infrastructure and a high level of trust—convinced the legislature to try a radically new approach. Within two years, six states had followed and both the governors and the president had endorsed what amounted to a new paradigm in the field of education. Concepts like choice and competition—fringe ideas when we began the research for this book—suddenly emerged as the president's and the governors' agenda. "When paradigms change," Kuhn tells us, "the world itself changes with them."

THE ENTREPRENEURIAL (R)EVOLUTION

In our study of public organizations, we have discerned a number of factors supportive of fundamental change. Not all need be present, but wherever we have seen wholesale reinvention, at least half have been in evidence:

A Crisis. Necessity is still the mother of invention. The most common form it takes in government is fiscal crisis, but economic crises, political crises, and even natural crises such as earthquakes can create demands for change. When no crisis is present, imaginative leaders sometimes create one. As Shakespeare wrote, "Sweet are the uses of adversity."

Leadership. Nothing is more important than leadership. Typically the leader is a mayor, city manager, governor, or president, but leadership can take many forms. In some places a group of leaders has acted together—some from the public sector, some from the private sector. At times leaders push government from the outside, as Martin Luther King, Jr., did; at other times they are internal department heads or managers. One important element of leadership is the ability to champion and protect those within the organization who are willing to risk change.

Continuity of Leadership. When leaders come and go, it is impossible to create fundamental change. In virtually every example we know, the key leaders—whether George Latimer in St. Paul or Rudy Perpich in Minnesota or Kimi Gray at Kenilworth-Parkside—have made a long-term commitment. Yet top leaders in government, particularly political appointees, are often too busy climbing the ladder of success to stay in any one position for more than a few years. No organization is going to risk reinventing itself if it senses that its leader might be gone in a year or two.

A Healthy Civic Infrastructure. John Parr, executive director of the National Civic League, uses the notion of civic infrastructure to describe the informal networks of civic commitment that differentiate strong communities from weak communities. Cities and states with healthy civic infrastructures are those in which citizens, community organizations, businesses and media outlets are committed to the public welfare. Governments that enjoy such commitment find it much easier to make fundamental changes.

Shared Vision and Goals. It is not enough that a leader has a vision of change; he or she must get other community leaders to buy into that vision. "The key element is a collective vision of a city or state's future—a sense of where it's headed," explains Parr. "If you haven't put that together, it's very difficult to make these innovative approaches work, because people are so confused about the role of government. They become very confused about why government is changing."

A shared vision is not the same thing as a consensus. Entrepreneurial leaders rally their communities to their visions, rather than accepting a least common denominator consensus. This does not eliminate conflict, it simply assures that enough of the community shares the leaders' vision to overcome the opposition.

Trust. When people embark on fundamental change, it helps if those with power trust one another: if the city council trusts the mayor, the business community trusts the governor, the union presidents trust the city manager. "If you look back at what it was that was really key in the development of civic and political institutions, it was trust that was based on personal relationships," says Scott Fosler, a former chairman of the Montgomery County Council, in Maryland, now a vice president of the Committee for Economic Development. "We've lost that today."

Outside Resources. Fundamental change is difficult and painful, fraught with uncertainty and risk. Most organizations that embark on the journey need outside help—from foundations, consultants, civic organizations, even other governments. The Citizens League in Minnesota, the Fund for the City of New York, the Lilly Endowment in Indianapolis—all were instrumental in creating change, whether through their expertise, their financial resources, or their political activism.

Models to Follow. Fundamental change occurs in an infinite variety of ways; there is no single mold everyone can copy. But institutions take great comfort when they can see what they are trying to create already in operation somewhere else. Not only does this give them mentors from whom they can learn, it gives them conviction that their goal is attainable.

A GLOBAL REVOLUTION

If the rise of entrepreneurial government is an inevitable shift rather than a temporary fad, as we argue, one would expect it to happen in other nations as well. And to a startling degree, it has. A similar process of transformation is under way throughout the developed world.

The British government, for instance, has forced local governments to put all services up for competitive bid, sold more than a million public housing units to tenants, and moved much of its publicly funded training system out of the public bureaucracy, using vouchers and contract arrangements. It has allowed choice of public schools and encouraged schools that want more autonomy to secede from their school districts and receive funds directly from the national government.

The British Audit Commission, originally designed to perform financial audits, now audits the performance of both national and local agencies, often comparing and ranking them according to their efficiency and effectiveness. In 1982, the national government adopted a set of financial management initiatives designed to create, in essence, organizations that understood their missions and measured their results. By the late 1980s more than 1800 output and performance measures were in use. In 1991, the British government restructured its National Health Service, separating policy management from service delivery and forcing hospitals and physicians' groups to compete for contracts.

One might ascribe Great Britain's movement to the conservative Thatcher administration, but the Social Democrats in Sweden have attempted many of the same things. "Our main efforts in the past have been to build the welfare structure," Finance Minister Kjell-Olof Feldt told the *New York Times* in 1989. "Now we're trying to remodel that building from the interior." The *Times* summed up Sweden's predicament this way:

The recognition that they cannot raise taxes forever is . . . causing the Social Democrats to rethink how to manage Sweden's huge public sector, and many of them are calling for a more market-oriented approach. As a result of the growing outcry about the uneven state of health care, education and day care, the Government is seeking to inject more competition into providing services to increase quality and efficiency.

Sweden's extensive employment and training system now bids out most training on performance contracts, treats "clients" as customers, and markets to industry. Public sector training providers compete directly with private, under the slogan "We have to earn it." Many taxpayers are given a choice of which hospital, day-care center, or other government service agency they want to use. The national government has adopted a three-year budget cycle, to support long-term planning. Once every three years, each agency undergoes an in-depth examination of its expenditures, performance, productivity, and outcomes.

Canada has given its federal departments authority to reallocate resources across line items and to carry over some of their capital funds from one year to the next. In exchange, departments are subject to more stringent use of performance measures.

Australia has adopted what it calls Program Management and Budgeting, as well as a Financial Management Improvements Program. "FMIP/PMB is shifting the focus of budgeting from the inputs used to the results achieved," says Allen Schick of the University of Maryland. "It seeks to change the operating culture of Australian public management from one which places a premium on compliance with externally-imposed rules to one which spurs managers to do the best they can with the resources at hand." The reforms required departments to cut their spending by 3.75 percent over three years, but gave them greater spending flexibility and the right to keep any money saved beyond the 3.75 percent.

Debates about school choice have aroused strong emotions in Canada, Great Britain, Germany, France, Belgium, the Netherlands, Australia, Israel, and Spain. Amsterdam is decentralizing not only its school system (moving to school site management) but its entire city government, by dividing the city into 16 administrative neighborhoods.

New Zealand has gone the farthest along the entrepreneurial path. Its Labor Party—still a socialist party according to its constitution—lead a total overhaul of New Zealand's welfare state during the 1980s. It restructured many of government's commercial functions as state-owned, for-profit enterprises—in energy, transportation, banking, insurance, forestry, construction, air traffic control, communications, broadcasting, and postal service. It sold other public agencies to the private sector, including an oil company, several banks, a shipping company, and the national airline. It separated the remaining government services into those with a policy management role, those with a regulatory role, and those with a social welfare role. The latter were thoroughly restructured, with new cost structures, increased reliance on user fees, increased contracting (with both public and private service providers), heightened competition, elimination of many regulations, and greater freedom for managers to manage.

In one fell swoop, New Zealand did away with its old civil service system, freeing department managers to negotiate their own contracts with their employees. It eliminated regulations that inhibited competition in both the private and public sectors—forcing government-owned businesses like the national railway, the telecommunications system, and the broadcasting corporation into more competitive markets. And it adopted a budget system focused on performance (called output budgeting) and an accrual accounting system modeled on business accounting.

Finally there is Eastern Europe, where bureaucracy and state monopolies have given way to markets and choice with a suddenness that was unthinkable five years ago. Change was impossible in Poland, but it happened. Change was impossible in the rest of Eastern Europe, but it happened. Change was impossible in the Soviet Union, but it happened. People and movements that were seen only a few years ago as hopelessly isolated and idealistic are now leading revolutions and governing nations.

In his 1991 inaugural address, Governor Pete Wilson of California articulated the central challenge of our age:

We will not suffer the future. We will shape it. We will not simply grow. We will manage our growth. We will not passively experience change. We will make change. **But to shape our future, we need a new vision of government.**

Our purpose in writing this book, as we made clear in the preface, was to offer our readers such a vision. Our governments are in deep trouble today. In government after government and public system after public system, reinvention is the only option left. But the lack of a vision—a new paradigm—holds us back. We hope the vision we have laid out will unlock the remaining gates—unleashing a paradigm shift throughout American government, from the smallest hamlet to the largest federal bureaucracy. We hope our road map will empower *you* to reinvent *your* governments.

Appendix A:
Alternative Service
Delivery Options

Once a government decides to look into the alternatives to service delivery by public employees, it faces an array of choices. Would contracting work best? Or would vouchers be more effective? Would a partnership be appropriate? Or would a quasi-public corporation do the job better? The 36 alternatives we have found in use across America include the following:

1. Creating Legal Rules and Sanctions. Surely the most common form of government action to encourage or discourage activity is the law. By making an activity illegal, government can minimize it; by making a formerly illegal activity legal, government can—with no other action by public employees—multiply the availability of that service a thousandfold. (Consider the impact of the Supreme Court's *Roe* v. *Wade* decision, in 1973, on the availability of abortions.) And by requiring an activity—whether affirmative action or pasteurization of milk—government can make that activity the norm.

2. Regulation or Deregulation. Momentous changes in service delivery can be accomplished with nothing more than a simple change in the regulations. When the federal government deregulated the express statutes governing the Postal Service—allowing competition for express delivery—an entirely new industry was born. Today Federal Express, United Parcel Service, and their competitors deliver millions of overnight packages every day. When states began requiring utilities to provide free energy audits to homeowners, what had been a tiny industry was transformed.

3. *Monitoring and Investigation*. The federal government inspects meat, milk, and other foods. The federal Occupational Safety and Health Administration monitors workplace safety. Other federal agencies monitor strip-mining, nuclear power plants, waste dumps, and other environmental hazards. State and local governments investigate complaints against businesses, monitor and investigate racial bias by landlords, and monitor buildings for compliance with fire and safety codes. With a small investment, governments can dramatically improve the quality of private goods or services simply by monitoring them and investigating complaints.

4. *Licensing*. By licensing activities, governments determine who can perform them and who cannot: who can drive a taxi and who cannot; what nurse practitioners can do and what they cannot; which buildings can be used for day-care centers and which cannot. By changing the licensing requirements, governments can increase or decrease service delivery almost overnight. When governments relax the licensing requirements for day-care facilities, nursing homes, and the like, thousands of nongovernmental providers spring into action.

5. *Tax Policy*. The federal government encourages people to buy homes and contribute to charities by allowing them to deduct their mortgage interest and charitable contributions from their taxable incomes. State and local governments offer tax breaks to entice industries to move into or expand within their boundaries. Pennsylvania encourages firms to hire welfare recipients by offering them a tax credit. On the other hand, governments often tax activity they want to discourage. The most common examples are "sin taxes" on items such as cigarettes and alcohol. Minnesota even requires drug dealers to buy "tax stamps" and affix them to drug packages, so as to have another count on which to prosecute drug traffickers and another way to confiscate their assets.

6. *Grants*. Virtually every American is eligible for a government grant at some point. Our governments give grants to artists, research scientists, low-income -housing developers, small businesses, schools, students, hospitals, community organizations, nonprofit corporations, and, of course, other governments. In 1987, the federal government dispensed $112 billion in grants.

7. *Subsidies.* Not only are all Americans eligible for subsidies at some point in their lives, most receive them. Social security is a subsidy. Welfare is a subsidy. Our farm programs provide subsidies. The tax deduction for home mortgage interest is a subsidy, administered through the tax system. A second category of subsidy goes not to individuals but to institutions, so as to lower the cost of service to the public. We subsidize educational institutions, hospitals, medical schools, developers of low- and moderate-income housing, and many, many others who produce services we consider beneficial to the public interest.

8. *Loans.* By 1987, the federal government had $234.2 billion in loans outstanding; state and local governments had untold billions more. These loans financed virtually everything imaginable. Some were at market interest rates; others offered subsidized interest rates (e.g., student loans); others provided some degree of loan forgiveness. Over the years, for instance, many medical students have received loans that were then forgiven if they served for an agreed number of years in the military or in an underserved area.

9. *Loan Guarantees.* Our governments guarantee private loans even more often than they lend money themselves. By absorbing part or all of the risk, they encourage private banks and other lenders to make loans that (theoretically, at least) accomplish public purposes. According to Lester Salamon, "loan guarantees became the principal growth vehicle" for federal domestic activism during the 1970s: by 1987 the federal government had more than half a trillion dollars' worth of loan guarantees outstanding. Our governments guarantee loans to students, businesses (from the smallest start-up to the Chrysler Corporation), home buyers, exporters, farmers, and many others.

10. *Contracting.* Contracting is older than the U.S. government itself. As E. S. Savas points out, "It was a private entrepreneur, under contract to the Spanish monarchs, who sailed to the

New World in 1492." When the federal government wanted to deliver mail west of the Mississippi River, it contracted with 80 horseback riders, known collectively as the Pony Express. Our governments have long contracted with private companies to build roads, sewer systems, buildings, and virtually every other element of our infrastructure. Our defense establishment employs 6 million people, 3.4 million of whom work for private contractors. Our Department of Health and Human Services contracts with Blue Cross/Blue Shield to administer Medicare for millions of people.

But contracting is hardly limited to such predictable tasks. The city of Chelsea, Massachusetts, has contracted with Boston University to run its school system. San Francisco contracts out its budget analysis to a private firm. Former Massachusetts Governor Michael Dukakis contracted out much of his state tax collection effort. Seventy-two cities in southern California, which have banded together in the Contract Cities Association, contract out most of their services to both public and private providers. (Many contract with the Los Angeles County Sheriff's Department to provide their police services, for example). The first contract city, Lakewood, has 73,000 residents today but only 170 employees. (For more on contracting, see chapter 1.)

11. *Franchising.* Franchising is contracting with a twist: government awards the franchise, but users of the service pay the producer directly. It is normally used when a service is a natural monopoly (or entry into the business is extremely limited) but government wants private companies to compete for the right to provide the service. Governments give franchises to restaurant chains to operate restaurants on turnpikes. They give franchises to utilities, cable television companies, bus companies, and concession firms.

12. *Public-Private Partnerships.* Like contracting, the use of partnerships exploded in the 1980s. Most cities of any size were involved in real estate deals of some kind, coventuring with developers. Indianapolis created a joint venture to burn 2,000 tons of trash a day and produce steam, which it sold as heat. Dade County, Florida, made deals with private companies to operate public schools on their property for the children of

employees. Seattle and many other cities created Adopt-a-Park programs, in which private companies helped fund and maintain public parks. Dallas did the same with libraries.

St. Paul created partnerships with for-profit firms, nonprofit organizations, and foundations. Mayor George Latimer found that when a foundation or for-profit firm brought substantial resources to the table, he could entice the city to do things it would never have tried on its own. "Once established, the machinery of city government is difficult to realign, no matter how rapidly social and economic circumstances change," he and Dick Broeker, his deputy mayor, wrote. "Foundation participation can make things happen outside conventional governmental restraints. . . . The trick is to skirt the paralyzed or outmoded bureaucracy and initiate direct action."

13. *Public-Public Partnerships.* Minneapolis and St. Paul joined together to create the nonprofit Family Housing Fund. Independence, Missouri, subsidizes the school system to keep its schools open 12 hours a day, to provide before- and after-school child care. Many governments share services, trade services, or contract with one another for services.

14. *Quasi-Public or Private Corporations.* When entrepreneurial governments want to accomplish tasks that are economic in nature, they often create private, nonprofit corporations, or the virtually identical quasi-public corporations. Baltimore pioneered the use of private, nonprofit development corporations to redevelop its Inner Harbor area. St. Paul created the Lowertown Development Corporation, the District Heating Development Corporation, and the Energy Resource Corporation, which performed energy audits and made loans to owners and landlords for investment in energy conservation. Phoenix created a nonprofit corporation to run a homeless shelter.

15. *Public Enterprise.* When the private sector will not or cannot provide some economic service—or public leaders feel the price is too stiff—governments at times create their own businesses. Municipally owned utilities are common. Dozens of cities own their cable television systems. Visalia owned a minor-league baseball team for six years. The public authorities created by many states and cities—for instance, port authorities, or bridge and tunnel authorities—are public enterprises. The federal government owns at least 30 public corporations, including the Tennessee Valley Authority, the Commodity Credit Corporation, and the Overseas Private Investment Corporation. (For more on public enterprise, see chapter 7.)

16. *Procurement.* In similar fashion, governments encourage certain activities by buying only from companies that engage in those activities. New York City buys payroll processing services from banks that make investments in low-income neighborhoods. Los Angeles gives preference to contractors who provide day-care facilities. Many governments set aside a percentage of their procurement for minority-owned firms or small businesses.

Government procurement policy can have an enormous impact; occasionally, it creates an entire industry. The federal government created the computer and semiconductor industries by funding the development of computers for military purposes during and after World War II, then asking for smaller and smaller units to put into its ballistic missiles and space vehicles. The General Services Administration gave a major push to the commercial development of air bags in cars by ordering 5,000 Ford Tempos equipped with air bags in 1984. Overall, federal, state, and local governments buy nearly $1 trillion worth of goods and services every year—18 percent of the gross national product.

17. *Insurance.* The federal government seeks to prevent financial panics by providing insurance for depositors in banks and savings-and-loan institutions. It also administers systems of unemployment insurance, workers' compensation insurance, and medical insurance for the elderly and poor. The state of Illinois fights racial segregation by authorizing the creation of home equity districts in Chicago, which can offer insurance against price drops caused by sudden racial turnover. Montgomery County, Maryland, struck a deal with Blue Cross/Blue Shield to offer catastrophic health insurance to county residents for $53.80 per family per year.

18. *Rewards, Awards, and Bounties.* When police departments or the FBI offer rewards for information leading to the arrest of criminals, they are using nongovernmental employees to help solve their problems. When governments award prizes and awards to private individuals and organizations, they are encouraging the behavior they reward—whether individual heroism or community development of low-income housing. Both of these approaches can harness private energies toward public goals, without increasing the use of public employees or tax dollars.

19. *Changing Public Investment Policy.* As noted in chapter 10, most governments are financial investors. By changing where and how they invest, they can encourage or discourage virtually any behavior: apartheid in South Africa; lending in minority communities here at home; even energy conservation. Public pension funds have become more deliberate about where they invest, and many governments have developed linked-deposit programs to put their cash only in banks that agree to meet some social objective. (See also chapter 10, p. 295.)

20. *Technical Assistance.* Governments often provide technical assistance to businesses, community organizations, and other governments, so they can better provide some service of value. The *Catalogue of Federal Domestic Assistance* lists 21 different advisory services for businesses. Many states fund technical assistance for local governments. Massachusetts created two quasi-public corporations that offer technical assistance to community-based development organizations. Pennsylvania pays outstanding community development organizations to work with others, so as to transfer their skills.

21. *Information.* Sometimes government can have a tremendous impact simply by providing information to the public. A 1989 study of bank lending patterns by the Federal Reserve Bank of Boston forced Massachusetts banks to promise $1 billion in new investments in minority communities. The surgeon general's 1964 report condemning smoking triggered a dramatic 25-year decline in the percentage of Americans who smoked. Information about cholesterol, fat, and other elements in food has had an effect as well. Columnist George Will has argued that "the most cost-effective thing government does is disseminate health information." (See also chapter 10, p. 292.)

22. *Referral.* Many governments operate referral services, steering people or organizations to those who offer the services they need. Many states offer referral services to businesses looking for help with exporting, financing, modernization of production technology, and the like. Connecticut operates a very effective referral service for day care; parents can get a list of everyone in their area who offers day care and talk to the state employee who monitors the quality of different facilities.

23. *Volunteers.* In a mid-1980s survey, almost three of every four cities surveyed reported using volunteers. More than 42 percent of the cities used volunteers in their fire departments. (Many small fire departments are in fact made up entirely of volunteers.) The Dallas Parks and Recreation Department used 1,200 volunteers on a regular basis and another 4,800 for special events. Many cities had full-time employees who coordinated the use of volunteers. In Florida, volunteers serve as tutors, interpreters, foster parents, drivers, speakers, and shopping, bookkeeping, and cleaning assistants. In Massachusetts, the Department of Environmental Protection has begun to use volunteer lawyers to mediate disputes involving the use of wetlands.

24. *Vouchers.* When governments want to give specific groups of people the ability to buy specific goods or services, they often use vouchers. The federal government gives poor people food stamps to buy groceries and housing vouchers to help pay their rent. Some states give low-income people vouchers to help pay for day care. More than 100 towns in Vermont and Maine give their high school students vouchers to attend private schools. Wisconsin provides up to 1,000 poor Milwaukee children with vouchers to attend private schools. (For a more thorough discussion of voucher mechanisms, see chapter 6.)

25. *Impact Fees.* In chapter 10, we described impact fees as a form of tax designed to impose the social cost generated by some activity, such as driving, developing real estate, or generating electricity, directly on those who benefit from the activity. By raising the cost of such activities, governments discourage them. They also ensure that people who benefit from them cannot shift their costs onto others, except their customers. Impact fees on developers are becoming common, and effluent fees on pollution are the subject of increasing discussion.

26. *Catalyzing Nongovernmental Efforts.* Los Angeles County helped organize a network of 1,200 churches and community groups, with 20,000 volunteers, that delivered 36 million pounds of food a year to poor families. When the public sector effort ended, 350 food pantries and soup kitchens remained in place. Minneapolis catalyzed the formation of a series of neighborhood networks involving community organizations and businesses, to get local corporations to hire low-income residents. (One city employee, whose salary was paid by the business community, acted as a coordinator and troubleshooter.) California's Contra Costa County Housing Authority brought banks and a nonprofit counseling agency together to help homeowners create second units in single-family neighborhoods, as an inexpensive way to expand the supply of rental housing.

27. *Convening Nongovernmental Leaders.* Often all government has to do is bring the key stakeholders together to solve a problem. Several states operate labor-management cooperation programs that do little more than convene groups of employers and union leaders. Boston Mayor Ray Flynn convened an Infant Survival Summit in 1990, to bring all those responsible for medical care in the city together to fashion a response to the rising infant mortality rate in Boston's black community. Mayors, governors, and presidents often convene conferences to focus attention on particular problems.

28. *Jawboning.* At times, convening is not even necessary; public leaders can make something happen simply by jawboning those involved. President Kennedy rolled back a steel price increase by jawboning. Governor Bruce Babbitt of Arizona stimulated the creation of at least 100 after-school daycare programs by drawing attention to the phenomenon of latchkey children. Mayor Art Agnos of San Francisco shamed the churches into opening their doors to the homeless.

29. *Seed Money.* St. Paul gave seed money to a nonprofit recycling program so it could extend its services to the entire city.

Visalia gave out seed money constantly: for a new swimming pool, for the Little League, for the Chamber of Commerce's economic development work. Arkansas gives communities $5,000 in seed money to bring their private employers together to organize Total Quality Management programs. Massachusetts and Pennsylvania have used seed money to catalyze the formation of networks of small manufacturers, to work on improving their productivity.

30. *Equity Investments.* At times, governments make equity investments to encourage or support a desired activity. The Michigan Strategic Fund has invested $12 million to $15 million in equity to catalyze the formation of private sector business and industrial development corporations. Pennsylvania's Ben Franklin Partnership has invested in five private seed capital funds. Many states encourage their public pension funds to invest in venture capital. The federal government held stock in Chrysler during the bailout.

31. *Voluntary Associations.* Some governments encourage neighborhoods, shopping districts, or groups of employers to form their own associations to provide services. Seattle contracts with neighborhood associations; St. Paul funds them to deliver certain services; Kansas City gives them a partial rebate on their property taxes if they opt out of city services; New York City and others give business owners in neighborhood shopping districts the power to tax their members to finance improvements.

32. *Coproduction or Self-Help.* Many governments help citizens produce services themselves. Urban homesteading programs in many cities let people buy houses for next to nothing if they will renovate them. Public housing authorities contract with residents to manage their own properties. And of course local governments provide support—if only the use of school grounds and parks—to people who organize baseball, soccer, and other sports leagues. Little League is a classic self-help operation.

33. *Quid Pro Quos.* When the tax revolt hit, governments quickly began to require businesses to pay for more services. Many developers now pay for new roads, highway interchanges, and other improvements in exchange for the right to

build their developments. (In San Antonio, Sea World agreed
to help pay for a new freeway.) Cities like San Francisco,
Oakland, and Boston use linkage programs, in which developers must invest in low-income housing or day care in exchange for the right to construct downtown office buildings.
Many governments put their cash reserves only in banks that
agree to maintain branches in poor communities or loan to
small businesses or minority-owned businesses. Montgomery
County, Maryland, even asks developers to build public
housing units in their private developments, in exchange for
zoning concessions.

34. *Demand Management.* Rather than spending ever more
to keep up with rising demands for services, some governments
focus on reducing demand for services. To cut down on demand
for water, Tucson and other cities mandate the use of ultralow-
flow toilets in all new houses. To cut down on demand for highways, governments raise tolls or fares during rush hour, provide
discounts to cars with three or more passengers, and provide
special lanes for buses and car pools. To cut down on ambulance and fire calls, some cities charge for calls that turn out to
be unnecessary. (For a more thorough discussion of demand
management, see chapter 10.)

35. *Sale, Exchange, or Use of Property.* Visalia enabled the
local school district to build a new school by arranging a four-
parcel land swap and sale. (See p. 198.) Orlando got itself a free
city hall by letting a developer build two office towers on the
same seven-acre parcel. (See p. 202.) Fairfax County, Virginia,
gave a private developer up to 146 acres of prime public land—
valued at $50 million to $70 million—in return for construction of a new county government center.

36. *Restructuring the Market.* As explained in chapter 10,
governments constantly shape the private marketplace to meet
citizens' needs. Zoning laws determine where development will
occur and what kind it will be. Federal agriculture programs
guarantee a set price and a market for many farm products.
Tariffs and import restrictions protect markets for domestic
producers. Building codes and rent control laws shape real estate markets.

CHOOSING THE BEST ALTERNATIVE

Entrepreneurial governments can choose not only from these 36 alternatives, but from among endless variations and combinations of the 36. With all these arrows in their quivers, they need to develop a methodology to find the right arrow for the target in question. As the Florida Speaker's Advisory Committee on the Future put it, "What is needed is a policy and an evaluation technique which can be routinely applied to each request for service initiation, continuation, or expansion. The question to be answered is 'where does the state get the best deal overall?' "

The best methodology—or analytical framework—we have found is presented in E. S. Savas's 1987 book, *Privatization: The Key to Better Government* (Chatham House Publishers, Chatham, New Jersey). Although an advocate of privatization, Savas distinguishes carefully between government's critical role in "providing" necessary goods and services and the separate question of who can best "produce" them. In other words, Savas is a pragmatic advocate of privatization, rather than an ideologue.

In his book, Savas divides goods and services into four categories: private goods, toll goods, common pool goods, and collective goods. He discusses the different options for providing each, then examines the strengths and weaknesses of 10 different service arrangements: government service, government vending, intergovernmental agreement, contracts, franchises, grants, vouchers, market systems, voluntary service, and self-service. Finally, he develops a list of criteria by which each arrangement can be judged and examines the strengths and weaknesses of each of his 10 alternatives in light of each criterion. The criteria are:

- "service specificity" (how specifically a service can be defined, so governments can tell private producers exactly what they want);
- "availability of producers" (are there enough, for instance, to ensure competition?);

- "efficiency and effectiveness";
- the "scale" of the service (how large an organization is necessary to produce it);
- "relating benefits and costs" (the degree to which those using the service pay directly for its benefits);
- "responsiveness to consumers";
- "susceptibility to fraud";
- "economic equity";
- "equity for minorities";
- "responsiveness to government direction"; and
- "the size of government" required by the service arrangement.

Another question public decision makers must ask, in deciding how to handle each service, is which sector would best produce it: the public sector, the private sector, or the third sector? Each of these sectors has its own set of strengths and weaknesses, as we pointed out in chapter 1.

For example, *public sector* institutions tend to be best at:

- policy management;
- regulation;
- ensuring equity;
- preventing discrimination or exploitation;
- ensuring continuity and stability of services; and
- ensuring social cohesion (through the mixing of races and classes, for instance, in public schools).

In contrast, even entrepreneurial public service providers are less adept at:

- performing complex tasks;
- replicating the successes of other organizations;

- delivering services that require rapid adjustment to change;
- delivering services to very diverse populations; and
- delivering services that become obsolete quickly.

Bureaucratic government organizations fall short on many other counts, as we have argued. They have trouble, for instance, with tasks that require flexibility, rapid change, customer responsiveness, and extensive customization of services.

The *private sector* is almost the opposite. It does very poorly at the first list of tasks above, but very well at the second. When tasks are economic in nature, or when they require an investment orientation, the private sector is far more effective than either the public or third sector. It is also far better at replicating successful experiments, because the profit motive attracts investors and drives private companies to imitate their successful competitors.

When there is little or no profit to be generated, on the other hand, the private sector is seldom interested or effective. One study of nursing homes, for instance, found that nonprofit institutions tended to offer high quality, but had no incentive to expand; for-profits had a great incentive to expand, but more often delivered poor-quality care.

For-profit businesses are more accustomed to innovating than public or nonprofit institutions, because they must often innovate to survive. For the same reason, they are far more accustomed to adapting to rapid change and to abandoning unsuccessful or obsolete activities. They also tend to use people with more expertise and more professional training than public or third sector organizations. Hence when tasks are extremely technical or complex, the private sector often has a great advantage. "A lot of snide remarks have been made about the risks of a manned lunar program consisting of the activities of thousands of profit-seeking, low-bidding private firms," William Niskanen wrote in 1971. Yet "the U.S. lunar program . . . has been one of the more spectacularly successful public activities in recent years."

On the other hand, large private firms, like large public organizations, are aggressive monopolists. They often have enough political clout to convince legislatures and city councils to give them virtual monopolies on production of a particular service or good.

The *third sector* tends to be best at tasks that:

- generate little or no profit margin;
- require compassion and commitment to other humans;
- require a comprehensive, holistic approach;
- require extensive trust on the part of customers or clients;
- require volunteer labor; and
- require hands-on, personal attention (such as day care, counseling, and services to the handicapped or ill).

The third sector is also best at enforcing moral codes and individual responsibility for behavior. Whether an institution is running homeless shelters, schools, or day-care centers, it must often enforce a code of behavior (shelter residents shall not use alcohol or drugs, for instance). Public institutions often have trouble doing this, because their employees have been inculcated with the idea that it is wrong for a government to impose any particular set of values on its citizens. For-profit firms have trouble doing this because it might cost them money—if they expel a paying student, for instance. But religious organizations, community groups, and the like—which typically exist to fulfill a mission—often have both a strong sense of values and a willingness to enforce them, despite the financial implications.

On the other hand, third sector organizations often choose to serve only certain people (only Catholics, or only poor people, or only Hispanics) and to exclude others. They are also less effective than government or business organizations at tasks that require them to generate extensive resources on their own, that require a high degree of professional expertise, or that benefit from economies of scale.

We have summarized the strengths and weaknesses of each sector in the following tables:

QUALITIES DESIRED IN
SERVICE PRODUCERS

(H = high; L = low; M = moderate level)

	Public	*Private*	*Third*
Public Sector Strengths			
Stability	H	L	M
Ability to handle issues outside central mission (e.g., affirmative action)	H	L	M
Immunity to favoritism	H	M	L
Private Sector Strengths			
Ability to respond to rapidly changing circumstances	L	H	M
Ability to innovate	M	H	M
Tendency to replicate success	L	H	M
Tendency to abandon the obsolete or failed	L	H	M
Willingness to take risks	L	H	M
Ability to generate capital	M	H	L
Professional expertise	M	H	M
Ability to capture economies of scale	M	H	L
Third Sector Strengths			
Ability to reach diverse populations	L	M	H
Compassion and commitment	M	L	H
Holistic treatment of problems	L	L	H
Ability to generate trust	M	L	H

TASKS BEST SUITED
TO EACH SECTOR

(E = effective, I = ineffective, D = depends on context)

	Public	Private	Third
Best Suited to Public Sector			
Policy management	E	I	D
Regulation	E	I	D
Enforcement of equity	E	I	E
Prevention of discrimination	E	D	D
Prevention of exploitation	E	I	E
Promotion of social cohesion	E	I	E
Best Suited to Private Sector			
Economic tasks	I	E	D
Investment tasks	I	E	D
Profit generation	I	E	I
Promotion of self-sufficiency	I	E	D
Best Suited to Third Sector			
Social tasks	D	I	E
Tasks that require volunteer labor	D	I	E
Tasks that generate little profit	D	I	E
Promotion of individual responsibility	I	D	E
Promotion of community	D	I	E
Promotion of commitment to welfare of others	D	I	E

Appendix B:
The Art of Performance
Measurement

Government is famous for its endless figures and forms. To an outsider, it seems like an industry that pays an enormous amount of attention to numbers. People in government are always counting something or churning out some statistical report. But most of this counting is focused on inputs: how much is spent, how many people are served, what service each person received. Very seldom does it focus on outcomes, on *results*.

This is true in part because measuring results is so difficult. Measuring profit in business is fairly straightforward. Measuring results in government is not. Normally it takes several years to develop adequate measures: an agency's first attempt often falls woefully short. It may measure only outputs, not outcomes. It may define outcomes too narrowly, driving employees to concentrate on only a few of the results the organization actually wants to achieve. It may develop so many measures that employees can't tell what to concentrate on.

Even Sunnyvale, California, perhaps the most sophisticated government we know when it comes to performance measures, still has some measures that cry out for refinement. As Sunnyvale, Phoenix, and hundreds of other government organizations have developed their measurement systems, however, they have learned a number of basic lessons:

1. *There is a vast difference between measuring process and measuring results.* When public organizations set out to measure performance, their managers usually draw up lists that measure how well they carry out some administrative process: how many people they serve; how fast they serve them; what percentage of requests are fulfilled within a set period of time. In essence, they measure their volume of output. But *outputs* do not guarantee *outcomes.* A vocational school might pump out more and more graduates of a welding program, for instance. But if those graduates cannot find jobs as welders, what good is the program? It may be generating impressive outputs without generating any positive outcomes.

The tendency to focus on process is natural: managers measure what their agencies do, and in rule-driven organizations, people think of their jobs as following certain processes laid down by the rules. If they follow those processes faithfully and produce the expected volume of output, they are doing their jobs. They rarely think of the outcomes: what impact the activity has on those the agency is designed to serve. Yet a perfectly executed process is a waste of time and money if it fails to achieve the outcomes desired.

The National Center for State Courts provides a good example. With the U.S. Department of Justice, it set out to create performance standards for trial courts. The purpose, stated explicitly, was to focus not on "the structures and machinery of the courts," but on "their performance (*what courts actually accomplish with the means at their disposal*)" (emphasis added). Yet the group found itself struggling constantly with what Dr. Ingo Keilitz, who staffed the project, calls "process creep." Some members assumed that "good management is an outcome," Keilitz remembers. "And we would say, 'But good management is not an end in itself.' We argued until we were blue in the face."

Process measures can be useful, of course. Good management is important, and process measures can help organizations get a handle on how they can improve their management. Organizations that use Deming's Total Quality Management, for instance, constantly measure their internal processes so they can see where problems lie and correct them. In addition, the outcomes desired by any given organization are often very difficult to measure, or will not become evident for a long time. In such cases, organizations often choose process measures that appear to be reliable proxies for the ultimate outcome. For example, Pennsylvania's Ben Franklin Partnership measures things like the amount of private investment attracted to match each of its grants—on the assumption that projects which attract significant private investment have a better chance of contributing to economic growth than projects that have difficulty attracting private investment.

The problem comes when organizations measure *only* process—as too many do. Fox Valley Technical College measures many process issues: the number of courses scheduled but later dropped; the use of evaluation techniques that stress skill competency rather than the ability to take written exams; the amount of computer-based instruction offered; and so on. If it did not also measure how many graduates got jobs in the fields for which they trained, their satisfaction, and the satisfaction of employers, however, it might create ever better courses that resulted in ever fewer job placements. Once robots have replaced welders, it makes no sense to keep working to improve one's welding courses.

2. *There is a vast difference between measuring efficiency and measuring effectiveness.* Efficiency is a measure of how much each unit of output costs. Effectiveness is a measure of the quality of that output: how well did it achieve the desired outcome? When we measure efficiency, we know how much it is costing us to achieve a specified output. When we measure effectiveness, we know whether our investment is worthwhile. There is nothing so foolish as to do more efficiently something that should no longer be done.

Both efficiency and effectiveness are important. But when public organizations begin to measure their performance, they often measure only their efficiency. Typically, a traditional Defense Department might measure how much it costs to house and feed its troops—and strive constantly to drive that number down. Yet as Bob Stone put it in his four-page "Department of

Defense Construction Criteria": "The goal is *not* to minimize the life-cycle cost of the facilities, but to maximize the performance of the people who use the facilities."

The public certainly wants efficient government, but it wants effective government even more. Citizens may be pleased that they spend less per student on education than other states, but if their schools are the worst in the country, they are not likely to be pleased for long. They may enjoy a low tax rate, but if that means they spend an hour getting to work on clogged highways, they usually vote to invest in a more effective transportation system.

Focusing on efficiency more than effectiveness also tends to alienate public employees. When governments stress the cost of each unit of work, they often develop a green-eyeshade mentality that belittles the intelligence and skill of their workers. Most employees want to be effective. Most will gladly do what is necessary to increase their organization's impact. But if their superiors concentrate solely on their efficiency—on how quickly they do each unit of work—they will begin to feel as if they are on an assembly line.

George Britton, a deputy city manager in Phoenix, notes that his city got heavily into efficiency measurement during the 1970s. "We thought every street sweeper ought to do 65 lane-miles a day," he says:

> *But that collapsed, because it got caught up in a green-eyeshade philosophy. And it lost track of asking the question: Why are we doing this service? Governments do a lot of services very efficiently, without asking why they do them. We lost the relationship between efficiency and effectiveness. You're only being effective if you're doing something that needs to be done.*

3. *There is an important difference between "program outcomes" and broader "policy outcomes."* When the National Center for State Courts developed its performance standards, it came up with outcome standards that measure public satisfaction with a court's accessibility, fairness, reliability, speed, political independence, and accountability. To measure these things so, courts use public surveys, focus groups, and the like. But none of these measures deals with the broader outcomes most important to the public: crime rates, public safety, conviction rates, recidivism rates, justice for victims of crime, or satisfaction with the way in which disputes are resolved. Judges would argue, of course, that the courts are not the only institutions responsible for things like crime rates, conviction rates, and public perceptions of safety. They would be correct. Yet these are the outcomes people care most about.

This dilemma confronts many public organizations. They can measure the outcomes of their specific program or activity, but those numbers are not as important as certain broader measures. A jobs program for welfare recipients might measure its job placement rate and the wages of those placed, for example. But what about the number of people coming onto the welfare rolls, the length of time they stay on, and the size of the overall caseload? Managers of the jobs program would argue that they should be held responsible for their job placement numbers, but not for the total caseload or the number of people signing up for welfare.

Again, they would be correct. The latter numbers are affected by broader policy questions: who is eligible; how attractive welfare is compared to low-skill, low-wage work; and how much low-wage work is available. Yet if the welfare department does not measure both sets of numbers, it may think it is doing a terrific job of getting people off welfare, while its rolls are actually growing! This is precisely what has happened to many states over the past decade. Massachusetts' Employment and Training (E.T.) Choices program is justifiably considered one of the best in the nation. Yet, although it placed roughly 10,000 people a year in jobs between 1983 and 1990, the department's AFDC caseload started at 90,000, never got below about 84,000, and headed past 100,000 when a recession began.

Statistics like this underscore the importance of measuring both *program outcomes* and *policy outcomes*. Programs like E.T. Choices need information on how well they are achieving their goals. Indeed, E.T. Choices' managers collected that information religiously and continually used it to refine and improve their efforts. But they also need information on broader trends, such as the percentage of the population on welfare and in poverty. With this information, it becomes clear that E.T. Choices is innovating within a broader welfare system that contains powerful incentives for people to get on and stay on welfare. At some point, one can hope, such information will trigger efforts to change the broader system, rather than simply more efforts to train and place people in jobs.

The table on pages 356–357 outlines the difference between outputs (process) and outcomes (results), between program outcomes and policy outcomes, and between efficiency and effectiveness. It then illustrates those differences for several different public services. To use street sweeping as an example, it illustrates that one would measure the *output*, or process, by measuring the number of miles swept. But if one wanted to measure the *outcome*, or result, one would have to measure the cleanliness of the streets—as rated, perhaps, by objective, trained observers. This latter measure would be the *program outcome*. A *policy outcome* would look at a broader question: how much litter do citizens leave on the streets, and how effective is public policy at minimizing this amount?

To determine *program efficiency*, an organization would simply measure the cost per mile swept. But to determine *policy efficiency*, it would have to measure the cost to achieve a desired level of street cleanliness, by whatever method—street sweeping, prevention, community self-help. Finally, to measure *program effectiveness*, a city might measure citizen satisfaction with the level of street cleanliness. But to measure *policy effectiveness*, it might ask citizens whether they wanted their money spent keeping the streets clean, or whether alternative uses, such as construction or repaving, would be preferable.

For those interested in learning more about performance measurement, a number of experts have written widely on the subject. Harry Hatry at the Urban Institute has published a series of books, particularly for local governments. Jack Brizius,

Michael Campbell, and Roger Vaughan have written about performance measurement in state government, for the Council of Governors Policy Advisers and the Corporation for Enterprise Development. In 1990, the Governmental Accounting Standards Board (GASB) released a research report on performance measurement, called *Service Efforts and Accomplishments Reporting: Its Time Has Come*, which provides a useful overview. GASB is also developing detailed research reports on a variety of specific fields, such as education, economic development, hospitals, mass transit, police, and water treatment. (See endnotes, p. 392, for specific citations.)

The experts tend to agree on a series of further lessons:

Do both quantitative and qualitative analysis. Some valuable results are impossible to quantify. Others require so much paperwork and expense that they are not worth quantifying. Still others are quantifiable, but no one can say for sure whether the program in question was responsible for producing them. For all these reasons, it is important to combine quantitative measurement with qualitative evaluation. Good managers can get enormous insight into performance by looking at relevant numbers, but they can get equally valuable insight by spending time observing the program, agency, or provider; talking with workers; and listening to customers.

If all performance evaluation is done through numbers, service providers may also learn to game the numbers. "We watch the [enrollment and job placement] numbers, but we don't want our centers obsessed with them," explains Suzanne Teegarden, director of Massachusetts' Industrial Services Program.

Our worst centers are those that are numbers-driven. One of them—if the goal is 250 people enrolled, you can be sure they'll enroll 252. They aren't very energetic, and they don't take risks. Our best centers are the ones that really care, that get creative, that do it first and ask questions later. We know the centers well, so we know what the numbers mean.

WHAT TO MEASURE?

	General Definition	Street Sweeping	Welfare: Job Training
Output (or process)	Volume of units produced	Miles swept	Numbers of people trained
Outcome (or result)	Quality/effectiveness of production: degree to which it creates desired outcomes	Cleanliness rating of streets	Numbers of people placed in jobs, working, and off welfare after six months, one year, and beyond. Impact on their lives.
Program Outcome	Effectiveness of specific program in achieving desired outcomes	Cleanliness rating of streets as a result of sweeping	Numbers placed in jobs, working, and off welfare after six months, one year, and beyond. Impact on their lives.
Policy Outcome	Effectiveness of broader policies in achieving fundamental goals	Measures indicating how much litter citizens leave on streets	Percentage of potential work force unemployed, on welfare, and in poverty; percent of welfare population on welfare more than one year, five years, etc.
Program Efficiency	Cost per unit of output	Costs per mile of streets swept	Cost per job trainee; placement; retained job; etc.
Policy Efficiency	Cost to achieve fundamental goals	Cost for X level of street cleanliness	Cost to achieve desired decrease in unemployment, poverty rate, welfare caseload, etc.
Program Effectiveness	Degree to which program yields desired outcomes	Level of citizen satisfaction with cleanliness of streets	Numbers placed in jobs, working, and off welfare after six months, one year, and beyond. Impact on their lives.

Policy Effectiveness	Degree to which fundamental goals and citizens needs are met	Do citizens want to use their money this way? E.g., would they rather spend it on repaving streets?	Effect on larger society: e.g., poverty rate, welfare caseload, crime rate, later spending to remediate poverty, etc.

Watch out for creaming. Service providers will usually deliver the numbers they're asked to deliver, even if they have to cut corners to do it. If they have to place 1,000 people in jobs in a year, they will find the 1,000 most employable people they can and give them training—a practice known as creaming. This is precisely what happened during the early years of the Job Training Partnership Act. One solution is to set goals for each of several different target populations: 250 placements from among people who have been out of work for at least two years; 250 from those who do not have high school degrees; and so on. Another is to set different reimbursement rates for different populations. The job training industry has learned to use such mechanisms without any great difficulty.

Anticipate powerful resistance. Hard information about efficiency and effectiveness can be extremely threatening to service providers who doubt their ability to compete. Florida repealed a program that rewarded individual schools for improved performance. Arizona defunded a program that publicized the job placement rates of graduates from all postsecondary education and training institutions. The community colleges and technical schools found the information extremely threatening, because it revealed how effective they were at preparing people for real jobs. "You had big winners and big losers," says George Britton, who helped devise the system while serving under Governor Bruce Babbitt. "Whenever you single out people at the top and at the bottom, in a governmental function, it's very threatening." (Publication of such data is not impossible, however. Florida now does it successfully.)

Involve providers and employees in developing the correct measures. The best way to deal with resistance is to bring providers and employees into the process of defining the appropriate measures. To use data effectively, after all, people have to buy into its value. They need to "own" the specific measures used—to feel that they provide useful, relevant information that will improve the service they deliver. Those who oppose the idea, or oppose particular measures, need a fair hearing. Saddling people with inappropriate measures in whose development they have had no input is a sure way to create resistance, destroy morale, and encourage cheating.

Subject measures to annual review and modification. No measures are perfect. Since governance is not a science, it is impossible to isolate measures that perfectly reflect the outcomes of government activity. All we can do is hope for a close approximation, often using the best proxies available. Therefore it makes sense to modify and refine performance measures often, particularly as their flaws are revealed in practice. It also makes sense to commission an independent audit of the measures periodically, to see if they in fact measure what one thinks they measure. (Once the measures are refined, however, it is best to keep some measures steady over time, so as to be able to compare performance from one year to the next.)

Don't use too many or too few measures. If an organization sets too few measures, they may not reflect all of its goals. Hence its service providers may be driven to emphasize some goals at the expense of others. If it sets too many, it will dilute the power of all measures. Providers may become confused about priorities and burdened with paperwork, and managers may be overwhelmed by detail. If employees and service providers participate in the development of measures, and if they are allowed to correct the measures periodically, they will usually be able to find the right balance.

Watch out for perverse incentives. The funding formula used to finance nursing home care in Illinois during the 1970s created an incentive to keep people bedridden, as we saw in chapter 5. The performance measures originally used by JTPA encouraged job training providers to cream. Perverse incentives like these can undermine the entire effort to measure performance. To avoid them, organizations should "game" new measures—anticipating how clever providers might respond—before imposing them.

Keep the measurement function in a politically independent, impartial office. If people are to rely on data, they must trust its objectivity. Hence it is a good idea to use an independent office, like the Phoenix City Auditor's Office, to do the measuring. In Florida, two private organizations, Florida TaxWatch and the Florida Council of 100 (a business group), have created a nongovernmental organization, Partners in Productivity, to develop performance measures for state government. In Great Britain, the national Audit Commission audits the performance not only of national government agencies but also of local governments. Because it publishes comparative information about efficiency and effectiveness, local governments pay close attention to its studies.

Focus on maximizing the use of performance data. Just developing measures does not guarantee that managers will use them to change what they do or that legislatures will use them to change what they fund. The Fund for the City of New York discovered, according to Greg Farrell, that "good measures and management information turned out to be much easier to conceive than to integrate into the conduct of government business. . . . Government managers are not, for the most part, *used* to having or using management information, especially for forward-looking purposes. And on many issues, political pressures are often so great that *data* seem to be beside the point when decisions are made." Hence while developing performance measures, organizations should try to develop budgets, management systems, and reward systems built around performance data, as discussed in chapter 5.

Notes

All quotations that are not attributed in the text or in these endnotes are from interviews with the authors. Only in cases where there might be some confusion about the source of a quotation have we indicated in a note that it came from an interview.

Preface

P. xvi "At one time, governments were active investors . . . ": See, for instance, Peter K. Eisinger, *The Rise of the Entrepreneurial State* (Madison: University of Wisconsin Press, 1988), pp. 331–32.

"The federal government actually gave . . . ": Congressman Byron L. Dorgan, "Disappearing Railroad Blues," *Progressive* (August 1984): 32–34.

P. xix Quotation from J. B. Say: Quoted in Peter F. Drucker, *Innovation and Entrepreneurship Practice and Principles* (New York: Harper & Row, 1985), p. 21.

P. xx "But as careful studies demonstrate . . . ": See, for example, David C. McClelland, "Achievement Motivation Can Be Developed," *Harvard Business Review* (November–December 1965), and David C. McClelland and David Winter, *Motivating Economic Achievement* (New York: Free Press, 1969).

Drucker quotation: Drucker, *Innovation*, p. 139.

P. xxi Drucker reference and quotation: Ibid., pp. 170, 178.

83,000 governmental units: U.S. Department of Census, *1987 Census of Governments,* vol. 3, no. 2 (Washington, D.C.: Bureau of the Census, 1991), p. v.

Figures on full-time civilian employees: Ibid., National Summary, p. 1, Table 1.

"After 10 years of education reform and $60 billion in new money, test scores are stagnant and drop-out rates are higher . . . ": U.S. Department of Education, personal communication. Test scores referred to are Scholastic Aptitude Test (SAT) and American College Testing Program (ACT).

P. xxii Proust quotation: Quoted in *The Homegrown Economy*, videotape prepared by the Latimer administration, St. Paul.

Introduction: An American *Perestroika*

P. 1 "Strangely enough, in the midst of change . . . " Speaker's Advisory Committee on the Future, *The Sunrise Report. Florida Sunrise: Which Tomorrow?* (Tallahassee: Florida House of Representatives, March 1987), p. 79.

    Time magazine cover: October 23, 1989.

    "By the late 1980s, only five percent . . . ": Derek Bok, "Why Graduates Are Shunning Public-Service Careers," *Sacramento Bee*, June 26, 1988, p. 1.

    "Only 13 percent of top federal employees . . . ": Susan B. Garland et al., "Beltway Brain Drain: Why Civil Servants Are Making Tracks," *Business Week*, January 23, 1989, pp. 60–61. The survey cited was conducted by the federal General Accounting Office (GAO).

    "Nearly three out of four Americans . . . ": Laurence I. Barrett, "Giving the Public What It Wants," *Time*, October 23, 1989, p. 34. From a Time/CNN poll, conducted October 9–10, 1989, by Yankelovich Clancy Shulman. The exact percentage was 73 percent.

P. 5 "Single mothers head . . . median income is $8,300": Raymond J. Domanico, *Education Policy Paper Number 1: Model for Choice. A Report on Manhattan's District 4* (New York: Manhattan Institute for Policy Research, June 1989), p. 3.

    "Twenty years ago . . . " and "Only 15 percent . . . ": Ibid., p. 10.

P. 6 "Incorrigible, recalcitrant, aggressive kids": John Falco, interview with authors.

    "By 1990, District 4 boasted . . . ": Ibid.

P. 7 Ed Rodriguez quotation: From his remarks, at "Choosing Better Schools: Regional Strategy Meetings on Choice in Education," an East Harlem conference sponsored by the U.S. Department of Education, October 17, 1989.

P. 8 Sy Fliegel quotation: Quoted in Robert Merrow, "Schools of Choice: More Talk Than Action," in *Public Schools By Choice*, ed. Joe Nathan (St. Paul, Minn.: Institute for Learning and Teaching, 1989), p. 118.

    "Reading scores are up sharply . . . ": Personal communication, District 4. See also Domanico, *Education Policy Paper Number 1*, p. 10. In 1989 the reading test manufacturer renormed the test to reflect heightened reading achievement nationwide and the percentage of children in New York City schools who read at grade level dropped below 50 percent. Using these new national norms, 43.1 percent of District 4 students read at grade level in May of 1991.

    "Writing skills have improved . . . ": Mary Ann Raywid, "The Mounting Case for Schools of Choice," in *Public Schools by Choice*, p. 27.

Statistics on admittance to selective public and private schools: John Falco, interview with authors, and Domanico, *Education Policy Paper Number 1*, pp. 15–17.

"Yet it has a waiting list . . . ": Joe Nathan, "Prime Examples of School-Choice Plans," *Wall Street Journal*, April 20, 1989.

"Perhaps the most telling statistic . . . ": John Falco, interview with authors.

P. 10   "In an experiment straight out of *In Search of Excellence* . . . ": See Thomas J. Peters and Robert H. Waterman, Jr., *In Search of Excellence* (New York: Warner Books, 1982), pp. 146–47.

For more information on the Model Installations program, see *Model Installations and the Graduate Program. A DoD Report to the President's Blue Ribbon Commission on Defense Management*, May 16, 1986, available from the Office of the Deputy Assistant Secretary of Defense for Installations.

P. 11   Data on the Unified Budget Test: *The Unified Budget Test* (Washington, D.C.: Deputy Secretary of Defense [Installations], March 1988).

P. 13   Weber quotation: H. H. Gerth and C. Wright Mills, eds., *From Max Weber: Essays in Sociology* (New York: Oxford University Press, 1958), p. 214.

P. 14   For a fascinating study of government buildings, see Charles T. Goodsell, *The Social Meaning of Civic Space: Studying Political Authority Through Architecture* (Lawrence: University Press of Kansas, 1988).

P. 16   Alfred North Whitehead quotation: Quoted in William Van Dusen Wishard, "What in the World Is Going On?" *Vital Speeches*, March 1, 1990, pp. 311–317.

" . . . by 1982, state and local governments had lost . . . ": According to Table 21 in *Significant Features of Fiscal Federalism*, vol. 2: *Revenues and Expenditures* (Washington, D.C.: Advisory Commission on Intergovernmental Relations, 1990), p. 21, federal grants to state and local governments totaled $77.9 billion in 1978 and $88.2 billion in 1982. Expressed in 1978 dollars, the 1982 figure would have been $59.6 billion. This is a reduction of $18.3 billion, or 23.5 percent, between 1978 and 1982.

P. 17   South Carolina's education reforms: Gary Putka, "South Carolina's Broad School Reform Includes Incentives or Punishment Based on Performance," *Wall Street Journal*, July 12, 1988, p. 62, and Terry Peterson, "Five Years and a Quantum Leap," *Entrepreneurial Economy Review* (December–January 1989), published by the Corporation for Enterprise Development, Washington, D.C.

P. 18   William Hudnut quotation: Quoted in Marjorie George, "Can a City Be Run Like a Business?" *San Antonio* (December 1986): 22–29.

Coopers & Lybrand survey: *Survey on Public Entrepreneurship* (Coopers & Lybrand, 1988).

P. 19   Neil Postman paraphrase: From Neil Postman, *Teaching As a Subversive Activity* (New York: Dell, 1987).

P. 21   Lou Winnick quotation: From "The Cleveland Conference on Fiscal Constraints/Constructive Responses/Action Steps," report on a conference held in Cleveland, April 21–23, 1982, sponsored by the Cleveland Foundation and the Hubert H. Humphrey Institute of Public Affairs, University of Minnesota. Available from Ted Kolderie, Center for Policy Studies, Minneapolis.

P. 23   Keynes comment: See, for instance, John Maynard Keynes, *The General Theory of Employment, Interest and Money* (London: Macmillan

and Co., 1936), Chapter 24.

Chapter 1: Catalytic Government: Steering Rather Than Rowing

P. 26   Statistics on Lowertown: From Weiming Lu, executive director, Lowertown Development Corporation, interview with authors. See also Ann E. Webber, "Lowertown: The Beginning," in *The Saint Paul Experiment Initiatives of the Latimer Administration: Case Studies in Metropolitan Reform*, ed. David A. Lanegran, Cynthia Seelhammer, and Amy L. Walgrave (St. Paul: City of St. Paul, December 1989), pp. 459–73. This book is an excellent and exhaustive source on the Latimer administration.

       Statistics on St. Paul's fiscal status: George Latimer, interview with authors, and J. J. Allaire, "Fiscal Policy and Budget Process," in *The Saint Paul Experiment*, pp. 407–425.

P. 27   "This was fine as long as tax revenues were rising . . .": Thomas E. Borcherding, "One Hundred Years of Public Spending, 1870–1970," in *Budgets and Bureaucrats: The Sources of Government Growth*, ed. Thomas E. Borcherding (Durham, N.C.: Duke University Press, 1977), pp. 19–43.

P. 28   William Hudnut quotation: From transcript of interview with Robert Guskind and Neal Peirce of the *National Journal*, provided to the authors by Guskind and Peirce.

P. 29   "Newark, New Jersey . . .": Howard Jurtz, "In an Era of Reduced Federal Aid, Newark Stays Afloat," *Washington Post National Weekly Edition*, June 20–26, 1988.

       "Massachusetts boosted . . .": Executive Office for Administration and Finance, Office of Purchased Services, *Progress Report to the House and Senate Ways and Means Committees, as of February 1, 1988* (Boston, 1988), p. 3.

P. 30   Salamon quotation: Lester M. Salamon, "The Changing Tools of Government Action: An Overview," in *Beyond Privatization: The Tools of Government Action*, ed. Lester M. Salamon (Washington, D.C.: Urban Institute Press, 1989), pp. 10–11.

       Cuomo quotation: From Martin Tolchin, "More Cities Paying Industry to Provide Public Services," *New York Times*, May 28, 1985, pp. A1, D17.

       Chiles quotation: From "Building Community Partnerships," campaign statement released by the Chiles campaign November 1, 1990.

P. 32   Drucker quotation: Peter F. Drucker, *The Age of Discontinuity* (New York: Harper Torchbooks, 1978), p. 233.

P. 35   Drucker quotation: Ibid.
         Kolderie quotation: Ted Kolderie, "The Puzzle of the 'Public Sector' and the Strategy of Service Redesign," in *An Equitable and Competitive Public Sector*, ed. Ted Kolderie (Minneapolis: Hubert H. Humphrey Institute of Public Affairs, University of Minnesota, 1984), p. 20.

P. 35   Keefe quotation: Quoted in Chris Black, "Question 2: Is It Still Bad for You?" *Boston Globe*, September 30, 1990, pp. A1-A4.
         "Many of the services . . . ": Ibid.

P. 37   "In 1986, a White House report . . . ": Cited by Sar A. Levitan, Garth L. Mangum, and Marion W. Pines, *A Proper Inheritance Investing in the Self-Sufficiency of Poor Families* (Washington, D.C.: George Washington University Center for Social Policy Studies, July 1989), p. 3.
         "Another study . . . ": Ibid.
         "As Lisbeth Schorr reports . . . ": Lisbeth B. Schorr, *Within Our Reach Breaking the Cycle of Disadvantage* (Garden City, N.J.: Doubleday, 1988).
         "The typical government loses . . . ": According to the federal Office of Personnel Management, the federal government loses roughly 10 percent of its employees each year. State and local governments with which we have been able to check this figure report similar attrition rates.

P. 38   "Los Angeles County . . . ": Kitty Conlan, "Contracting Out: A Labor Perspective," *Urban Resources* 2, no. 4 (Summer 1985): 19.

P. 40   "Ohio uses local boards . . . ": For more information, see Nancy D. Kates, "Pam Hyde and Ohio Mental Health: Shifting Control of Inpatient Care," a case study prepared for the John F. Kennedy School of Government, Harvard University, 1987.
         "In Pittsburgh . . . ": Gwen Ifill, "Pittsburgh Finds Diversity Works in Fight on Homelessness," *Washington Post*, March 31, 1990, p. A3.
         "Montgomery County, Maryland . . . ": C. Kenneth Orski, " 'Managing' Suburban Traffic Congestion: A Strategy for Suburban Mobility," *Transportation Quarterly* 41, no. 4 (October 1987): 471-472, and personal communication with Transporation Management District.

P. 41   "This method has reduced the cost . . . ": *Behavioral Health Service System Description* (Phoenix: Arizona Department of Health Services, Division of Behavioral Health Services, February 1989).

P. 41   For more on CODAMA, see David Osborne, *Laboratories of Democracy* (Boston: Harvard Business School Press, 1988), pp. 122-128.

P. 43   Cleveland quotation: Harlan Cleveland, *The Knowledge Executive* (New York: E. P. Dutton, 1985), p. 82.
         "By 1982, nonprofit organizations . . . ": Gabriel Rudney, "The Scope and Dimensions of Nonprofit Activity," in *The Nonprofit Sector: A Research Handbook*, ed. Walter W. Powell (New Haven: Yale University Press, 1987), pp. 55-56.

"Between 1972 and 1982 . . . ": Ibid., p. 56.

"A 1989 Gallup survey . . . $170 billion": Personal communication with the Independent Sector, Washington, D.C., which commissioned the Gallup poll.

P. 44 "In 1985, Blue Cross Blue Shield . . . ": Mitchell Zuckoff, "Blue Cross Reports $30 Million Profit in 1990," *Boston Globe*, March 5, 1991.

"This sector . . . ": More than 20 years ago, Peter Drucker used a similar definition. He called such organizations "nongovernmental, autonomous institutions" that acted as "agents of social performance." He prophesied, in 1968, that their design might "become a central job for tomorrow's political architects." Drucker, *Age of Discontinuity*, p. 240.

Salamon quotation: Lester Salamon, "Partners in Public Service: The Scope and Theory of Government-Nonprofit Relations," in *The Nonprofit Sector*, p. 113.

"It existed . . . particular problems": Lester Salamon, "Of Market Failure, Voluntary Failure, and Third-Party Government: Toward a Theory of Government-Nonprofit Relations in the Modern Welfare State," in *Shifting the Debate· Public/Private Sector Relations in the Modern Welfare State*, ed. Susan A. Ostrander and Stuart Langton (New Brunswick, N.J.: Transaction Books, 1987), pp. 29–49.

"To this day . . . Johnny-come-lately": See Gwen Ifill, "Pittsburgh Finds Diversity Works in Fight on Homelessness," *Washington Post*, March 31, 1990, p. A3.

"Even a decade . . . source of income": Salamon, "Of Market Failure," p. 30.

P. 47 Kolderie quotation: "Let's Not Say Privatization," *Urban Resources* 2, no. 4 (Summer 1985): 14.

Drucker quotation: Drucker, *Age of Discontinuity*, pp. 241–42.

Chapter 2: Community-Owned Government: Empowering Rather Than Serving

P. 49 Brown quotation: Neal R. Peirce, "Police As Neighborhood Organizers: Chief Brown's Momentous Innovation," Washington Post Writer's Group, March 13, 1988. On community-oriented policing, see also James Q. Wilson and George L. Kelling, "Making Neighborhoods Safe," *Atlantic* (February 1989): 46–52; several articles in the July 1990 issue of *Public Management* (published by the International City Management Association, Washington, D.C.); John F. Persinos, "The Return of Officer Friendly," *Governing* (August 1989): 56–61; and Richard Lacayo, "Back to the Beat," *Time*, April 1, 1991, pp. 22–24.

P. 50 Wilson quotation: Wilson and Kelling, "Making Neighborhoods Safe."

Diamond quotation: Persinos, "Return of Officer Friendly," pp. 64–65.

Notes to Pages 50–58 367

National Association of Town Watch figures: "Neighbors Join to Roust the Criminals in the Streets," *Insight*, November 28, 1988, p. 9.

P. 51 Williams quotation: Ibid., p. 20.

Latimer quotation: *The Saint Paul Experiment Initiatives of the Latimer Administration*, ed. David A. Lanegran, Cynthia Seelhammer, and Amy L. Walgrave (St. Paul: City of St. Paul, December 1989), p. xxii.

P. 52 Latimer quotation: George Latimer, "1986 State of the City Address."

P. 53 On recycling in Seattle, see Randolph B. Smith, "Aided by Volunteers, Seattle Shows How Recycling Can Work," *Wall Street Journal*, July 19, 1990, pp. 1, A5; and "Recycling Life's Debris," *Governing* (October 1990): 47. Two years after the program began, Seattle was recycling 38 percent of its waste stream.

P. 54 Chubb quotation: John E. Chubb, "Why the Current Wave of School Reform Will Fail," *Public Interest*, no. 90 (Winter 1988): 40.

Statistics on Chicago schools: *Closer Look* (published by Designs for Change, Chicago), no. 1 (February 1991): 5.

P. 55 On New Haven, see Sharon Elder, "The Power of the Parent," *Yale* (Alumni Magazine) (October 1990): 50–54.

For an excellent article on Head Start in which the remarks quoted here appear, see Liza Mundy, "The Success Story of the War on Poverty," *Washington Monthly* (December 1989). As Mundy reports, a careful long-term study of one Head Start center, in Ypsilanti, Michigan, found that children who attended were more likely than their counterparts in the community to finish high school, to go on to college or vocational training, and to become self-supporting, and they were less likely to be detained or arrested or to become pregnant as teenagers. A cost-benefit analysis showed that every dollar spent on the center saved $6 in later special education, social service, court, and prison costs.

Clinton quotation and data on HIPPY: Bill Clinton, "Repairing the Family," *New Perspectives Quarterly* (Fall 1990): 12–15.

P. 56 Wisniewski quotation: From Gregg McCutcheon, *In Their Own Words* (Boston: Industrial Services Program, 1990), p. 8.

Data on San Francisco Community Boards: *Rebuilding American Community* (New York: Project for Public Spaces, August 1988).

P. 57 "Florida paroles . . . law-abiding citizens": Peter Drucker, *The New Realities* (New York: Harper & Row, 1989), pp. 200–203.

The "House of Umoja": Stuart Butler and Anna Kondratas, *Out of the Poverty Trap* (New York: Free Press, 1987), pp. 77, 124; and Lynn A. Curtis, "Neighborhood, Family and Employment," in *American Violence and Public Policy*, ed. Lynn A. Curtis (New Haven: Yale University Press, 1985), p. 208.

P. 58 Home health care a $7 billion industry: Mary Sit, "Lifetime Corp: House Calls with a Hug," *Boston Globe*, June 13, 1989, pp. 57, 58.

Washington Monthly article on AIDS care: Katherine Boo, "What Mother Teresa Could Learn in a Leather Bar," *Washington Monthly* (June 1991): 34–40.

P. 60   For more on Kenilworth-Parkside, see David Osborne, "They Can't
         Stop Us Now," *Washington Post Magazine*, July 30, 1989, pp. 12–19,
         27–31, from which this discussion is drawn.

P. 62   "At one point, 120 residents . . . ": *Cost Benefit Analysis of the Kenil-
         worth-Parkside Public Housing Resident Management Corporation.
         Executive Summary* (Washington, D.C.: National Center for Neigh-
         borhood Enterprise, May 1986). This report was based on a cost-
         benefit analysis done by the consulting firm Coopers & Lybrand.

P. 63   "By 1987, rent collections were up to 75 percent . . . ": Dennis Eisen,
         a real estate consultant hired to prepare a financial plan for resident
         ownership at Kenilworth–Parkside, interview with authors.

P. 64   "By 1989, the crime rate . . . ": Sergeant Robert L. Prout Jr., Wash-
         ington, D.C., police department, interview with authors.
              "In 1986 . . . additional savings": *Cost Benefit Analysis of the Ken-
         ilworth-Parkside Public Housing Resident Management Corporation.*

P. 66   McKnight quotation: John L. McKnight, "Regenerating Commu-
         nity," *Social Policy* (Winter 1987): 58.
              "McKnight provides an illuminating series . . . ": Ibid., pp. 56–58.
              Gillette quotation: From McCutcheon, *In Their Own Words*,
         pp. 22, 45.

P. 67   McKnight quotation: From "The Cleveland Conference on Fiscal
         Constraints/Constructive Responses/Action Steps," report on a con-
         ference held in Cleveland, April 21–23, 1982, sponsored by the
         Cleveland Foundation and the Hubert H. Humphrey Institute of
         Public Affairs.

P. 68   Rhoads quotation: Steven E. Rhoads, *The Economist's View of the
         World* (Cambridge: Cambridge University Press, 1985), p. 192.
              One Church, One Child: see John Herbers, "And a Little Child
         Shall Lead Them," *Governing* (October 1989): 34–35.

P. 69   "Florida saves $180 million . . . ": Florida TaxWatch, *Cost Savings
         in Florida Government 1980–89* (Tallahassee: Florida TaxWatch,
         1989), p. 20.
              "In fact, the state . . . ": *Behavioral Health Service System Descrip-
         tion* (Phoenix: Arizona Department of Health Services, February
         1989), p. 3.
              McKnight quotation: John L. McKnight, testimony before the U.S.
         Senate, Subcommittee on Aging, Family and Human Services, Sep-
         tember 17, 1981.
              Cook County study: Diane Kallenback and Arthur Lyons, *Govern-
         ment Spending for the Poor in Cook County, Illinois Can We Do Bet-
         ter?* (Evanston, Ill.: Northwestern University Center for Urban
         Affairs and Policy Research and Center for Economic Policy Analy-
         sis, April 1989).
              New York City study: McKnight, "Regenerating Community,"
         pp. 55–56. The study was *New York City's Poverty Budget*, done by
         the Community Services Society of New York, 105 East 22nd Street,
         New York, NY 10010.

"Sister Connie Driscoll . . . as we do": Bryan Miller, "House of Hope," *Reason* (May 1991): 50–53.

P. 70 McKnight quotation: McKnight, testimony, pp. 2–3.

P. 73 "By 1989, three out of four Americans . . . ": Richard Morin and Dan Balz, "Majority in Poll Criticize Congress," *Washington Post*, May 26, 1989, p. A8.

P. 74 "Many people have recommended . . . ": In his book, *Strong Democracy· Participatory Politics for a New Age* (Berkeley: University of California Press, 1984), Benjamin R. Barber outlined an ambitious set of proposals, including weekly or monthly neighborhood assemblies, town meetings using two-way televised communications, a national initiative and referendum process, and the use of interactive video communications to hold frequent straw polls and plebiscites as a way to spur discussion of important issues.

For more information on "futures projects," see Clement Bezold, ed., *Anticipatory Democracy* (New York: Vintage Books, 1978).

"We already have 504,404 . . . ": Richard Morin, "A Half a Million Choices for American Voters," *Washington Post National Weekly Edition*, February 6–12, 1989, p. 38. According to the *Statistical Abstract of the United States 1990* (Washington, D.C.: Bureau of the Census, 1990), p. 263, table 440, 91,595,000 votes were cast in 1988. This works out to one elected official for every 182 voters.

For more on St. Paul's district councils, see *The Saint Paul Experiment*, pp. 388–405.

Chapter 3: Competitive Government: Injecting Competition into Service Delivery

P. 76 Moffitt quotation: Quoted in Scott Lehigh, "Privatization Would Be Far-reaching," *Boston Globe*, April 29, 1991, p. 1.

P. 78 " . . . the city auditor estimates savings of $20 million . . . ": Phoenix City Auditor's Office, "Estimated Cost Impact of Competitive Service Delivery for Fiscal Year 1989–90 Management Summary," June 29, 1990. The precise number is $19.9 million.

P. 79 Creech quotation: Quoted in Jay Finegan, "Four-Star Management," *Inc* (January 1987): 42–51.

P. 80 "If competition saves money . . . ": Some governments specify a minimum wage contractors must pay. Some require minority hiring. Others, such as Phoenix, find that in services like garbage collection, the private sector pays just as well as government. A 1984 study done for the federal Department of Housing and Urban Development by Ecodata, a New York research company, found that in low-skill jobs, such as janitorial services, governments tend to pay more than contractors, but in more high skill occupations, such as asphalt paving, contractors pay considerably better. Barbara J. Stevens, ed., *Delivering Municipal Services Efficiently A Comparison of Municipal and*

Private Service Delivery (Washington, D.C.: U.S. Department of Housing and Urban Development, Office of Policy Development and Research, June 1984).

Savas quotation: E. S. Savas, "Implementing Privatization," *Urban Resources* 2, no. 4 (Summer 1985): 41.

P. 81 · "They show, he says . . . ": Interview with authors. But see E. S. Savas, *Privatization: The Key to Better Government* (Chatham, N.J.: Chatham House, 1987).

"James Q. Wilson . . . ": James Q. Wilson, *Bureaucracy What Government Agencies Do and Why They Do It* (New York: Basic Books, 1989), pp. 350–51. See also Robert M. Spann, "Public versus Private Provision of Governmental Services," in *Budgets and Bureaucrats The Sources of Government Growth*, ed. Thomas E. Borcherding (Durham, N.C.: Duke University Press, 1977), pp. 71–85.

"Not surprisingly, Massachusetts . . . ": Doug Bailey, "Study Blames Regulators for High Auto Rates," *Boston Globe*, August 30, 1989, pp. 69, 70.

P. 82 "We all know the Postal Service . . . ": Carol Matlack, "No Pickup, No Delivery," *National Journal*, June 4, 1988, p. 1484.

"In 1988, it met . . . ": President's Commission on Privatization, *Privatization: Toward More Effective Government* (Washington, D.C.: President's Commission on Privatization, 1988), p. 107.

"The trade association of bulk mailers . . . ": Matlack, "No Pickup, No Delivery."

"In 1971 . . . 12 percent": John Judis, "What's Wrong with the Post Office," *New York Times Magazine*, September 15, 1988.

Douglas quotation: From Roger Douglas, "National Policy-Makers' Experience—New Zealand" (address to World Bank Conference on Privatisation, Washington, D.C., June 11–13, 1990).

P. 83 " . . . the survival of the helpful . . . ": David Miller and Saul Estrin, "Market Socialism, a Policy for Socialists," in *Market Socialism*, ed. Ian Forbes, Fabian Society pamphlet 516.

Savas quotation: E. S. Savas, *Privatizing the Public Sector* (Chatham, N.J.: Chatham House, 1982), p. 136.

P. 85 "When Tennessee recently decided . . . ": Elizabeth Neuffer, "Cost of Private Prisons Debated," *Boston Globe*, May 6, 1991, pp. 15, 18.

New York City's Sanitation Department material: Ronald A. Contino, "Waging Revolution in the Public Sector: Operational Improvements Through Labor/Management Cooperation," unpublished paper, available from Ronald A. Contino, Surface Transit, New York City Transit Authority.

"To handle 4,500 . . . post offices": President's Commission on Privatization, *Privatization*, p. 121.

P. 86 "In Massachusetts in 1989 . . . ": Bruce Mohl, "Insurance Costs Shackle State," *Boston Globe*, December 8, 1989, pp. 1, 18.

SRI International study on Arizona: Nelda McCall et al., *Evaluation of the Arizona Health Care Cost Containment System: Final Report* (Menlo Park, Calif.: SRI International, January 1989).

P. 87   "Studies in Wisconsin . . . ": Timothy Tyson, *An Evaluation of the Medicaid Health Maintenance Organization Program· 1987–1989* (Madison: Wisconsin Office of Policy and Budget, December 1989), and *The Medicaid Health Maintenance Organization Program: Its Impact on Cost, Utilization and Access* (Madison: Department of Health and Social Services, Division of Policy and Budget, January 1988).

"We didn't slash any benefits . . . ": John F. Persinos, "The Good Old Days of Generous Health Benefits Are Starting to End," *Governing* (March 1989): p. 60.

"By 1987, the federal government . . . ": President's Commission on Privatization, *Privatization,* p. 129.

" . . . state and local governments contracted . . . ": John R. Miller and Christopher R. Tufts, "Creative Management Through Privatization," *American City and County,* (September 1988): 82.

"The average city . . . ": E. S. Savas, "Private Enterprise Is Profitable Enterprise," *New York Times,* February 14, 1988.

"The AFL-CIO has filled books . . . ": See, for example, *America . . . Not for Sale· A PED Guide for Fighting Privatization* (Washington, D.C.: AFL-CIO Public Employee Department, October 1989).

"To do it right . . . ": Stevens, *Delivering Municipal Services Efficiently,* pp. 9–10.

P. 88   "Privatizing to a monopoly . . . ": See Harry P. Hatry, *A Review of Private Approaches for Delivery of Public Services* (Washington, D.C.: Urban Institute Press, 1983), p. 74.

Starr quotation: Paul Starr, "The Meaning of Privatization," *Yale Law and Policy Review* 6 (1988): 34.

"Marion Barry's administration . . . ": Michael Willrich, "Department of Self Services," *Washington Monthly* (October 1990): 28–36.

P. 89   "It works best . . . ": Jeffrey L. Katz, "Privatization Without Tears," *Governing* (June 1991): 40.

"A 1989 survey . . . 30 percent": Jonathan Marshall, "Troubled Cities Put Services Out to Bid," *San Francisco Chronicle,* June 3, 1991, pp. 1, 6.

P. 90   Savas quotation: Savas, *Privatizing the Public Sector,* p. 136.

For more on Minnesota's Department of Administration, see Michael Barzelay and Babak J. Armajani, "Managing State Government Operations: Changing Visions of Staff Agencies," *Journal of Policy Analysis and Management* 9, no. 3 (1990): 307–338; and Michael Barzelay and Pamela Varley, "Introducing Marketplace Dynamics in Minnesota State Government," a case study prepared for the John F. Kennedy School of Government, Harvard University, 1988.

P. 92   Hale quotation: From Sandra J. Hale, "Reinventing Government the Minnesota Way" (address to National Public Sector Productivity Conference, Albany, N.Y., September 10, 1990).

"Between 1987 and 1990 . . . saving the state $3.6 million": Sandra Hale, Judith Pinke, and others in the Minnesota Department of Administration, interviews with the authors.

P. 93   Drucker quotation: Peter Drucker, *The New Realities* (New York: Harper & Row, 1989), p. 235.

P. 94   Thompson quotation: From Nancy Paulu, *Improving Schools and Empowering Parents: Choice in American Education* (Washington, D.C.: U.S. Department of Education, Office of Educational Research and Development, October 1989), p. 44.

P. 95   Chubb quotation: From "The Right to Choose: Public School Choice and the Future of American Education," Manhattan Institute for Policy Research Policy Paper, June 1989, pp. 8–13.
          Wagner quotation: Ibid., p. 29.
          Chubb quotation: Ibid.

P. 97   "In the program's first year . . . college courses": Jessie Montano, "Choice Comes to Minnesota," in *Public Schools by Choice,* ed. Joe Nathan (St. Paul, Minn.: Institute for Learning and Teaching, 1989), pp. 165–180.

P. 98   "By 1987, 5,700 students . . . ": Ibid., pp. 176–177.
          "Roughly a quarter . . . ": Joe Nathan, "Prime Examples of School-Choice Plans," *Wall Street Journal,* April 20, 1989.
          "In three years . . . television instruction": Montano, "Choice Comes to Minnesota."
          "In its first two years . . . just two years": Joe Nathan, in "The Right to Choose," p. 22.

P. 99   "Once they entered . . . ": Peter Hutchinson, Babak Armajani, and John James, *Enterprise Management. Designing Public Services As if the Customer Really Mattered* (Minneapolis: Center of the American Experiment, 1991), p. 14.
          Statistics on participation in open enrollment options: Minnesota Department of Education.

P. 100   Kolderie quotation, "School choice alone . . . ": Ted Kolderie, *Beyond Choice to New Public Schools: Withdrawing the Exclusive Franchise in Public Education* (Washington, D.C.: Progressive Policy Institute, November 1990).

P. 101   "When Governor Perpich . . . 60 percent did": Nathan, "Prime Examples."
          "Even more revealing . . . ": Rebecca Woosley, "School Choice Benefits Students, Teachers," *Wingspread Journal* (Fall–Winter 1990): 1–5.

P. 105   Dallas hospital study: Elizabeth Hudson, "Stemming the Tide of Patient Dumping," *Washington Post Weekly Edition,* April 4–10, 1988, p. 35.
          "Careful studies indicate . . . ": Stevens, *Delivering Municipal Services Efficiently*
          "But some studies suggest . . . ": Jonathan Marshall, "Troubled Cities Put Services Out to Bid," reporting a 1989 study by the National Commission for Employment Policy.

P. 106   Donahue quotation: John D. Donahue, *The Privatization Decision* (New York: Basic Books, 1990).

"In mass transit . . . ": See Elliott D. Sclar, K. H. Schaeffer, and Robert Brandwein, *The Emperor's New Clothes Transit Privatization and Public Policy* (Washington, D.C.: Economic Policy Institute, 1989), pp. 19–24.

"Even in day care . . . ": Bill Jameson, former director of Arizona's Department of Economic Security, told us: "The private, for-profit day care centers did everything they could to keep us from contracting with mothers who took in a few kids. My goal was, the more kids we can get in day care homes the better, because it's a good environment. But they went to the legislature and tried to prohibit us from putting kids in those homes. They also tried to keep us from doing business with schools, for after school care. They said that was unfair competition from the public sector, because the schools are subsidized. . . . They succeeded one year in striking down any attempt to license schools, but that's been taken care of."

"The postmasters sent . . . ": Associated Press, "Post Offices Use Free Mail to Lobby," *Boston Globe*, July 5, 1990.

P. 107   "Public police forces are losing ground . . . ": William C. Cunningham, John J. Strauchs, and Clifford W. Van Meter, *Private Security Trends 1970 to 2000: The Hallcrest Report II* (Boston: Butterworth-Heinemann, 1990), pp. 229, 230.

Chapter 4: Mission-Driven Government: Transforming Rule-Driven Organizations

P. 108   Patton quotation: Quoted in Roger Vaughan, "Is It Working," *Entrepreneurial Economy Review* (published by the Corporation for Enterprise Development, Washington, D.C.) (July–August 1989): 3.

P. 110   Wilson quotation: James Q. Wilson, *Bureaucracy* (New York: Basic Books, 1989), p. 342.

P. 111   "When the Federal Aviation Administration . . . 9 to 12 months": President's Commission on Privatization, *Privatization: Toward More Effective Government* (Washington, D.C.: President's Commission on Privatization, 1988), pp. 67–68.

"When the Massachusetts Revenue Department . . . ": Chris Black, "Civil Service Feels the Strain," *Boston Globe*, August 26, 1987, pp. 1, 83.

Logue quotation: Charles A. Radin, "High Cost Seen in Adhering to Ward Reforms," *Boston Globe*, December 26, 1989.

P. 112   Stein quotation: Andrew Stein, "The Board of Education Surrenders to Janitors," *New York Times*, November 6, 1987.

P. 113   "St. Paul, Visalia . . . ": "The Top 50 Cities: 5th Annual Financial Report," *City and State*, November 19, 1990, p. 12.

"As Morton H. Halperin . . . ": James Q. Wilson, *Bureaucracy* (New York: Basic Books, 1989), p. 179.

"All the research shows . . . ": For a review of the research literature, see Mary Anne Raywid, "The Mounting Case for Schools of

Choice," in *Public Schools by Choice*, ed. Joe Nathan (St. Paul, Minn.: Institute for Learning and Teaching, 1989), pp. 26–27.

Fliegel quotation: Remarks at East Harlem conference sponsored by the U.S. Department of Education, October 17, 1989.

"When a Philadelphia youth gang . . . ": Stuart Butler and Anna Kondratas, *Out of the Poverty Trap* (New York: Free Press, 1987), pp. 130–131.

P. 114 "Even today, McDonald's . . . ": Wilson, *Bureaucracy*, p. 114.

P. 115 Rural Electrification Administration: James Bennett, "Power Failure," *Washington Monthly* (July–August 1990): 12–21.

P. 116 "When Common Cause surveyed . . . ": *The Status of Sunset in the States· A Common Cause Report* (Washington, D.C.: Common Cause, 1982). Cited by Jonathon Rose, "The Arizona Sunset Experience: The First Two Cycles, 1978–82," *Arizona State Law Journal*, no. 2 (1985): 321–423.

P. 118 "In one branch . . . ": *The Unified Budget Test* (Washington, D.C.: Deputy Secretary of Defense [Installations], March 1988).

"At one military base . . . in the mud": Ibid.

P. 121 "By 1991 . . . its revenues": *City of Fairfield, California, 1991/92 Annual Budget and Ten-Year Financial Plan* (Fairfield: City of Fairfield, May 30, 1991), p. 29.

P. 122 "Sweden, Canada, Britain . . . ": Allen Schick, "Micro-Budgetary Adaptations to Fiscal Stress in Industrialized Democracies," *Public Administration Review* (January–February 1988): 523–532; and Allen Schick, "Budgeting for Results: Recent Developments in Five Industrialized Countries," *Public Administration Review* (January–February 1990): 26–33.

P. 123 Peters and Waterman quotation: Thomas J. Peters and Robert Waterman, Jr., *In Search of Excellence* (New York: Warner Books, 1982), p. 144.

P. 125 "No issue . . . ": Black, "Civil Service Feels the Strain."

"In San Francisco . . . ": Stephen Schwartz, "SF Proposal to Reform Hiring, Firing," *San Francisco Chronicle*, May 18, 1991.

"When E. S. Savas . . . ": Interview with authors. For more, see E. S. Savas and Sigmund G. Ginsberg, "The Civil Service: A Meritless System?" *Public Interest*, no. 32 (Summer 1973): 70–85.

P. 126 "Federal employees cannot . . . ": Wilson, *Bureaucracy*, pp. 145–146.

"James Q. Wilson . . . ": Ibid.

P. 127 "When New Jersey . . . ": Matthew Cooper and Paul Glastris, "Laughing at the Hangman," *U S News and World Report*, June 17, 1991, p. 28–29.

Rosenthal quotation: Ibid.

"While their unions . . . ": *The St Paul Experiment*, ed. David A. Lanegran, Cynthia Seelhammer, and Amy Walgrave (St. Paul: City of St. Paul, December 1989), pp. 376–377.

"Scott Shuger . . . ": Scott Shuger, "How to Cut the Bureaucracy in Half," *Washington Monthly* (June 1990): 38–51.

"With 17.5 million . . . ": Figures on public payroll: *Statistical Abstract of the United States 1990*, Table 487, reports a total monthly payroll of $32,382,000,000 in 1987—roughly $388 billion a year. As of 1992, this is the most recent figure available. Adjusting for inflation between 1987 and 1992, the figure should be close to $500 billion.

"Benefits add . . . ": In the federal government, benefits total 23 percent of payroll, according to the Office of Personnel Management. Applying the 23 percent figure to $500 billion, benefits for all governments would be $115 billion a year.

"One study found . . . ": T. E. Borcherding, W. C. Bush, and R. M. Spann, "The Effects on Public Spending of the Divisibility of Public Outputs," in *Budgets and Bureaucrats. The Sources of Government Growth*, ed. Thomas Borcherding (Durham, N.C.: Duke University Press, 1977), pp. 221–224.

P. 128 "Mayor Latimer pushed . . . ": See *The St. Paul Experiment*, pp. 372–387.

The China Lake Experiment: Wilson, *Bureaucracy*, pp. 146–148.

P. 130 "Even 50 years ago . . . ": Ibid., pp. 97–99.

Couper quotation: David C. Couper and Sabine H. Lobitz, *Quality Policing: The Madison Experience* (Washington, D.C.: Police Executive Research Forum, 1991), p. 24.

P. 131 "In 1989, Representatives Lee Hamilton . . . ": Morton Kondracke, "How to Aid A.I.D.," *New Republic*, February 26, 1990, pp. 20–23.

P. 132 "When George Latimer . . . ": See *The Saint Paul Experiment*, pp. 57–71, 317–328.

P. 135 Gen. Gray quotation: "CMC Blasts Zero-defect Mentality," *Graduate Gazette*, n.d., published by the Office of the Assistant Secretary of Defense for Installations.

In his book, *Bureaucracy*, pp. 14–16, James Q. Wilson describes a fascinating example of a mission-driven organization: the German Army in World War II. The central concept the Germans used to build a military capable of blitzkrieg tactics was *auftragstatik*—a "mission-oriented command system":

"An army that could probe enemy defenses, infiltrate weak points, and rapidly exploit breakthroughs with deep encircling moves could not be an army that was centrally directed or dependent on detailed plans worked out in advance. . . .

Commanders were to tell their subordinates precisely what was to be accomplished but not necessarily how to accomplish it. . . . The German army . . . had remarkably little paperwork. Orders were clear but brief.

The result was an organization well adapted to the task of getting men to fight against heavy odds in a confused, fluid setting

376 Notes to Pages 135–143

far from army headquarters and without precisely detailed in-
structions."

P. 135 "Florida's *State Management Guide* . . . ": Governor's Management
Improvement Program, *State Management Guide* (Tallahassee: Administration of Governor Bob Graham).

P. 137 Drucker quotation: Peter Drucker, *The Age of Discontinuity* (New
York: Harper Torchbooks, 1978), p. 229.

Chapter 5: Results-Oriented Government:
Funding Outcomes, Not Inputs

P. 139 For more on the Illinois system of rating nursing homes, see *Innovations in State and Local Government, 1986*, report of the Ford Foun-
dation/John F. Kennedy School Awards Program, p. 13.

P. 140 " 'Pleasing the voters is our performance evaluation' ": Quoted in
Katherine Barrett and Richard Greene, "The Forgotten State
House," *Financial World*, April 17, 1990.

Blumenthal quotation: Quoted in James Q. Wilson, *Bureaucracy*
(New York: Basic Books, 1989), pp. 195, 197. Originally from Michael Blumenthal, "Candid Reflections of a Businessman in Washington," *Fortune*, January 29, 1979, p. 39.

Fountain quotation: Quoted in "Tracking Bang for the Buck," *Governing* (April 1991): 13–14.

P. 141 "Fountain's organization . . . ": See Harry P. Hatry et al., eds., *Ser-
vice Efforts and Accomplishments Reporting: Its Time Has Come: An
Overview* (Norwalk, Conn.: Governmental Accounting Standards
Board, 1990).

P. 142 "Six states are testing performance standards . . . ": See Commission
on Trial Court Performance Standards, *Trial Court Performance
Standards with Commentary* (Williamsburg, Va.: National Center for
State Courts, 1990); *Measurement of Trial Court Performance 1990
Supplement to the Trial Court Performance Standards with Commen-
tary* (Williamsburg, Va.: National Center for State Courts, 1990); and
Beatrice P. Monahan, *Public Perceptions of Access to Justice* (Wil-
liamsburg, Va.: National Center for State Courts, 1990).

"Some offer performance bonuses . . . ": Ted Kolderie, *An Equitable and Competitive Public Sector* (Minneapolis: Hubert H.
Humphrey Institute of Public Affairs, University of Minnesota,
1984), p. 61; and Kolderie, "Let's Not Say Privatization," *Urban Resources*, 2, 4 (Summer 1985): p. 13.

"Boston Edison pays . . . ": Gordon McKibben, "Edison, State Set
Rate Pact," *Boston Globe*, October 4, 1989, pp. 1, 26.

P. 143 Sunnyvale performance standards: From City of Sunnyvale, *Resource Allocation Plan. 1989–90 to 1998–99 Fiscal Years, 10-Year Operating Budget.*

P. 146   "Scorecard" and related performance measurement: See *Fund for the City of New York, Three-Year Report, 1979–81* (New York: Fund for the City of New York, 1982).

P. 147   Farrell quotation: Ibid., p. 3.

Spanbauer quotation: Stanley J. Spanbauer, *Quality First in Education . Why Not?* (Appleton, Wis.: Fox Valley Technical College Foundation, 1987), p. 48.

"Smaller, more entrepreneurial . . . ": For a good example, see Mark Muro, "Agencies Find That Small Is Vulnerable," *Boston Globe*, May 30, 1989, pp. 15, 19.

"When the Bush administration . . . what we've bought": Paul M. Barrett, "Federal War on Drugs Is Scattershot Affair, with Dubious Progress," *Wall Street Journal*, August 10, 1989; p. 1.

P. 148   "One sage . . . ": Stan Jordan, chairman of the school board, Duval County, Florida.

"When the Federal National Mortgage Association . . ": Brian Dumaine, "Making Education Work," *Fortune*, Education 1990 Issue, p. 13.

"When wealthy New Orleans oilman . . . ": Ann Reilly Dowd, "How Washington Can Pitch In," *Fortune*, Education 1990 Issue, p. 62.

P. 149   "In 1989, the state . . . ": Ibid., and "Arkansas Adopts Taylor Plan," *New Concepts* (newsletter published by the Exchange Foundation, Birmingham, Ala.) 4, no. 9 (Spring 1991): 3, 4.

Fliegel quotation: Quoted in Robert Merrow, "Schools of Choice: More Talk Than Action," *Public Schools by Choice*, ed. Joe Nathan (St. Paul, Minn.: Institute for Learning and Teaching, 1989), p. 119.

"One study . . . ": In 1986, Metro United Way in Louisville published *Incentives for Working*, which used a $7 an hour figure. (Indeed, it became known as the "$7-an-hour study.") In December 1988, a University of Kentucky report said the figure had increased to $9 an hour: Lucinda R. Zoe and Lynne S. Kelly, *Status of Child Care in Kentucky* (Lexington, Ky.: University of Kentucky College of Business and Economics, Center for Business and Economic Research, Dec. 1988).

P. 150   "Minnesota's Learnfare initiative . . . ": *Access to Excellence, Education in Minnesota* (St. Paul: Minnesota Department of Education), p. 14.

P. 151   Drucker quotation: Peter Drucker, *Innovation and Entrepreneurship* (New York: Harper & Row, 1985) p. 37.

For more on Transitional Employment Enterprises and America Works, see David Osborne, *Laboratories of Democracy* (Boston: Harvard Business School Press, 1988), pp. 198–200.

P. 153   Community Mental Health Centers story: Andrew Bates, "Mental Health Spas," *Washington Monthly* (December 1990): 26–29.

P. 155   Florida TaxWatch quotation: "TaxWatch Survey Shows Strong Public Support for Increased Transportation Funding IF Tied to Increased DOT Performance," *Florida TaxWatch Briefings*, April 24, 1990. Available from Florida TaxWatch, Tallahassee, Florida.

P. 157   "James Q. Wilson . . . ": James Q. Wilson, *Bureaucracy* (New York: Basic Books, 1989), p. 162.

P. 158   "The Urban Institute's Harry Hatry . . . ": Harry P. Hatry and John M. Greiner, *Issues and Case Studies in Teacher Incentive Plans* (Washington, D.C.: Urban Institute Press, 1985), p. 115.

   Shanker proposal and quotation: Edward B. Fiske, "Lessons," *New York Times*, July 26, 1989, p. B8.

P. 159   "As one Rochester teacher . . . ": Quoted in Jerry Buckley, "Blackboard Juggle," *U S. News and World Report*, December 24, 1990, p. 56.

P. 160   Scholtes quotation: Peter R. Scholtes, *The Team Handbook* (Madison, Wis.: Joiner Associates, 1988), pp. 1–11, 1–12.

P. 165   "Great Britain, Denmark . . . ": See Allen Schick, "Budgeting for Results: Recent Developments in Five Industrialized Countries," *Public Administration Review* (January–February 1990): 26–33.

Chapter 6: Customer-Driven Government: Meeting the Needs of the Customer, Not the Bureaucracy

P. 166   Couper quotation: David Couper and Sabine Lobitz, *Quality Policing The Madison Experience* (Washington, D.C.: Police Executive Research Forum, 1991), p. 65.

P. 167   Forsberg quotation: In Peter S. Canellos, "Undaunted by Dire Straits," *Boston Globe*, December 23, 1990, pp. 25, 31.

P. 169   Fliegel quotation: Remarks at East Harlem conference sponsored by the U.S. Department of Education, October 17, 1989.

P. 170   Kearns quotation: David T. Kearns and Denis P. Doyle, *Winning the Brain Race A Bold Plan to Make Our Schools Competitive* (San Francisco: Institute for Contemporary Studies, 1988), pp. 21–22.

   Drucker quotation: Drucker, "What Business Can Learn from Nonprofits," *Harvard Business Review* (July–August 1989): 328–333.

   "The Dallas Parks and Recreation Department . . . ": See *Innovations in State and Local Government 1987*, report of the Ford Foundation/John F. Kennedy School Awards Program, p. 12.

P. 172   Sensenbrenner quotation: Joseph Sensenbrenner, "Quality Comes to City Hall," *Harvard Business Review* (March–April 1991): 65.

P. 174   For more on Fox Valley Tech, see Stanley J. Spanbauer, *Quality First in Education . Why Not?* (Appleton, Wis.: Fox Valley Technical College Foundation, 1987); and Stanley J. Spanbauer, *Quality: A Business Prescription for America's Schools* (Milwaukee: Quality Press, forthcoming).

P. 177   Florida TaxWatch quotation: *Building a Better Florida: A Management Blueprint to Save Taxpayers over $1 Billion* (Tallahassee: Florida TaxWatch, 1986), p. 15.

P. 178   "It discovered that social problems . . . ": Adult Literacy Task Force, *Countdown 2000· Michigan's Action Plan for a Competitive*

Workforce (Lansing, Mich.: Governor's Cabinet Council on Human Investment, March 1988), p. 49.

"And it learned that . . . ": "Creating a Strategic System for Human Investment: The Michigan Opportunity System," Michigan Human Investment Fund, January 1990.

Electronic mail in Santa Monica: M. J. Richter, "The Real Advantages of Putting Government On Line," *Governing* (May 1991): 60.

P. 179   "Many high schools . . . ": Jerry Thomas, "High School Gives Warrantees," *Boston Globe*, June 1, 1991.

Drucker quotation: Peter Drucker, *The Age of Discontinuity* (New York: Harper Torchbooks, 1978), p. 256.

"Sweden . . . by 1988": Sam Zagoria, "Ombudsmen Can Clear the Air Between Citizens and City Hall," *Governing* (November 1988): 82. A former *Washington Post* ombudsman, Zagoria wrote *The Ombudsman: How Good Governments Handle Citizens' Grievances* (Bethesda, MD: Seven Locks Press, 1988).

P. 182   Coleman quotation: From "The Right to Choose: Public School Choice and the Future of American Education," Manhattan Institute for Policy Research policy paper, June 1989, p. 29.

"James Q. Wilson . . . like McDonald's": James Q. Wilson, *Bureaucracy* (New York: Basic Books, 1989), pp. 135–136.

P. 183   Raywid quotation: Mary Anne Raywid, "The Mounting Case for Schools of Choice," in *Public Schools by Choice*, ed. Joe Nathan (St. Paul, Minn.: Institute for Learning and Teaching, 1989), p. 32.

Nathan quotation: Joe Nathan, "Introduction," in *Public Schools by Choice*, p. 9.

P. 184   "Even a majority . . . ": Poll funded by Metropolitan Life, released in October 1989.

"Education research . . . satisfaction": Raywid, "Mounting Case for Schools of Choice."

P. 185   "Studies done in Wisconsin . . . ": E. S. Savas, *Privatizing the Public Sector* (Chatham, N.J.: Chatham House, 1982), p. 142.

P. 187   "In 1989, the assistant secretary . . . ": U.S. Congress, Select Committee on Children, Youth, and Families, *Opportunities for Success Cost-Effective Programs for Children Update, 1990* (Washington, D.C.: U.S. Government Printing Office, 1990), p. 159.

Youngstown story: Terry F. Buss and Roger J. Vaughan, *On the Rebound: Helping Workers Cope with Plant Closings* (Washington, D.C.: Council of State Policy and Planning Agencies, 1988), and interviews with authors.

Vaughan quotation: Interview with authors.

P. 188   "*Those who avoided*": Personal communication from Dr. Terry Buss and Dr. Roger Vaughan.

Vaughan quotations: interview with authors.

P. 192   "Power and his colleagues . . . ": *Creating a Human Investment System* (Lansing: Michigan Job Training Coordinating Council, 1989), p. 10.

P. 193   "A recent *Governing* . . . for Tasha": Kathleen Sylvester, "New Strategies to Save Children in Trouble," *Governing* (May 1990): 32–37.
     "Even the AFL-CIO . . . funding streams": *Making Government
Work* (Washington, D.C.: AFL-CIO Public Employee Department,
1991).

Chapter 7: Enterprising Government:
Earning Rather Than Spending

P. 195   Wilson quotation: In Ray Vicker, "Fairfield, Calif., Relies on Busi-
ness Savvy to Raise Revenues in Wake of Tax Revolt," *Wall Street
Journal*, November 24, 1982, p. 56.
     FERC story: Dale Rusakoff, "The Government's Not Like You or
Me," *Washington Post*, February 15, 1990, p. A23.
P. 196   1984 Olympics: See Peter Ueberroth, *Made In America* (New York:
William Morrow and Co., 1984).
P. 197   "Chicago turned . . . the privilege": Katherine Barrett and Richard
Greene, "American Cities: A Special Report," *Financial World*, Feb-
ruary 19, 1991, p. 22.
     "The St. Louis County . . . police department": Fred Jordan, *Inno-
vating America* (New York: Ford Foundation, 1990), p. 48.
     "Paulding County . . . operating costs": Tom Watson, "Lockups
for Lease," *Boston Globe*, May 16, 1991.
P. 200   Figures on Fairfield mall and other development projects: Interviews
with Fairfield development staff.
P. 201   "Lest you think . . . ": Lawrence M. Fisher, "Cities Turn into Entre-
preneurs," *New York Times*, April 4, 1987, pp. Business 1, 19.
P. 202   Frederick quotations: From Mayor Bill Frederick, 1991 State of City
Address, p. 6.
     Orlando city hall: See Lewis Oliver and Eric Smart, "Orlando's
City Commons," *Urban Land* (January 1990): 21–25; and Rowland
Stiteler, "The Deal That Built City Hall," *Orlando Magazine* (December 1990): 53–74.
P. 203   Oliver quotation: In Stiteler, "Deal that Built City Hall," p. 55.
     "Fairfield has made . . . ": Charles Long, Fairfield city manager,
interview with authors.
     "Sunnyvale generates . . . ": City of Sunnyvale, *Resource Alloca-
tion Plan. 1989–90 to 1998–99 Fiscal Years, 10-Year Operating Budget*, p. xxxix.
     "The average local government . . . ": Steven D. Gold, *Reforming
State-Local Relations: A Practical Guide* (Denver: National Conference of State Legislatures, 1989), pp. 51–52.
     "They are particularly common . . . ": Harry P. Hatry, "Using Fees
and Charges to Adjust Demand," in *The Entrepreneur in Local Government*, ed. Barbara Moore (Washington, D.C.: International City
Management Association, 1983).

Shannon quotation: In Penelope Lemov, "User Fees, Once the Answer to City Budget Prayers, May Have Reached Their Peak," *Governing* (March 1989): 26.

P. 204   "What is fair about subsidizing golf . . . ": Neal R. Peirce and Robert Guskind, "Fewer Federal Dollars Spurring Cities to Improve Management and Trim Costs," *National Journal*, March 1, 1986, p. 506.

"To solve this problem . . . ": For examples, see Lemov, "User Fees,", p. 28.

Mikesell quotation: Ibid., p. 27.

P. 205   King quotation: Norman R. King, "Managing Demand for Government Services: Toward a New Public Administration Ethic" (address delivered to Michigan City Management Association, February 17, 1988), p. 12.

P. 206   "Careful studies have estimated . . . ": See U.S. Congress, Select Committee on Children, Youth, and Families, *Opportunities for Success· Cost-Effective Programs for Children Update, 1990* (Washington, D.C.: U.S. Government Printing Office, 1990), pp. 70–71, for summaries of several studies.

P. 210   "Phoenix typically gets 1,000 . . . ": Interviews with Phoenix Personnel Department.

P. 211   Cisneros quotation: Marjorie George, "Can a City Be Run Like a Business?" *San Antonio* (December 1986): 22–29.

Drucker quotation: Peter F. Drucker, "The Innovative Organization," *The Frontiers of Management* (New York: Harper & Row, 1985), pp. 263–264.

Pinchot quotation: Gifford Pinchot III, *Intrapreneuring* (New York: Harper & Row, 1985), p. 275.

P. 212   "Local governments have . . . ": Lawrence "Chip" Pierce, "Hitting the Beach and Running: Minibonds," *Government Finance Review* (August 1988): 29–31.

P. 213   Armajani quotation: In Michael Barzelay and Pamela Varley, "Introducing Marketplace Dynamics in Minnesota State Government," a case study prepared for the John F. Kennedy School of Government, Harvard University, 1988, p. 6.

P. 214   Pensacola quotations: From Steve Garman, "Divesting Local Functions in Pensacola," in *The Entrepreneur in Local Government*, p. 170.

Martinez quotation: Peirce and Guskind, "Fewer Federal Dollars Spurring Cities To Improve Management and Trim Costs," *National Journal*, March 1, 1986, p. 506.

P. 216   Von Raesfeld quotation: From transcript of Santa Clara City Council meeting, January 31, 1984, attached to "Deposition of Mr. Donald R. Von Raesfeld," in Casimer Szlendak and Gerald I. Waissman vs. Marriot Corporation, City of Santa Clara, Redevelopment Agency, et al., January 22, 1988, vol. 2.

P. 217   "One study of 68 cities . . . ": E. S. Savas, "How Much Do Government Services Really Cost?" *Urban Affairs Quarterly* 15, no. 1 (September 1979): 23–42.

Chapter 8: Anticipatory Government:
Prevention Rather Than Cure

P. 219 Dator quotation: "State Judicial Foresight in the '80s and '90s," in
"Governing with Vision: State Government Foresight in the '90s"
(Washington, D.C.: Council of Governors Policy Advisers and Insti-
tute for Alternative Futures, unpublished draft).

P. 220 "Homicide is . . . remained level": Neal Peirce, "Brady Bill Will
Help Save the Children," *Philadelphia Inquirer*, April 1, 1991.

"Every year . . . preventing it.": Howard Wolpe and Claudine
Schneider, "Reducing Hazards, Cutting Costs," *Northeast-Midwest
Economic Review*, March 6, 1989, pp. 5–6.

"The United States ranks . . . during pregnancy": National Commission to Prevent Infant Mortality, 1988 statistics, (most recent
available), personal communication.

"Careful medical studies prove . . . ": See U.S. Congress, Select
Committee on Children, Youth, and Families, *Opportunities for Suc-
cess. Cost-Effective Programs for Children Update, 1990* (Washington,
D.C.: U.S. Government Printing Office, 1990), pp. 26, 35–36, 43.

"Yet 20 million . . . ": Kathleen Sylvester, "Infant Mortality: It's
As American As Apple Pie," *Governing* (July 1988): 56. Sylvester
cites analysis by the New York–based Alan Guttmacher Institute.

P. 221 "In 1991 . . . the debt": As of September 1991, the federal Office of
Management and Budget estimated fiscal 1991 net interest (interest
paid on the federal debt minus interest payments made to the federal
government) at $197 billion. It estimated the total federal debt at
$3.6 billion.

Toffler quotation: Alvin Toffler, *Future Shock* (New York: Bantam
Books, 1970), p. 471.

Donaldson quotation: From transcript of interview with Robert
Guskind and Neal Peirce of the *National Journal*, provided to the
authors by Guskind and Peirce.

P. 222 Wilson quotation: In Neal Peirce, "Two New GOP Governors Try
New Approaches to Old Problems," *Philadelphia Inquirer*, April 8,
1991, p. 11-A.

P. 223 "New Jersey . . . welfare hotels": Gwen Ifill, "New Jersey Battles
Homelessness by Preventing It," *Washington Post*, March 14, 1990,
p. A1.

"In Europe . . . ": Ted Kolderie, "The Declining Need for the 'Fire
Department,'" Public Services Redesign Project, Humphrey Institute, University of Minnesota.

P. 224 "Fresno, California . . . ": Ibid.

P. 225 "It even saves . . . ": personal communication from Rural Metro,
Scottsdale, Arizona.

"Passed when only . . . ": "Innovations of Cities," September 14,
1988, memo provided by city of Scottsdale, p. 7.

"The result . . . ": Rural Metro and city of Scottsdale, interviews with authors.

"It has safer . . . ": Rural Metro, interview with authors.

"Other forms of prevention . . . ": See *Fund for the City of New York, Three-Year Report, 1979–81* (New York: Fund for the City of New York, 1982), pp. 24–25; and *Fund for the City of New York, Three-Year Report, 1982–84* (New York: Fund for the City of New York, 1985), pp. 52–53.

P. 226 Cooperative Home Insurance Program: See Charles W. Thompson, "Municipal Home Insurance," in *The Entrepreneur in Local Government*, ed. Barbara H. Moore (Washington, D.C.: International City Management Association, 1983), pp. 195–204.

"During the 1970s . . . ": Clement Bezold, "An Image of Health Care in 2010," in "Governing with Vision."

"Air pollution . . . ": From Elliott Sclar, K. H. Schaeffer, and Robert Brandwein, *The Emperor's New Clothes· Transit Privatization and Public Policy* (Washington, D.C.: Economic Policy Institute, 1989), p. 5. The authors cite *Transit 2000· Interim Report of the American Public Transit Association Transit 2000 Task Force* (October 1988).

"Stress costs . . . ": William Van Dusen Wishard, "What in the World Is Going On?" *Vital Speeches*, March 1, 1990, p. 314.

"A research team . . . ": Ibid.

"In 1983, we spent . . . ": U.S. Congress, Office of Technology Assessment, *Technology and the American Economic Transition Choices for the Future*, OTA-TET-283 (Washington, D.C.: U.S. Government Printing Office, May 1988), p. 41.

P. 227 Kitzhaber quotation: In Richard A. Knox, "Oregon Strips Its Medicaid Plan," *Boston Globe*, July 9, 1990, p. 28.

Governing quotation: Laura Ost, "Governing Guide: Cleaning Up," *Governing* (April 1991): 41.

P. 228 "Nearly 30 jurisdictions . . . ": Reid Lifset and Marian Chertow, "Changing the Waste Makers: Product Bans and the New Politics of Garbage," *American Prospect* (Fall 1990): 83–88.

"Dupont, Procter & Gamble . . . ": Tom Arrandale, "Plastics Recycling: Industry Buys In," *Governing* (May 1991): 21.

P. 229 "Dow Chemical . . . to Dow": Wolpe and Schneider, "Reducing Hazards, Cutting Costs."

P. 230 Toffler quotation: Alvin Toffler, "Introduction," in Clement Bezold, ed., *Anticipatory Democracy* (New York: Vintage Books, 1978), pp. xiv–xv.

P. 231 Goals for Dallas, including all quotations: See Robert B. Bradley, "Goals for Dallas," in *Anticipatory Democracy*, pp. 58–87.

P. 232 "Alternatives for Washington . . . ": See Robert L. Stilger, "Alternatives for Washington," in *Anticipatory Democracy*, pp. 88–99.

P. 233 Bryson book: John Bryson, *Strategic Planning for Public and Nonprofit Organizations* (San Francisco: Jossey-Bass, 1988).

"The Tokyo Metropolitan Government . . . plan": See Mary Mc-
Cormick, "What's Produced in Tokyo That Will Play in New York?
Lessons in Public Management from Japan," *Public Papers of the
Fund for the City of New York* 7, no. 1 (May 1988).

P. 234   Gretzky quotation: From John M. Bryson, "A Strategic Planning
Process for Public and Non-profit Organizations," *Long Range Planning* 21, no. 1, (February 1988): p. 73.

Bryson quotation: Bryson, *Strategic Planning for Public and Nonprofit Organizations*, p. 2.

P. 235   "As a mayoral assistant . . . ": Gregory Farrell, "Helping Government Do Better with Less," in *Fund for the City of New York, Three-
Year Report, 1979–81*, p. 2.

Peirce quotation: Neal R. Peirce, "New Horizons for Nebraska,"
(address at conference sponsored by Nebraska State Legislature), October 25, 1987.

Rose quotation: Charlie Rose, "Building a Futures Network in
Congress," in *Anticipatory Democracy*, p. 105.

P. 237   "The 10-year projections . . . ": Quoted in Clint Page, "Small Computers Solve Big Problems," *Nation's Cities Weekly*, March 22, 1982,
p. 6.

"There is no way . . . ": John Mercer, "Only Poor—and Thrifty—
Cities Should Get Federal Aid," *San Jose Mercury News*, September 6,
1985.

P. 242   "The *Boston Globe* found . . . ": "Weld to Revamp Day Care Despite
Cuts in Budget," *Boston Globe*, May 31, 1991, pp. 1, 10.

Schorr quotation: In Eileen Shanahan, "Attacking the 'Nothing
Works' Notion," *Governing* (December 1989): 65. The book is
Within Our Reach Breaking the Cycle of Disadvantage (Garden City,
N.J.: Doubleday, 1988).

State rainy day funds: See Tony Hutchison and Kathy James, *Legislative Budget Procedures in the 50 States. A Guide to Appropriations
and Budget Processes* (Denver: National Conference of State Legislatures, September 1988).

P. 243   Oklahoma: Larry Tye, "Oklahoma Charted a Course Out of Its 1980s
Budget Crisis," *Boston Globe*, February 25, 1990.

Leonard quotations: Herman B. Leonard, *Checks Unbalanced· The
Quiet Side of Public Spending* (New York: Basic Books, 1986), pp. 9,
170, 208–212.

P. 245   Antonio quotation: In Jonathan Walters, "The Books and the Bottom
Line," *Governing* (November 1989): 61.

"A member . . . ": Ibid., p. 62.

P. 246   Latimer quotation: George Latimer, "Public Administration," in
The St. Paul Experiment, ed. David Lanegran, Cynthia Seelhammer,
and Amy L. Walgrave (St. Paul, Minn.: City of St. Paul, December
1989), p. 314.

P. 249   Toffler, "Introduction," pp. xii-xiv.

Chapter 9: Decentralized Government: From Hierarchy to Participation and Teamwork

P. 250　Contino quotation: Ronald A. Contino, "Waging Revolution in the Public Sector: Operational Improvements Through Labor/Management Cooperation," unpublished, 1988, p. 34.

P. 251　Toffler quotation: Alvin Toffler, "Introduction" in Clement Bezold, ed., *Anticipatory Democracy* (New York: Vintage Books, 1978), pp. xvii–xviii.

P. 252　Contino quotation: Ibid., pp. 33–34.

　　　　"Their biggest surprise . . . ": John Herbers, "The Innovators: Where Are They Now?" *Governing* (October 1989): 33.

P. 253　Cleveland quotation: Harlan Cleveland, *The Knowledge Executive* (New York: E. P. Dutton, 1985).

P. 254　Pinchot quotation: Gifford Pinchot, *Intrapreneuring* (New York: Harper & Row, 1985), p. 304.

P. 255　"According to military . . . ": Martin van Creveld, *Command In War* (Cambridge, Mass.: Harvard University Press, 1985), p. 270.

　　　　On the Tactical Air Command, see Jay Finegan, "Four-Star Management," *Inc* (January 1987): 42–51; and General W. L. Creech, "Leadership and Management—The Present and the Future" (address at the Armed Services Leadership and Management Symposium, October 11–14, 1983), available from the Office of the Assistant Secretary of Defense for Installations, in the Pentagon.

P. 256　Creech quotations: "The U.S. military . . . ": Finegan, "Four-Star Management," p. 42; " 'one size fits all' ": Creech, "Leadership and Management," p. 17; "Control was at the top": Ibid., p. 10.

P. 257　Creech quotations: " . . . if equipment is shabby . . . ": Finegan, "Four-Star Management," p. 48; "We actively stressed . . . ": Creech, "Leadership and Management," p. 34.

P. 258　Creech quotations: "What was it primarily?": Ibid., p. 33; "When I left TAC": Finegan, "Four-Star Management," p. 51.

P. 259　"Manufacturing businesses . . . ": See, for instance, John Hoerr, "Getting Man and Machine to Live Happily Ever After," *Business Week*, April 30, 1987, pp. 61–62.

　　　　Pinchot quotation: Pinchot, *Intrapreneuring*, p. 200.

　　　　New York City Sanitation Department story: See Contino, "Waging Revolution."

P. 260　"Madison's first quality team . . . ": Joseph Sensenbrenner, "Quality Comes to City Hall," *Harvard Business Review* (March–April 1991): 68.

P. 261　Madison Police Department: See David Couper and Sabine Lobitz, *Quality Policing: the Madison Experience* (Washington, D.C.: Police Executive Research Forum, 1991).

P. 262　"Before its recent decentralization . . . ": Joe Nathan, *Free to Teach* (Minneapolis: Winston Press, 1983), p. 61; and "Improving

Education: Lessons from the States," *State Backgrounder* (Washington, D.C.: Heritage Foundation, October 24, 1988), p. 1.

"Yet study after study . . . ": See, for example, John E. Chubb, "Why the Current Wave of School Reform Will Fail," *Public Interest*, no. 90 (Winter 1988); or John E. Chubb and Terry Moe, *Politics, Markets and America's Schools* (Washington, D.C.: Brookings Institution, 1990).

Clinton quotation: From address to Democratic Leadership Council, November 1989, published in the DLC's magazine, *Mainstream Democrat* 2, no. 2 (December 1989).

P. 263   "When the consulting firm . . . ": *Survey on Public Entrepreneurship* (Coopers & Lybrand, 1988).

P. 264   Contino quotation: In *Work Worth Doing*, documentary available from the City of New York Department of Sanitation.

Bureau of Motor Equipment story: Contino, "Waging Revolution."

"And in Madison . . . ": Sensenbrenner, "Quality Comes to City Hall."

P. 265   "As Peters and Waterman . . . way up": Thomas Peters and Robert Waterman, Jr., *In Search of Excellence* (New York: Warner Books, 1982), p. 313.

P. 266   Quality Circles: For a useful handbook on Total Quality Management, see Peter R. Scholtes, *The Team Handbook* (Madison, Wis.: Joiner Associates, 1988).

P. 267   Washington's Teamwork Incentive Program: See James L. Perry, "Unleashing the Power of Teamwork," *Government Executive* (July 1990): 40.

P. 268   Peters and Waterman quotation: *In Search of Excellence*, p. 126.

Drucker quotation: Peter Drucker, *The Age of Discontinuity* (New York: Harper Torchbooks, 1978), pp. 289–290.

P. 269   Harrison quotations: Roger Harrison, "Understanding Your Organization's Character," *Harvard Business Review* (May–June 1972): 119–128.

Kanter quotations: Rosabeth Moss Kanter, *The Change Masters* (New York: Harper & Row, 1983), pp. 75–76, 143.

P. 270   Madison story: Sensenbrenner, "Quality Comes to City Hall."

P. 271   "In Madison, managers . . . ": Ibid.

P. 272   Krim quotation: Robert M. Krim, "Quality of Worklife Programs in the Public Sector: Toward a More Effective Management Paradigm," unpublished, pp. 22–23.

P. 273   Andres quotation: Recollection of Peter Hutchinson, interview with authors.

For more on STEP, see Sandra J. Hale and Mary M. Williams, eds., *Managing Change A Guide to Producing Innovation from Within* (Washington, D.C.: Urban Institute Press, 1989).

P. 274   STEP lessons: Ibid., pp. 151–158.

P. 275   Creech quotation: Creech, "Leadership and Management," p. 34.

"In 1990, the Governor's . . . ": Governor's Management Review Commission, *Operational Review of Training* (Trenton, N.J.: Department of Personnel, July 27, 1990), p. 5.

P. 276 "Between 1963 and 1980 . . . local governments": John E. Chubb, "Federalism and the Bias for Centralization," in *The New Direction in American Politics*, ed. John E. Chubb and Paul E. Peterson (Washington, D.C.: Brookings Institution, 1985), pp. 279–281.

"Despite severe funding cuts . . . ": David Rapp, "Nervous Partners in the Block Grant Minuet," *Governing* (May 1991): 58.

P. 277 "Let us simply . . . ": Gold, *Reforming State-Local Relations* (Denver: National Conference of State Legislatures, 1989).

P. 278 For more on the Ben Franklin Partnership, see David Osborne, *Laboratories of Democracy* (Boston: Harvard Business School Press, 1988), chap. 2.

Chapter 10: Market-Oriented Government: Leveraging Change Through the Market

P. 280 Corporation for Enterprise Development quotation: Robert Friedman and Doug Ross, *The Third Wave in State Economic Development* (Washington, D.C.: Corporation for Enterprise Development, 1990), draft.

P. 281 " . . . half a million fewer . . . throughout New York State": "Before and After: Streets and Parks and the Returnable Container Law," *Public Papers of the Fund for the City of New York* 4, no. 3 (November 1985).

" . . . broken glass prevalent . . . ": David Arnold, "Neglect by City, Abuse by Vandals Mar Boston's Parks," *Boston Globe*, June 17, 1985, pp. 1, 16.

P. 285 Power and Urban-Lurain quotations: *Creating a Human Investment System* (Lansing: Michigan Job Training Coordinating Council, 1989), pp. 4–5.

P. 286 "One state development program . . . ": Roger Vaughan, "Is It Working," *Entrepreneurial Economy Review* (July–August 1989): 3–7.

P. 287 Power and Urban-Lurain quotation: *Creating a Human Investment System*, p. 5.

P. 288 "Head Start, long acclaimed . . . ": Associated Press, "Senate Moves to Boost Head Start," *Boston Globe*, June 2, 1991.

"The Michigan Strategic Fund . . . ": For more, see David Osborne, *Laboratories of Democracy* (Boston: Harvard Business School Press, 1988), pp. 158–161.

P. 289 "Yes, Minister" quotation: Quoted in Roger Vaughan, "Bridge over Garbled Waters," unpublished manuscript.

"Ralph Tyler . . . ": "Education Guru Is Optimistic About Future," *Stanford Observer* (January–February 1990): 8–10.

P. 290 "Today school districts . . . ": see David Armor, "After Busing: Education and Choice," *Public Interest*, no. 95 (Spring 1989): 24–37.

P. 292   "Other states, including New York . . . ": Jacob Sullum, "Totaled!" *Reason* (November 1990): 30–35.

"Three states have driven . . . backfired": Peter Spiro and Daniel Mirvish, "Whose No-Fault Is It, Anyway?" *Washington Monthly* (October 1989): 24–28.

"When California required companies . . . ": Cass R. Sunstein, "Remaking Regulation," *American Prospect* (Fall 1990): 80.

"In San Francisco . . . real estate": Kathleen Sylvester, "Global Warming: The Answers Are Not Always Global," *Governing* (April 1990): 48.

P. 293   "Seattle, San Diego, and Tampa . . . ": On Seattle, see Robert H. McNulty, R. Leo Penne, Dorothy R. Jacobson, and Partners for Livable Places, *The Return of the Livable City* (Washington, D.C.: Acropolis Books, 1986), p. 287. On incentive zoning in general, see Terry Jill Lassar, *Carrots and Sticks New Zoning Downtown* (Washington, D.C.: Urban Land Institute, 1989).

P. 294   "Many of Japan's . . . ": Peter Drucker, *The Age of Discontinuity* (New York: Harper Torchbooks, 1978), p. 134.

For more on Pennsylvania's and Michigan's strategies, see Osborne, *Laboratories of Democracy*.

P. 295   "In 1982, when . . . ": Ibid., pp. 154–158.

For more on Massachusetts' Bay State Skills Corporation, see ibid., pp. 206–207.

P. 296   "According to the Rand Corporation . . . ": George Will, "Constructive Irritability," *Boston Globe*, July 16, 1989.

King quotations: Norman R. King, "Managing Demand for Government Services: Toward a New Public Administration Ethic" (address delivered to Michigan City Management Association, February 17, 1988).

P. 297   "After Florida's 1985 . . . ": Associated Press, "Study: Fees Not Able to Pay All Costs of Growth," *Miami Herald*, November 30, 1990, p. 28.

"By 1988, 58 percent . . . ": William E. Schmidt, "Developers Paying New Fees for Public Services," *New York Times*, October 31, 1988.

King quotation: "Managing Demand for Government Services: Toward a New Public Administration Ethic."

P. 298   "According to economist . . . ": Steven A. Morrison, "Pricing the Crowds off the Roads," *Boston Globe*, May 14, 1991.

P. 299   "Half of all Americans . . . ": David Callahan, "The Greening of the Tax System," *American Prospect* (Fall 1990): 90.

"Studies suggest that other methods . . . ": Sunstein, "Remaking Regulation," p. 77.

P. 300   "The original Clean Air Act . . . a storm": "A Clean-Air Era," *Boston Globe*, November 19, 1990.

P. 301   "Even the EPA's own . . . ": Laura Ost, "Cleaning Up: A Governing Guide," *Governing* (April 1991): 36.

Wilson quotation: James Q. Wilson, *Bureaucracy* (New York: Basic Books, 1989), p. 13.

P. 302 Drucker quotation: Peter Drucker, *The New Realities* (New York: Harper & Row, 1989), pp. 135–136.

P. 303 "European nations . . . other products": See Susan Owens, Victor Anderson, and Irene Brunskill, *Green Taxes. A Budget Memorandum* (London: Institute for Public Policy Research, 1990), cited by Callahan, "Greening of the Tax System."

"Iowa, Minnesota and Oregon . . . ": Callahan, "Greening of the Tax System," p. 92.

P. 304 "Oregon and New Jersey . . . ": "Recycling Pays, But Not in Cash," *Governing* (March 1989): 65.

Seattle: See Randolph B. Smith, "Aided by Volunteers, Seattle Shows How Recycling Can Work," *Wall Street Journal*, July 19, 1990, pp. 1, A5; and "Recycling Life's Debris," *Governing* (October 1990): 47.

"This stimulated only a limited market . . . ": Robert Hahn and Robert Stavins, "Incentive-Based Environmental Regulation: A New Era from an Old Idea?" *Ecology Law Quarterly* 18, no. 1 (1991).

"The EPA estimated that the trading program . . . ": Ibid.

P. 305 Stavins study: Robert N. Stavins et al., *Project 88—Harnessing Market Forces to Protect Our Environment Initiatives for the New President* (Washington, D.C.: Project 88, December 1988). For more on market-based approaches to environmental regulation, see Robert N. Stavins et al., *Project 88—Round II, Incentives for Action Designing Market-Based Environmental Strategies* (Washington, D.C.: Project 88, May 1991).

Stavins quotation: In "The Most Fascinating Ideas for 1991," *Fortune*, January 14, 1991.

P. 306 Hayes quotation: "Guidance Planned for Green Consumer," *Boston Globe*, June 15, 1990.

P. 307 King quotation: King, "Managing Demand."

Kolderie quotation: Ted Kolderie, "Education That Works: The Right Role for Business," *Harvard Business Review* (September–October 1987): 56–62.

Chapter 11: Putting It All Together

P. 311 Drucker quotation: Peter Drucker, *Innovation and Entrepreneurship* (New York: Harper & Row, 1985), pp. 186–187.

P. 314 For a good description of the German medical system, see a three-part series, "Health Crisis: The German Cure," that ran in the *Boston Globe* May 12, 13, 14, 1991.

P. 315 Urbanski quotation: Diego Ribadeneira, "Educators Say School Reform Is Not Enough," *Boston Globe*, November 13, 1990.

"Drop-out rates . . . ": U.S. Department of Education, personal communication.

"Scores on the two . . . ": Ibid.

"In tests used . . . ": David Pierpont Gardner, "If We Stand, They Will Deliver," *New Perspectives Quarterly* (Fall 1990): 4. Gardner, president of the University of California, chaired the commission that produced *A Nation at Risk*.

Education Summit: "The President's Education Summit with Governors, University of Virginia, September 27–28, 1989, Joint Statement," p. 4.

P. 317 Blue Hills Regional Technical School: Amy Callahan, "Postgrads Enroll at Blue Hills," *Boston Globe*, October 15, 1989, South Weekly Section, pp. 1, 4.

P. 318 Kearns quotation: In Edward B. Fiske, "Lessons," *New York Times*, July 26, 1989, p. B8.

"Indeed, 150 different studies . . . ": Herbert Walberg, "Educational Productivity and Choice," in *Public Schools by Choice*, ed. Joe Nathan (St. Paul, Minn.: Institute for Learning and Teaching, 1989), p. 87.

"Even the president . . . market economy": Albert Shanker, "Letting Schools Compete," *Northeast-Midwest Economic Review*, November 13, 1989, pp. 4–8.

P. 319 "Since 1960 . . . in the world": Tim Weiner, "Senate Unit Calls US 'Most Violent' Country on Earth," *Boston Globe*, March 13, 1991, p. 3. Weiner cited a report by the U.S. Senate Judiciary Committee.

"While the prison . . . ": Steven D. Gold, *The State Fiscal Agenda for the 1990s* (Denver: National Conference of State Legislatures, 1990), pp. 78–79. Gold reports that state corrections spending tripled between 1980 and 1988.

P. 320 "They might even encourage . . . ": In *Bureaucracy* (New York: Basic Books, 1989), p. 352, James Q. Wilson reports a study showing that after allowing for differences in population, crime rates, and other factors, "the operating expenditures (per capita) of a sheriff's department were lower in counties where contracting was common." He cites Stephen L. Mehay and Rudolfo Gonzalez, "Economic Incentives Under Contract Supply of Local Government Services," *Public Choice* 46 (1985): 311–325.

P. 321 Kuhn book: Thomas S. Kuhn, *The Structure of Scientific Revolutions*, 2nd ed. (Chicago: University of Chicago Press, 1970).

P. 322 Kuhn quotation: Ibid., p. 113.

P. 323 Kuhn quotation: Ibid., p. 77.

Kolderie, quoting Andersen: Ted Kolderie, ed., *An Equitable and Competitive Public Sector* (Minneapolis: Hubert H. Humphrey Institute of Public Affairs, University of Minnesota, 1984), p. 29.

P. 324 Kuhn quotation: *Structure of Scientific Revolutions*, p. 90.

P. 325 Kuhn quotation: Ibid., p. 111.

P. 328 "In 1982 . . . in use": Allen Schick, "Budgeting for Results: Recent Developments in Five Industrialized Countries," *Public Administration Review* (January–February 1990): 26–33.

"In 1991, the British government . . . ": Francis H. Miller, "Socialized Competition—British Style," *Boston Globe*, August 16, 1991, p. 15.

Kjell-Olof Feldt quotation and *New York Times* quotation: Steven Greenhouse, "Sweden's Social Democrats Veer Toward Free Market and Lower Taxes," *New York Times*, October 27, 1989, p. A3.

P. 329 "The national government . . . outcomes": Schick, "Budgeting for Results."

Schick quotation: Ibid.

"Debates about school choice . . . ": Charles Glenn, "Parent Choice and American Values," in *Public Schools by Choice*, pp. 44–45.

P. 330 For more on New Zealand, see Graham Scott, Peter Bushnell, and Nikitin Sallee, "Reform of the Core Public Sector: The New Zealand Experience," *Governance: An International Journal of Policy and Administration* (April 1990).

Appendix A: Alternative Service Delivery Options

P. 334 "In 1987, the federal government . . . ": Donald Haider, "Grants As a Tool of Public Policy," in *Beyond Privatization The Tools of Government Action*, ed. Lester M. Salamon (Washington, D.C.: Urban Institute Press, 1989).

"By 1987, the federal government . . . ": Lester M. Salamon, "The Changing Tools of Government Action: An Overview," in *Beyond Privatization*, p. 5.

"According to Lester Salamon . . . ": Ibid., pp. 5, 10.

Savas quotation: E. S. Savas, "The Key to a Better Society," *World and I* (January 1988): 22.

P. 335 "Our defense establishment . . . ": Wendell M. Hannaford Jr., "Peace May Be the Only Dividend," *State Government News* (August 1990): 25.

"The first contract city . . . ": Jonathan Marshall, "Troubled Cities Put Services Out to Bid," *San Francisco Chronicle*, June 3, 1991, pp. 1, A6.

P. 336 Latimer and Broeker quotation: George Latimer and Richard Broeker, "Recycling an Older City with Foundation Support," unpublished, August 1981.

P. 337 "The federal government owns . . . ": Lloyd D. Musolf, "The Government-Corporation Tool: Permutations and Possibilities," in *Beyond Privatization*, p. 231.

"The General Services Administration . . . Gross National Product": Ralph Nader, "Big Consumer," *Mother Jones* (November–December 1990): 21–22.

P. 338 "The *Catalogue of Federal Domestic Assistance* . . . ": Salamon, "The Changing Tools of Government Action: An Overview," in *Beyond Privatization*, p. 7.

Will quotation: George F. Will, "Access to Fashion," *Boston Globe*, January 8, 1989.

P. 339 "In a mid-1980s survey . . . ": Sydney Duncombe, "Volunteers in City Government: Advantages, Disadvantages and Uses," *National Civic Review* (September 1985): 356–364. The survey was conducted by the University of Idaho's Bureau of Public Affairs Research.

"In Florida, volunteers serve . . . ": Keon S. Chi, "Private-Public Alliances Grow," *State Government News* (January 1986): 10–13.

"In Massachusetts . . . ": James L. Franklin, "Volunteers to Mediate Environmental Cases," *Boston Globe*, September 18, 1990, pp. 25, 56.

P. 343 Florida Speaker's Advisory Committee quotation: *Florida Sunrise Issues and Options Choosing Strategies for the Future, Issue Paper Notebook*, vol. 1 (Tallahassee, Fla.: Speaker's Advisory Committee on the Future, July 1987), p. 204.

P. 345 "One study of nursing homes . . . ": Joe Nathan, *Free to Teach* (Minneapolis: Winston Press, 1983), p. 154.

Niskanen quotation: William A. Niskanen, Jr., *Bureaucracy and Representative Government* (Chicago: Aldine-Atherton, 1971), p. 217.

Appendix B: The Art of Performance Measurement

P. 350 National Center for State Courts material: See Commission on Trial Court Performance Standards, *Trial Court Performance Standards with Commentary* (Williamsburg, Va.: National Center for State Courts, 1990), p. 1.

P. 353 "Yet although it placed . . . ": See David Osborne, *Laboratories of Democracy* (Boston: Harvard Business School Press, 1988), pp. 200–206; and Scot Lehigh and M. E. Malone, "Weld: Revenue Loss Threatens '92 Budget," *Boston Globe*, April 23, 1991.

P. 354 Works on performance measurement: See, for instance, Harry P. Hatry, Louis H. Blair, Donald M. Fisk, John H. Greiner, John R. Hall, Jr., and Philip S. Schaenman, *How Effective Are Your Community Services? Procedures for Monitoring the Effectiveness of Municipal Services* (Washington, D.C.: Urban Institute and International City Management Association, 1977); Jack A. Brizius and Michael D. Campbell, *Getting Results* (Washington, D.C.: Council of Governors' Policy Advisors, 1991); Richard E. Brown, Meredith C. Williams, and Thomas P. Gallagher, *Auditing Performance in Government. Concepts and Cases* (New York: Ronald Press, 1983); Harry P. Hatry et al., eds., *Service Efforts and Accomplishments Reporting Its Time Has Come An Overview* (Norwalk, Conn.: Governmental Accounting Standards Board, 1990); and Roger Vaughan, "Is It Working," *Entrepreneurial Economy Review* (July–August 1989): 3–7.

P. 359 Farrell quotation: Gregory Farrell, "Helping Government Do Better with Less," in *Fund for the City of New York, Three-Year Report, 1979–81*, pp. 5–6.

Index

Massachusetts, 29, 36, 66, 146, 242,
290, 293, 335, 338; car insurance,
81–82; child care, 181, 242; civil
service, 125; crime, 57;
education, 93, 155; Employment
and Training (E.T.) Choices, 353–
54; health care, 86; Industrial
Services Program, 56, 66; job
training, 56, 296, 317; pollution
control, 228; Taxpayers
Foundation, 125; Transitional
Employment Enterprises (TEE),
151–52. See also Boston
Mattress display tags, 115
"Meals on Wheels," 68
Medicare and Medicaid. See Health
care
Mental health. See Health, mental
Mercer, John, 237
Mesa, Arizona, 197
Miami, 85, 262
Michigan, 17, 126, 188–93, 288,
294, 308; Commerce Department,
84, 131, 172, 179, 252;
education, 178; Human
Investment System, 189–192,
283, 285, 306; Michigan
Modernization Service, 157, 160,
177, 178; 263; Opportunity Card
and Shops, 190–93, 295, 306;
Strategic Fund, 341; Treasury
Department, 295
Mikesell, John, 204
Military bases, 9–11, 115, 118, 122,
166. See also Department of
Defense
Mills, Jon, 232
Milwaukee, 87, 197, 339
Minneapolis, 44, 81, 138, 336, 340;
Family Housing Fund, 109–10
Minnesota, 115, 181, 247, 248, 333;
budgets, 240, 241; Department of
Administration, 90–92, 198–99,
205, 213; education, 55, 93, 96–
102, 150, 169, 325; highways,
142; parks, 178, 273–74;

pollution, 228, 303; STEP
program, 177, 267, 272–75. See
also Minneapolis; St. Paul
Mission-driven budgets, 117–24,
210–11
Mission-driven government, 108–
37; advantages of, 113–14;
creating, 114–19
Missouri, 258, 336
Model Cities, 53
Model Installations Program, 10–
11, 115, 259
Moe, Terry, 94
Monopoly suppliers, 34, 88, 216
Montclair, New Jersey, 94
Montreal, 196
Moore, Don, 54
Moreno Valley, California, 205, 296
Morris, David, 223
Morrison, Cliff, 58
Morrison, Steven A., 298
Mosgaller, Tom, 261, 309
Motor Vehicles Registry, 168, 182
Mudd, John, 132
Murray, Alice, 70

Nadel, Robert, 8
Naperville, Illinois, 177
Nathan, Joe, 97, 183
National Association of Town
Watch, 50
National Center for State Courts,
350, 351
National Center for Neighborhood
Enterprise, 65
National Center for Policy
Alternatives, 72, 206
National Commission for
Employment Policy, 89
National Conference of State
Legislatures, 229, 242, 277
National Governors Association,
245
National Institue of Justice, 173
National Science Foundation, 81,
105

San Antonio, Texas, 178, 202, 210–11, 240, 342
San Bruno, California, 214–15
San Diego, California, 128, 293
San Francisco, 29, 56, 128, 292–93, 340, 342; and AIDS, 58–59; budget, 123–335; civil service, 125, 128
San Jose, California, 94, 209, 218, 223
Santa Clara, California, 215, 223; amusement park, 208–9
Santa Monica, California, 178, 295
Savas, E. S., 25, 80–81, 83, 90, 105, 125, 244, 281, 334, 343
Savings, retained in budgets, 3, 5, 10, 209–11, 242, 265
Say, J. B., xix
Schick, Allen, 329
Scholtes, Peter R., 160
Schools. See Education
Schorr, Lisbeth, 37, 242
Schrader, George, 231
Schulman, David, 57
Schumacher, Ernst, 222
Schwarzkopf, Norman 255
Scotts Valley, California, 121
Scottsdale, Arizona, 221, 224–25, 293
Sea World, 342
Seattle, Washington, 53, 74, 94, 293, 341
Sensenbrenner, Joseph, 172, 270
Services, delivery of, 17, 27, 29, 32, 140, 145, 186, 215, 186, 220, 287; alternative options, 31, 332–48; competition, 76–107; costs, 216–18; and steering organizations, 39–42
Shanker, Al, 158–59, 318–19
Shannon, John, 203
Shuger, Scott, 127
Shycoff, Don, 165
Silver Spring, Maryland, 40–41
Sims, Renee, 62
Singapore, 298

Small Business Administration, 294
Smoking, 226, 338
Social Security Administration, 130
Softball teams, Visalia, 199–200
South Africa, 338
South Barrington, Illinois, 170
South Carolina, 17, 50
Soviet Union, 330
Spain, 329
Spanbauer, Stan, 147, 174–76
Sparacino, Jennifer, 209, 215
Speaker's Advisory Committee on the Future. See Florida
Springmeyer, Roy, 136
St. Paul, Minnesota, 17, 25–27, 29, 38, 109–10, 113, 210, 267, 293, 326, 340, 341; civil service, 127. See also Latimer, George
St. Louis, Missouri, 197, 248
St. Petersburg, Florida, 177
Starr, Paul, 88
Stavins, Robert, 305
Stein, Andrew, 112
STEP (Strive Toward Excellence in Performance). See Minnesota
Stone, Bob, 8–11, 23, 115, 122, 132–35, 165, 166, 259, 351
Street maintenance, 4, 146, 239, 259–60, 354, 356–57
Stumberg, Robert, 72, 206–7
Sullivan, Louis, 312
Sunnyvale, California, 217, 233, 240–41, 349; community surveys, 177; long-term budget, 233, 237–41; performance measurement and budgeting, 142–45, 148, 156, 158, 159, 161, 163, 349; user fees, 203
Sunset laws, 116
Surveys, 18, 173–74, 177, 184, 232, 263, 266, 274. See also Customer-driven government, Performance measurement
Sweden, 122, 151, 165, 179, 328–29

Tacoma, Washington, 221

Tactical Air Command, 79, 255–59, 265, 267
Taft, William Howard IV, 11
Tampa, Florida, 112, 214, 293, 294; Community Redevelopment Agency, 38–39; health care, 109
Tarnowski, Kathy, 75
Taxes, 22, 27, 333; and voters, 33, 140, 299; federal, 221; Florida, 116, 232; gasoline, 296; green, 283, 299, 303–5; Orlando, 213; St. Paul, 25, 26; tax collections, 206; tax revolt, 23, 29, 76, 154–55, 195–96, 199, 202, 322, 341. See also Proposition 13
Taylor, Patrick F., 148
Teachers. See American Federation of Teachers, Education
Teegarden, Suzanne, 355
Television, 221; cable, 214–15, 335, 336
Tennessee, 85, 224; Tennessee Valley Authority, 337
Texas, 49, 130, 224, 299. See also Dallas, San Antonio
Texas Instruments, 212
Thatcher, Margaret, 328
Theme park. See Amusement park
Third sector organizations, 43–47, 344–48; definition of, 44
Thomas, David, 214–15
Thompson, Tommy, 94
Thornburgh, Richard, 278
Time magazine, 1
Toffler, Alvin, 221, 230, 249, 251
Toll-free phone numbers. See Hotlines
Total Quality Management (TQM), 17, 21, 159–63, 172, 174, 176, 260–61, 264, 266, 270, 309, 341, 350
Traffic, 40–41, 208–9, 223, 298. See also Highways
Transitional Employment Enterprises (TEE), 151–52
Truman, Harry, 289

Tsongas, Paul, 28–29
Tucson, Arizona, 342
Tulsa, Oklahoma, 50
Turkey, 289
Tyler, Ralph, 289

Ueberroth, Peter, 196
Unemployment. See Job training, Layoffs.
Unified Budget System, 11, 122
Unions, 41, 76, 78, 87, 104, 106–7, 125, 127, 188, 193, 263–64, 266
United Parcel Service, 82, 107, 332
Universities. See College, Education
Upward Bound, 60
Urban Development Action Grants, 25
Urban Institute, 44, 158, 354
Urban-Lurain, Jan, 285–86
Urbanski, Adam, 315
User fees, 203–5, 297–98
Utah, 93
Utilities, 81, 333, 335.

Van Creveld, Martin, 255
Vaughan, Roger, 187–88, 355
Vermont, 93, 247, 339; education, 155; pollution control, 228
Veterans Administration, 186
Vierra, Ernie, 4
Vietnam, 255
Virginia, 342
Visalia, California, 2–5, 31, 113, 115, 122, 123, 130, 136, 158, 177, 210, 264, 276, 336, 341, 342; Expenditure Control Budget, 3–5, 122–23, 210; Employee Development Program, 226; energy efficiency ratings, 292, 306; invention policy, 267; profit generation, 198–200, 216
Voinovich, George, 19
Volcker, Paul, 275